D1560348

Man, Mind, and Science

A History of Anthropology

Man, Mind, and Science

A History of Anthropology

Murray J. Leaf

New York Columbia University Press 1979

Library of Congress Cataloging in Publication Data

Leaf, Murray J
. Man, mind, and science.

  Bibliography: p.
  Includes index.
  1. Anthropology—History. I. Title.
GN17.L39   301.2′09   78-27724
ISBN 0-231-04618-9

Columbia University Press
New York   Guildford, Surrey

Copyright © 1979 Columbia University Press
All rights reserved
Printed in the United States of America

Sections from the *Prolegomena to Any Future Metaphysics* by Immanuel Kant, edited
by Lewis White Beck, copyright © 1950 by The Liberal Arts Press, are reprinted by
permission of the Bobbs-Merrill Company, Inc.

Contents

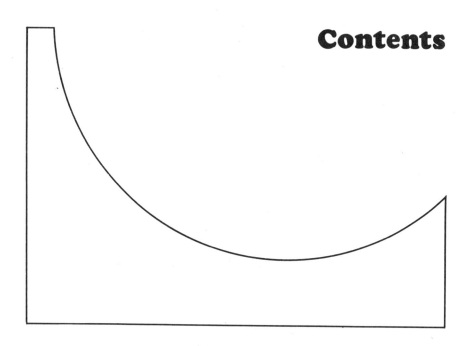

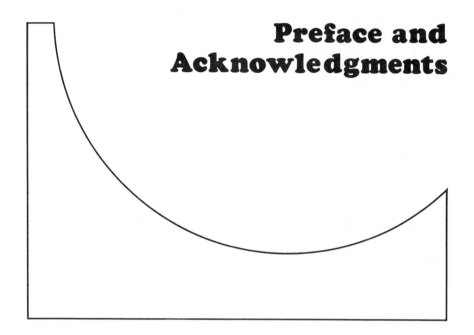

Preface and Acknowledgments

This book has developed into an intellectual history in the broad tradition of Lovejoy's *Revolt Against Dualism* (1930) and *Essays in the History of Ideas* (1948). The convergence is welcome and provides a kind of reassurance, but the real point of origin lies in another quarter.

My first exposure to the literature of the history of anthropology, in an undergraduate course in 1959, came with Lowie's 1937 *History of Ethnological Theory*. The fact that this more than twenty-year-old work was still a popular text itself bespoke a certain attitude of anthropologists toward their past. Lowie's preoccupation with the conflict between diffusionism and evolutionism may have reflected major concerns current when his book was first written, but twenty years later it was hardly relevant to any of the major theoretical debates. Even more importantly, the organization of Lowie's work suggested that anthropology had been built up by the gradual accumulation of separate truths, with no evident critical awareness of the general problem of establishing truth and developing theory—problems that were well represented in almost all other aspects of the anthropological literature.

The instructor in that first course, David French, had presented the deeper open questions quite clearly in other contexts, so it was natural to ask him about the discrepancies. His reply, in part, was to recommend David Bidney's *Theoretical Anthropology* (1953). It was easy to see how one might think that Bidney was addressing these more basic issues, and in a way perhaps he was, and I was expecting to have too many questions answered at once. He was taking terms that had profoundly disputed meanings in philosophy, and finding parallels in anthropology; but the way the parallels were assigned glossed over the disputes, so the sense of probing the limits of what could be known or established was lost. At the same time, Bidney was not attempting history. The parallels he described between anthropological and philosophical concepts were treated as though they were in a sense fortuitous, interesting, or useful coincidences.

The juxtaposition of these two works, and their place in the field at the time, made it clear that the history of anthropology was not then seen as a vehicle by which one could examine and separate its fundamental assumptions; and its fundamental assumptions were not thought of as having anything very direct to do with the systems of thought that had been developed over the centuries in the larger world of ideas, and grouped loosely under the label "philosophy." If anything, most anthropologists appeared to agree with what Lowie, and in a different way Bidney, suggested: that the theoretical problems in the field were relatively minor, temporary, and wholly internal to it. Earlier positions in philosophy were considered irrelevant. There was no admission of the possibility that the difficulties that anthropologists were experiencing in building their theories (and many were recognized), or even in deciding what theory, proof, or truths were, might be but new versions of much older debates, new growths from the intellectual seeds anthropologists had carried perhaps unknowingly in their baggage to what they thought was a new and virgin world. Personally, I doubted that the difficulties of the past were that easily avoided. That doubt has been strengthened by subsequent events and forms the first foundation of the present work.

In the later 1960s, the surface complacency in regard to the history of the discipline was churned by several opposed currents. One was reflected in, and stimulated by, Marvin Harris' *Rise of Anthropological Theory* (1968). Its basic plan was like Lowie's, ignoring classical systems of thought or concurrent developments that tied anthropological fashions and assumptions to those of other fields, and evaluating a series of past anthropological writers with respect to their contribution or opposition to a single substantive view of culture—the author's own. Yet it was far from an updating of the earlier work. Where Lowie had opposed evolutionism, Harris was for it; and among those Lowie saw as the closest to the truth, Harris suggested the existence of politically motivated anti-scientific conspiracy, at the heart of which was the "historical particularism" of Franz Boas (whom Lowie had represented, equally unfairly, as a functionalist in basic sympathy with A. R. Radcliffe-Brown). Many accepted Harris' characterization; many others agreed with the need to stir things up; and a few were stirred into independent research by his interpretations.

For that latter group of scholars, an important countercurrent was represented by George Stocking's *Race, Culture, and Evolution,* also published in 1968. Stocking, too, concentrated heavily on Boas. But his concern was not to argue for or against any particular theoretical camp so much as to document the development of an idea. His problem was with showing originality and its context. His methods, aimed at the kind of thoroughness that could establish the existence of innovative thinking, were necessarily confined to a limited conceptual area. In consequence, Stocking's work lacked the scope of Harris', but pointed a road that others could follow. The significant contrast between Harris and Stocking went beyond method alone, and far beyond their views of the contribution of Boas. Stocking also made the first major break with the custom of ignoring external intellectual currents, showing the relevance of literary movements, broad political trends, and developments in other scientific disciplines. In the process he provided direct documentation of Boas' self-conscious and explicit interest in the philosophy of Immanuel Kant, and his identification with a group of Kantian scholars in Berlin at the beginning of his anthropological career. While this was a minor point in Stocking's argument, it was very important to me. It snapped into focus not only many features of Boas' argument that neither Lowie nor Harris had seemed able to represent accurately, but beyond that it seemed to account for Harris' polemical antipathy itself. It was an example of precisely the sort of inherited philosophical dispute that Harris and others like him had intimated were not important in the modern discipline.

Alongside the great expansion of perspective in the literature on the history of anthropology as such, there was an increase in the historical and philosophical content of debates in many areas of linguistic and ethnological theory. Lévi-Strauss' description of his own position as "Hegelian"; Chomsky's "rationalism" and "Cartesian" theory; the reliance of the "new archeologists" on the positivism of Karl Hempel; the use of positivist theories of meaning by componential analysts; and of course the "Marxism" of Harris himself and many of his colleagues all suggested histories. In fact, they were tied to specific versions of history, that themselves had histories—in most cases going back to the philosophers named. Of course, these versions of history conflicted with one another, and in many instances they were demonstrably wrong.

To provide an alternative to Harris' disinclination to see major historical figures' individual claims in terms of their own most basic assumptions, to expand on Stocking's beginnings, and to provide a documented framework for the many historical claims passed on in the course of theoretical argument or the received wisdom of the field, it seemed that a history that traced major theoretical assumptions back to their roots in philosophy and other disciplines, and that related them to ongoing developments in these sister fields, could be of service.

Because of the focus on the overall structure of arguments rather than on any specific terms or facts, it has been necessary to select only a relatively few major works to look at in relatively greater detail than one finds in most anthropological histories. I have tried to select authors who are at once well recognized, who have argued their cases fully and consistently, who have written before other authors with similar basic positions, and whose writing makes their positions relatively easy to illustrate. I have also cleaved to theories in linguistics, kinship, and social organization, partly because they were the earliest distinctively anthropological concerns to take form, and partly because they show the longest consistent development. I have avoided writings that are merely suggestive or programmatic, or that are or have proved to be highly ambiguous, subject to unusually conflicting interpretations. Perhaps arbitrarily, I have also avoided positions when my analysis of them would only repeat points made in discussing earlier positions, even if in some cases the two positions may not be immediately recognized as closely related. These selection criteria inevitably slight some currently popular authors. I am sure the judgments may in some cases be quite legitimately questioned. But I hope it will be apparent that any other selection would be equally liable to such objections, and that most anthropologists will therefore bear with me. The aim of the work is not, after all, to record the relative strength of current interests, nor to decide or assign relative importance to current or past writers. It is to describe very basic contrasting forms of argument, and their histories.

The aim of the work is to increase the general appreciation of some truly fundamental choices anthropologists have inherited and must eventually make. It is not to argue for any particular theoretical position in anthropology, although it will argue against certain theoretical positions insofar as they make historical claims that understate the richness of our legacy and of the options we have for the future.

This has, necessarily, become a rather complex work. Anthropology is an enormously complex field, with not one history but many. It would not have been possible to proceed without relying on an increasingly large number of both more substantively and more narrowly focused historical works (Carroll 1956; Firth 1957; Hays 1958; Lowie 1959; Mead 1959; Mead and Bunzel 1960; Wolf 1964; Penniman 1965; Helm 1966; Brew 1968; T. Kroeber 1970; Leach 1970; Hymes 1974; Stocking 1971, 1974; Willey and Sabloff 1974), as well as many reissues of classic works and the recent *Encyclopedia of Philosophy*. The histories by Malefijt (1974) and Voget (1975) reached me too late to be of great assistance, but their much wider than usual scope and many parallel interpretations were often comforting.

Once my general plan was formed, its implementation owed much to the students in my history of anthropology course at the University of California, Los Angeles, taught between 1969 and 1974. Those who made definite contributions through their papers, classroom and after-class criticisms, and direct discussions of the project are too numerous to be listed individually. They will recognize their ideas in these pages. It is to them especially that the manuscript owes its present double concentration on the relationship between the content of specific theoretical ideas and the logical structures of the arguments which they appeared in. Also at UCLA, it is a pleasure to acknowledge the criticism and suggestions of Marlys McClaran and Dwight Read, and the informal conversations with Professors Joseph Birdsell, Ralph Beals, Walter Goldschmidt, Hilda Kuper, and the late Harry Hoijer about their own careers and experiences. Additional extended discussions with Triloki Nath Pandey and Milton Singer (who graciously provided a manuscript analysis of the relationships between the ideas of Radcliffe-Brown and Bertrand Russell that confirmed and expanded my own readings) were of immense substantive and procedural value.

The first complete manuscript began a process of reiterative review and revision that involved a number of scholars who unfortunately remain anonymous to me. Nevertheless, the debt to them is great, each materially influencing the form of the manuscript as much material was cut out, other added, and arguments were pared to what would be most meaningful and directly intelligible. It was one of these readers who pointed out the relevance of Lovejoy. In this phase, a special debt is due to Professor Dell Hymes, whose trenchant and extensive criticism in many ways brought together the several lines of thought that Stocking had originally stimulated.

In the end, this work relies so much on the dedication and knowledge of so many scholars, it almost amounts to a team effort. But the responsibility for the overall direction, and for any errors, remains my own, as does the unhappy responsibility for many necessary omissions.

Preparation of material for the study was aided by a small grant from the Academic Senate, UCLA, and early drafts were expertly prepared by the UCLA stenographic bureau.

The final manuscript was prepared for typing by my wife, Michelina, who also materially aided and supported me in all earlier phases of the work. The final typescript was cheerfully and ably prepared by the secretaries of the School of Social Sciences of the University of Texas at Dallas, especially Florence Cohen, Ruth Cole, and Evelyn Stutts.

Murray J. Leaf
University of Texas at Dallas
October 1978

Man, Mind, and Science

A History of Anthropology

1.
Introduction

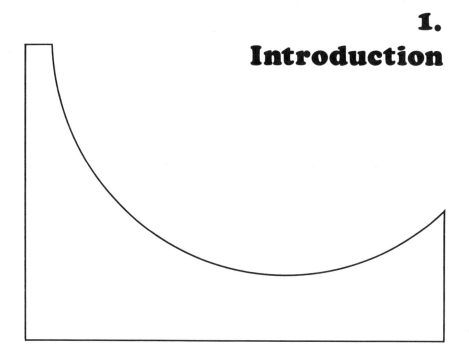

To explain people of cultures different from their own in kind, in space, and, often, in time, anthropologists have had to become concerned with cross-cultural comparison as a general problem. To non-anthropologists it may seem a relatively simple matter to go to a place, describe what the people do, and contrast it to whatever benchmark one chooses. It seemed rather simple to anthropologists for a while. But it does no longer.

From the late 1930s and up to about 1955, major anthropologists like Ruth Benedict, Ralph Linton, Margaret Mead, A. R. Radcliffe-Brown, E. E. Evans-Pritchard, Robert Redfield, and Clyde Kluckhohn adopted a style of writing that spoke confidently of anthropological theory and method, as if all anthropologists already understood and agreed upon the fundamental issues and it only remained to convey their understanding to the general public. When deficiencies were admitted, they were easily blamed on the preoccupation with wartime matters, the relatively small numbers of anthropologists then in existence, the denial of access to data that lay in combat areas, or, later, the need for reconstructing pre-war traditions rather than studying the impact of the war and its consequences.

But as more anthropologists were trained and began work in more areas, it became more and more evident that the early optimism was unjustified. The once plausible claims began to look like pretension. In the area of culture and personality, for example, it was not only that the relationships between culture and personality were harder to find than had been suggested; those who looked for them quickly found they didn't know what to put under the heading of "culture" as against "personality." When talking to an informant, did one divide the answers into the two categories? Whose culture did one look at as typical? Whose personality did one take as representative among individuals? How did one characterize either a culture or a personality? If one looked at child-rearing, how did one justify saying that such-and-such child behavior was the counterpart of such-and-such adult behavior? If one looked at the ideas about society present in one family or group of families, how did one relate it to a "whole" like Japan, or even Dobu?

Similarly, in social structure and kinship, it was not only that kinship systems were harder to find than one might think, but that the act of looking for them made anthropologists aware that they didn't know what their most basic concepts meant. There developed a fierce debate over what a "kinship term" was: "father" surely, but what about "child" or "parent"? Was "grandfather" (the English term) one term or two? It became evident that there was no way to resolve such a debate—no way to settle the issues in a manner that all concerned would regard as scientific or objective. And there were even greater problems regarding the relationships between kinship terms and kinship "systems," "rules," "rights," "units," and so forth. Similar difficulties developed in studies of religion, politics, economics, ecology, and, later, in symbolism and semantics.

By the late 1950s and early 1960s, optimism in the literature began to give way to a deepening recognition of difficulties yet to be faced. In 1961, E. R. Leach called for "rethinking" major issues in social anthropology, especially what he considered to be the basic concepts of kinship, as well as the aims and methods of theorizing. Also in 1961, E. E. Evans-Pritchard presented, in a major lecture, what many saw as a startling abandonment of earlier claims for the generality and universality of social structural analysis when he argued that the difference between history and social anthropology was "one of orientation, not of aim" (in 1962:191). At about the same time, a large number of American cultural and social anthropologists were turning to the sociological theory of Talcott Parsons and a number of his associates in the School of Social Relations at Harvard, in the evident belief that theory in anthropology fell far short of what Parsons' sociology had to offer—even though Parsons' theory was explicitly non-empirical, and was offered with the idea that one had to begin by establishing a set of logically circular conventions, tautologically related to one another (1951:17, 18).

By 1968, the belief that anthropology lacked coherent general theory was so widespread that a great many anthropologists were willing to accept Marvin Harris' explanation for the supposed deficiency, which characterized Franz Boas as fundamentally anti-theoretical, and as having in effect created a whole anti-theoretical generation of anthropologists dedicated to "historical particularism" (1968:250–318). Still more recently the wave of interest that has developed in the "structuralism" and "idealism" of Claude Lévi-Strauss has been based on a similar willingness to see anthropological theory as excessively crude, particular, and piecemeal. But this time the blame is placed on the "positivism" of Radcliffe-Brown, which Lévi-Strauss and his followers seem to construe as being an overly descriptive and classificatory orientation. And most recently, there has been a new kind of indictment of the past: essays brought together by Dell Hymes in a radical critique called for "reinventing anthropology," associating the inadequacy of current theory (variously diagnosed) with the interests of the Western social and economic systems that have served as anthropology's main sponsors (1969).

Clearly, anthropology is in trouble, but there is very little agreement on the way out. There is even a substantial body of argument, though only obliquely represented in print, to the general effect that anthropologists are inherently bound by the parameters of their culture. They can never escape it to see the world of those they study from an indigenous viewpoint, so that "objective" theory or culture-free theory is unobtainable in principle. All one can have is a more or less arbitrary approximation of the ideas of one culture in terms of another. This amounts to saying that a science of culture, or a science of man, is impossible in principle—at least as "science" is normally understood.

At first glance the most direct way to attack such doubts would seem to be to publish a general theory that explains human behavior with equal ease in any society, and which neither depends upon nor is limited by the cultural background of the analyst using the theory. But in anthropology such an approach is difficult for reasons over and above the inherent complexity and scope of the subject matter itself. The fact is that there are in the field at the present time quite different ways of thinking about theory, about culture, and about cultural comparison. The differences are so great, and so basic, that the strong points of a theory advanced in terms of one of them will not be apparent in terms of the other—in fact the proposal may not appear to be a theory at all.

There is a problem of ''tradition-centrism,'' a theoretical version of precisely the kind of thinking anthropologists recognize as ''ethnocentrism'' in other contexts.

Every anthropological theory must form a notion of three key issues: man, mind, and science. It must form or assume some conception of human nature; it must form a conception of what human thought, or mind, is and how it operates; and it must form or assume some conception of ordered scientific knowledge itself, about its power, bases, and limits. And every consistent theory must be applied or be applicable both to those the anthropologist studies and to the anthropologist himself. The human nature he attributes to those he studies should be related to what he attributes to himself; the mental processes he attributes to those he studies should have some relationship to what he sees in himself; and the conceptions of the power and basis of the knowledge he hopes to provide should have some relation to the systems of knowledge built up by those he wishes to understand. No complete theory can do only part of this, and every major writer has at least touched upon all the points.

Theories form traditions when they differ in detail, but make the same fundamental assumptions in their treatment of these basic issues, together with whatever other issues may be seen as equally basic from time to time. Debate becomes tradition-centered when scholars form the habit of defending their own specific theory only against others in the same general family, arguing over fine points but not defending, often not even explaining, the basic assumptions. Eventually in such debates, some scholars lose sight of their roots entirely and assume that the problems of their tradition are problems of knowledge in general. This is part of the problem in anthropology.

The optimistic theories dominant through the 1950s in fact represented a single tradition, but by the end of the period the tradition had moved sufficiently far from its points of origin that its common assumptions were no longer explicitly debated. Its followers became preoccupied with issues defined only within it, and in consequence when its difficulties were realized they were assigned to these debated but superficial points instead of the fundamental assumptions that generated the debates. At the same time, histories of the field written within the context of the same tradition, from Lowie's to Harris', saw other positions in its terms, which reinforced the tradition-centrism.

The principal casualties of the drift obscuring the origin of the recently dominant tradition (and hence the alternatives to it) were the theoretical views of Franz Boas and Bronislaw Malinowski. Despite their lack of mutual regard, these two scholars were in fact co-heirs to quite a different set of fundamental assumptions about man, mind, and science than Redfield, Radcliffe-Brown, Evans-Pritchard, and the others named, a tradition that had itself been dominant in ethnology and several related fields in the late nineteenth century. These two traditions, each with its fundamentally distinct conceptualizations of man, mind, and science, are the central concern of this work.

An idea that is fundamental to a tradition is, in part, an idea that lies unchallenged in a series of arguments where other ideas are subjected to attack—what remains unquestioned when all the questions are listed. But it is more than that. We can without much difficulty find lowest common denominators of general acceptance of the meanings of many individual terms that anthropologists use in their arguments: couvade, berdache, cross-cousin, kinship, lineage, sanction, right, exchange, reciprocity, alliance, ecology, system, culture, structure, or whatever. And we could, as others have done, build a history by taking a set of such terms and finding the earliest occurrences of these assigned meanings, one at a time. But there would be no guarantee that such meanings were in fact important or historically real bases of argument, retaining integrity over time. And more to the point the impression that anthropology is nothing but an accumulation of such ideas and definitions one at a time is quite misleading, a precise counterpart of the view of science as accumulation that Kuhn has argued against in the history of the physical sciences (1962:1–3).

Fundamental assumptions are not single definitions of terms. They are *systems* of ideas. In any argument, many ideas remain unquestioned. One cannot define every term used. But everything that is unquestioned is not of equal importance to the outcome. What is important are the unquestioned groups of interrelated ideas that mark the path from beginning to end. They even mark what a "beginning" and "end" should be. They define what an argument should contain, what a "fact" that can be included is, what relevance is, and what a conclusion is. These ideas determine the significance to be assigned the more isolated, individualized concepts. The ideas we will trace here are fundamental in just this sense. They are simple enough to be passed on and used in many different ways; but they are complex enough to form systems with considerable power and obvious integrity, so we can be assured that we are identifying real historical entities—seeing history from the point of view of those within it, not from the point of view of present impressions only.

The fundamental assumptions of the tradition shared by the optimistic pre- and postwar theories can be described appropriately under the general label of "dualism." The tradition associated with Malinowski and Boas, rejecting determinism and focussing on the free and purposive individual, can be characterized as "monism." Both labels reflect widely established usage, although the neatness of the contrast they suggest should not be taken as indicating that the two positions are in any sense simple opposites of each other, or that they logically exhaust all the possible assumptions that may be made. There have been quite different sets of assumptions offered from time to time, as in the radical historical determinism of Giambattista Vico, but they have been of much less importance.

It is possible to characterize both traditions quite simply, although a simple description runs the risk of being construed too narrowly, and therefore of conveying only part of the whole phenomenon. It should be remembered first that what one is hearing is only a general formula, the bare premises of an argument that can underlie many specific subject matters. Second, the description does not apply only to something "out there"; it also defines the perspective from which the entities "out there" are approached.

The dualistic tradition goes back to the philosophy of Socrates and Plato—so much so that it cannot be described without using the concepts and terms that these two men and their immediate followers invented. It is built upon three basic concepts that are employed together, as a single system, fundamentally to divide a shifting and unreliable world of individual beliefs and perceptions from a world of timeless and absolute truths that lie beyond the individual, his beliefs, and his perceptions: the concepts of the dichotomy, the doctrine of forms, and the doctrine of essences.

Philosophers commonly present the dichotomy as all but an item of common sense, much too innocuous to be a major assumption in its own right. But it nevertheless takes a major role in the dualistic tradition by being treated as if it were the only basis of logical thought, and by being used as the basis of the concept of a "class" in traditional systems of formal logic. A dichotomy is a division between two classes, in such a way that each class is the opposite of the other, and both classes together make up a "universe," with nothing left over. Formally, this means that if the two classes are A and B, B is the same as the negation of A. Everything which is not an A is *therefore* a B. This elaborates the concept of negation into what appears to be undoubtable objective truth. Obviously, no matter what A is taken to be, one can confidently assert that everything in the universe is either it or something else.

The doctrine of essences is that each thing has one and only one unique defining characteristic (which is its essence), which it shares identically with all other things of that class or type, and with them only. These defining essences are specifically distinguished from "mere" appearances, as something underlying them, and are in fact in most versions of this tradition considered to be somehow more "real" than surface appearances. This creates a radical separation between "reality" and "perception": the world of stable classes from the world of shifting and changing appearances. The aim of scholarship then becomes to transcend change, and arrive at the unchanging basis of it. Finally, the doctrine of forms was the link between the two other concepts: it was the idea that there was a basic dichotomy between "form" and "matter," and that forms (but in some later versions, matter) were essences. Objects as we know them were imperfect attempts of form to manifest itself in matter, on the model of an architect's plan that he tries to manifest in the materials of construction. The plan is inherently separate from the material, and prior to the construction, even though it cannot be perceived apart from matter in the final artifact. In Plato's own writings the dichotomy between form and matter was equated with the distinction between good and evil, reason and its objects, mind and the world of perception, perfection and imperfection, light and darkness, and the orders of enlightened rulers as against the sometimes unwilling subordinate citizens who must follow them. Aristotle added the dichotomies between formal logical analysis and description and between *a priori* analysis and analysis *a posteriori,* and with them he codified Plato's dialectic into the systematic deductive method of "division," or syllogism.

Since Plato's and Aristotle's time, the most characteristic focus of activity in this tradition has been the elaboration of new counterparts to form and matter, and new ways of arranging them in a deductive argument based on a hierarchy of increasingly general dichotomies.

In the monistic tradition, the world of appearances is taken as the only world there is. Truth, and more fundamentally human reason itself, is created by people in the course of their interaction. It is not an entity or quality sought by a single individual in isolation from context and circumstance. In this system of thought, there are no absolute principles used deductively as in the dualistic tradition, but there is a fundamental belief, taken more as an observation than a doctrine. In the famous phrase of the sophist Protagoras, it is that "man is the measure of all things."

The variability and instability of the perceived world, and the relativity of individual perspective, are not to be set aside in reaching knowledge. They are rather taken as the fundamental basis and cause of all knowledge, of actors and analysts alike. Knowledge itself is considered to be nothing but the result of efforts to order this individualistic and relativistic flux of perceptions by imposing, through social institutions, invented conventional categories upon it, in the context of everyday behavior. Accordingly, in this view, concepts like those of essences, gods, or logical rules are equally human creations, and none can be assigned a privileged status or reality apart from what can be shown in practical human affairs. The "truth" (another human concept) of an idea was always relative and would last only so long as it was consistent with the aims and purposes of those using and depending on it. In ethics, this led Protagoras to the view that what people in a community considered proper was proper so long as they considered it so—an early cultural relativism that Aristotle attacked bitterly. As a mode of argument it led to practical and experimental demonstration, as a way of gaining assent through controlling individual perception, rather than deduction or appeals to extra-experiential authority. Finally, knowledge had to be useful, and was in this respect treated as a commodity—what Socrates disassociated himself from in ringing terms as "teaching for money, and making the worse case appear the better" (The Apology).

Over the centuries many claims originally made in one tradition have been replicated within the other; and many attacks that have been developed in each against the other have been borrowed and redirected in turn. It is very difficult to find a clear point of difference that proponents of both traditions will acknowledge. So that one winds up arguing that some point—for example, recognition of individual freedom—is more fundamental to one tradition, and stated in more realistic and forceful ways within it, than in the other. But one point of difference is still very clear, and very germane to the current theoretical difficulties within anthropology. Namely, the dualistic tradition does not apply the same standards to, or offer the same description of, the knowledge of the analyst (or philosopher) as opposed to the knowledge of the people he is describing, whether it be the people of a specific community or all human beings in general. The analyst's knowledge is not part of the same system of knowledge as those he describes, or instructs, and it is not knowledge of the same kind. The monistic tradition, by contrast, is built upon providing exactly the same description to the knowledge of the analyst and those he is trying to understand. His knowledge and theirs is always described as exactly and without qualification of the same sort, with no privileged status, and it makes no difference if one is describing one's "own" society or another's. This diffrence has been the source of many of the most profound disagreements (for those who were aware of it explicitly) and misunderstandings (for those who were not).

From the monistic point of view, the inability of the dualistic tradition to apply uniform standards for verification to itself and to what it purports to describe is a fundamental inherent inconsistency, an admission that in practical terms theories within this tradition are not verifiable or applicable in principle. One either accepts them on personal faith, or in response to external authority, or one does not. But from the dualistic point of view, monistic schemes seem inconsistent for the opposite reason: they do not proceed systematically and consistently from premises that can be held as secure "objective" truths, beyond the vagaries of personal experience.

Abstract as these ideas may seem, they translate directly into theoretical issues in anthropology that are still unresolved. The optimism of the forties and fifties was commonly based on the identification of society or culture with a set of dualistic classes or categories which contained and shaped individuals as form shaped matter. This conveyed the too simple impression that all the anthropologist had to do was to find the specific social units that society was divided into, and those classes would automatically "show the essential basis" of the behavior of the people who occupied them. By contrast, Malinowski's conception of customs as "social charters," invented and maintained for their "function" for individuals in the community, was built upon the monistic conception of knowledge as a created, purposeful convention.

In another vein, the idea that one can never break out of one's own culture and see another is based on seeing the categories of one's own culture as knowledge *a priori,* a dualistic basis of classification that can itself never be transcended or side-stepped. This interpretation is reinforced by seeing the analyst as the subject and the observed culture as the object in a dichotomous subject-object relation. Again, in contrast, the monistic conception of the equality of all perspectives led both Boas and Malinowski, among others, to regard the ethnologist's field work, in practice, as the counterpart of the native's own methods of learning his culture. The only requirement for anthropological method to transcend the limits of the analyst's own culture would be to record diligently the situations within which he was taught each specific custom or usage of the people he was studying, making sure that such situations corresponded to those within which the natives themselves learned their systems, and being careful not to attribute more importance to the knowledge than the learning situation would warrant.

There are many reasons for reviewing these assumptions historically. First, it is by far the most straightforward and natural way to show the power of the simple ideas that the traditions are founded on—the way they recur and re-form over time, in constantly new and seemingly widely divergent applications. A second reason is that the order of their past development is directly related to their currency at the present, and thereby to the relationships between anthropology and other scholarly disciplines—from theology and philosophy through the other social sciences. Finally, by looking at the persistence of these traditions in time we can form a conception of an issue that is for most people of much greater interest than anthropological history as such—the way a tradition generally constrains its adherents and limits their originality, even while it provides a background against which the originality can be described.

There would be no point in writing a history like this if one believed that we could not overcome the difficulties of the past. In actual fact, the established difficulties in the comparative method, and in attaining our theoretical aims in general, are assignable not to our ''culture'' itself, but to specific elements of our academic traditions, and if we identify them and understand their operation, we can reformulate our aims and methods in such a way as to avoid them.

To reduce what might seem to be repetitious detail and concentrate on the branches of the development of these two traditions and their mutual interaction that are most directly related to current concerns, it is necessary to go back in the dualistic tradition to the philosophical rationalism founded by Descartes, and in the monistic tradition to the skeptical social and legal theory of Montesquieu, partly because philosophical positions invoked in modern debates seldom go back farther, and also because with them, philosophy, including social philosophy, ceased to apologize for its dissimilarity to religion and began to apologize for its dissimilarity to the sciences. After them, arguments about the nature of man and of thought came to be more and more fully entangled with explicit arguments about the nature of science in the precise frame of reference that is still current, and still not fully explored.

Since each of the following chapters describes one sequence of developments within one of the two major traditions that leads into modern anthropology, they fall into groups that overlap chronologically. Chapters 2 and 3 describe rationalism and monistic skepticism. The next five chapters describe several separate sub-traditions that overlapped, in steps, through the nineteenth century: chapter 4 describes the origins of sociology in the beginning of the nineteenth century; chapter 5 describes the contemporary beginnings of the comparative method that anthropologists were later to use; chapter 6 describes the influence of the comparative method on biology, centering on the last half of the century; chapter 7 describes the uses of the comparative method in anthropology in the same period, indicating the beginnings of several major technical areas that have been carried directly into the modern discipline; and chapter 8 briefly describes the way an initially rather unimportant western cultural and legal concept, that of the "tribe," developed into a major touchstone of theoretical debate in academic anthropology at the beginning of the present century.

The remaining chapters deal with this century and with anthropology as an academic discipline in the modern sense. Chapters 9 and 10 describe contrasting major early theories reflecting, respectively, the monistic orientation descending from skepticism and the dualistic theories descending from rationalism, mainly by way of sociology. Chapter 11 attempts to indicate by a few examples the arguments by which the assumptions of the monistic tradition were submerged, in general opinion, within the conceptual framework of dualism, centering on the period around the Second World War. Chapter 12 indicates the proliferation of dualistic schools during the same period, culminating around 1950. Finally, turning to the period since 1955, chapter 13 describes the way a number of leading authors reconstructed or re-stimulated much of the monistic position, but stopped short of rejecting dualism or recognizing their own arguments in their most general terms; and chapter 14 describes the most recent development of a series of arguments that in effect finished the process of criticism and reestablished the old debate in its full scale.

It is not my purpose to argue for monism and against dualism. That would require the use of types of evidence and modes of argument that are inappropriate in a history. But it is my purpose to show, historically, that dualistic assumptions involve, in themselves, severe and inherent problems, and that the acceptance of these assumptions by a large number of anthropologists has led to the quite mistaken belief that these problems are unavoidable in principle. I further hope to suggest that the monistic tradition avoids these limitations, but has suffered from limitations of another sort—namely that it requires certain factual understandings of the mechanism of human perception that have been beyond definitive investigation for most of the history of the tradition. Finally, I should like to convey my own hope that this situation has recently changed quite dramatically, and that anthropology now stands in a position capable not only of avoiding the difficulties of dualistic assumptions, but of establishing a series of understandings of man, mind, and science that will be like monistic positions of the past in many of its assumptions, but quite unlike them in the extent to which it is experimentally demonstrative rather than partially speculative. Far from being unable to escape the bonds of our own culture, we may be at the point of obtaining, as a trans-cultural experimental discipline, a new level of the special freedom that consists in understanding human understanding itself.

2.
Philosophical Foundations, Part I
Rationalism

Plato and his associates founded dualism in order to reject monism. Almost two thousand years later, Descartes and his associates offered their revised dualism for the same reason—as an attack against a series of new monistic positions that consciously invoked the memory, and even the names, of the earlier arguments.

In founding the dualistic tradition, Socrates, Plato, and Aristotle arrayed themselves against a series of established monistic philosophical systems going back to the Miletians, and including sophism and Pythagoreanism. After dualism was established, sophism continued into Roman ethics and statecraft, while Pythagorean mathematics was supplanted by the mathematics of such Alexandrian scholars as Euclid, Eratosthenes, and Archimedes—all holding that mathematics was both natural and conventional, observational and practical. At the same time, Plato's own school gave rise to monistic skepticism when the Socratic method of analysis (originally borrowed from the sophists in any case) was turned against two obvious targets that Socrates and Plato had neglected—the concept of essences and the doctrine of forms. Only the analytic method itself was left standing, and therefore framed a kind of sophism by default. But while monism was thus spreading in several technical and scholarly areas, dualism was spreading in cosmology and religion. It came, through Neoplatonism, and the stoic concept of "seminal reason," to supply the philosophical basis of formal Christian theology. Then, as the Roman Empire became the Holy Roman Empire, it became the official justification for the political authority that was claimed by the major political powers in Europe. Using this power, Church and state together eventually combined to suppress the monistic systems and schools, as well as dualistic schools offering opposing doctrines. Plato's own Academy was closed with other "pagan" schools by the emperor Justinian in A.D. 529.

By the late sixteenth and early seventeenth centuries, however, the ancient monistic traditions were reviving strongly in the context of a major argument over the scope of the competence of Church philosophy. The revival had begun in the thirteenth century with the first translations and publications in Europe of Euclid. Original developments by Europeans themselves soon followed and were abetted as mathematics gradually replaced logic in university curricula, especially in the Italian city-states. With many improvements in measuring instruments, including the invention of the telescope, this development eventually included the work of Copernicus and his great Italian defender and advertiser, Galileo Galilei. Copernicus' posthumous works were placed on the Index of Forbidden Books in 1616. In 1632, Galileo published his *Dialogues Concerning the Two Chief World Systems,* which purported to be a defense of the "Aristotelian" doctrines of the Church against what Galileo called Copernicus' "Pythagorean doctrines." In reality, of course, it was systematic exposure of all the weaknesses of the Church position, what Einstein has acutely called a "downright roguish" parody (Drake 1953:5). The Church, of course, was not amused. The book joined Copernicus' on the Index the same year it was published. In the next year Galileo was summoned to Rome, threatened with torture by the Inquisition, recanted, and was sentenced to indefinite imprisonment. This use of force was widely recognized as exposing the intellectual bankruptcy of the Church in matters of experimental science, and was almost without doubt the immediate stimulus to Descartes's effort to recast both dualism and mathematics in such a way as to remove the sense of conflict between them.

Modern treatments of Descartes and rationalism often suggest that it was part of the skeptical opposition. In fact, it was an attempt to save the bases of Church theology by meeting the skeptical challenge halfway, with a new "method of doubt," integrated in a framework of dualistic assumptions and principles. Descartes never responded to criticism he considered "atheistic."

After Descartes set out the general orientation, the principal modifications of the tradition that bear upon modern anthropology were made by Thomas Hobbes, who founded social contract theory; J.-J. Rousseau, who gave contract theory a historical and ethnographic interpretation; John Locke, who developed Hobbes's psychological views into philosophical "empiricism" (the basis of modern logical positivism); and Leibnitz, who reacted against the contradictions of Locke's position to found idealism, which in turn gave rise, combined with Rousseau's historicism, to the social idealism of Hegel.

Among the many ideas in current use that obtained their sense and justification in this literature are the distinctions between materialism and idealism as two opposed systems of thought, and between induction and deduction as two modes of reasoning. It also produced the so-called "mind-body" problem, as well as the idea that mathematics is purely deductive and universal, and the related idea that science is empirical observation that is generalized by being placed in a mathematical language. By way of social contract theory, it also generated the idea that perception consists in the imposition of mental constructs upon physical "sense impressions," a conception of human motivation that lays stress on personal fear and greed as opposed to more altruistic and social motives, and a special concept of social "law" as a quasimathematical system of rules based on *a priori* principles constructed by the analyst, yet which determine the behavior of people within society, and which constitute a total organization of the society.

René Descartes (1596–1650)

Descartes's philosophy was, in his own view, closely connected to his analytic geometry. He invented the technique of using a graphic representation in two dimensions to define what is now known as a Cartesian coordinate system, and of using this system in turn to define, at least in principle, any algebraic function. Since the coordinates are themselves defined in terms of Euclid's geometry, and since graphic curves and lines can define geometrical figures, this integrated algebra and geometry, formerly distinct fields of mathematics, into a single system. For Descartes, this synthesis accomplished nothing less than a formalization of the analysis of all of the material world. The argument supporting this claim, and placing the analysis of the material world in the context of a still larger analysis of both material and immaterial entities, is based on the dualistic assumptions, and constitutes the overall framework of Cartesian philosophy.

The analytic geometry was published by Descartes as one of three appendices to his *Discourse on Method: To Properly Conduct the Reason and to Seek Truth in the Sciences* (1637). This was followed in 1641 by his perhaps most famous *Meditations on First Philosophy: In Which the Existence of God and an Immortal Soul Is Demonstrated.* Roughly, these two works stand in about the same relationship to each other as Aristotle's *Categories* (prior analytics) stand to his *Metaphysics* (posterior analytics). The *Discourse* deals with the problem of adequate bases of inquiry and reasoning, the *Meditations* with the problem of applying the inquiry to the description of basic "substances."

The first three sections of the *Discourse* recount Descartes's desire to develop a method of analysis that would provide conclusions that were certain, withstanding all doubt. The shift to positive argument begins in the fourth section and develops rapidly:

> In practical life, as I had long observed, it is sometimes necessary to follow opinions which we know to be highly uncertain; . . . but as I was then minded to give myself entirely to the search for truth, I thought that . . . I ought to reject as downright false all opinions which I could imagine to be in the least degree open to doubt—my purpose being to discover whether, after so doing, there might not remain, as still calling for belief, something entirely indubitable. (Descartes 1637:118)

On this basis he rejected the evidence of the "senses," of "mathematical demonstration" and all specific thoughts. Then:

> But I immediately became aware that while I was thus disposed to think that all was false, it was absolutely necessary that I who thus thought should be somewhat; and noting that this truth *I think, therefore I am,* was so steadfast and so assured that the suppositions of the skeptics, to whatever extreme they might all be carried, could not avail to shake it, I concluded that I might without scruple accept it as being the first principle of the philosophy I was seeking.
>
> Next . . . from this very circumstance that I thought to doubt the truth of those other things, it very evidently and very certainly followed that I was, whereas I had only to cease to think for an instant of time and I should then . . . have no ground for believing that I can have existed in that instant. From this I know that I was a substance whose whole essence or nature consists entirely in thinking, and which, for its existence, has no need of place, and is not dependent on any material thing; so that this I, that is to say, the soul, by which I am what I am, is entirely distinct from the body, and is indeed more easy to know than the body, and would not itself cease to be all that it is, even should the body cease to exist.

I then . . . judged that I could take as being a general rule, that the things we apprehend very clearly and distinctly are true—bearing in mind, however, that there is some difficulty in rightly determining which are those we apprehend distinctly.

Reflecting in accordance with this rule on the fact that I doubted, and that consequently my being was not perfect—I resolved to inquire whence I had learned to think of something more perfect than I myself was; and I saw clearly that it must proceed from some nature that was indeed more perfect. (118–120)

Here are the basic elements of the Cartesian philosophy. The system is built on a series of dichotomies beginning with "truth" as the negation of "falsehood," and concluding with the immaterial soul and a perfect God as opposed to the physical body and the material world.

Using the truth-falsehood dichotomy the argument equates dubitability with falsehood—suggesting that anything that can ever be doubted therefore cannot be true, since empirical verification is necessarily circumstantial. Also note that the statement Descartes begins with as the most undoubtable truth has the form of a traditional logical proposition "A therefore B," suggesting (what he elsewhere spells out) that his most general intellectual tool is to be Aristotelian class-inclusion logic and the associated theory of essences. Descartes's own uses of this logic are original and are especially important historically. First, he puts "I am"—a form of the verb "to be"—in the place where Aristotle would put a predicate, like "is red," designating a quality or characteristic of a class. This equates the truth of the proposition with the bare *existence* of its subject, a point medieval logicians had always refrained from asserting. In this case, the subject is "I." By this logical innovation, Descartes asserted the *a priori* existence of "I," apart from perception and perceptual problems. He thus accomplished at the outset what Aristotle's entire apparatus had been designed to establish as an end point. The line of development that Descartes had in mind for this concept is suggested in the continuation of his remark after the point is introduced—first in the idea that he was a "substance" that consists *only* of thinking "entirely distinct from body," and then in the idea that his thinking substance must reflect a higher "more perfect" being of the same substance, equally distinct from "body" or "place."

In the *Meditations*, Descartes developed the general idea that "all things we judge clearly and distinctly are true in that very mode in which we are judging them" (Descartes 1641:171). Then, holding that we had a clear and distinct idea that mind was separate from body, he argued that the world was radically divided between substances that were indivisible (mind and God) and those that were divisible (corporeal bodies). Within this framework, his analytic geometry was an analysis of divisibility—reducing all figures and motions to points which cannot be themselves divided and, hence, were the ultimate constituents of all bodies.

Extending the geometrical analogy, Descartes evidently thought of mind as being "within" body in the same way a point is "within" a line in geometry—where lines are thought of as being made up of points even though lines are divisible and points are not. But a line is not a body, and despite the geometrical metaphor, the actual effect of Descartes's system was to raise the mind-body problem to the forefront of this new system of philosophy. At the same time, the system makes the problem unsolvable *in principle*. If the existence of mental entities can be inferred from the fact of thinking alone, and thinking alone is sufficient to guarantee their existence and nothing else, then it follows that his premise necessarily leads to the conclusion (which is contained in it) that thinking exists. Further, if material objects are radically separated at the outset from objects of thought, then it follows, by definition, that there is no necessary guarantee of the existence of material objects within the premises of the system (that is, on the basis of knowledge of thinking alone). Finally, in terms of the system, no guarantee (necessary connection) is tantamount to no connection at all, for it is Descartes's contention that he is building a system on undoubtable logical inference. Therefore, asking how mental entities and material entities are connected, given the way they are defined, is precisely like asking how many angels (immaterial objects) can stand on the head of a pin (a material object). Eventually this problem led most of those who accepted Descartes's assumptions to cleave to one or the other of two extreme positions: to attempt to derive matter, or perception, from mind (idealism), or mind from matter (empiricism).

Thomas Hobbes (1588–1679)

Common opinion places Thomas Hobbes second in importance to Descartes in the formation of rationalist philosophy. But the two major subtraditions that Hobbes founded, social contract theory and the empirical theory of knowledge, have had far more direct bearing on current concerns than strict Cartesian rationalism. Both embody elements Descartes never suggested, and have a complexity and force beyond anything in his system. Philosophical empiricism in the technical sense, resting on Descartes's mind-matter dualism, was an attempt to see mind as wholly internal to the individual and to derive its content as ''impressions'' of external matter operating in accordance with natural laws. Social contract analysis was built on an application of geometrical reasoning, like Descartes's system, to frame an analysis of civil society as an agreement between the ruler and those ruled, or between citizens and the state. It is the first system of analysis specifically aimed at the state, a social organization, rather than at law in general, or the conduct of rulers.

On the surface Hobbes's works are a defense of the powers of monarchy. But it is a defense that agrees with many of the enemies of monarchy in refusing to grant it any religious status. The argument turns on the concept of a state or ''common-wealth'' as created by ''covenant'' only, where a covenant is understood to be ''artificial,'' or man-made (*Leviathan,* part 2, ch. 17), as opposed to divine.

Hobbes's concept goes back to a dispute between Epicurean and Stoic philosophers concerning the origin of human law (continuing the debates of Aristotle and Plato; see Windelband 1958:1:174 ff.), as it had been reflected especially in the works of Niccolò Machiavelli (1469–1527) and Hugo Grotius (1583–1645). In medieval and Renaissance jurisprudence, the dispute had given rise to the general distinction between ''civil'' (local and arbitrary) and ''canon'' (universal and necessary) law. The Church claimed exclusive authority only in the latter area, while the first was considered a matter of local custom and convenience. Without challenging this framework, Machiavelli had developed his system of statecraft based on fear and greed—a view perfectly consistent with the Augustinian conceptions of life in the ''city of man'' rather than the ''city of God.'' But against the established view, Grotius (more akin to the skeptical tradition) had argued that the law of war, which was taken as being universal (international), was actually not divine but artificial, just like local law, on the ground that states acted on a large scale just as individuals did on a small scale. The state was simply the individual writ large. Hobbes's system combined a Cartesian method with these two key earlier ideas: Machiavelli's concept of motivation, and Grotius' conception of the state as man in the large—which Hobbes called Leviathan.

Hobbes published *De Cive* in 1642 or thereabouts (in Latin). His second major work was published by his friends as *Human Nature* and *De Corpore Politico* in 1650. *Leviathan* was published in 1651 (Windelband:341) and is a popularized and expanded version of the same arguments. Other works were projected but not completed, apart from one on optics published in 1644. Hobbes remained the center of bitter controversy throughout his long life.

Like geometrical proofs, Hobbes's arguments can be stated in a brief formula, or in a highly expanded version. A concise summary is presented in the dedicatory of *De Cive*. He begins, like Descartes, by stating his reasons for beginning philosophical study. Given this, he mentions certain questions of procedure and fact which he next had to deal with, and he arrives at the statement of his central concern: "the foundation of justice"—a view he shared with Aristotle, but not with Machiavelli. This "formulation" is what he saw in turn as the consent of men in regard to the "enclosure" of their individual rights from one another. From this point, he moves to the question of how his enclosure came about:

> And I found the reason was, that from a community of goods there needs must arise contention whose enjoyment should be greatest, and from that contention all kinds of calamities must unavoidably ensue, which by the instinct of nature, every man is taught to shun. Having therefore thus arrived at two maxims of human nature, the one arising from the concupiscible part, which desires to appropriate to itself the use of those things in which all others have a joint interest, the other proceeding from the rational, which teaches every man to fly a contranatural dissolution as the greatest mischief that can arrive to nature; which principles being laid down, I seem from them to have demonstrated a most evident connection, in this little work of mine, first the absolute necessity of leagues and contracts, and hence the rudiments both of moral and civil prudence. (Lamprecht 1949:5–6)

This "fundamental question" has the same status in Hobbes's scheme that the question of describing how a linear figure can be inscribed in a circle has in Euclid's scheme. It contains in its own formulation the assumptions necessary to answer it.

By identifying civil society as an "enclosure" of rights, Hobbes introduces the critical assumption that the absence of social organization, of civil society, is the absence of such enclosed rights. This very simple and straightforward dichotomy rests on the geometrical distinction between a line that crosses itself and one that does not—exhausting the universe of possible forms of lines. A curve may intersect itself and "lose" both its end points, or not intersect itself and retain its end points, by the definition of a line and of enclosure, for us and for Hobbes. Therefore "enclosure" must be either affirmed or denied, present or absent. There is no matter of degree, and no other alternative. Hobbes's problem was merely to find a plausible way of connecting the idea of "rights" to that of enclosure, of describing the logical construction of the enclosed state from the unenclosed state.

Besides the enclosure of rights a second major dualistic component of Hobbes's argument is the dichotomy "will" versus "reason." This idea had evolved purely in a context of theological simplification of Aristotle's and Plato's psychology, principally in the hands of Augustine and John (Duns) Scotus Erigena (see Windelband, vol. 1, part iii, ch. 2, p. 26). As indicated in Hobbes's contrast with the "concupiscible part," reason has the same disembodied and "indivisible" character that it had for Descartes.

Once we recognize that Hobbes's "community of goods" is, by definition, nothing but the condition of unenclosed rights, the logical structure of the argument is clear. Based on the geometrical dichotomy between enclosed and unenclosed rights and the theological dichotomy between will and reason, Hobbes argues that in a state of nature (absence of enclosure) any claim by any person to any good is necessarily a claim to all goods—it cannot be distinguished from such a claim by others. Therefore requirements of basic individual survival would lead inevitably to a "war of all against all"—the "contranatural dissolution" referred to above. Such a "war," however, is itself inimical to the survival of those who created it (hence *contra*-natural—against natural law, the social counterpart of a self-contradiction). From this it follows that it cannot be maintained as a "natural" or stable condition. The instability ends when people end the community of goods—by "partitioning" (same as "enclosing") rights. This enclosure at once limits each person's claims to something tolerable by others, and provides a basis for cooperation and "contracts." In dividing rights, the possibility of exchanging them is automatically created.

In the transition from a "community of goods" to "civil society" and its consequences, Hobbes defined the state of nature as a state where every person retains his own will to act—he acts only under his own power. By contrast, he views a state of enclosed rights as a state where one no longer retains one's own will.

Hobbes's argument was that if a person retains his will, he retains it to do whatever he wishes—without restriction. Such a person logically could not truly participate in any division of rights, or engage in any true contract. On the other hand, if one did participate in such a division of rights and engage in contracts, it implied that one had given up the will to act freely. One was accepting the terms of the division, or of the contract, in place of one's own will. Hobbes next argued that since the will was indivisible, one either gave it all up or one did not give it up at all. He further argued, by a series of postulates, that will could not be given up to something that was not itself active—such as a paper instrumentality. Rather it had to be given up only to something (necessarily some person or group) that could itself act upon it and enforce the contracts one wished to make. The "social contract" as Hobbes thus came to define it was nothing but the initial contract that set up the initial transference of will. The government or "monarch" was that which the will was transferred to (the term "body politic" was not an idle metaphor). Civil society was the resultant condition. Civil law was based on the assumption of an external embodiment of the general will. Natural law was that minimal law that made no such assumption. It was purely individual law that allowed no basis for contractual relationships or exchanges.

The argument is a steel trap. For Hobbes, the only condition that would automatically void the "social contract" was its failure to provide the end for which it was set up—failure to provide an improvement over the war of all against all. Specifically, the relation of any person to the social contract was voided if—and only if—the repository of the general will endangered his life.

At the time of the Long Parliament and demands for religious and civil rights, this must have seemed a very slim concept of the responsibility of the state to its citizens. Whatever its logical force might have been as a defense against the enemies of unlimited monarchy, it was hardly likely to win political friends for the royalist cause. But the complementary position that this entailed on the relation of the subject to sovereign was even more upsetting. Since the sovereign was established by the handing over of will, it followed that any act whatever that was not consonant with the will of sovereign amounted to a resumption of one's own will. This in turn was a dissolution of the social contract, and a return to a state of "war" of all against all. In this case, the individual was of course alone against his former sovereign who was now a simpler but stronger "individual" in the state of nature, unconstrained by the terms of any agreement, with all the resources he might control. This logical condition would last until a contract was reestablished on any terms that would preserve the life of the individual, or until one of the parties was destroyed. In effect, anyone who dissented in any degree was an enemy of the sovereign and of the body politic. There was no loyal opposition, and no means of redress save a struggle of wills and resources. Lamprecht, commenting in his edition of De Cive, was not the first to see this position as "ruthless" (p. xxix).

The principal difference between De Cive and Leviathan is the incorporation of Hobbes's psychology in the latter. Recognizing that his view of the agreement among different individuals' conceptions of what was necessary in the state of nature was otherwise arbitrary, Hobbes constructed a mechanistic psychology to provide a basis for it. This is empiricism, and lest a paraphrase be taken for a parody, the following remarks from the first part of the *Leviathan* will let Hobbes speak for himself:

> Concerning the thoughts of man, . . . singly, they are every one a representation or appearance of some quality or other accident of a body without us which is commonly called an object. Which object works on the eyes, and other parts of a man's body, and by diversity of working produces diversity of appearances . . . The cause of sense is the external body or object which presses the organ proper to each sense, either immediately as in the taste or touch, or mediately as in seeing, hearing, and smelling; which pressure, by the mediation of the nerves and other strings and membranes of the body continued inward to the brain and heart, causes there a resistance or counterpressure or endeavor of the heart to deliver itself, which endeavor because *outward,* seems to be some matter without. . . . So that sense, in all cases, is nothing else but original fancy, caused, as I have said, by the pressure— that is, by the motion—of external things upon our eyes, ears, and other organs of thereunto ordained. (1651:25, 26)

Hobbes was especially concerned with differentiating this position from the "Aristotelian" view of the Church that there were separate "essences" of objects for each of the senses, and that these objects, "coming into the understanding, make us understand" (p. 26). That is, for Hobbes only *substances* are objective, qualities arise in the mind, as against the idea that qualities are inherent in the thing and impress themselves on the mind. But of course this position still utilizes the ancient dichotomy between substances and qualities.

Hobbes's dualism rendered his scheme unprovable from the start, but it also made it seem simple and natural to those who already accepted such notions in other areas. At the same time the way in which it differed from other dualistic psychologies would not have seemed at all small or fine to those who accepted the framework as the only possible one. Hobbes promised to make the mathematical advances of Descartes and others applicable not only to the world of objects in a crude sense, and to astronomy, but to an integrated theory of law, society, perception, and psychology as well. Once Descartes and others had provided calculi that could give mathematical statements for any object in motion in any context, it must have seemed to Hobbes that by reducing perceptions of sense to such objects and their motions, he could adapt the new mathematical apparatus to underpin his individual psychology, and ultimately to his analysis of the state as an "artificial man." It was a powerful vision.

John Locke (1632–1704)

John Locke accepted Hobbes's basic technique of treating the foundation of society as an enclosure of rights. He differed with Hobbes, within this framework, by arguing that such an enclosure can come about in a state of nature, on the basis of natural law alone. In the course of argument he expanded and elaborated Hobbes's psychological views, and unintentionally exposed, therefore, their basic internal inconsistencies. Locke's psychology in turn provided the starting points for economics, associationist psychology and modern "behaviorism," and, as noted, "empiricism" as a philosophy of science. All of these applications have carried forward the original difficulties.

Locke's two most influential works were *An Essay Concerning Human Understanding* and *Two Treatises on Civil Government,* both written more or less concurrently, and published in 1690. The first essay of *Two Treatises* is a rejection of a then-influential defense of absolute monarchy. The second is "An Essay Concerning the True Original, Extent and End of Civil Government." The *Essay Concerning Human Understanding,* though less formally divided, also included treatments of two distinct topics: the first was his psychology, and the second his theory of "knowledge and probability," beginning at about Book 4.

It had been widely recognized that Hobbes failed to state all the links necessary to complete his argument, connecting the "workings" of external "bodies" to the actual ideas in the mind. Locke undertook to complete the scheme. To do this, he proposed to work backwards, from thought to sensations. He first divided ideas into "simple" and "complex." The former were supposed to correspond directly to "sensations"; the latter to be made of simple ideas. And to show how this happened, he took a number of important philosophical ideas (going back to Aristotle's *Metaphysics* in most cases), classified them as either simple or complex and, if complex, resolved them into simple ideas. Complex ideas dealt with in this manner included God, self, and infinity—all later recognized as major problems by Kant—as well as relation, substance, will, and power. The last was a major focus of Hume's attack, and was in turn the principal concept that Thomas Reid, James Beattie, Dugald Stewart, and other "common sense" Scottish philosophers attempted to defend against Hume.

Locke framed his analyses with an extended attack on the possibility that such ideas could be "innate," recognizing that this was the only logical alternative to his own materialistic explanation of agreement between individual minds within the Cartesian mind-matter dichotomy (which saw mind as only "within" the individual without reference to learning or convention). But this led to confusion. For example, in order to account for similarity among different individuals' ideas, such as that of "God," without arguing that they were simple and corresponded to direct sensations, Locke had to argue that such ideas were built up in each person's mind by a uniform process. Yet to avoid a doctrine of innate ideas, he had to argue that the mind that did this building was entirely passive. He tried to support this interpretation with the idea that "relations" by which simple ideas were compared and arranged were themselves impressed upon the mind by nature, but to do this he had to argue that "relation" was both a simple idea (otherwise how would *it* be built up?) and a complex idea (because it obviously does not correspond to an impression on a sense). In the end, the argument is a hopeless tangle, but it showed how difficult it can be to account for some of our most ordinary concepts.

Locke's empiricism was built directly upon his psychology, stressing the distinction between ideas in the mind and sensations of objects in nature. Locke held that truth was the "right joining or separating of signs, i.e., ideas or words" (1690a: book 4, ch. 5, sec. 1), and that knowledge therefore consisted of propositions that were determined to be true, false, or probable (thus combining logical and mathematical reasoning in one system). To determine which of these or in what degree, one had to know what types of proposition one was dealing with:

> . . . it appears that there are two sorts of propositions. (i) There is one sort . . . concerning the existence of anything answerable to such an idea: as, having the idea of an elephant, phoenix, motion, or an angel in my mind, the first and natural inquiry is, whether such a thing does anywhere exist. And this knowledge is only of particulars . . . (ii) There is another sort of proposition, wherein is expressed the agreement or disagreement of our abstract ideas, and their dependence on one another. Such propositions may be universal and certain. (ch. 9, sec. 13)

With the doctrine that "particulars" must ultimately be stated in terms of sensations, in Hobbes's sense, this formulation provides what

W. V. O. Quine not long ago characterized as the "two dogmas of empiricism": the analytic-synthetic distinction and "reductionism," and they exist today without substantial change (a point that Quine obscured in the same essay when he attributed the distinction to Hume and Kant and failed to mention Locke) (Quine 1953:20).

This psychology provided Locke with a means for seeing ownership as based on the simple and immediate perception of one's own force or labor transferred to an object, while his logic provided for natural law based on the concepts of the relative magnitude of this labor within objects, "without any express compact of all the commoners" (1690: ch. 5, sec. 15).

> He that is nourished by the acorns he picked up under an oak, or the apples he gathered from the trees in the wood, has certainly appropriated them to himself. Nobody can deny but the nourishment is his. I ask, then, when did they begin to be his—when he digested, or when he ate, or when he boiled, or when he brought them home, or when he picked them up? And 'tis plain if the first gathering made them not his, nothing else could. That labor put a distinction between them and common; that added something to them more than nature, the common mother of all, had done, and so they became his private right . . . And the taking of this or that part does not depend on the express consent of all the commoners . . . The labor that was mine removing them out of that common state they were in, hath fixed my property in them. (sec. 28)

From here, the argument is obvious: the quantity or intensity of labor in an object gave it its value and provided a basis for trading under natural law. A fair trade was a trade of a quantity of labor (of oneself) for its equal. And finally, money was invented as a repository for value to delay trade: "And thus came in the use of money—some lasting thing that men might keep without spoiling, and that, by mutual consent, men would take in exchange for the truly useful but perishable supports of life" (sec. 47). With all this established without a social contract, it was easy to continue to argue that basic laws pertaining to property could be developed and enforced on a similarly "natural" basis. "Civil government," when finally recognized as necessary in the argument, was no more than a limited court of equity, set up as a mutual convenience by two contending parties who recognized they could not agree among themselves.

With the various qualifications Locke added in order to preclude, for example, wanton killing of game or wastefully amassing goods others could better use or claim, the Utopian conception of a self-regulating natural system where everyone was rewarded according to his labor, and no oppressive government was required, exercised a powerful influence on a series of subsequent thinkers.

At bottom, Locke uses the same dichotomy between divided and undivided property that Hobbes invented and, beneath this, the same mind-substance dichotomy as the basic framework of his argument. Without these assumptions, there is no point in most of what he says. How else, for example, can one construe labor as a *quantity*, a thing? And why else would anyone go to such lengths to ignore consensus as a *basis* of organization? Locke is operating in a dichotomized world where explanation must come from mind or matter; there is no other alternative. Given this, he not only can but must set up a world of "real" relations quite apart from what participants in the world may actually see or believe, and he not only can but must urge these upon the participants as what they *ought* to be doing. In the content of what he urges, Locke is very different from Plato, Augustine, and Hobbes. In the manner of his urging, and the privileged position he claims for it, he is not different at all.

Idealism: Leibnitz (1646–1716)

The doctrine of innate ideas that Locke tried to reject was adopted as the principal alternative to his position in the second major rationalist sub-tradition, called, generally, idealism. George Berkeley (1685–1753) was the principal British idealist, and is probably still considered the greatest enlightenment proponent of this position. But Baron Wilhelm Gottfried von Leibnitz, an associate of Descartes, was in most respects the idealist with the greatest impact on social theory.

Rigorously adhering to Descartes's premises, Leibnitz came to the conclusion that there could not be certain or "necessary" knowledge of material substances. Instead, the only certain knowledge was of "immaterial substances," which were nothing but different aspects of Descartes's thinking "I" whose "whole substance" was thought alone. This selection from his 1702 essay "On the Supersensible Element in Knowledge, and on the Immaterial in Nature," written as a letter to Queen Charlotte of Prussia, indicates Leibnitz' general argument quite clearly:

> Thus what the ancient Platonists have observed is very true, and is very worthy of being considered, that the existence of intelligible things and par-

ticularly of the *Ego* which thinks and which is called spirit or soul, is incomparably more sure than the existence of sensible things; and that thus it would not be impossible, speaking with metaphysical rigor, that there should be at bottom only these intelligible substances, and that sensible things should be but appearances. . . . This conception of *being* and of *truth* is found therefore in the Ego and in the understanding, rather than in the external senses and in the perception of external objects. (in Weiner 1951:359–60)

Leibnitz recognized explicitly that he was in sharp conflict with both the associational psychology of Hobbes and Locke, as well as the then widely discussed parallelism of Spinoza, within the framework of their shared dualistic assumptions. In his *New Essays on the Human Understanding* (written in 1704, first published in 1765), he specifically contrasted Locke's "Aristotelianism" to his own "Platonism," attacking and rejecting Locke's conception of mind as a *tabula rasa* acted upon by matter in motion, in favor of his own idea of mind as an active "soul" (Weiner:367ff.).

Leibnitz' concept of mind as active rather than passive had an important bearing on the monistic philosophies of both Kant and Hume, as well as the strict dualism of Hegel. So did an important point Leibnitz made in arguing against Locke and for his system: one does not find the basic categories of thought in complete form in perception alone. It is not so paradoxical as it may first appear that the "dogmatic slumbers" from which Kant "awoke" to attack the entire dualistic tradition were Leibnitzian slumbers in particular.

Jean-Jacques Rousseau (1712–1778)

After Locke's diversion, social contract theory was re-focused on an analysis of society by Jean-Jacques Rousseau, in a form that stimulated Kant and led directly to Hegel, and thence to Comte and Durkheim.

Rousseau's work cannot be characterized as a whole. It was far too inconsistent, and parts can easily be placed in the monistic tradition. He was obviously following the Skeptical writers in approaching the analysis of society through the reconstruction of progressive historical sequences incorporating a developmental sense of individual psychology. But the part of his argument that is dualistic is so to the core, fundamentally and not superficially. His conception of society as a "general will" is based squarely on the three dichotomies: will versus reason, particular versus general, and divisibility versus indivisibility in Hobbes's and Descartes's sense.

In *The Social Contract* (1762), Rousseau argued, in direct contradiction to Hobbes, that individuals could not give up their will. Will was inalienable. The argument was weak and boiled down to saying, arbitrarily, any group of individuals who gave up their wills to a monarch would have to be a "nation of madmen," and "madness creates no right" (*Social Contract*, book 1, ch. 5). But the idea itself was powerful. Rousseau construed it to put the ruler in precisely the position that Hobbes had placed a disobedient subject. Like Hobbes, Rousseau saw the general will as unified and active. But he also saw it as infallible— as inherently right in any action (book 2, ch. 3). Therefore, if a monarch acted against the general will, he had no legitimate claim to be followed, no legitimate power, and in effect should be eliminated as a traitor or criminal. Any ruler, any "particular will," who stood apart from the general will, stood automatically against it, and was entitled to no protection or privileges (book 2, ch. 10). All law also was seen to derive its claim only from the general will, and hence could not be held to stand above the general will.

This concept of the general will has no logical relationship to the better known historical parts of his argument that portray society as becoming increasingly complex, and increasingly removed from natural simplicity and directness, in time. The general will has no role in this development; nor is it described as itself evolving.

The general will is the seed of the dualistic tradition that has dominated academic anthropology in this century. Rousseau's concept of the general will portrayed society as a single whole, determinant of the behavior of all its members but not reducible to them. Yet it was an invention of the analyst and not a construct or creation of the members in any conscious or deliberate sense, and the analysis contained a provision for the dismissal of the behavior of individuals who failed to exhibit the hypothesized universal pattern.

Conclusion

Rationalism is complex and many-sided enough to provide parallels to any modern position, if one focuses only on the differences between its opposed sub-traditions and ignores their similarities. Almost every sort of religious opinion is represented, a range of political views from religious autocracy through secular autocracy to radical democracy (if that is an accurate view of Rousseau), and epistemologies from relatively strong materialism (Locke) to absolute idealism. Yet in a larger view, the similarities are equally striking and show a common front against the monistic tradition, rejecting every argument the monists advanced. The rationalists all phrased their problems, various as they were, in terms of a single individual surrounded by a perceived world, total and undivided. They explained their conceptions of the individual so conceived, and his relation to the world, by positing yet another world beyond both the individual and his perceptions. Finally, their conception of proof involved appeals to consistency in deduction from premises that were supposed to be beyond experimental challenge— always a distinctive set of concepts wherein the images and concepts of mathematics, especially geometry, were used to define dichotomous classes of relations, types of rights, positions in regard to social groups, or types of objects. The greater the number of debates based on these assumptions, and the more bitter they were, the more important the assumptions themselves inevitably appeared to be.

3.
Philosophical Foundations, Part II
Skepticism

As the revival of skepticism did not put an end to dualism, but forced it to develop new arguments, so the rise of rationalistic dualism in turn did not destroy skepticism so much as it gave it new issues to address. One of these issues was the status of mathematics.

Descartes, Leibnitz, and Hobbes treated mathematical reasoning as a new version of Aristotle's formal logic—a new basic framework for dividing the universe into dichotomous classes for analysis. Where Aristotelian logic divided classes by distinguishing substance and qualities, the new method of division involved mathematical distinctions: divisible versus indivisible; extended versus unextended; lines that intersect versus lines that do not intersect. In this view mathematics was knowledge *a priori*, true apart from and prior to any experience, flowing from the character of "mind" itself.

Skeptics, however, persisted in their quite different conception of mathematics as conventional formalization of observation, and in their avoidance of the idea that anything was true absolutely and before all possible experience. In 1662, Robert Boyle's *Sceptical Chemist* extended Galileo's attacks on theological "Aristotelians." In 1687, Newton's *Philosophiae Naturalis Principia Mathematico*—Mathematical Principles of Natural Philosophy—began a long series of arguments against Descartes, Leibnitz, and other dualists on a wide range of issues. Against Descartes's wave theory of light, Newton argued that light consisted in "bodies" (a position that left no way for them to be perceived by "mind" in Descartes's sense). Against Newton's conception of gravity, Leibnitz and others argued that some necessary basis had to be provided for accepting the hypothesis, and against this in turn Newton argued that no such ultimate basis was necessary. It was sufficient that the concept best fit the experimental evidence, and that no evidence contradicted it. Additional issues in the debate ranged from the calculus itself (Newton's won out) to the interpretation of the Old Testament.

Like monistic natural philosophy, monistic social philosophy too responded to rationalism, and as in natural philosophy, skepticism was the preferred label for the tradition as it developed. In social philosophy, skepticism goes back at least to Montaigne. His *Essays,* the first of which were published in 1580, were explicitly based on the model of a chemical or geological analysis (an "assay"—in French, *essayer*), as well as a "trial." Avoiding deduction from first principles (in the manner of Augustine or the contemporary Utopian literature in the tradition begun by Thomas More), or comparison with stipulated ideals, Montaigne's method was to describe the evidence and opinions in favor of the possible explanations (often of the origin or source of a custom or act) and then to draw the conclusion only according to that evidence. Irony and paradox were not precluded by this method, and Montaigne's often dry writing gave way eventually to the equally skeptical (in a technical sense) but far more entertaining essays of Voltaire (1694–1778) and the pseudo-Utopian literature of Swift and many others down to the present time.

The modern academic tradition of skeptical analysis, however, begins not with the essayists but with Voltaire's contemporary, Montesquieu, who turned back to a more extended expository mode of writing, and incorporated a concept of demonstration as the basis of all knowledge, for actors as well as analysts, into a pattern of social analysis that differed from social contract theory in every fundamental respect.

Montesquieu (1689–1755)

The Spirit of the Laws (1748) of Charles Louis de Secondat, Baron de Montesquieu, viewed the role of law in human society very much the way Galileo, Boyle, and others viewed mathematics in science—not as a universal and timeless system of rules that nature had to follow, but as an evolved system of human conventions for ordering situations of observation and communication.

Like the social contract theorists, Montesquieu was concerned with describing natural and civil law and their relationships to each other. But as a skeptic, he could not argue that any specific substantive law is natural or universal without claiming a special status for his own knowledge, and denying equal weight to the opposite opinions of others. In effect, the rationalists had described natural law by example; to take into account the relativity of individual human perceptions, Montesquieu has to describe natural and civil laws *in principle,* in a way that will let us see quite different actual laws as instances of such natural law or civil law, or as illustrating the relationship between them. This is of course precisely the same problem as that of recognizing cultural relativity without imposing an arbitrary set of categories from one culture on all others—and without falling into solipsism.

The way in which Montesquieu does this can be illustrated with two quotations. The first is from the first paragraphs of *Spirit of the Laws;* the second is a remark in passing after the argument has been well developed.

Law in general is human reason, inasmuch as it governs all the inhabitants of the earth: the political and civil laws of each nation ought to be only the particular cases in which human reason is applied.

They should be adapted in such a manner to the people for whom they are framed that it should be a great chance if those of one nation suit another.

They should be in relation to the nature and principle of each government: whether they form it, as may be said of politic laws; or whether they support it, as in the case of civil institutions.

They should be in relation to the climate of each country, to the quality of its soil, to its situation and extent, to the principal occupation of the natives, whether husbandmen, huntsmen, or shepherds: they should have relation to the degree of liberty which the constitution will bear; to the religion of the inhabitants, to their inclinations, riches, numbers, commerce, manners, and customs. In fine, they have relations to each other, as also to their origin, to the intent of the legislator, and to the order of things on which they are established; in all of which different lights they ought to be considered.

This is what I have undertaken to perform in the following work. These relations I shall examine, since all these together constitute what I call the Spirit of Laws. (Bk I, Ch. 3)

But on the other hand: "Mankind are influenced by various causes, by the climate, by the religion, by the laws, by the government, by the precedents, morals, and customs; from whence is formed a general spirit of nations'' (Bk. xix, Ch. 4).

As these statements suggest, the argument involves two major themes. The most prominent is the idea of a "spirit" of laws that reflects the nature of the people who live under them—especially that reflects their social relationships; and people have a "spirit," presumably the same, that is influenced by their laws and institutions. This "spirit," *ésprit*, is not a mystical notion but may best be thought of under the heading of "attitude"—some moral orientation and sense of coherence and purpose that varies with each community and set of laws. It is clearly not any one explicit formula or ideology that all laws should represent or conform to. As the quotations indicate, the "spirit" does not cause the laws, nor do the laws create the spirit. There is no determinism and no reductionism, but each is influenced by the other. As a person grows up in a society, his attitudes and relations are shaped in part by the laws of the society; as laws are made and modified in society, they are influenced by the "spirit" that pervades or reflects the institutions and social relations of its people.

The second major theme is the problem of saying what natural law is in principle. The phrase "Law in general is human reason" is part of his solution. But what is "human reason"? Since any sort of substantive definition (like Hobbes's geometrical framework) would violate his premises, Montesquieu takes a different approach, and this is where the idea of demonstration fits in. Reason is not defined by some single principle at all. It is, instead, treated as a sense of fit between things in society that anyone can recognize once it is pointed out, just as one can recognize order in physical nature once it is demonstrated. Reason is thus not a belief of a certain kind, but a demonstrable order (and the ability to see order) of a certain kind. One rather famous example of this argument is his treatment of the British and French laws on false witness, another is his treatment of monogamy.

In France, it was a capital offense to make a false accusation. In Britain, it was a minor offense. But Montesquieu argued that one could not assess the difference in isolation; it was necessary to know the other laws that formed systems with each of these. In France, accusation alone could cause a person to be summoned and tortured, and the accused could not in turn call his own witnesses to counter the accusation. An accusation alone could therefore do great harm, so the law against false witness was a necessary check on the abuse of such power. In the English courts, by contrast, an accused could not be tortured and could call his own witnesses. A single accusation could therefore do little harm, and it was necessary for many accusers to come forward to make a case. Hence the law was designed to encourage witnesses to come forward without fear (book 29, ch. 11). Despite their differences, each law was equally "natural," and equally reasonable, in its place.

The comparison of polygamy and monogamy is partly responsible for the current notion that Montesquieu was an environmental determinist. He argued that in the hotter countries, women attained their full beauty earlier in life and before they were intellectually capable of exploiting it, while in colder countries women matured physically at a slower rate. In consequence, men in hot countries were attracted to the beauty of women who could not provide full intellectual partnerships. These women stayed on in the houses when their intelligence increased but their beauty faded, and they had to acquiesce when the men took subsequent wives. In cold countries, a woman could exploit her beauty more effectively, because of her greater intellectual maturity, and could serve as a fuller partner of the man throughout their lives as both matured together. Hence polygamy was the "extremely natural" arrangement from both male and female viewpoints in hot countries, and monogamy was equally natural in cold climates (book 16, ch. 11). (In other sections, relative birthrates were also discussed in this connection.) In this case, Montesquieu's facts are wrong; all people in hot countries are not polygamous, nor all those in cold countries monogamous. But unlike a contradiction in a deductive system, this sort of error is not fatal. It can easily be corrected within the framework of analysis.

The simplest characterization of the view of society that emerges from the juxtaposition of hundreds of comparisons of this sort is radical pluralism. It is pluralism because laws pertaining to criminal procedures are separated from laws regarding property, and these again from laws in relation to religion, and these again from areas of custom rather than law, and so forth. Government itself is spoken of as involving legislative and executive functions that can be combined or separated in various ways; government and religion are sharply separated; government and the state are separated, and so on—not absolutely, of course, but rather in specific examples. In modern jargon, one might say that Montesquieu sees the order in society as existing at the level of subsystems, not total systems. But the point in calling his pluralism "radical" is that it seems quite clear that he is saying there are in fact no total systems at all. Society, as that which people in a cultural or regional community share, is not *one* system or entity of any sort, but a loose and constantly changing collection of common usages, including but not limited to laws of various kinds. The people create them, and the usages in turn influence the action and attitudes of their creators.

But while there is no sense in which society is a single entity for Montesquieu, there is a sense in which it is a single idea for the people he describes. It is a condition laws are aimed at creating, a kind of ideal people raise for themselves, and hold themselves up to. Unlike the rationalists, Montesquieu did not attribute to people any single "natural" or dominant motive. He saw human impulses as complex, fluid, and many-sided. People were selfish, but also selfless; fearful, but also courageous; greedy, but also benign; and so forth. He saw it as natural and reasonable for people to seek to create ways to encourage their own better impulses and to suppress their destructive or unkind sides. He saw their manipulation of the laws, of government, and of customs as primarily having this end in view: to instruct and encourage more people to adopt more sociable attitudes, and to create situations where individuals can do best by subordinating their personal interests to the interests of others. In this sense, society, or perhaps better sociability, is an aim of the laws—it is what laws are intended to bring about. But of course the individuals who make the laws in order to create this sociability learn to value it by growing up in situations where it is valuable. This is no contradiction for Montesquieu, but plain fact. Montesquieu's psychology is a strictly *social* psychology. Each person grows up in a social setting and develops his ideas in it. As he attempts to implement these ideas, he contributes to the situation where his successors obtain their ideas. They again will do the same in turn, through constantly evolving cycles of learning and teaching, absorbing, examining, reflecting, choosing, and acting.

The points of Montesquieu's arguments flow so naturally, and the sentiments and observations are often so familiar, that it requires a conscious effort to realize that they do not occur in the rationalist tradition. They not only do not; they can not. Montesquieu's central problem of the mutual fit, from the point of view of individuals, among purposes, needs, values, laws, institutions, and climate is ruled out by the very structure of the rationalist arguments, and by their adoption of a fixed psychology as a starting point in their deduction—a psychology that does not depend on the *felt* perceptions and desires of those to whom it is attributed.

Montesquieu gave skepticism a productive set of starting points analogous to a series of "demonstrations," that lead "naturally" to a long and still by no means exhausted series of important real-world problems and solutions.

The Scottish Moralists

The Spirit of the Laws has many parallels in the writings of the "Scottish moralists," centering on David Hume (1711–76), Adam Smith (1723–90), and Adam Ferguson (1723–1816).

The major concern of Smith's *Theory of Moral Sentiments* (1759) was to explain why and how the better sentiments, the moral sentiments, came to be socially commended and institutionalized, while the more selfish sentiments were condemned. Like Montesquieu he saw this as the problem of showing how society served as a human means to human betterment. But Montesquieu was not mentioned (very few people were), and it is hard to find clear paraphrases. He does, however, talk of a "spirit of system . . . apt to mix itself with a public spirit that is founded upon the love of humanity" (part 6, Sec. 2, chap. 2).

In the more influential *Wealth of Nations* (1776) the influence of Montesquieu is more obvious. Smith's treatment of the going money price of a good as its "natural" value in that place and time, and many details of his treatments of the relationship between the supply of coinage and money to prices, and between the relative wealth of countries and their trade and laws directly correspond to Montesquieu's treatments of the same topics in the latter parts of *The Spirit of the Laws,* as do Smith's general views of the ways laws can encourage or discourage trade and commerce. There is also a deeper parallelism in their mutual view that the wealth of a nation consists precisely in this commerce, which was a direct measure of the welfare of its citizens, and not in "treasure" held in store. And finally, there is a still deeper parallelism in the fundamental idea expressed in the phrase "division of labor": an ordered social differentiation constructed by individuals pursuing their own ends, establishing patterns of interdependence rather than authority, and creating overall social order as if by the operation of what Smith called an "invisible hand."

Smith's relativism was not complete, however. Side by side with his idea of the market price as the natural value of a good and the implicit notion that the value of money was the good it bought was an adaptation of Locke's labor theory of value as the real basis for a person's willingness to accept a price for a good (though not for the price itself). This labor theory was in turn related deterministically to his concept of the division of labor. He saw it as an essential or necessary property of labor that it increased in value by being concentrated on specific tasks, and organized, for it was this property that caused the increase in national wealth over time. Ricardo and then Marx were to fasten on this value theory and the associated mechanistic causality to the exclusion of social psychology and its associated psychological and social relativism. Later, when the labor theory was rejected, the exclusion still remained. Economics has continued to be cut off from one of the principal sets of concerns and assumptions of its acknowledged founder.

Smith's concept of the division of labor was developed in close cooperation with Adam Ferguson, whose *Essay on the History of Civil Society* (1767) also used the phrase and gave it the same basic meaning. Ferguson's use of the idea shows the links to Montesquieu even more clearly. Like Smith, Ferguson saw the increase of occupational specialization, the differentiation of occupational groups, and the increase of trade as interrelated aspects of the evolving complexity of society. But he went beyond this to sound the theme that was to be the starting point of Comte's positivism. He saw this differentiation as leading to the possibility of the moral breakdown of society—of the development of increasingly differentiated and specialized personal moral outlooks, losing the overriding sense of belonging to a single community that he saw as characteristic of simpler societies—be they Sparta or the Highland Scots. Moral alienation of the individual from society could then follow as the price of progress and comfort, and this alienation was itself a proper concern of legislation and instruction. The invisible hand would not do everything by itself.

Ferguson closely followed Montesquieu, and differed from Smith, in setting up no universal categories or explanations for the social and moral differences that concerned him. There was no absolute theory of value to explain its accumulation, and no absolute scale of social complexity. He used the rough division between "savagery" or "barbarism" and "civilization" or "polished society", as Montequieu had, to set up his discussion, but the actual measure of complexity and differentiation employed was always the number and arrangement of social and occupational categories that the natives themselves recognized. The parallelism between the Highland Scots and the ancient Greeks that ran through the book turned on the point that the concepts of the citizen-warrior in the two societies were similar; that the ways agriculture was managed in the two areas were similar; that the ways the two responded to climate and topography were similar; and that in consequence the "fit" between these things was similarly tied to an ethical outlook that placed its premium on individual strength and integrity, coupled with individual willingness to sacrifice oneself for the community as a whole—a moral outlook quite the same as the "virtues" that Montesquieu had associated with each major type of modern government. In fact, at a theoretical level, there is no point of disagreement between Ferguson and Montesquieu. Ferguson is merely concerned with a slightly different regional comparison, and with morality in a general sense rather than law.

Although both Smith and Ferguson have influenced the history of anthropology, David Hume was ultimately the most important of the three. Hume wrote a history of England and a rather whimsical *Natural History of Religion* (1757). The first was popular in its time, the second has had some influence on later anthropological treatments of religion. But his most important works described neither religion nor society as such. They were philosophical in a fairly strict sense—in fact they were extended attacks on the rationalists' psychological theories and concepts of truth, especially on those of Locke, in the light of the relativism of Montesquieu. The way these attacks were carried out and the conclusion Hume came to laid the philosophical basis for the theoretical study of custom, and it was as the study of custom rather than society (or economics) that anthropology first took form as a theoretically well-grounded group of interests in the early nineteenth century.

The main attacks on rationalism are in the *Treatise on Human Nature* (1738) and the *Inquiry Concerning Human Understanding* (1750), which is in many respects a rewritten version of the *Treatise*. Similar arguments, variations on the original themes, appear in still other, later, works. A good deal of the current misunderstanding of Hume, which portrays him as a supporter of Locke rather than an opponent, stems from the fact that Hume begins his arguments by quoting and seeming to accept a number of Locke's important concepts. He accepts the analytic-synthetic distinction—that some truths reflect relations of ideas and some reflect matters of fact. He accepts the idea that mathematical propositions are of the first sort and he accepts the idea that such truths depend only on the law of contradiction. But unlike Locke, he seems to view such truths as mainly matters of sticking to one's definitions and of relatively little importance. Hume considered that the main problems in philosophy were with the second sort of propositions, propositions of fact. Again seeming to echo Locke, he argued that the fundamental concept in relation to such propositions was cause and effect. For Locke, of course, this was true in two senses. First, the "associations of ideas," in the case of such propositions, would have had to reflect real relations of cause and effect. And second, the presence of such knowledge in the mind, according to Locke, could only arise by necessary relations of cause and effect from objects in nature producing sense impressions, which in turn created ideas in the mind. Then finally, still seeming to follow Locke, he accepts the idea that all knowledge of cause and effect comes from "experience": "I shall venture to affirm, as the general proposition which admits of no exception, that the knowledge of this relation is not, in any instance, attained by reasonings *a priori,* but arises entirely from experience, when we find that any particular objects are constantly conjoined with each other" (1750:42).

On the surface, it appears that Hume intends to go on to succeed where Locke failed, to remedy the major weakness of Locke's system and eliminate forever the spectre of innate ideas. But notice the odd phrase "when we find . . . objects . . . constantly conjoined." How do "we find" such conjunction? Shouldn't he rather say simply "arise when particular objects are constantly conjoined"? The reason for the odd phrase is that Hume means just what he says. It arises from experience, but not the experience of the constant conjunction itself. That is, Hume is going to give the term "experience" a new meaning, quite unlike Locke's. First Hume rejects the idea that, looking at an object for the very first time, one might infer anything about its causes or effects. Look at a ball suspended in the air; there is no way to know it should fall when it was released. Then

> Suppose again that he has acquired more experience and has lived so long in the world as to have observed similar objects or events to be constantly conjoined together—what is the consequence of this experience? He immediately infers the existence of one object from the appearance of the other, yet he has not, by all his experience, acquired any idea or knowledge of the secret power by which the one object produces the other, nor is it by any process of reasoning he is engaged to draw this inference; but still he finds himself determined to draw it, and though he should be convinced that his understanding has no part in the operation, he would nevertheless continue in the same course of thinking. There is some other principle which determines him to form such a conclusion.
>
> This principle is *custom* or *habit.* For wherever the repetition of any particular act or operation produces a propensity to renew the same act or operation without being impelled by any reasoning or process of the understanding, we always say that this propensity is the effect of *custom.* By employing that word we pretend not to have given the ultimate reason of such a propensity. (1750:56–57)

This is indeed a "skeptical" solution. It rejects the idea that it was necessary for philosophers to establish the ultimate reality of cause and effect and, by implication, all those other articles of belief that were considered as the foundations of knowledge in the dualistic psychologies of Hume's time. Where the rationalists had sought to explain and justify popular beliefs by assigning them to enduring and unchanging underlying entities or causes that *by definition* lay beyond perception, Hume proposed to explain the existence of a basic metaphysical category by reference to custom—popular established belief and practice. We can easily see the implications of this for social analysis. In the former view, social analyses must follow from the axioms that control all human perception. Cultural differences, as such, can only be dealt with as variations on the general themes. In Hume's view, especially as buttressed by Smith and Ferguson, there is instead the possibility that social science as an experimental science would become the basis upon which one would explain why people postulate any type of philosophical system.

Hume's treatments of moral knowledge corresponded directly to his treatment of empirical knowledge, again emphasizing "experience" but again seeing experience not in the perception of properties of things or relations as such so much as in what we learn from each other about them.

Kant (1724–1804): Critical Philosophy

Hume stopped his philosophical criticism without developing these concepts of "custom" and "experience," and without examining one major idea he shared with Locke: the principle of contradiction. But Kant saw his criticism as the natural basis of a new, non-speculative system of metaphysics. As Kant put it, Hume had only "suggested" such a system "in his doubts": "Yet even he did not suspect such a formal science, but ran his ship ashore, for safety's sake, landing on skepticism, there to let it lie and rot; . . . . (*Prolegomena:*262–63).

Before Kant "awoke" (his term), at the age of fifty-two, in response to Hume's criticism, he had written several works on the history of science and on anthropology (his own term) dealing with cognition, sense perception, the relation between physiology and character, and the relation between physiology and environment, and had planned a "handbook of anthropology." He had also taught a course on "anthropology" and lectured on "physical geography" from 1756 to 1796.

Kant's lectures in physical geography, especially his Introduction, gave him a major position in the history of that discipline. At the same time, geography was directly complementary to anthropology, as the two subdivisions of "sensory knowledge" (as opposed to knowledge obtained through "pure reason"). Geography was the study of "nature" or the world as perceived through the "outer senses," while anthropology was the study of man, or the soul, as perceived through the "inner senses." Geography was, further, knowledge of nature organized in time and space, as opposed to an organization by a system of rational categories, like the *Systema Naturae* of Linnaeus. As such, geography was inherently historical; or rather history was continuous geography.

Kant's divisions of geography were Mathematical Geography (describing the form, size, and movement of the earth), Moral Geography (describing the different customs and characteristics of peoples), Political Geography (describing the relationship between political units and their physical backgrounds), Commercial Geography (examining trade and relative surpluses and scarcities), and Theological Geography (looking at variations in theological traditions in different environments) (Taylor 1957:38–41). Anthropology was, in a sense, the inside view of these same topics: it was concerned with developing a consistent view of human nature and of the conceptions of the self that would underpin the observations of geography.

After Kant's "awakening" he wrote a number of additional works on history and law. His last publication was *Anthropology from a Pragmatic Point of View* (*Anthropologie in pragmatischer Hinsicht*) in 1798, which tried to integrate early material from his course with later thinking. But in the center of the chain came the foundations of the new system, the works dealing with "pure reason" itself: the great *Critique of Pure Reason* (1781), the *Prolegomena to Any Future Metaphysics* (1783), that explained the *Critique,* the most fundamental *Critique of Practical Reason* (1788) and the *Critique of Judgment* (c. 1790).

Kant took Hume's critique as raising the question of "whether such a thing as metaphysics be even possible at all" given that "metaphysics" by definition had to be a study of knowledge independent of "physics," in the classical sense of all empirical knowledge (Introduction to the *Prolegomena*). He undertook to answer the question by showing the kind of metaphysics that was "possible" given the strictures of Hume's critique, distinguishing it from the kinds that were not. He considered that such metaphysics would be "science" (meaning Galilean demonstrative science of the kind he had been concerned with as a historian) and therefore would be totally different from the speculative metaphysics up to that point.

The *Critique* and the *Prolegomena* both deal with two quite definite topics. The first is what might be described as a simple perception—something directly before one, such as a table in a room. The second is the step above that, the sense that the table and the room can exist as "objects" apart from the act of perception itself—and the way we extract aspects of direct perception and assign them to such objects. Kant calls such simple perceptions "judgments," while the objects that seem to be perceived are called "transcendental"—not because they transcend all reality in a dualistic sense, but because they transcend the simple judgments, the direct perceptions. Kant's later works proceed to still larger perceptual units and the problems in delineating them precisely.

At first, the *Prolegomena* does not directly suggest its basically psychological interests. The Preamble starts almost idealistically, as Kant defines metaphysics as *"a priori* knowledge, coming from pure understanding and pure reason" (*Prolegomena:*265–66). However, the next section (and the corresponding Introduction to the *Critique of Pure Reason*) makes three related points. They pertain to the distinction between judgments which are "analytic" and judgments which are "synthetic," as a distinction associated with, and parallel to, the distinction between knowledge which is *a priori* and knowledge which is empirical (*a posteriori*). The first of these sections is a general discussion of the distinction, which is important enough to quote directly:

> *On the Distinction between Analytical and Synthetical Judgments in General.*—The peculiarity of its sources demands that metaphysical knowledge must consist of nothing but *a priori* judgments. But whatever be their origin or their logical form, there is a distinction in judgments, as to their content, according to which they are either merely *explicative,* adding nothing to the content of knowledge, or *expansive,* increasing the given knowledge. The former may be called *analytical,* the latter *synthetical,* judgments.
>
> Analytical judgments express nothing in the predicate but what has been already actually thought in the concept of the subject, though not so distinctly or with the same (full) consciousness. When I say: "All bodies are extended," I have not amplified in the least my concept of body, but have only analyzed it, as extension was really thought to belong to that concept before the judgment was made, though it was not expressed. This judgment is therefore analytical. On the contrary, this judgment, "All bodies have weight," contains in its predicate something not actually thought in the universal concept of body; it amplifies my knowledge by adding something to my concept, and must therefore be called synthetical. (*Prolegomena:*266–67)

The argument continues that "all analytical judgments depend wholly upon the law of contradiction, and are in their nature *a priori* cognitions, whether the concepts that supply them with matter be empirical or not" (p. 267). This is important in part because, first, it seems to leave little basis for assigning any great importance to such analytic cognitions. Secondly, it contains the idea that the "matter" of an analytical judgment may be either substantive or non-substantive. This, in turn, implies (against Locke's view) that the analytic-synthetic dichotomy is not necessarily coordinate with the *a priori-a posteriori* dichotomy. This is spelled out directly in the next section, introducing a critical and distinctive Kantian notion—the idea of knowledge that is "synthetic *a priori*," which becomes his main concern.

The description begins:

Synthetical Judgments Require a Different Principle from the Law of Contradiction.—There are synthetical *a posteriori* judgments of empirical origin; but there are also others which are certain *a priori,* and which spring from pure understanding and reason. Yet they both agree in this, that they cannot possibly spring from the principle of analysis, namely, the law of contradiction alone. They require a quite different principle from which they may be deduced, subject, of course, always to the law of contradiction, which must never be violated, even though everything cannot be deduced from it. I shall first classify synthetical judgments. (*Prolegomena:* 267–68)

With this, Kant has used two of the more important dualistic dichotomies to create a very nondualistic division of judgments into three basic classes: analytic *a priori,* synthetic *a priori,* and synthetic *a posteriori.*

Kant proceeds in the next subsection to argue that judgments of experience are always synthetic, and that mathematical judgments are non-experiental (*a priori*) but also synthetic. Finally and most importantly, "Metaphysical judgments, properly so-called, are all synthetic" (p. 272). Since Kant defined metaphysical judgments as *a priori* at the outset, this means that they are both *a priori* and synthetic. The law of contradiction applies to determining their truth, but so do other criteria. They are true on the basis of "intuitions as well as concepts" (pp. 273–74). This in turn completes Kant's framework by raising the question of an "intuition" as a basic philosophical problem: ". . . the generation of *a priori* knowledge by intuition as well as by concepts, in fine, of synthetic propositions *a priori,* especially in philosophical knowledge, constitutes the essential subject of metaphysics" (pp. 273–74).

The Preamble concludes by dividing the treatment of this essential subject matter into four subquestions; each to be considered in one subsequent chapter:

1 How is pure mathematics possible?
2 How is pure natural science possible?
3 How is metaphysics in general possible?
4 How is metaphysics as a science possible?

(Prolegomena: 279–80)

The section that takes up the first of these questions has a heading: "First Part of the Main Transcendental Problem." This indicates that the answer to the question involves "transcending" our ordinary experience to seek a "product of pure reason," "resting on no empirical grounds." But to say that it "rests" on no empirical grounds is for Kant (as for Hume) not the same as saying that experience is not relevant. He merely takes *a priori* literally—*before* experience, but still in it. The discussion of the "possibility" of mathematics in this section makes this point in its simplest and most acceptable form. The historical development of mathematics, which Kant has in mind, clearly indicates that it does not spring by necessity from individual perception alone, nor is it inherent in the mind for each individual, but rather it is prior to experience, applicable to experience, but not strictly experiential in itself.

Kant begins to develop a second main thread of his overall argument while describing these aspects of mathematics. This is a reconsideration of the relation between the *subject* of thought and its *object*. It is in part a reconsideration of the nature of "objective" entities, and it is carefully constructed to avoid the dualistic division between perceived objects and their true natures or essences. Kant begins to draw a sharp line between "things in themselves" and our perceptions of them—or rather their appearances in perception. Here Kant agrees with Leibnitz and Hume at once, in holding that such things in themselves are not knowable *directly*, but only through our representations of them. (Although Kant does not suggest that therefore they do not exist.) Basic categories of mathematics, among which he argues we should include time and space, are not properties of things in themselves so far as we can know, because we cannot know things in themselves. They are, however, properties of our understanding, of the way objects appear in our (human) perception. The "intuitions" by which we judge mathematics, in addition to the rules of contradiction, consist in just such aspects or objects of perception that are in this sense "subjective" (part of the perceiving subject) rather than purely "objective" (wholly detached from the perceiving subject) in themselves.

Kant's discussion of causation illustrates the general argument. Causation, he argues, involves the idea of a sequence of events, and therefore is based on concepts of space and time. He then concentrates on space and time, and steers his argument between two extremes. He rejects on one hand the view that his categories are "actual qualities inherent in things in themselves" (which would be the position of Locke and Hobbes) (p. 284–85). On the other hand, he rejects the idea that his own position reduces space and time to the status of "illusions," or a "mere fiction" (the position of idealism) (pp. 284–88). Most modern readers will probably find the first point familiar, but the second difficult to grasp. In fact, however, they are closely interrelated. The argument for subjective appearances of such categories as causation being more than illusions or "mere" appearances rests precisely on the lack of any possible knowledge of things in themselves apart from perception. Two selections from his first "remark" on this part of the *Prolegomena* (a discussion of the formal solution to the problem) shows the connection:

> Sensibility, the form of which is the basis of geometry, is that upon which the possibility of external appearance depends. . . .
> It would be quite otherwise if the senses were so constituted as to represent objects as they are in themselves. For then . . . . The space of the geometer would be considered a mere fiction, and it would not be credited with objective validity because we cannot see how things must of necessity agree with an image of them which we make spontaneously and previous to our acquaintance with them. But if this image, or rather this formal intuition, is the essential property of our sensibility by means of which alone objects are given to us, and if this sensibility represents not things in themselves but their appearance, then we shall easily comprehend, and at the same time indisputably prove, that all external objects of our world of sense must necessarily coincide in the most rigorous way with the propositions of geometry; because sensibility, by means of its form of external intuition, namely, by space, with which the geometer is occupied, makes those objects possible as mere appearances. (*Prolegomena:*287–88)

Again:

> . . . thought space renders possible the physical space, that is, the extension of matter itself; that this pure space is not at all a quality of things in themselves, but a form of our sensuous faculty of representation; and that all objects in space are mere appearances, that is, not things in themselves but representations of our sensuous intuition. (*Prolegomena:*288)

Having given time and space the status of subjective judgments that were nevertheless real and not illusory, Kant had to say what a *merely* subjective judgment in the usual sense would be like in terms of his scheme, and the criterion he uses is best described as social. In the *Prolegomena,* this question and its answer are developed in Part Two, dealing with the possibility of a "Pure Science of Nature." Kant's solution to this is characteristically original, and empirical. It is also crucial to his impact on the development of anthropology:

> All our judgments are at first merely judgments of perception; they hold good only for us (that is, for our subject), and we do not till afterward give them a new reference (to an object) and desire that they shall always hold good for us and in the same way for everybody else; for when a judgment agrees with an object, all judgments concerning the same object must likewise agree among themselves, and thus the objective validity of the judgment of experience signifies nothing else than its necessary universal validity. And conversely when we have ground for considering a judgment as necessarily having universal validity (which never depends upon perception, but upon the pure concept of the understanding under which the perception is subsumed), we must consider that it is objective also—that is, that it expresses not merely a reference of our perception to a subject, but a characteristic of the object. For there would be no reason for the judgments of other men necessarily agreeing with mine if it were not the unity of the object to which they all refer and with which they accord; hence they must all agree with one another.
>
> Therefore objective validity and necessary universality (for everybody) are equivalent terms, and though we do not know the object in itself, yet when we consider a judgment as universal, and hence necessary, we thereby understand it to have objective validity. (*Prolegomena:*298–99)

Kant is not saying that objectivity comes from universal validity of perception, or conversely that universal validity of judgments comes from objectivity. What he is saying is that they are two sides of the same coin, two aspects of one larger cognitive phenomenon. A judgment which we expect to have objective validity is by that very fact alone a judgment we expect to have universal validity, and vice versa. By "universal validity," it should be clear, Kant means universally *shared*—a judgment we expect anyone else to agree to. The judgment of objectivity is a *social* judgment.

How do we as individuals know a judgment will be shared? Kant's position is that the categories of perception—the synthetic categories *a priori*—themselves provide the basis whereby a universal judgment is distinguished from a *merely* subjective one. One makes a judgment that a perception is "objective," inherent in an object, when the perception (or different aspects of the perception) unite under categories that *we know* are synthetic *a priori,* when for example they form a pattern under the concepts of space and time. The judgment appears to be *merely* subjective when the perceptions only come together in "the same subject" (the perceiver as he is perceived by himself) (pp. 299–300). That is, we expect judgments to be universally shared if they are about qualities we expect to be universally recognized.

In proposing this solution to the problem of distinguishing objective universal from non-universal judgment, Kant was of course aware that it increased the importance of being able to say exactly what the synthetic *a priori* categories were. This is done in section 21 of the second chapter of the *Prolegomena,* in three related tables. The first two tables are also in chapter 1 of the "Transcendental Analytic" of the *Critique of Pure Reason,* while the third comes from a subsequent portion of this work. The first two tables are parallel to each other. Each presents four groups of three categories. The headings of the groups in each table are the same: "quantity," "quality," "relation," and "modality." The first table is titled a "Logical Table of Judgments," where the term "Judgments" corresponds to Hume's "sense perceptions." The term "Logical" indicates the fact that these headings are traditional classifications for the types of predicates that may be assigned to a subject in a proposition of formal logic. The second table is titled "Transcendental Table of the Concepts of the Understanding." The formidable title merely means that the categories do not depend upon experience but rather "transcend" it. These categories are imputed to experience, in order to give it the appearance of reflecting objects, and correspond to Hume's relations of ideas that have an existence beyond the moment of perception alone—such categories as "unity" (under the heading "quantity") or "reality" (under "quality"). The third table, "Pure Physical Table of the Universal Principles of the Science of Nature," refers to judgments we make about judgments themselves—that they are "axioms of intuition," "anticipations of perception," "analogies of experience" or "postulates of Empirical Thinking generally." In the *Prolegomena,* they are explained in a rather cryptic discussion in section 26 that follows (after describing the other two together, and after declaring that he had shown how it was possible to have a pure science of nature).

With these three tables, Kant moves from the problem of saying how we make individual judgments of perception and assign objectivity to them to the quite different problem of how we assign whole series of judgments to "objects" in the sense of things or entities in a world— objects like people, or stones. The tables are intended to be a list of the categories under which multiple perceptual judgments are integrated into synthetic wholes (rather than remaining discrete) within the flow of experience. The analysis bears on some of the technical problems that were very perplexing in Locke's sensationalism, and Leibnitz' response to it. And here again, Kant's approach, showing its skeptical roots, has a stong social or cultural component.

Kant concludes his argument for this portion of his analysis by pointing out what was already implicit in the idea that the bases of judgment are shared. It is that the categories are not merely logically related headings one may personally use or not; they have an inherently normative aspect, and *by the same token* apply not only to some (or even all) past experience but to all *possible* experience: "Judgments, when considered merely as the condition of the union of given representations in a consciousness, are rules" (*Prolegomena:*305). In relation to experience (as a thing perceived), this means:

> The principles of possible experience are then at the same time universal laws of nature, which can be known *a priori*. . . . the principles, by means of which all phenomena are subsumed under these concepts, constitute a physical system, that is, a system of nature which precedes all empirical knowledge of nature, and makes it possible. It may in strictness be denominated the universal and pure science of nature. (*Prolegomena:*306–07)

And in relation to "nature" (also a thing perceived) it means:

> How is nature itself possible? This question—the highest point that transcendental philosophy can ever reach, and to which, as its boundary and completion, it must proceed—really contains two questions.
>
> First: how is nature in the material sense, that is, as to intuition, or considered as the totality of appearances, possible; how are space, time and that which fills both—the object of sensation—possible generally? The answer is: by means of the constitution of our sensibility, according to which it is in its own way affected by objects which are in themselves unknown to it and totally distinct from those appearances. This answer is given in the *Critique* itself in the "Transcendental Aesthetic" and in these *Prolegomena* by the solution of the first general problem.
>
> Secondly: how is nature possible in the formal sense, as the totality of the rules under which all appearances must come in order to be thought as connected in experience? The answer must be this: it is only possible by means of the constitution of our understanding, according to which all the above representations of the sensibility are necessarily referred to a consciousness, and by which the peculiar way in which we think (namely, by rules) and hence experience also are possible, but must be clearly distinguished from an insight into the objects in themselves. (*Prolegomena:*318–19)

Like so many of Kant's previous answers, this one introduces a new conception that requires further explanation of its own. In this case, the

answer is that to bring our perceptions into an ordering, we each postulate "a consciousness" for ourselves.

In modern, if imprecise, terms this accounts for the way we bring
unity to a "perceptual field," and is the way we might have a science of
that unity. The next step, for Kant, is to ask how we can come to think
of nature as a system of *objects,* beyond the totality of our perceptions,
and his answer, logically enough, is to say that we do this by postulating a "self," or a "reason" for ourselves, as a repository of consciousness—and then a transcendant nature as object. This naturally raises a
still more basic question: How do such postulations, self as subject and
nature as object, come to be made? And the first question that has to be
answered in this regard is how the problem can be investigated. Kant's
answer, in effect, is not by dogmatic or deductive means so much as by
critical observation of our own perceptual and conceptual practices:

> . . . the transcendent cognitions of reason cannot either, as Ideas, appear in
> experience or, as propositions, ever be confirmed or refuted by it. Hence
> whatever errors may slip in unawares can only be discovered by pure reason
> itself—a discovery of much difficulty, because dialectical by means of its
> Ideas; and this unavoidable illusion cannot be limited by any objective and
> dogmatic researches into things, but only by a subjective investigation of
> reason itself as a source of ideas. (*Prolegomena:* 328–29)

What he is saying is actually simple, although to avoid confusion it is
necessary to bear in mind that Kant is using the term "idea" in a special
technical sense, that distinguishes it from "category." Roughly, a category is an aspect or component of perception, or of a judgment, while
an idea is an aspect or component of "pure reason," or of mind. Hence
ideas (or the idea of ideas) are themselves constructs, transcendental entities. Accordingly, ideas like "self" *by definition* cannot wholly appear
in experience or be confirmed by it, since they are stipulated, in a sense,
as being larger than any experience, or as lying beyond any. This is an
"illusion," but it is one that can only be uncovered or explained by
reason, subjectively. When he attempts the discovery, he concludes that
these ideas evolve as reifications of three forms of logical argument, just
as the categories of perception evolve as reifications of logical forms of
predication:

> As I had found the origin of the categories in the four logical forms of all the
> judgments of the understanding, it was quite natural to seek the origin of the
> Ideas in the three forms of syllogisms. For as soon as these pure concepts of
> reason (the transcendental Ideas) are given, they could hardly, except they be
> held innate, be found anywhere else than in the same activity of reason,
> which, so far as it regards mere form, constitutes the logical element of

syllogisms; but, so far as it represents judgments of the understanding as determined *a priori* with respect to one or another form, constitutes transcendental concepts of pure reason.

The formal distinction of syllogisms renders necessary their division into categorical, hypothetical, and disjunctive. The concepts of reason founded on them contain therefore, first, the Idea of the complete subject (the substantial); secondly, the Idea of the complete series of conditions; thirdly, the determination of all concepts in the Idea of a complete complex of that which is possible. The first idea is psychological, the second cosmological, the third theological; and as all three give occasion to dialectic, yet each in its own way, the division of the whole dialectic of pure reason into its paralogism, its antinomy, and its Ideal was arranged accordingly. Through this deduction we may feel assured that all the claims of pure reason are completely represented and that none can be wanting, because the faculty of reason itself, whence they all take their origin, is thereby completely surveyed. (*Prolegomena:*329–30)

The "formal distinction of syllogisms" Kant refers to here means the traditional classification of syllogisms according to the type of proposition upon which they are based. There are, classically, three such types of propositions. "Categorical" propositions are of the form "All *A*'s are B"; "hypothetical" propositions are of the form "Some *A*'s are B" (or "if an object is an A, it may or may not be a B"); and "disjunctive" propositions are of the form "No *A*'s are B" (or either an object is A or it is B, but not both). These categories or types of propositions, as one can easily see, form a system, and were generally considered to be both exhaustive and exclusive. Evidently Kant takes the idea of a complete self as the limiting condition implied in the first form, the idea of a complete series of conditions as the limiting condition implied in the if-then hypothetical form, and the idea of a complete set or series of possibilities as the limiting condition implied in the either-or form. Because the forms constitute a complete system, these three limiting assumptions also constitute an exclusive list of three possible bases for inferring noumena, which he calls "hyperbolical objects . . . or pure beings of the understanding" (*Prolegomena:*Sect. 48).

All noumena are either "psychological," that is, postulated complete selves; "cosmological," that is, postulated objects with definite sets of attributes; or "theological," that is, postulated total complexes, or universes. Kant proceeds to describe the way the noumena are generated by dialectic. He does this by describing the logical structure of the ideas upon which they are based or patterned. Each basic idea has a slightly different logical structure, reflecting the syllogistic form that corresponds to it. The idea of self is built up by the device of "paralogisms" from experience; the idea of a complete series of conditions involves "antinomies" in their relation to experience, and the idea of a total complex is related to experience as an ideal (I am somewhat over-clarifying). Each of these processes of reasoning produces paradoxes, and can support a number of alternative versions of the basic categories (such as alternative dualistic philosophies) with equal force. This means, in part, that no one consistent metaphysical system can be generated by the categories alone, any more than it can come directly from experience. There is no suggestion whatever that the ideas thus generated are "true," or that reason can provide "truth" in any sense that a rationalist would want to agree with.

The idea of an antinomy can illustrate the reasoning of this portion of Kant's argument. The concept itself is very important, but very simple. It means what its etymology suggests—"against rule." The antinomies of pure reason consist in sets of logically contradictory but universally relevant ideas, that it is possible to deduce by syllogism from each of the basic cosmological ideas—that is, from the possible ways to specify the attributes of an object. For example, the cosmological complex freedom-or-nature produces the deduction that "there is no freedom but all is nature" as well as the idea that freedom and nature can exist together. Similarly, the pair of propositions "in the series of the world-causes there is some necessary being," and its antithesis, "there is nothing necessary in the world, but in this series all is contingent," are both equally derivable from the cosmological idea of a cause and effect, and each is equally provable—and equally paradoxical—as the history of philosophy itself bears witness. The critique of psychological and theological ideas is less schematic, but comes to the same point. All such transcendent propositions or beliefs rest on a dialectical extension, by reason, of ideas pertinent to experience. But all such extensions necessarily go beyond what is provable, and beyond the ideas' original bounds or necessary uses. They are exaggerations.

This is "how" transcendental objects come to be postulated. The obvious final question is "why"? Why do people extend categories of perception in this way? Kant's answer in the *Prolegomena* is what defines the scope and aim of anthropology in his system. It is short enough to quote in its entirety. Read it slowly:

> Thus we have fully exhibited metaphysics, in its subjective possibility, as it is actually given in the natural predisposition of human reason and in that which constitutes the essential end of its pursuit. Though we have found that this merely natural use of such a predisposition of our reason, if no discipline

arising only from a scientific critique bridles and sets limits to it, involves it
in transcendent and specious inferences and really conflicting dialectical inferences, and this fallacious metaphysics is not only unnecessary as regards
the promotion of our knowledge of nature but even disadvantageous to it,
there yet remains a problem worthy of investigation, which is to find out the
natural ends intended by this disposition to transcendent concepts in our nature, because everything that lies in nature must be originally intended for
some useful purpose.

Such an inquiry is of a doubtful nature, and I acknowledge that what I can
say about it is conjecture only, like every speculation about the ultimate ends
of nature. Such conjecture may be allowed me here, for the question does
not concern the objective validity of metaphysical judgments but our natural
predisposition to them, and therefore does not belong to the system of metaphysics but to anthropology.

When I compare all the transcendental Ideas, the totality of which constitutes the proper problem of natural pure reason, compelling it to quit the
mere contemplation of nature, to transcend all possible experience, and in
this endeavor to produce the thing (be it knowledge or fiction) called metaphysics, I think I perceive that the aim of this natural tendency is to free our
concepts from the fetters of experience and from the limits of the mere contemplation of nature so far as at least to open to us a field containing mere
objects for the pure understanding which no sensibility can reach, not indeed
for the purpose of speculatively occupying ourselves with them (for there we
can find no ground to stand on), but in order that practical principles [may be
assumed as at least possible]; for practical principles, unless they find scope
for their necessary expectation and hope, could not expand to the universality
which reason unavoidably requires from a moral point of view. (*Prolegomena:*362–63)

This, finally, introduces the idea of the "practical" purpose for postulating such entities as God, the self, and the universe in their various
forms. The concept of "practicality," like most Kantian concepts, is
not used casually. Nor is its parallelism to "anthropology" in their respective paragraphs to be taken lightly. It receives considerable development in Kant's *Groundwork of the Metaphysics of Morals* (1785) and
the *Critique of Practical Reason* (1788). Practical reason is contrasted
regularly with "pure" reason. Practical reason recalls the earlier skeptical treatments of legislation and the creation of order. It presupposes
freedom of the will, for which pure reason provides no guarantee, but
only an antinomy—a self-contradiction. Practical reason presupposes a
possibility and need for control, and morality. In the *Critique of Practical Reason,* Kant also specifically repeats the theme of "hope." The
postulated noumena provide unity and continuity to principles that indi-

viduals use, deliberately and purposefully, to organize and control their day-to-day expectations, perceptions, and actions—principles which they themselves (not nature or God) must create for this use.

This idea has basic implications for what we would now call the problem of social control and social order. It sees individual actions not isolated as "natural" behaviors, but as self-conceptualized activities that arise only in contrast to a background of felt options and limits that must, because their parameters are historically evolved and publicly learned, be shared by other individuals as well.

It is easy to see the excitement that Kant's argument could have engendered, remembering that those who read him were highly likely to have also read at least Rousseau, Hume, and Locke, and quite probably Montesquieu. They would almost necessarily have seen Kant as once again relating individual psychology to a view of social order, but at a radically different level and in a different way.

Society is clearly not the state but rather a set of conventions that are "rules." It is not an external, objective, almost material entity that helps people organize their material affairs by enforcing their rights. Rather, it is a foundation of individual perception and cognition, a part of the "subject," and a source of indispensable intellectual tools whereby individuals place their perceived action in an evolved common framework of felt totalities. Kant articulated the implicit skeptical version of the way in which the limits of individual human experience, the inability of experience alone to provide for such unity, is itself a stimulus and cause for the creation of extra-perceptual bases for the organization of opinion. One can read Kant and suddenly see what was never seen before in a major recognized philosopher of the Western tradition— a detailed account of the processes of thought through which the limits of human perception, the very inability of individual perception alone to supply itself with the concepts to give it organization and manageability, could itself be the cornerstone on which *society as a cognitive system* is and must be built.

The Idea of a Universal History (1784), whose full title adds the phrase "From a Cosmopolitan Point of View," applies the analysis directly to treating the state itself. The treatment is non-technical, but the concept of the state indicates that Kant places it under his general metaphysical category of "cosmology"—a classified object. Here he argues for the eventual necessary development of a universal "culture" and a universal republic. The essay *Perpetual Peace* (1795) extends the argument of the *Idea of a Universal History*. Together, the two works are a script for writing historical analysis. At the same time, by his arguments, they are also a script for the historical development of culture itself, by conscious human action, conforming to Montesquieu's and Ferguson's conception of history as involving increasing freedom. It is a suggestion for the promulgation of useful noumena to bring such freedom about.

Kant's last two major works were of the greatest and most direct relevance to what became ethnology: the *Metaphysics of Morals* and *Anthropology from a Pragmatic Point of View*. By the time they were written, however, Kant seems to have lost his power of relentless consistency, and both works reintroduce distinctions and concepts formerly rejected (although they do not require them). At the same time both have an inherent defect that Kant himself would surely have acknowledged. They fall under the broad category of "anthropology" used in the *Critique of Practical Reason,* and therefore inherently require factual information which Kant himself did not command.

The *Metaphysics of Morals* was published in two parts in 1796 and 1797 (both bearing the date 1797). The title in German was *Metaphysik der Sitten,* and it should be noted that *Sitten* has a meaning somewhere between "morals" (or "mores") and "customs." It has been translated with the former term in these philosophical works, but the same German term is what was rendered as "custom" when it was used ethnologically. More importantly, the *sense* that Kant gave this term made it one of the hallmarks of the dominant monistic tradition in the nineteenth century, setting it apart from the concern with "society," or the "state," with quite a different sense, that marked the dualistic traditions descending mainly from Hegel.

The first part of the *Metaphysik der Sitten* was titled *Metaphysische Anfangsgründe der Rechtslehre,* the second was *Metaphysische Anfangsgründe der Tugendlehre.* The first title has been recently rendered as the *Metaphysical Foundations of Jurisprudence,* the second as the *Metaphysical Foundations of Ethics,* but it should be noted that here too the German words have somewhat broader meanings than these glosses suggest. The noun *"Lehre"* means an example or a pattern, so that *Rechtslehre* has the sense of a legal pattern, while *Tugendlehre* has the sense of a moral or ethical pattern. The overall idea is that custom consists of patterns for people to follow; law consists in one general subtype of such patterns, ethics in another. But *Rechtslehre* itself is still a broad category, of which law in a strict sense is only one form.

The argument of the *Metaphysical Foundations of Jurisprudence* was a general critique of social contract theory, utilizing concepts drawn from Roman law, interpreted in the framework of his general conceptions of practical reason and morality. A passage from the Introduction, giving a few definitions that later became important in comparative law, will indicate the scope and manner of Kant's reasoning:

> Natural and Positive Laws—Obligatory Laws for which an external legislation is possible, are called generally External Laws. Those External Laws, the obligatoriness of which can be recognized by Reason *a priori* even without an external legislation, are called NATURAL LAWS. Those Laws, again, which are not obligatory without actual External Legislation, are called POSITIVE LAWS. (General Introduction, Sect. IV)

That is, external laws are laws we *follow,* recognizing that they originate outside of ourselves. But of these, some are followed because it is reasonable to do so, so that even though they may be legislated, legislation is not necessary—such "laws" might be "Do not leave your hand in fire," or perhaps even "Do not lie incessantly," or "Do what is right." But other laws are followed because they are legislated, and they must be legislated because although there are a number of things that might equally be right under some circumstances, one of them must be chosen. Uniform distress signals and all sorts of "rules of the road" are obvious examples, as in the last analysis are most laws, whether written or customary, of inheritance, marriage, property, and welfare.

Kant's *Anthropology* (1798) obviously carries over many ideas from his early course, before the critiques, and was not wholly re-written to incorporate his newer more consistent monism. Still, it shows the kind of behaviorally oriented social psychology that follows from his system. For example, note the way the idea of universality of objective judgments is applied to formulate the social aspects of hallucinations:

> The one universal characteristic of madness is the loss of *common sense* (*sensus communis*), and the substitution of a *logical private sense* (*sensus privatus*) for it; for example, man sees in broad daylight a lamp burning on his table that another man present does not see; or hears a voice that no one else hears. For we have to attach our own *understanding to the understanding of other men* too, instead of *isolating* ourselves with our own understanding and still use our private ideas to judge *publicly,* so to speak. This is a subjectively necessary criterion of the correctness of our judgments generally, and so too of the health of our understanding. (1798, trans. Gregor 1974:88)

Overall, Kant did not do many things that had formerly seemed natural and even necessary, while he did do some things that no one had been able to do or had seen a need for. Although he argued for God and noumenal reason, he did not infer from the existence of his own reason to the presence of a more perfect external reason—as Descartes and many others had done as the bases of their systems. Although he talked about phenomena, perceptions, subjects, and objects, he did not divide the world between mind and matter, or substance and quality. He discussed pure reason with cold accuracy, and called that the object of the highest philosophy. But he did not credit it with the ability to discover real entities beyond perception, and he considered pure reason itself (taken as a totality) to be simply a practically necessary postulation. He talked about the mental and physical objects that lie beyond perception, but reversed their causal relationship to perception. In the *Critique of Practical Reason,* he makes it quite clear that practical reason has "primacy" over perception of nature in the ordering of human thought. He talked of laws of nature, and saw their role as useful *putative* explanations of perceptions; but he did not see them as real causes of perception.

Although there was never a time in the history of the Western academic tradition when there were no disputes and perfect harmony reigned, there were few times when there were so many disputes that werc at once so clearly defined and so clearly basic.

One modern tradition of interpretation, most commonly attributed to Edmund Husserl, holds that Kant based his system somehow on Newton's *Physics,* and that Kant is therefore now obsolete in the way that Newton's system is. If this is meant to suggest that Kant accepted or relied upon the "real" absolute space and time, it is clearly wrong, as the quoted material indicates. Kant did accept the categories of space and time as fundamental intuitions. But he also, at the same time, was accepting the same kinds of limits for philosophical knowledge that Newton had accepted for physical knowledge. Since many systems of formal conceptualization could articulate any one intuition, the formal system in use at any one time was always subject to change, and good "only" temporarily, not timelessly.

Many philosophers since Kant have not accepted Kant's own view of his work—that he was clarifying the pretensions of philosophy in order to make real progress more likely. They have instead seen Kant as limiting knowledge itself, and Husserl is among them. Academic anthropology has inherited the disagreement, and it is still both fundamental and undecided. Is science fundamentally deductive and aimed at absolute and nonrelative principles, like Descartes's system? Or is it an evolving system of concepts grounded in observation and the practicalities of human perception and communication, like Kant's system?

Conclusion

   Skepticism was fundamentally relativistic and historicist (or develop-
mentalist) in its social theory. However, it is most important to realize
this relativism was not at all the same thing as the nihilism or radical
idealism one finds in the dualistic tradition—the notion that all one
knows are one's own thoughts. Quite the contrary. Relativism of perception was offered as an *observable fact*. Anyone who does not believe
that fact, or accept that fact, can feel perfectly free to refuse to accept
the systems. Skeptical social psychology was built on the fact of relativism, and on the further fact that people everywhere, in practice, recognize it. People see their own relativism of perspective, and have
recourse to common consensus to overcome it in creating ordered affairs. All of Kant's concepts for analyzing judgments involve consensus
in different ways. The law of contradiction is simply the rule that one
should use concepts consistently—in one way for one purpose, a rule
implicit in any concept and learned as part of learning the concept. Intuitions are perceptual orderings embodying learned systems of parameters, expressed "formally" in such obviously evolved systems of conventions as mathematics, science, and theology. Judgments are made to
adhere to "things" and given long-term significance by the stipulation
of noumena of various classes—selves, series, or totalities—following
certain evolved tricks of reason that enable one to infer plausible (but
never provable) extra-perceptual entities from the flow of perception itself. One has to learn the law of contradiction, one has to learn the
parameters of judgment, one has to learn to have a "self" apart from
other things in a world, and one learns each from people as a matter of
convention. Continuing series of people learn such things as they grow
and teach them to others as they live.
   The historicism is present in two senses, both already indicated: individuals are not seen as having fixed properties once and for all but as
developing through their lives; and their lives in turn are seen as part of
the larger and longer historical sequence that makes up the growth and
transformation of culture. It is no accident that so many more of the
principle philosophers of this tradition than of the dualistic tradition
have written major historical works: Montesquieu's *Causes of the
Greatness and the Decadence of the Romans* was published in 1734. It
was closely followed in content and orientation, as well as time, by
Voltaire's *The Age of Louis XIV*. Hume's *History of England* was a
major effort published in installments from 1750 to 1762. Ferguson's

History was, of course, historical from the outset, and Kant's historically oriented works, which include his *Anthropology,* as well as his early work in the history of science, have been mentioned. If one looks closely at Gibbon's *The Decline and Fall of the Roman Empire* (1788), a work of vast importance for later social thought, its assumptions and premises too will be seen to follow in this same skeptical tradition.

Whether Kant was riding a wave or leading it is in most respects a moot question. What is important is that he articulated assumptions being made very commonly in a wide and powerful movement of thought that carried into the nineteenth century, where it generated the first clear versions of the debates and issues that still concern anthropology.

4.
Social Determinism to Sociology

Every scholarly discipline is defined by what it is and by what it is not. What anthropology was in the nineteenth century will be described in the next two chapters. One of the main things it was not is described here: it was not sociology. Those who called themselves sociologists favored a conception of man, mind, and science that the main founders of anthropology chose to avoid, ignore, or oppose.

The sociological conception was both mechanistic and deterministic. It portrayed society as a totally integrated entity, analogous to a physical or biological system, that entirely determined the behavior of the people "within" it. Such a system was at the same time equated with the scientific "laws" of the analysts, that is, with their theoretical models—regardless of how the people concerned might describe themselves. The term "sociology" was invented, and given this set of associations, by August Comte, and was popularized by Herbert Spencer. Comte was working in a tradition that defined itself as coming mainly from Hegel, while Comte's impact on the English-speaking world was influenced by the interpretation of him advanced by John Stuart Mill. Therefore, as the basis of describing an important tradition that nineteenth-century anthropology defined itself by avoiding, it is necessary to sketch briefly the main features of the arguments of these four men: Hegel, Comte, Mill (as he relates to positivism), and Spencer.

It should be borne in mind that each of these men was in fact the leader of a distinct social movement. Hegel, in his later life, was actually the official State Philosopher in Bavaria. The others created their positions through writing and lecturing, as they took part in a large system of popular causes and popular societies in the nineteenth century that ran from the Royal Geographical Society in Great Britain at one extreme to the International Workingmen's Society at another.

G. W. F. Hegel (1770–1831)

Forty-six years Kant's junior, Hegel began publishing his major works shortly after Kant's were available, although much of the present Hegelian corpus consists of material published after his death, based on his (generally quite complete) lecture notes. Hegel's works incorporated versions of many of the major Kantian ideas or themes, including the idea of society evolving with increasing individual freedom, the importance of noumena in relation to human purpose, and indeed the whole idea of a *social* psychology. But in doing so he gave them fundamentally dualistic definitions. These ideas were developed consistently both in Hegel's social theory, and in his concept of an encyclopedic integration of knowledge. But the social theory, in point of time, came first.

Hegel's first major publication was *The Phenomenology of the Spirit,* in 1807, and its title indicates both its links to Kant and its fundamental departure from him. Hegel's title suggests that Kant's phenomenology was not, as Kant claimed, a total approach to all knowledge but rather only a phenomenology of individual human perception. Hegel's own phenomenology pertains to observation and analysis of the "spirit," or as Hegel would say, "The Spirit," as something apart from the individual.

Hegel begins the argument by describing Anaxagoras's ancient concept of *"nous"* as the earliest appearance or recognition of "spirit." Then, working like a prestidigitator within the folds of some of the darkest and most obscure writing in the whole of the history of German romantic idealism, he adds to this idea by degrees all of the dualistic accretions it had obtained in the Neoplatonic, and then theological, systems up to the time of Rousseau. "Spirit" magically became *nous,* "Law," "Force," "Reason," "Self-contained and Self-subsistent," "ruler of the world," "God," "the Divine Will," and "embodied in

Nature''; and since it ''was'' all these things, it allowed Hegel to claim to integrate all past discussions ''of'' them into a single new system of philosophy, in his view broader than any before. He viewed the entire Christian theology as a subordinate form of his own more general scheme, and explicitly claimed to be generalizing and broadening the claims that theology had made about the nature of God.

Since several of the things Hegel takes as ''Spirit'' are clearly noumena, rather than phenomena, both in the sense that they are defined by him as existing beyond direct perception and in the sense that Kant explicitly identified them as noumena in his own critiques, how could Hegel really have a ''phenomenology'' of the spirit? The answer in the *Phenomenology of the Spirit* is given partly by describing how he came to the study of the Spirit by observing his own thought. In addition, he argues that there are ranges of phenomena within which we see the Spirit at work, and which we cannot construe as organized in any other way. Nature was one of these ranges. The other, more important for us, is ''World History,'' recalling, of course, Kant's own distinction between nature and history as two sets of phenomena to which we must attribute two sets of organizing categories. But Hegel goes on to merge two fundamentally different levels of Kant's analysis as he argues that Reason itself, with the properties assigned to it in the above list, can only be organized by itself, and therefore has an internal structure of thesis, antithesis, and synthesis based on the concept of the dichotomy (recalling Kant's association of formal logic with the dialectic of pure reason). This he construes as having a general temporal order and form: thesis being Reason itself, antithesis being the negation of itself or the division of itself (which only it can accomplish), and synthesis (the new and entirely anti-Kantian element) being the reconciliation that is inherent in the fact that assertion and negation are not independent but only aspects of the larger whole. Successive dialectical assertions, negations, and syntheses are the means by which Reason progressively ''forces itself'' in history, using a different ''World Historical People'' in each phase. These properties in turn are the very ones he sees as laws by which History advances and Nature is differentiated.

Any reasonably sophisticated student of Kant should recognize that ''World History'' is no more a phenomenon in Kant's sense than ''Nature'' is. Rather both are, strictly speaking, noumena, whose existence may be postulated as a matter of practical need, but which cannot be considered to be known from nature or (reason) alone. Hegel is actually arguing for one noumenon on the basis of another, and not analyzing phenomena at all.

How does Hegel avoid this objection? In one, strict, sense, he never does. But in another sense, he avoids it by diverting attention from it with an idea that is both ingenious and audacious: precisely the idea of social determinism itself. It appears in the form of the doctrine that the State and not the individual is the phenomenal object in which reason manifests itself (this idea was used by Kant in a strictly limited sense in his *Idea for a Universal History*—that is in the sense that no noumenon could be reduced to individual perceptions alone). "World History" is thus the history of states and their development of progressively more rational constitutions. This is the heart of Hegel's social analysis, and of his impact on us.

In effect, Hegel suggests that the reason Kant could not see the operations of Reason clearly (i.e., Reason by itself) was that he looked only at individuals, while in reality the individual alone is not where Reason manifests itself. Hegel has reinterpreted Kant's idea that the judgment of objectivity is a judgment of universal validity in the light of his own premise that all judgments have to be either wholly individual or wholly independent of the individual—precisely what Kant had rejected.

In the *Philosophy of History* and *Reason in History,* both based on lectures and published posthumously, Hegel applies the phenomenology to the analysis of the "Oriental World," the "Greek World," the "Roman World," and the "German World" as successive phases of World Reason. In this, and implicitly in the *Phenomenology* as well, there is a new version of Rousseau's conception of the "general will" as something particular wills can be set off from, thereby losing their status as part of the social contract. The concept provides a general rationale for dismissing any action at an individual level that does not conform to his analysis.

The Introduction to the *Philosophy of History,* written as a lecture to introduce his course, is considered his best known and most lucid exposition: "The State is the Idea of Spirit in the external manifestation of human Will and its Freedom. It is to the State, therefore, that change in the aspect of History indissolubly attaches itself; and the successive phases of the Idea manifest themselves in it as distinct political *principles*" (1900:47).

Reason rules the development of states just as natural law rules the planets, even though "neither the sun nor the planets, which revolve around it according to these laws, can be said to have any consciousness of them" (p. 415). The only difference between Nature and History, Hegel says, is that "History in general is therefore the development of 'Spirit' in *Time,* as Nature is the development of the Idea in *Space*"

(p. 483). As the State responds to Reason in its formation and has the power only to be corrupt or to be the vehicle of Reason (on the model of the Neo-platonic idea of matter as the embodiment of form), so it logically follows that it cannot respond to men. Hegel argues for this at length and in a number of ways. He describes such men as Alexander and Napoleon, whom one might think of as creative of States and constitutions, as mere tools of History. They are great men only because they "had an insight into the requirements of the time—*what was ripe for development*" (p. 436). But this they did only because "that Spirit which had taken this fresh step in history is the innermost soul of all individuals; but in a state of unconsciousness which the great men in question aroused" (p. 436). And lest there be any doubt that Hegel means to say that this consciousness is the causative entity, and not the men, he makes a point of observing that:

> If we go on to cast a look at the fate of these World Historical persons, whose vocation it was to be agents of the World Spirit—we shall find it to have been no happy one. They attained no calm enjoyment; their whole nature was nought else but their master-passion. When their object is attained they fall off like empty hulls from the kernel. (p. 31)

As for other individuals, Hegel sees them too on the model of matter that is unimportant without form. Men exist insofar as they are "free," he argues (again beginning with a Kantian idea). But then he also argues that they are free insofar as they participate in the Divine Will as manifested in the State.

> Society and the State are the very conditions in which Freedom is realized (p. 41).

> The State is an *abstraction,* having even its generic existence in its citizens; but it is an actuality, and its simply generic existence must embody itself in individual will and activity (p. 43).

> For Law is the objectivity of Spirit; volition in its true form. Only that will which obeys Law, is free; for it obeys itself—it is independent and so free. (p. 39)

But lest we then think the State is also a product of its citizens, Hegel assures us that:

> . . . . it is a dangerous and false prejudice, that the People *alone* have reason and insight, and know what justice is; for each popular faction may represent itself as the People, and the question as to what constitutes the State is one of advanced science, and not of popular decision. (p. 43)

Insofar as people do not act "freely" in Hegel's sense, that is, act in conformance with the law of the State, they do not act or exist at all. They are not historically significant. They are "thus sacrificed, and their happiness given up to the empire of change, to which it belongs" (p. 33). "The particular is for the most part of too trifling value as compared with the general: individuals are sacrificed and abandoned. The Idea pays the penalty of determinate existence and of corruptibility, not from itself, but from the passions of individuals" (p. 33).

The assumptions are thoroughly dualistic: individuals are matter, the State is Form. The argument turns in a grand circle: History is the manifestation of the Idea by its internal processes of development. The State is the embodiment of History. It encompasses all human acts that are historical, because only those acts which follow Reason have pattern and are historical. Therefore History must be the manifestation of the action of Reason through the development of States.

Hegel's analysis of Reason in Nature rather than in History appeared in two principal works: the *Science of Logic* (two volumes) in 1812 and 1813, and *The Encyclopedia of the Philosophical Sciences in Outline* (1817). The *Encyclopedia* was greatly expanded in 1827. Meanwhile, *Natural Law and Statecraft in Outline* applied the scheme to the analysis of classic problems in law such as occupied the social contract theorists (1821; generally titled in English *Philosophy of Right*). It consigns literally every facet of life that is "general" to the State, and views this generality only as an aspect of the State manifest in individuals—all concepts of law, of property rights, of social relations, and of moral obligations (precisely the theme Durkheim later takes as the basis of his *Elementary Forms of the Religious Life*). A passage from its Preface shows the connection between the encyclopedic and social analyses very clearly. The link is Hegel's "method":

> . . . the chief difference between this manual and an ordinary compendium lies in the method which constitutes their guiding principle. But in this book I am presupposing that philosophy's mode of progression from one topic to another and its mode of scientific proof—this whole speculative way of knowing—is essentially distinct from any other way of knowing. It is only insight into the necessity of such a difference that can rescue philosophy from the shameful decay in which it is immersed at the present time. (p. 2)

This "mode of progression" is precisely the technique of grouping all topics, one after another, under the general headings of "Reason" and the "State," as he defines them—this is his "systematic" philosophy, and he equates this philosophical speculation with science, and this with the organization of material: "What we have to do with here is philosophical *science*, and in such science content is essentially bound up with form" (p. 2). And form, of course, springs from pure reason itself.

When we draw the arguments from their protective convolutions, the defense of every statement in the system ultimately rests on a tautologous relationship between it and other statements, while the basic terms remain not only non-phenomenal but in large measure undefined. Freedom is acting according to the law of the State—but what are "law" and the "state" in this scheme? What is a "world-historical people"?—apart from a group who can be described intuitively as exhibiting Hegel's laws? What, for that matter, is History itself? To say that it is organized in time as nature is organized in space is to say less than nothing—since time and space, after all, are not separately known.

The circularity is related to a ruthlessness in Hegel that goes far beyond Hobbes's concept of the obligation to obey a monarch so long as one's life is guaranteed. Hegel says, in effect, individuals and their lives in themselves do not have intrinsic importance or reality. The only significance they have at all is that they can and should exhibit conformance to the laws of the State, which are also the laws of Hegel's own speculative analysis.

An extremely important modern counterpart of this doctrine is the willingness to study a people, to claim to be discovering the "social determinants" of their behavior, but to disregard any of their own actions, conceptions, or values that do not confirm the patterns one expects to find. Whether we speak of "History," or of "society," the modes of argument that let us ignore behavior that does not represent the structural patterns we claim to seek as explanations of behavior spring from Hegel's equation of the State with Reason, of this reason with his own reason, and of Reason so construed as equal to all general order and to natural law, while non-conforming behavior is construed as non-patterned and non-reasonable, and therefore as irrelevant to science, rather than as negative evidence that can require an analysis to be rejected.

Auguste Comte (1798–1857) and Positivism

Using Hegel's ideas of science and the state, Comte created the idea of a "sociology," and two major images or themes that have been carried from it into modern anthropology: the conception of "organic" society, and the conception of a "positive" philosophy.

From August of 1817 to 1824, Comte served as secretary to Claude Henri de Rouvroy, Comte de Saint-Simon, while Saint-Simon was developing his conception of "socialism," with strong overtones of Hegel's state philosophy. Socialism involved the idea that all morality referred to society, which was the same as the state, and that the state itself should be the focus of a new religion, organized as a scientific successor to the medieval Church. Saint-Simon's *New Christianity* appeared in 1825—the last year of his life.

Later, after his association with Saint-Simon, Comte corresponded extensively with John Stuart Mill, and Mill supported his work both intellectually and financially. Comte's life seems to have been one of constant annoyance and trials over an inability to manage "trifles"— money, marriage, position, and the like. At a few points, one being his critical first attempt to give a course of public lectures on his philosophy in 1826, he suffered what Viscount Morely called "a severe attack of cerebral derangement" (1911: p. 815).

Comte's *Cours de philosophie positive,* in six volumes, was completed in 1842. Ten years later, the ideas of the *Cours* were expanded in the work of principal interest to social science, his second large effort, the *Système de politique positive.* The title can legitimately be translated either as *System of Positive Policy* or *System of Positive Polity:* the French words and the content of the work are both ambiguous. This is a massive affair of some 1,600 pages, in three volumes, including a *General View of Positivism* appended to the first volume. The titles of the volumes, in order, are *Introductory Principles, Social Statics,* and *Social Dynamics.* The sub-title of the whole is "Treatise on Sociology, Instituting the Religion of Humanity."

Comte's aim was to create a "Republic of Western Europe" consisting of the Italian, Spanish, British, and German populations grouped around France as its "natural center" (*General View of Positivism* 1875:67). This involved the moral and social "regeneration" of Europe (Preface, 1875 ed., 1:xxv), based on acceptance of his Positive Religion, and the establishment of a dictatorship (his term) to guarantee liberty of speech and discussion (see 1875:89–92) and to avoid what he called at one point "the delusions of constitutionalism" (Preface, 1875 ed., 1:xxii).

"Positive Religion" involved the integration of all the sciences, and was in turn a religion based on science: "The primary object, then, of

Positivism is two-fold: to generalize our scientific conceptions, and to systematize the art of social life. These are but two aspects of one and the same problem'' (Introduction, *General View of Positivism,* 1875:2).

Comte's solution to the problem involved three separate theoretical conceptions. The first was his view of social unity as depending upon religious unity. The second is a general theory of social evolution, or universal history. And the third is a concept of a "logical" reconstruction of sciences and religion. While the first two concepts have monistic parallels, Comte gives them a fundamentally dualistic meaning. The third concept is pure Hegel. Sociology was Comte's name for the reasons he gave for accepting his positive "Religion of Humanity.'' His ideas of a state apart from a religious system are actually extremely rudimentary, and fall back mainly on historical allusions. His contention was that the present ills of society were in large measure due to feudal Catholicism having become "retrograde" due to "intellectual incoherence" (vol. 3, chap. 6), so that it failed to unify the productive and military aspects (or classes) of society. His recommendations blended social and religious ideas in arguing for a new kind of "theocracy" directed by a "positive committee'' (*General View*) that would control industrial society as theologians (in his view) had controlled medieval society. The ideas that linked religion to the rest of each "stage" were: unity of society involved or required unity of public opinion, such opinion had to pertain to matters of morality, matters of morality were matters of religion, and religion required doctrine, or dogma (see vol. 1: *Introductory Principles*). In his new Republic, uniform public opinion had to be based on a "general system of education which positivism will introduce, and the principal function of the new spiritual power'' (*General View,* 1875 ed.:136). What Comte wanted to create, in effect, was a new version of the medieval Church as he understood it to have operated.

The important term "organic," associated with a biological analogy, was consistently used in connection with this complex of ideas: religious doctrine, uniformity of public opinion, and the integration of society. One example of many is when Comte describes the role of the working class as the "innervation of the social Organism" (his capitalization, in the first volume of *Positive Polity,* 1875 ed.:299).

Comte described the second element of the scheme as his "fundamental theory of Evolutions" (Introduction, 1875 ed., 3:5). The plurality of "Evolutions" is significant, for the argument involves the idea that science and religion have naturally evolved divergently, which is why positivism is required to bring them together.

In volume 3, the *Social Dynamics,* Comte describes his theory as "based on the systematic demonstration of three grand Laws of Sociology" (p. 5), all of which have as their "true principle" that "Progress is the development of Order" (p. 5). Two of these laws are evidently the "Law of Filiation of Concepts" and the "Law of Classification." (One cannot be sure because there is continual vague discussion of three laws being reduced to two without saying which are which. This confusion is further compounded by the fact that the general outline for the section actually describes four laws, and the discussion further involves numerous "principles" described in grandiose language.) The third law, it seems, relates "to the fundamental progress of the Intellect itself" (p. 14). It is the "Law of Intellectual Progress" (p. 14).

Apparently, the content of the first law—of "Filiation"—is that "the nobler phenomena are everywhere subordinate to those which are grosser but also simpler and more regular" (p. 15) and its extension or corollary (for Comte), that there is a "necessary and continual subordination of our Subjective Conceptions to the Objective Materials from which they are constructed" (p. 15). It may help indicate what Comte has in mind by noting that he says "without this rule Subjectivity runs wild, and the mind tends toward madness" (p. 19), and that in the "Normal State" of human reason (to be brought about by Positivism) "Subjective Reason in a regenerated form will resume its rightful empire" (p. 19). He is going to use this law to argue that individual minds, to be saved from disorder, have to be brought into uniformity by simple general ideas imposed from above.

The second Law is intended to "classify the sciences as a matter of doctrine" (pp. 33–34). Although the discussion is horribly confused, this classification seems to involve mainly the distinction among cosmological, biological, and mental sciences, with sociology being an aspect of the last. These classifications involve the idea of an "encyclopaedic hierarchy" of decreasing generality and increasing complexity (p. 35). For example, the laws of physics are very simple and cover many phenomena. All phenomena involve physical aspects. By contrast the laws of sociology are very complex, but involve only a few of the total range of phenomena. Many physical things are not social, but all social things are also physical.

Finally, the "Law of Intellectual Progress" seems to be the same as the "Law of Three Stages"—which is the idea that "each class of postulations" passes through three *successive* stages of development: *Theological, Metaphysical,* and *Positive* (p. 34). Generally (according to a common reading—I find Comte unclear on the points myself), theological explanations seem to involve explanations of the type "a god made it happen," metaphysical explanations involve ideas like "opium makes one sleepy because it contains a soporific principle," and positive explanations are the type of inductively and deductively justified explanations that his own scheme would generate (whatever they are).

Comte argued that the cosmological and biological sciences, which together made up "Natural philosophy," evolved in order of their hierarchical relations, that is in order of decreasing generality, increasing complexity, and increasing subordination of the subjective to the objective. This further amounted to a successive development of theological and metaphysical explanations, and went along with the larger use of theology and metaphysics in the stages of society surrounding them. Cosmology was associated with theology, from Greek "Polytheism" to medieval monotheism. Biology arose next, with secular metaphysics. In the last phase, positivism, mental science would be developed. It is still more complex and less general than the most complex biological science, and would control the others. It would be controlled in turn by the positive religious establishment that used its principles.

Comte's use of Hegel's conception of the "logic" of a science, in the form of his own "positive logic," came into play at this point. Its application depended in turn on a further idea of the division between "abstract" observations, laws, and/or science, and "concrete" observations, laws, and/or science (*Positive Polity*, vol. 1, ch. 1). Concrete observations deal with "beings," abstract observations (or laws, or science) deal with "events" (*Positive Polity*, 1875 ed., 1:343). Concrete observations are "composite and reducible to others," while abstract observations are "simple and irreducible" (p. 344). Thus distinguished, only abstract laws were required by Comte for his purpose (p. 30). It is evidently these laws, or the set of such laws that make up a science, that contain the logic of that science (I say "evidently" because the term is not precisely defined—it only seems to interchange with the phrase "abstract laws" in this sense). The debt to Locke, and associationism, is obvious. Abstract laws correspond to idealistic counterparts of "sensations"; concrete ideas correspond to objects.

In Comte's view, all the logics of the cosmological and biological sciences were "objective" logics, produced by objective methods and coming from the world to man. "Positive logic," by contrast, was a "logic of feeling," a "subjective" logic reflecting moral sentiments and going from man to the world (p. 329). This is what will give it the power to encompass the logics of the several sciences and of religion, and this is precisely why the integration must come from religion, as the expression of man's inner social and mental life and as the agency of uniform public opinion.

Leaving aside Comte's lack of coherent detailed documentation, it is obvious that the entire scheme depends on the dualistic (from Locke) idea of logic, the related distinction between "abstract" and "concrete" observations and laws and the subordinate distinction between "inside" the person and "outside," equated with the contrast between "feeling" and "reason," and between "subjective" and "objective" reality.

What makes Comte a minor philosopher is that he never did define or describe these conceptions clearly—much less avoid the difficulties already identified for most of them. So that unless one already accepts them without question, one cannot accept the scheme built upon them. What makes Comte a representative of the dualistic tradition is that these dichotomies are patterned after the classic form/matter distinction, and are used deductively and as the basis of what Comte repeatedly called a system of "rational" principles or laws that become totally general when they were "divested of everything empirical"—and thus reflect the "constitution of Human Nature" itself (see 1875 ed., 3:5).

Reading Comte, especially the more personal prefaces and the scattered autobiographical remarks, one has the uncomfortable feeling that one is in the presence of a lunatic. Yet, compared with Hegel, Mill, or Spencer, he probably had the most detailed impact, by the largest number of well-defined routes, on the development of modern academic anthropology, both in the short and the long run.

"Positivist" societies were founded in a number of important European cities. They debated "sociological" issues, just as the comparable Utilitarian and Communist societies of several types debated "economic" ones. Their popular activities, and many publications, in turn stimulated and encouraged more scholarly efforts.

One scholarly line involves the start of academic "sociology" itself. Herbert Spencer's "Synthetic" philosophy is part of this growth, and borrows much from Comte even while attacking him, as will be described in a moment. Another line leads to Durkheim; another to E. B. Tylor. These will be reviewed below. But none of the reactions to Comte among English-speaking readers can be understood without understanding his relationship to John Stuart Mill.

John Stuart Mill (1806–1873)

Mill published his evaluation and explanation of Comte in his *Auguste Comte and Positivism* (1865), which was itself in important respects an attempt to answer Spencer's criticisms of Comte that Mill thought unfair and misleading. This short but very persuasive work focused mainly on the *Cours de philosophie positive,* which Comte published before the *Positive Polity.* As his title indicates, Mill treated Comte not as the creator of positivism but as a contributor to it (1865:5), the first of many misrepresentations that appear in the work and were passed on from it.

Mill argued that Comte's "most fundamental theory" was the idea of the three successive stages of thought from theological to metaphysical and finally to positive (pp. 12–13). He connects this to a broad argument between "nominalist" and "realist" ideas of explanation, and aligns it as nominalist. In the process he also aligns Comte with Hume, and against Kant, whom he calls Hume's "great adversary" (p. 8). The realist position, which he equates with "theological" explanations, is mistaking words for things, products of the mind for aspects of nature (p. 15), in which connection he says that Kant "peremptorily asserted (the) existence . . . of things in themselves." By contrast, in Mill's view, Comte's "doctrine condemns all theological explanations and . . . thinks them destined to be replaced, by theories which take no account of anything but an ascertained order of phenomena" in the final historical phase (p. 13). After some considerable discussion of examples of "theological" thinking, Mill works toward the conclusion that Comte did not really show how to avoid such thinking. "He therefore needs a test of inductive proof; and in assigning none, he seems to give up as impracticable the main project of logic properly so-called" (p. 56). Comte's religious program and program for social reform is dismissed as an aberration not connected to his historical theories (p. 118), and possibly as a derangement brought on by an intervening romantic disappointment (p. 131). Comte's "positive logic" (which was not inductive, but was obviously intended to serve sociology the way dialectical logic had served theology and analytic geometry served physics) is not commented on, although the related idea that the study of natural laws must have a social "destination" is firmly rejected (pp. 62, 130 ff.). This characterization portrays Comte as nothing more or less than a benighted Mill, whose social philosophy would be assimilated in Mill's utilitarianism, even as his philosophy of science should be seen as a poor version of Mill's *System of Logic* (1843), which greatly expanded Locke's empiricism into a comprehensive set of rules for scientific "induction."

In short, Mill takes a small portion of Comte's scheme, assimilates it to the British tradition he himself represents and then says, in effect, what Comte has contributed and what he has left undone. He thus seriously distorts Comte and his actual context, as is recognized in at least one major history of recent philosophy (Passmore, 1957:14).

While Mill's version of Comte was not Comte, in a larger view it still was very Comte-like. It too embodied a nominally "scientific" version of post-Kantian dualistic philosophy. Despite congratulating Comte for "relativism" and avoidance of the idea of "absolute knowledge" (p. 6) (which he could do with some justice), Mill assumes that there was a clear distinction between inductive logics and deductive logics, and that logic itself was a matter of saying how statements *should* be verified (apart from knowing what the statements were about). He also assumes that there was in fact a clear and absolute distinction to be made between artifacts of the mind and "phenomena." This, along with the misunderstanding of Kant and a number of other important clues, marks Mill, like Comte, as a thinker who inherited much of Kant's language and conceptual apparatus, but assimilated it loosely and inconsistently to precisely the dualistic assumptions it was intended to reject.

Herbert Spencer (1820–1903)

Herbert Spencer, who began by following Mill, became a major adapter of Comte's sociology to English religious and political tastes. At the same time, by a series of accidents and opportunities, he came to be regarded as major spokesman for Charles Darwin. Many of the social ideas associated with social "Darwinism" would in fact be more accurately called sociological Spencerism. Spencer was born six years before Comte gave his abortive first series of lectures. Spencer's first publication was *Social Statics*, in 1850. He described the evolution of society in ways that recalled both Comte and Lamarck (who will be described below)—but not, of course, Darwin, who had not yet published. Spencer circulated the syllabus of his *Synthetic Philosophy* (projected to cover ten volumes), which was in good measure a reply to Comte, in 1859—one year after the publication of Darwin's *The Origin of*

Species. In it, Spencer described himself as both an evolutionist and a sociologist. A large international readership accepted him as the general philosopher of both important movements, but his scheme always remained in its broad plan more akin to Hegel and Comte than to Darwin.

Spencer's education was idiosyncratic and self-directed, but he had a genius for integrating ideas that combined high popularity and high plausibility, from the most diverse sources, into a scheme that seemed to suit an incredible range of individual tastes.

Spencer's *First Principles* is the first volume of his ten-volume *Synthetic Philosophy.* His *Principles of Sociology,* in three volumes, made up the sixth through the eighth segments, between *Principles of Psychology* and *Principles of Morality.* In the whole work, like both Hegel and Comte, Spencer attempts to derive his conceptions of the basis of knowledge and the limits on knowledge from a consideration of the development of thought in human history, as he reconstructs it. Like them, he connects the history of knowledge of the most basic source of order in nature with the history of knowledge of God, and therefore sees religion, or morality, as extended by his own works. But he differs from both Hegel and Comte—especially Comte—when he comes to identify the ultimate source of order as a "Power" in all things, that is itself "inscrutable"—an almost pantheistic idea that he shared with Coleridge and other contemporary Romantics and that comes very close to being a materialistic version of Hegel's World Reason. The idea also directly recalls a point Kant made in the *Critique* to the effect that some objects of our perception perceivably resist our will. It also recalls, of course, the definition of "things in themselves" as lying beyond our possible experience. But in the last analysis Spencer did not share Kant's basic assumptions, so that despite his use of Kantian phrases and ideas individually, his argument as a whole falls precisely into the traps Kant would have guided him away from. The following is a sample of his argument in the *First Principles:* "If Religion and Science are to be reconciled, the basis of reconciliation must be this deepest, widest, and most certain of all facts—that the Power which the Universe manifests to us is utterly inscrutable" (1862:39). To identify the universe as singular, and the inscrutability of Power as fact, is to talk nonsense in phenomenal (phenomenological) terms. As a *totality* the universe can never be more than a noumenon—a "hyperbolical entity."

Spencer's misunderstanding of Kant is directly related to his often-noted "materialism," which corresponded directly to Locke's and Mill's "empiricism." He assumes throughout that ideas are subjective and mental—"internal" states—while anything known as a fact is necessarily an external object, and therefore necessarily material:

To say that Space and Time exist objectively, is to say that they are entities. The assertion that they are non-entities is self-destructive; non-entities are non-existences; and to allege that non-existence exists objectively, is a contradiction in terms. Moreover, to deny that Space and Time are things, and so by implication to call them nothings, involves the absurdity that there are two kinds of nothing. Neither can they be regarded as attributes of some entity; seeing, not only that it is impossible really to conceive any entity of which they are attributes; but seeing further that we cannot think of them as disappearing, even if everything else disappeared; whereas attributes necessarily disappear along with the entities they belong to. Thus as Space and Time cannot be either non-entities, nor the attributes of entities, we have no choice but consider them as entities. (p. 39)

Spencer did recognize here that his position differed from Kant's and went on to criticize, and further misrepresent, the Kantian position:

Shall we then take refuge in the Kantian doctrine? Shall we say that Space and Time are forms of the intellect—'a priori laws or conditions of the conscious mind'? To do this is to escape from great difficulties by rushing into greater. The proposition with which Kant's philosophy sets out, verbally intelligible though it is, cannot by any effort be rendered into thought—cannot be interpreted into an idea properly so called, but stands merely for a pseudo-idea. In the first place, to assert that Space and Time, as we are conscious of them, are subjective conditions, is by implication to assert that they are not objective realities: if the Space and Time present to our minds belong to the *ego,* then of necessity they do not belong to the *non-ego.* (p. 40)

This objection makes sense in terms of Locke's assumption that all phenomena were either "within" the single individual or "outside" in the rest of the world, but it makes no sense whatever in Kant's terms, where *a priori* meant only that it provided a necessary learned assurance that one's perceptions could be shared. After rejecting Kant in this manner, Spencer came to his full position: "It results therefore that Space and Time are wholly incomprehensible. The immediate knowledge which we seem to have of them proves, when examined, to be total ignorance . . ." (p. 41). From a Kantian point of view, the "incomprehensibility" Spencer attributes to the universe as an objective property is in practice the outcome of his own inability to recognize that it is generated by his own dualistic assumptions.

Given his assumption that all things were either subjective states (attributes) or external objective entities, it is hardly surprising that Spencer's concept of evolution was stated in terms of the physical movement and aggregation of bodies. He saw the universe as permanent, with parts of it rhythmically interacting, at different rates, between integration and disintegration in accordance with a general "law" of "transformation and equivalence'': as matter concentrates, motion dissipates. Bodies aggregate as the motion of their component parts is reduced, and vice versa (p. 72).

Like Comte, Spencer saw the subject matter of the sciences arranged in a developmental hierarchy, and saw the sciences themselves as ranked in importance reflecting the hierarchy. The order of realms of organization was, as is well-known, Inorganic, Organic, Superorganic. Like Comte's levels, the Organic of Spencer is higher than the Inorganic, and its objects encompass the first. The Superorganic is yet a higher level of organization, a state of less motion, embodying more latent force, and its objects encompass both Organic and Inorganic. The principal difference between Comte and Spencer is that Spencer regards the higher levels and their sciences as inherently more generalized, rather than more specialized, than the lower levels.

Notwithstanding the idea of cosmic balance that ought to result from the trade-off between motion and order, Spencer goes on to argue for ''evolution'' in the things that affect humans by the operation of the general ''principle'' that a single cause tends to produce a multiplicity of effects. Water flowing over rocks produces many shapes; a seed produces many parts of a plant; a sperm cell produces many organisms and motions; and (as he rephrases it in Darwin's terms in a footnote in the fourth edition) natural selection produces different forms of new species out of more homogeneous early forms (Sec. 159, p. 376). This became an extremely popular idea, and was often added to Mill's ''nominalism'' and Hegel's theoretical circularity in producing a justification for highly speculative and arbitrary analyses that allowed no possible decisive role for negative evidence.

Spencer's application of his general ideas to the ''Superorganic'' involves little in the way of social theory that is new in comparison to the ideas that can be found in either Hegel or Comte, except for the very important version of a Darwinian conception of a competitive struggle among offices, institutions, and societies. But undoubtedly Spencer's form of expression, especially his use of physical or mechanical imagery, was widely influential, and its use was precisely dependent on the loose relationship to data that was produced by the idea of multiple causes for one effect. For example:

> The successive phases through which societies pass very obviously display the progress from indeterminant arrangement to determinate arrangement. A wandering tribe of savages, being fixed neither in its locality nor in its internal distribution, is far less definite in the relative positions of its parts than a

nation. In such a tribe the social relations are similarly confused and unsettled. Political authority is neither well established nor precise. Distinctions of rank are neither clearly marked nor impassable. And save in the different occupations of men and women, there are no complete industrial divisions. Only in tribes of considerable size, which have enslaved other tribes, is the economical differentiation decided.

Any one of these primitive societies, however, that evolves, becomes step by step more specific. Increasing in size, consequently ceasing to be so nomadic, and restricted in its range by neighboring societies, it acquires, after prolonged border warfare, a settled territorial boundary. This sharpness of definition, growing both greater and more variously exemplified as societies advance to maturity, is extremest in those that have reached their full development or are declining. (*First Principles,* sec. 134)

Spencer envisions individual societies that are integral wholes, "superorganic" structures, created either by growth from within or absorption of groups from without, precisely like Comte's organic state. Beyond them, or surrounding them, are general levels or states of development, containing similar societies, at similar levels of complexity and order (precisely the idea recently revived by Leslie White as levels of energy). Finally, beyond them, are the general laws of development that they illustrate and obey in common with other evolving entities.

Nineteenth-Century Sociology and Anthropology

The next chapter will make it plain enough that the nineteenth-century traditions leading most directly to modern anthropology either ignored or rejected the ideas of Hegel, Comte, Mill, and Spencer. Later, however, the two separate streams converged, so that to a very large extent the movement toward dualism in modern anthropological theory has been based on the adoption of theory, and assumptions about theory, from sociology.

5.
Beginnings of the Comparative Method

When the first indisputably anthropological works were written in about the middle of the nineteenth century, their common distinctive feature was what their authors called the "comparative method." Although the phrase now has many meanings, in terms of both dualistic and monistic assumptions, the form that these first scholars invoked was distinctively monistic, and very precisely defined.

To be exact, there were two monistic versions of the comparative method in the first part of the nineteenth century, and both eventually influenced anthropology. One form was based on the distributional orientation of Kant's geography, and on the way he separated the different types of institutions for separate description (a method quite incompatible, for example, with Comte's idea of a single "organic" state). The second comparative method, of about equal age, was more structural than distributional, and pertained to language and linguistic history. It too is traceable to Kant, but indirectly, through Johann Gottfried von Herder and Friedrich Karl von Savigny. The linguistic method was important to anthropology first; then the geographic method, while something of a combination of the two was adopted in biology.

In all discussions of the comparative method throughout the nineteenth century, it is important to bear in mind that there has been, between then and now, a revolution in our conceptions of the time over which the earth and man on it have developed. In the nineteenth century, there were many more open questions. There were reasons to believe that the earth could have been much older than we now think, or very much younger. The significance that could be attached to any method of historical reconstruction based on data then available varied greatly according to different assumptions about this absolute age of the earth and its geological subdivisions.

As late as 1911, E. B. Tylor in the *Encyclopaedia Britannica* had held for what he thought of as a long view of "between twenty and a hundred thousand years" for the "first appearance of man"—the very first appearance of human progenitors (2:115). Such estimates are often attributed to acceptance of religious opinion, but there were other and stronger reasons. In about 1854, Lord Kelvin argued that the entire age of the earth could not be more than 50 million years, dating from the point of its separation from the sun and assuming the sun shrinking inward from the orbit of the earth to its present position. He further estimated that it could not have been more than 20 million years since the earth changed from a molten mass to its present condition—based on rates of cooling projecting from rates of contraction in relation to the diminishing surface radiating heat into space (see Asimov 1960:1:44 ff. for a concise review). This is about 1/250th of present estimates—easily ten times as wrong as Tylor's estimate for human history. Geologists, calculating on the basis of erosion rates, argued that such estimates were much too small and held for far longer periods—some long even by modern standards. But the field was open. Translated into social terms, it came down to this: known history—say from Homer to the present—was quite possibly a very large portion of total human history. If so, it should be possible to infer backward from present evidence to the earliest human conditions. Conversely, if one wanted to discuss any kind of mechanism of social development, any sort of theory of historical dynamics in society, one had to take some position on the first state of society almost as a matter of course, if only to argue that the mechanism proposed had room to operate, whether or not one was interested in defining such an original condition *per se.*

In the framework of the possibility of a short chronology, the "comparative method" had all the features that Thomas Kuhn ascribes to a "paradigm" around which a science is organized. It embodied quite definite models of scientific research; it had a definite theory; it carried a definite conception of "scientific law"; and it was tied to quite definite procedures for data collection and manipulation. The "theory" was the still-familiar image of a branching evolutionary tree, beginning at some

time in the past and branching into divisions, some of which survive to
the present while others die out, with no re-combination, and no second
starts or unaccounted modifications. The concept of "law" focused on
the branching, saying how, out of any one set of usages, a division
would arise by a systematic change in a portion of it. And the model of
research was a specific conception of how one collects the material
representing branches, at any point in time, organizes it, and treats it to
infer earlier conditions.

Monistic Beginnings

The linguists most closely identified with the comparative method are
Rasmus Rask and the Grimm brothers, who became active in the first
quarter of the century. The first anthropologists to espouse it were J. J.
Bachofen, Henry Maine, Lewis Morgan, and John F. McLennan, all of
whom had published major works by 1860. Tylor, Frazer, and the many
other well-known anthropological names came later. The mutual cita-
tions, personal histories, and the phrases and ideas of both these first
two groups lead back in turn to two major earlier sources: Herder and
Savigny. Both men drew directly on Kant and Montesquieu, and carry
forward their conception of social investigation.

Johann Gottfried von Herder (1744–1803)

Between 1762 and 1764 Herder was a student of Kant at
Königsberg—indeed a protegé. He attended Kant's lectures, and Kant
introduced him to the work of Hume, Montesquieu, and Rousseau. His
first publication of major importance in relation to anthropology was
Essay on the Origin of Language (*Abhandlung über den Ursprung
der Sprache*), offered in a prize competition sponsored by the Berlin
Academy in 1772. Between 1784 and 1791, he published *Reflections on
the Philosophy of the History of Mankind,* which articulated a special
version of Kant's conceptions that was to be of continuing importance
throughout the century. Kant reviewed the work, and commended it in
the main. But he criticized one important feature. He said that Herder's

argument *could* be restated to leave out purpose, and to construe human development mechanistically. He objected to the consequent suggestion that individuals, seen historically, might not be responsible for the morality of their actions.

Herder eventually attacked Kant in turn, but despite the recriminations, those of Herder's ideas that were important for the comparative method rested squarely on Kant's development of the monistic tradition.

Herder's *Essay on the Origin of Language* begins with an attack on theories of language that rested on dualistic assumptions—mainly on the sensationalism of Locke that was taken over by Condillac, and on the "contract" theory of Rousseau. Against sensationalism, Herder argued, with Kant, that language could not designate perceptions that occurred merely in the flow of sensations—in the kind of ongoing perceptions humans share with animals. Nor could it come from automatic vocal responses to sensations—like cries of pain or grunts of effort (it might more easily be seen to come from gestures, which were more obviously voluntary). Against Rousseau, he argued that to suppose that language arose by agreement was circular, since there would be no way for agreement to come about without language in the first place. It had to be something more basic, within the individual. Tying both these points together, he argued in effect that language originates in "reflection," which itself comes from the fact that humans, compared to other animals, are what we would now call comparatively unspecialized. They are wide ranging and widely adaptable and hence have the capacity to select adaptations. Herder expressed this with the idea of freedom:

> Man manifests reflection when the force of his soul acts in such freedom that, in the vast ocean of sensations which permeates it through all the channels of the senses, it can, if I may say so, single out one wave, arrest it, concentrate its attention on it, and be conscious of being attentive . . . He thus manifests reflection if he is able not only to recognize all characteristics vividly or clearly but if he can also recognize and acknowledge to himself one or several of them as distinguishing characteristics. The first act of this acknowledgement results in a clear concept; it is the first judgment of the soul— . . . (1966:116)

A "reflection" is a "judgment" which Herder describes in the Kantian sense that presumes freedom of the will, and that involves setting off oneself as perceiver from an object that is not only perceived but is in a sense free of time—perceiv*able* in principle. He recognized that it was a major problem to show why human language is primarily vocal after all, and he spent the largest part of the essay on precisely this point (this part of the argument was also in a sense the weakest, since Herder had none of the modern evidence, from ape learning, human evolution, and comparative anatomy, that his position really requires).

Herder's conception of language provides a logical basis for expecting inherent internal variation, variation over space, and development over time. He went on to argue that different languages embodied different systems of distinctions, with primitive languages embodying fewer and less distinct conceptions than more advanced languages. This suggested a descriptive aim for linguistic research that was quite in contrast with the universalistic and normative purposes of current dualistic theories, and it was this that especially led Otto Jesperson (1924:27), among others, to see Herder and not his predecessors as the philosopher who signals the start of modern linguistic theory.

Herder's *Reflections* extended the approach of the *Essay* to the development of culture in general. There are, especially in chapter headings and conclusions, many key paraphrases of Kant's *Prolegomena* and the *Critique of Practical Reason*. But the *Reflections* lays greater stress on a second, potentially quite non-Kantian, theme that was also present in the *Essay*—a special romantic, but mechanistic, argument for constant and rapid change and adaptation:

> And since man is no independent substance, but is connected with all the elements of nature; . . . shall not he also be changed by it? It is far too little, to compare him to the absorbing sponge, the sparkling tinder: he is a multitudinous harmony, a living self, on whom the harmony of all the powers that surround him operates.

> The whole course of a man's life is change: the different periods of his life are tales of transformation, and the whole species is one continued metamorphosis. (1791:book 7, ch. 1)

This was not at all an incidental or innocent way of speaking. A large part of Herder's argument for the rapid and complete adaptation of people's ideas and behaviors to their environment rested directly on it. This is evidently just what Kant had in mind when he criticized Herder's mechanistic implications, and as Kant predicted, it did indeed eventually blur the explanatory importance of the technical concepts of purpose and freedom, and eventually blurred the lines between Kantian and Hegelian positions.

Friedrich Karl von Savigny (1779–1861)

Karl von Savigny was not a direct student of Kant as Herder had been, but in all respects he followed Kant and Montesquieu with fewer extraneous and contradictory assumptions, and in the end had a more direct influence on the development of the comparative method in anthropology proper. He was the teacher of the Grimms, and later of Bachofen, and directly and indirectly influenced Maine, McLennan, Morgan, and Bastian. He was the founder of the tradition that anthropologists generally call "comparative law," and that legal scholars call the "historical school" of jurisprudence.

Savigny began teaching law in 1800 at Marburg, and moved to Berlin when the University was founded there in 1810. His monumental *History of Roman Law in the Middle Ages* was published from 1814 through 1834, describing the transformation, persistence, and spread (and extinction) of Roman legal institutions and concepts in Europe between the fifth and sixteenth centuries. The sources of data were mainly legal documents, from edicts and compendia to records of actual cases, as well as the history of Rome published by B. G. Neibuhr in 1812, which he praised at length. Savigny's interpretations paid particular attention to the ritual forms recorded in the documents, such as the forms of witnessing, the types of assemblies indicated, and the titles and modes of address applied to the parties. Savigny exhibits all of Montesquieu's pluralism and relativism in his effort to see institutions from the viewpoint of those who used them, and to see the way changing institutions, in their turn, would lead to changing viewpoints over time. One of his major theses was that Roman institutions and legal offices survived as the Roman territorial law was transformed into a personal law on the model of the personal law of the German conquerors. Each German was part of a "nation" by birth, and other tribes respected his national law when he moved into their areas. Once Roman law was recognized by Germanic rulers on this analogy, it evolved differently in different regions. A second, different, set of arguments, traced the survival of other aspects of Roman law in ecclesiastical law.

The publication of the *History* was accompanied, in 1814, by *Of the Vocation of Our Age for Legislation and Jurisprudence,* a pamphlet intended to draw out the lessons of the larger work, especially in relation to projects then afloat to codify German law on the basis of "natural" law, as the utilitarians (and then Hegelians) had proposed. Savigny argued that the law had no "rational" or "natural" basis but arose from the patterns of life of the people, and it had evolved too slowly to cover too many subtle ramifications for such a violent replacement from above to work as well. Note the comparison between the body of law and language:

> (In the) youth of nations . . . we . . . find symbolical acts universally employed where rights and duties were to be created or extinguished: it is their palpableness which externally retains law in a fixed form; and their solemnity and weight correspond with the importance of the legal relations themselves, which have been already mentioned as peculiar to this period . . . These formal acts may be considered as the true grammar of law in this period; . . . (ch. 2) (in Morris 1959:290)

Then, in his view:

> . . . With the progress of civilization, national tendencies become more and more distinct, and what otherwise could have remained common, becomes appropriated to particular classes: the jurists now become more and more a distinct class of the kind; law perfects its language, takes a scientific direction, and, as formerly it existed in the consciousness of the community, it now devolves upon the jurists, who thus, in this department, represent the community. Law is henceforth more artificial and complex, since it has a two-fold life; first, as part of the aggregate existence of the community, which it does not cease to be; and secondly, as a distinct branch of knowledge in the hands of the jurists. (ch. 2) (Morris: 290)

Savigny's concept of law has obvious similarities to Hume's "custom," to Montesquieu's concept of law and legislation, and to Kant's definitions of positive law as a type of custom (*Sitte*). Savigny is simply extending Kant's investigation to show how such legislation comes about—how it evolves and what its media are. Jurisprudence, in a strict sense, represents an advanced development in the legislative process. Taking "custom" as a set of symbols embodying positive law, legislation *sensu strictu* was just one way of creating custom, and jurisprudence was one way of acting upon legislation.

Jakob Grimm had become a law student at Marburg in 1802, and his brother Wilhelm joined him a year later. Jakob began working directly with Savigny as a research assistant in 1805, helping with the preparation of the *History of Roman Law*. The Grimms' first edition of the famous *Kinder- und Hausmärchen* (*Household Tales* and *Children's Tales*) came out in 1812, and they provide nothing if not material for an extension of Savigny's analysis of German law back into the still more distant past, by looking for symbolic usages that would embody it at a period in history of the Germanic peoples before they became a part of the Roman empire. It was their chronological ordering of these tales that brought criticism from Rasmus Rask. This ultimately forced Jakob Grimm into Indo-European linguistics, where he contributed substantially to its special and very important form of the comparative method.

Linguistics

Because of their own monistic assumptions, the schemes of Herder and Savigny were preadapted to integrate and articulate the technical accomplishments of a most important foreign monistic tradition: the indigenous South Asian linguistic analysis that evolved around the preservation and interpretation of Vedas and later philosophical poetry and commentary.

The Indian tradition never held the ancient texts to be anything but human creations; their value lay in the experience and wisdom they embodied on that account. For this very reason, it was important to preserve the original texts as accurately as possible, in both sound and sense. Gradually, from about the sixth century B.C., a system was developed to do this, epitomized by the work of Panini, who may have lived in the fourth century B.C. As described in a recent article by Staal (in Hymes 1974), the system involved two coordinated levels of analysis. First, each line of verse was remembered as a running text. Secondly, against this, all the elements of each line that were considered compound were broken up into the elements that they were considered to be derived from—the root forms and combining affixes and suffixes, prepositions and postpositions. Separately, general rules for combinations were stated, down to rules stating the order in which rules were to be applied. Long after Panini, the method was set down in a writing system that used a clearly defined phonemic alphabet that made it very easy to recover the way words were actually pronounced, and to see changes in articulation over time. All of this together provided a complete linguistic analysis of Sanscrit, including paradigms for the grammar, and rules for the construction of "words" within it. The system was in some important ways more comprehensive and exact than traditional European systems (actually going back to Aristotle) using abstract "parts of speech"—taking Greek and Latin as implicit ideal languages.

The Sanscrit analysis provided a model for reducing the massive complexity of all that we call "language"—everything anyone might say in one or about one—to a few powerfully generative components. These components, reflecting their original discoverers' concern with letting the parameters of analysis rise from the material itself, provided not only a new basis for reconstruction and interpretation but also for comparing several languages with one another with the assurance that what was being compared was actually the same thing in the two cases.

The first two major figures generally described as initiating the modern type of linguistic analysis, that combined the monistic assumptions of Kant with the monistically grounded linguistic tradition of South Asia, are Sir William Jones and Friedrich von Schlegel.

Jones had been a noted Orientalist for many years before he studied law in the early 1770s. In 1784, after admission to Temple bar and a brief but notable career in England, he began a career as Magistrate in Calcutta, India. He founded the Asiatic Society of Bengal and served as its president until his death.

Jones called attention to the importance of Sanscrit for historical studies and its relation to other languages in a series of presidential addresses, as well as in some translations of major philosophical works from the ancient Indian literature, including the *Ordinances of Manu* (1794). His third address contains the remarks usually quoted in histories of linguistics, taken as previsioning both the delineation of the Indo-European family of languages and later scholarly approaches to it. It was published in his collected works in 1799:

> The Sanscrit language, whatever be its antiquity, is a wonderful structure; more perfect than the Greek, more copious than the Latin and more exquisitely refined than either; yet bearing to both of them a stronger affinity, both in the roots of verbs and in the forms of grammar than could possibly have been produced by accident; so strong, indeed, that no philologer could examine them all without believing them to have sprung from some common source, which, perhaps, no longer exists. There is a similar reason, though not quite so forcible, for supposing that both the Gothic and the Celtic, had the same origin with Sanscrit; and the old Persian might be added to the same family. (in Lehmann 1967:15)

Here is evolution on a genetic analogy long before such a conception was accepted in biology. But two further aspects of the address, equally important historically, are not accurately suggested by this quotation. First, a good part of Jones's argument was not linguistic in a strict sense but rather referred to early Hindu conceptions and institutions and their parallels in other ancient cultures. Secondly, the ultimate scope of Jones's historical ambitions was much broader than the Indo-European family:

> Of these cursory observations on the Hindus, which it would require volumes to expand and illustrate, this is the result: that they had an immemorial affinity with the old Persians, Ethiopians, and Egyptians, the Phenicians, Greeks, and Tuscans, the Scythians or Goths, and Celts, the Chinese, Japanese, and Peruvians; whence, as no reason appears for believing, that they were a colony from any one of those nations, or any of those nations from them, we may fairly conclude that they all proceeded from some central country, to investigate which will be the object of my future Discourses . . . . (Lehmann:20)

Schlegel followed Jones in associating Sanscrit with culture as well as language in a strict sense, but he held for more narrowly linguistic criteria in deciding upon historical relationships.

Schlegel had studied in Paris, which had become a center of Sanscrit studies pursuant to French efforts to compete with British influence in South Asia. In 1808, he published *On the Language and Wisdom of the Indians* (in German), arguing first that one could not base historical relationships on leaps between modern and ancient languages using arbitrary or "logical" rules for the alteration or recombination of sounds. The parallels had to show identity, or be based on demonstrated intermediate links at all points. Then, partly as a further constraint, and partly to indicate how such demonstrations of relationship should be framed, he argued that there were basically two distinct types of languages, using two distinct principles of grammatical construction that were reflected in different classes of linguistic elements. The type of grammar represented by Sanscrit was "inflectional," meaning that words were made up of root forms and combining elements, like affixes, that changed their shape in various combinations to indicate variations of meaning. The second type of language, exemplified by Chinese, used only simple particles as words, generally (in Schlegel's description), monosyllabic, which were merely juxtaposed in building sentences, and which did not actually combine or change their form in any way. Schlegel considered such languages inherently more primitive, less able to indicate complex shadings of meaning, notwithstanding the otherwise high level of Chinese cultural attainments.

On the basis of these two broad types, Schlegel actually delineated three major families of languages—the Indo-European languages, which were inflectional, the Arabic, which combined elements but which were not inflectional in the same way as the Indo-European languages, and the Tartar languages including Chinese (see the excerpts translated in

Lehmann 1967:21–28). Explicitly against Jones, he argued that no overall unity could be demonstrated among them.

Schlegel's work was quickly followed by Franz Bopp's *Über de Conjugationssystem der Sanskritsprache* . . . (1816), Rasmus Rask's *Undersogelse om det gamle nodiske eller islandske sprogs oprindelse* (1818, but submitted in response to an essay prize contest in 1814), and Jakob Grimm's *Deutsche Grammatik* (1819). The latter two works enunciated the "sound law," which provided a completely explicit procedure for describing connections of the sort Schlegel had insisted on, and Jones guessed at—the comparative method in its most powerful form.

Schlegel had remarked that certain terms in modern languages appear to involve direct exchanges of letters from terms in ancient languages, like the initial consonant of *dies* in Latin that changes into the initial consonant of *giorno* in Italian, and he was willing to see such differences, when regular, as not disproving a connection between them. Rask's treatment of Icelandic turned the qualification into an important insight, noting that transformations of this sort, when they occurred regularly, provided a coherent way to link forms from different time levels to one another, and to separate such linked terms from borrowings or rediscovered terms:

> When in such words one finds agreements between two languages, and that to such an extent that one can draw up rules for the transition of letters from one to the other, then there is an original relationship between these languages; especially when the similarities in the inflection of languages and its formal organization correspond. (From *Undersogelse,* pp. 49–51, in Lehmann:30)

He gave a series of examples of regular correspondences between Greek and Latin, and went on to state formal transformations from Greek and Latin to Icelandic, assuming that where Greek and Latin were the same, they represented a common ancestral language he called "Thracian" (Lehmann:33–34). This is the concept of the sound shift, although the fact that Rask admitted many exceptions makes his statement of it weak enough so that further credit for its invention also has to go to Grimm, who developed it as a "law."

Rask's sound shifts involved only consonants. Grimm held that vowels varied regularly but according to "laws" as "yet undisclosed." The "liquid" consonants were not subject to change (Lehmann:48) and the spirants "remain essentially unchanged throughout all the German dialects." But the stops showed regular shifts from Greek through Gothic to Old High German, and these he summarized in a simple table:

Gk	Goth.	OHG	Gk	Goth.	OHG	Gk	Goth.	OHG
P	F	B(V)	T	TH	D	K	–	G
B	P	F	D	T	Z	G	K	CH
F	B	P	TH	D	T	CH	G	K

But this statement itself, compressed though it is when one re-members that it intended to deal with all occurrences of these "letters," and not just some, was not yet the "law." The law was that, in the shift from Gothic to German: ". . . the Gothic . . . tenues correspond to the High German aspirates; the Gothic media correspond to the High German tenues; and the Gothic aspirates to the High German mediae" (Lehmann:49).

In other words, representing each category by its initial (following Jesperson 1924:44): T goes to M goes to A. And the same law applied to the "step" from Greek to Gothic, so that in no trivial sense the law may be described as characterizing the *line* of the development of German from Greek. Other laws would characterize other lines and branches within lines.

The exact phonetic meaning of Grimm's terminology is not clear, but he apparently considered that tenues were very "hard" sounds, gener-ally corresponding to voiced explosive stops; "media" meant seemingly less hard or strong sounds, such as the unvoiced stops; and "aspirate" did not mean what we would now mean, but rather the softest range of sounds, including both what we would actually call aspirates (like *h* in "hat") as well as such continuents as are represented frequently by the letter *f* and the initial *th* in "thus." That is, the idea was that each con-sonant at each step is pronounced more weakly, until it is an aspirate that decays to the point where it has to be replaced by returning to the strongest series.

From Grimm and Rask, pursuit of further sound shifts carried through the phonetics of Rudolph von Raimer to the "new grammarians" of the 1870s. This work clarified phonetics and drove the "exceptions" into smaller and smaller corners, discovering more and more sound laws, af-fecting more consonants, the vowels, and even subtleties of stress. Each advance produced a change in the conceptions of language history. But the general relationships between sound laws, word formation, gram-matical forms, and the arrangement of languages into historical sequences continued to be as Rask and Grimm stated them. In a very strong sense, the substance of the evolutionary tree of languages re-mained not the languages themselves, in some loose sense, but the

sound laws they exemplified. The separation of major groups of languages was articulated by stating their unique sound laws, and within
groups the order of languages (and the argument for any particular
linguistic item between placed at any point of time) depended on the
state of the laws they exemplified.

Beginning with Franz Bopp, a dualistic tradition began to take shape
that eventually offered a quite different framework for interpreting the
new data and techniques. Bopp, like Schlegel, was a Sanscritist. But
unlike Rask or Grimm he was interested in finding the ultimate origin of
grammatical forms. His approach depended on the Aristotelian conception of a sentence consisting of a subject, a predicate stating the quality
of the subject, and a cupola joining the subject and quality. As with the
medieval logicians, Bopp's cupola was the verb "to be," and his proposal, following from this, was that complex verbs develop from some
root indicating a quality or state plus a particle derived from "to be" (in
the language in question, of course). These roots and their combinations
have different forms in different language families (Bopp began following Schlegel in his ideas here), but the underlying processes were supposed to be the same.

Bopp's influence is especially clear in two other great Sanscritists
who worked before the new grammarians came to dominate the scene:
Wilhelm von Humbolt (1767–1835) and August Schleicher (1821–68).
Both were especially interested in basic issues in the philosophy of language. Humbolt was one of the most self-consciously Kantian of the
linguists of the period; Schleicher was conspicuous as one of the first
self-consciously Hegelian.

Humbolt became an associate of Goethe and Schilling, and he espoused their construction of Kant's conception of freedom to stress the
paramount importance of the inherent worth of the individual. He was
the principal founder of the University of Berlin, while he served in the
ministry of religious and educational affairs in that city. He was also in-
strumental in establishing there the first Professorship in Sanscrit, and in
making it a major center of scholarship in the broadly liberal, Kantian
tradition. In addition to Savigny, scholars there who identified themselves with Kant included Karl Ritter (after 1820) and Alexander von
Humbolt (Wilhelm's brother; after 1827) in Geography (see Taylor
1957:43–77), as well as Rudolf Virchoff, the anatomist (after 1847),
who had a strong second interest in anthropology, and was one of the
founders of the Berlin Anthropological Society. In 1866, with Bastian,
he was also a founder of the Museum für Volkerkunde—the first major
ethnological museum.

In political as well as linguistic philosophy, Humbolt's aim was to define structures that were "organic," which meant very much what "natural" meant to Montesquieu: an embodiment of human freedom and, by that fact, human intelligence. Languages were "organic" if they permitted conceptual sophistication to develop by elaboration or growth from within rather than by the accretion of new and arbitrarily associated elements from without:

> . . . as in the designation of the manifold associations of thought, language needs freedom; and one can regard it as a secure sign of the purest and most successful linguistic structure if in it the formation of words and constructions undergoes no other limitations than are necessary to combine regularity with freedom, that is, to assure for freedom its own existence through limitation. For the course of development of intellectual capability generally stands in natural harmony with the correct course of development of language. (Humbolt 1836, ch. 9; in Lehmann:64)

The type of language that best provided these conditions was "inflectional," in Schlegel's sense:

> Compared with the process of incorporation and loose attachment without a true word unity, the method of inflection seems to be a principle of genius, proceeding from the true intuition of the language. For while such languages are anxiously concerned with uniting the individual entity into a sentence, or with the representing sentence immediately unified, the method of inflection indicates directly the components in accordance with a particular thought construction, and by its nature cannot separate the relationship of a component to the thought in speech. (ibid.; Lehmann:65)

Many threads in Humbolt reappear later in the modern tradition associated most closely with Edward Sapir (as recently discussed, for example, by Miller [1968]). Humbolt's criteria for "organic" language, for example, are virtually identical with Sapir's conception of "genuine" rather than "spurious" culture.

Schleicher differed from Humbolt precisely in the way his Hegelian loyalties would suggest. Instead of seeing language structure wholly in relation to the freedom and development of the speakers, he saw it as based on absolute limits to the structure of root forms—all being based in the first instance on three vowels and three consonants. He carried his affection for three-way distinctions through all phases of his analysis— from types of grammar through stages in history. Side by side with this, seeing languages as distinct objective beings, Schleicher was also the first to explicitly draw out, graphically, the "family tree" of the Indo-European languages, in his *Compendium of the Comparative Grammar of the Indo-European, Sanskrit, Greek and Latin Languages,* first published in 1861 (see Lehmann:87–96).

The many-sided technical developments that these broad ideas epitomize provided an obvious model for the comparative method in biology, and were very closely involved with a series of developments in archeology, which were parallel to, and interacted with, developments in anthropology proper.

Archeology

Archeological advances were closely linked to linguistic advances, and gave added importance to the underlying method. Several archeologists had accompanied Napoleon on his expedition to Egypt in the years 1798 to 1801. Among the objects they brought back to France was a basalt stele found near Rosetta, the "Rosetta stone." It is inscribed with hieroglyphic, demotic Egyptian, and Greek versions of a decree of the priests assembled at Memphis in favor of Ptolemy V. The presence of these three records of the same text enabled Champollion, in 1821, to decipher the entire stone and, for the first time, to show how the hieroglyphics could be read (until that time it was not known that the language they transcribed was Egyptian). This gave scholars the ability to study the history of the Egyptian language, which was an early representative of the major non-Indo-European group Bopp called "Arabic," and this in turn clarified vistas of history far more distant than those familiar up to that time. The discoveries also gave new validation to such well-known materials as Herodotus' history and the Old Testament, and suggested new lines for integrated use of archeological and linguistic methods to reconceptualize and expand the study of history.

A series of efforts by Sir Henry Rawlinson, Paul Botta, and George Smith opened cuneiform to interpretation, and brought to light still more material on classical history and the Old Testament (see Penniman 1965:160–64). Paul Delroux, following Herodotus' ancient account, made the first Scythian discoveries near Kertch in 1830 (ibid.; p. 160). And perhaps the best-known and most spectacular of all, Schliemann eventually discovered the ruins of Troy, by working from his own reading of Homer, in 1879. He also found the remains of Minoan civilization on Crete and Mycenaean ruins concurrent with those of Troy.

Such accomplishments, in the context of the linguistic advances, conveyed the impression to many that scholarship was on the verge of a comprehensive understanding of all of human history.

6.
The Comparative Method in Biology
The Evolutionary Paradigm

The current accusation that nineteenth-century anthropology was "racist" or "social Darwinian" (Harris 1968:Chs. 4, 5) conveys the impression that it somehow developed out of evolutionary biology. It is true that in some countries the term "anthropology" nearly *meant* biologically based theories of cultural development (and still does). But these traditions had little bearing on the ethnological thinkers who led most directly to modern social and cultural anthropology.

Fundamentally, the traditions leading to modern anthropology and the beginnings of evolutionary biology were separate but parallel adaptations of the comparative method to different problems, even if to somewhat overlapping subject matters. Part of the parallelism included the presence of opposed dualistic and monistic traditions. In fact, in biology there were two such oppositions. The first and best-known revolved around opposed interpretations of the arrangement of biological classifications. The dualistic tradition, derived in this case mainly from Christian theology, held the categories to be arbitrary reflections of God's reason; while the skeptical tradition held that the classes were natural, and corresponded to a developmental sequence—this was the position of Darwin (apparently reluctantly) and his close defenders. The second debate revolved around the relative influence of "nature" versus "nurture" in human behavior, and the permanence or importance of race. In addition to these two rather complex debates, a third set of interests revolved around the search for the "missing link." It was neutral with respect to the broadly opposed views of man, mind, and science of the dualistic and monistic traditions, but added a great deal to their apparent general importance.

Biological Classification

The publication of Charles Darwin's *Origin of Species* in 1859, and its subsequent successful defense by Lyell, Huxley, Romanes, and others, was not simply a matter of taking a paradigm that had been developing in linguistics and suddenly grafting it onto the set of interests that went sometimes by the name of biology and sometimes by the name of geology. It was more that the continuing linguistic and archeological developments tipped the balance toward evolution in an argument that was already underway. In biology, a strong skeptical tradition began with Hook's cell theory (1662) and Harvey's experimental demonstration of the circulation of the blood (1628). But their assumptions had been opposed by the clearly dualistic tradition articulated most forcefully by Linnaeus (1707–78), and by the nineteenth century his views appear to have been dominant.

Carl von Linné, or Linnaeus, was born in Rashult, Smäland, Sweden, the eldest son of the parish co-minister, later pastor. In 1726, his father wanted him to become an apprentice tailor or shoemaker. But with the help of a medical friend, he began studies at the University of Lund in 1727, and transferred to Uppsala in the next year. He encountered Vaillant's *Sermo de Structure Florum* (1718, Leiden) and became interested in the pistils and stamens of plants.

In 1732, Linnaeus, with a grant of 530 copper dollars (about 25 pounds sterling), began a series of travels exploring Lapland and covering over 4,600 miles. He took an advanced degree at Haderwijk, and later, when his funds were almost gone, traveled to Leiden, where he called on Jan Frederick Gronovius (1690–1762). He showed Gronovius the manuscript for his *Systema Naturae*. The latter, according to Jackson, was "so greatly astonished at it" that he had it published at his own expense (Jackson 1911:733).

The *Systema,* written in Latin, remained the most important of Linnaeus' great classifying works, and he produced several expansions and revisions. It is considerably more than a zoological catalogue. It begins by setting out the "Imperium Naturae" and its divisions. The first division was between God and the World (*Mundus*) in a broad sense. Under the latter in turn he placed: Stars, Elements, the planet Earth, Natural Law (immutable and created by God), and Nature (natural objects). This last category in turn was further divided into three "Kingdoms": animal, vegetable, and mineral. Man (*Homo Sapiens*), Angels, and some analytic categories also were defined as part of the "Empire," outside the Kingdoms.

Within each Kingdom, Linnaeus first gives the characteristics of the Kingdom, then of each "class" (of Animals: Mammalia, Aves, Amphibia, Pisces, Insecta, and Vermes). Classes in turn were broken down into "orders," Genera, Species, and finally into local races. *"Primates"* was an order of the class *Mammalia,* and *Homo* was one of four *genera* within the order. This genus is further divided into two species. The first species, *Homo Sapiens* has six local races, beginning with "wild" (*ferus*), "American" (*Americanus*), and "European" (*Europaeus*). The second species, *Homo Troglodytes,* consists of one race, *Homo Sylvestris*—Orang. Outang. (1767:28–33). Among the many characteristics listed, the former species was described as "diurnal" in its habits, the latter as nocturnal. Footnotes argue for the various points when necessary. At the species level, in all the orders, the detailed descriptions were made manageable only by a physiological shorthand based on the general anatomical form—as for the different numbers of rays in the fins of fishes. The work was monumental in scope and execution, and a surprising amount of it still stands (but not *Homo Troglodytes*).

By the time he died, Linnaeus had given the world a comprehensive system of classification applicable to all known living things. His was the concept of species based on morphology and the capacity to interbreed, and the method of comparative morphological analysis that appeared to show pattern after pattern to support and reinforce each correct classificatory conclusion. But there was no suggestion in Linnaeus' work that today's species was tomorrow's genus, or that the families of today descended from a species of former times. It was seen by Linnaeus entirely as an "arbitrary" exercise in the logical construction of classes and subclasses (like Aristotle's *Categories* and *Metaphysics*) that happened to work. The system of nature, as declared by the introduction of several psalms of David sprinkled through the opening pages, was a perfect and ample work of God, understood by man, His own perfect and immutable creation on earth. The human mind simplified nature by the imposition of reason, and no more.

Baron George L. C. Cuvier (1769–1832) continued Linnaeus' attacks on skepticism, added the level of "phylum" to the scheme beyond that of "order," and applied the Linnaean system to fossils as well as to living organisms. The discovery of the Archeopeterix at the same time, midway between reptile and bird, could only have intensified the need for asking why the scheme worked so consistently, with new forms always fitting the established pattern.

The more advances that were made, the more unreasonable it seemed, at least to many people, to repeat that human reason had such power because it was capable of seeing the divine plan in nature. But this was precisely the position of Louis Agassiz (1807–73) both before and after Darwin published his conclusions.

Like Linnaeus, Agassiz was the son of a pastor—in this case of the parish of Motier, near the lake of Neuchâtel, in Switzerland. In 1828, Agassiz fell heir to the place of J. B. Spix in a project of classification of fishes collected in Brazil on an expedition directed by C. P. von Martius. In 1830 he published a prospectus of a *History of the Freshwater Fishes of Central Europe*. In 1831–32 he began the work under Cuvier at Paris, which led him to his lifetime study of living and fossil fishes. He went on to reclassify basic fish types and to do important work with aquatic reptiles and with such diverse related matters as annelids and glaciers.

Agassiz recognized, after Cuvier, fossil as well as living forms. He noted the adaptation of species to their geographical circumstances, and he is the author of the observation that "ontogeny recapitulates phylogeny," which Darwin made good use of (Darwin 1859:338). Yet for all this, he staunchly maintained that each species was "specially" created by a unique act of God—in fact by a "thought of God" (Himmelfarb 1959:281). After Darwin's work was published, he took pains to oppose it, for example, in a series of public talks on "The Structure of Animal Life"—six lectures on the "Power, Wisdom, and Goodness of God, as manifested in His Works" (Himmelfarb:268). In Agassiz's view, the recapitulation of phylogeny in ontogeny, of the history of the species in the developing embryo of a member of the species, was no more than a revelation of the divine plan on which that species was constructed, of its own unique history, but did not on that account suggest that one species shared its history with others.

It must be noted that there is a strict logical consistency to Agassiz's position, quite apart from its religious basis. He is generally accused by later biologists of cutting his species too fine, of denying variation within species by the process of making any variation the basis of assigning·a new species category. But so long as Agassiz followed this procedure of dividing species consistently, making any detected difference a new species differentiation, then each species was in a very real sense the product of an act of reason, and there was no species variability. Each really is unique as a category of perception and could therefore quite consistently be attributed to divine intervention, if one believed God to be the basis of one's own thought.

The rich recent literature on Charles Darwin makes it unnecessary to review his work in detail here (see Glick 1972; Himmelfarb 1959). The main point is that by the time he published the *Origin of Species* (1859), he had both predecessors and allies on most key features of his scheme up to—but not including—his centrally important conception of the mechanism of "natural selection" that enabled evolution in biology to be seen on the model of evolution in languages. In addition to Lamarck (1744–1829), Darwin was much influenced by the ideas of Thomas Robert Malthus (1766–1834) and Charles Lyell (1797–1875).

Jean Baptiste Lamarck was a botanist whose professional life overlapped Linnaeus' and resembled it in many respects, but with a tragic coloration. His first major publication was the *Flore Françoise* (1778), followed in 1785 by contributions in botany to the *Encyclopédie méthodique,* in his capacity as holder of the title of Botanist to the King (he was then forty-four years old). At the age of forty-nine, because of changes in the organization of the Jardin du Roi (where he held his position), he was moved to a zoological chair and called on to lecture on the classes "Insecta" and "Vermes" of Linnaeus. But at this point, driven to develop a difficult new research field, his eyesight began to fail and he soon became blind. Nevertheless, his important *Histoire naturelle des animaux sans vertèbres* was published between 1815 and 1822, as a supplement to his earlier *Philosophie zoologique.* In the preface, he described the theory of the work as one which "recognized in nature the power to make something, even the power to make all which we observe . . ." (1815:iv). The purpose of his proposed classification was to "explicate the general distribution most conformable to the different known animals, the principles on which that distribution must be founded, and the true disposition that it is necessary to give to the entire order so that it will conform to that which nature has followed" (p. xiii). Elsewhere, he rephrased this even more clearly, describing his central problem as an explanation of the progressive origin of diverse forms of life from its simplest beginnings (p. 165). But note that this was after Jones, Rask, and Grimm had used similar imagery in linguistics.

Flatly contradicting Linnaeus, Lamarck argued that these laws are not about God, but about the properties of living bodies themselves, in the way they react to their environment. In this connection he enunciated his famous "four laws" of the inherent properties of living bodies:

1. Life by its own forms tends continually to increase the volume of all bodies which possess it, and to extend the dimensions of its parts, up to a limit which it brings about itself.
2. The production of a new organ in an animal body results from the supervention of a new need (*besoin*) continuing to make itself felt, and a new movement which this need gives birth to and encourages.
3. The development of organs and their force of action are constantly in ratio to the employment of these organs.
4. All which has been acquired, laid down, or changed in the organization of individuals during the course of their life is conserved by generation and transmitted to the new individuals which proceed from those which have undergone those changes. (1815: 181–82; Part 3 of Intro.)

Every one of these principles save the last was used by Darwin, and, in effect, he came very close to the last. But even though the influence seems inescapable, Darwin argued not for a refinement of Lamarck but in most cases directly against the catastrophists and advocates of special creation, as if Lamarck had never written. It should be said, however, that Lamarck's writing is often rather difficult and not well organized or clearly documented. He, like Comte (who considered him a pioneer of Positive Biology [1875:459]), has not a few laws but a welter that seem to stumble over one another.

Darwin's debt to Thomas Malthus is far more specific, and more specifically acknowledged, than his debt to Lamarck. Malthus' *Essay on the Principle of Population* (1798) offered the general "law" that while human population expands "exponentially," the food supply expands only "arithmetically." Darwin recognized that the idea of *different* rates in this argument is specious—food is produced by the same biological mechanisms as those who consume it. But this very point led to the deeper recognition that both Darwin and Alfred Wallace (whose almost identical views, sent to Darwin for comment, finally forced Darwin to publish) cited as the key to both their theories.

By Darwin's own account, the relevance of Malthus was not apparent to him until after he had become absorbed in the effort to explain the data he had collected. In the meantime, the plan of his work showed the obvious and direct influence of Charles Lyell. Lyell's *Principles of Geology* was published in 1830—one year before Darwin left on the voyage of the Beagle. The *Principles* argued, convincingly enough for most, that the fossil species that Cuvier and others had ranged alongside modern species were, in general, systematically different from modern living forms. By an application of precisely the same reasoning comparative philologists used, Lyell argued that they were in fact ancestral forms—they were generally simpler, and they contained a full range of organs that were either lacking or divergently modified in living species. Why he did not go on to the next step and link the fossil and ancestral forms into larger tree-like patterns is difficult to understand. But what he did was enough to narrow Darwin's problem. Within reasonable limits, Darwin could assume the existence of at least some groups of known ancestral and descendant species. Thus the problem that remained was not to show that a species at one time level can give rise to divergent forms at a later time level, and thus define a genus or family, but specifically to show the *mechanism* by which such descent comes about.

The thoroughness with which Darwin, on his voyage (1831–36), accumulated the evidence for such relationships as Lyell described leaves no room to doubt that the general idea of evolution was in his mind from the outset. The wonder is not that Darwin invented so much, but that he added so little to what was already established, and that he took twenty-four years to publish his results, in 1859. In the end, his own contribution was not evolution in general but the notion of "natural selection" in particular, based on the idea that "as more individuals are produced than can possibly survive, there must in every case be a struggle for existence, either one individual with another of the same species, or with the individuals of distinct species, or with the physical conditions of life . . ." (1859:64). This struggle works on the inherent variability within species, and results in the selection of those traits that better enable the individual to survive, while the traits less conducive to survival are lost with the individuals that exhibit them.

The evolutionary arguments by the immediate associates of Darwin in the decades following the publication of the *Origin of Species* were aimed at bringing biology into the group of disciplines using the comparative method, and sharing a generally skeptical or experimental frame of reference.

Nature Versus Nurture: Anthropometry

The nineteenth-century theoretical line most deserving the label "racist" in a strict sense was anthropometry, which emerged from "somatology," a widespread interest in racial origins and the association between physical type and behavior, in the first decades of the century.

Most somatology was pursued by anatomists and physicians like J. F. Blumenbach (1752–1840) in Germany, J. C. Pritchard (1786–1848) in England and S. G. Morton (1799–1844) in the United States. Its basic theoretical framework was usually Lamarckian, with deterministic overlays.

Anthropometry differed from most somatology in its emphasis on statistical methods, by which racial or other hereditary groups were to be discovered and defined. Its line of progress consists not in a developing argument about evolution (such as the arguments for the single origin of all modern races), or a developing system of physical measurements, so much as a developing system of mathematical techniques for describing populations and samples, and the properties of statistical measures themselves. These statistical concepts were framed in a larger system of conceptions of perception and the philosophy of science that were strictly dualistic, in the tradition of Locke and Mill. These included the idea that statistical inference corresponded to the major (and later, the only) form for the valid scientific induction of generalized laws from particular instances, and that statistical "significance" was tantamount to scientific significance in general. We no longer accept racial determinism, but this metatheoretical explanation of the value of statistical inference is still very much alive.

The principal theoretical foundations of anthropometry were provided by Lambert Adolphe Jacques Quetelet (1796–1874), Francis Galton (1822–1911), and Karl Pearson (1857–1936). Quetelet, originally an astronomer, wrote *On Man and the Development of His Faculties* in 1835, followed by *Of the Social System and the Laws Which Rule It* (1848). *Anthropometry,* from which the tradition takes its name, was published in 1871. The earlier works argued that individual measurements of individual characteristics are regularly grouped around measurements representing the "average man" (the population mean), in a way that exactly corresponds to the probability of drawing each measure from a population of that size with that mean. This formulation permitted the definition of the mathematical theory of probability to be applied to a description of population characteristics. In *Anthropometry,* he stressed the use of the binomial theorem to predict the distribution or "shape" of the measures of a feature in a group of samples around the mean of all samples. This provided, among other things, a way to describe a race without requiring a pure or representative racial type (assuming there could be agreement on the relevant features to measure), or any knowledge of the actual mechanism of inheritance, which was hotly disputed at the time.

Galton, the grandson of Erasmus Darwin and cousin of Charles Darwin, is most responsible for the identification of Darwinism with racial determinism and Comte-like programs for imposing social reform from above by a scientific elite. He was trained in medicine, but spent his life in explorations, in meteorology, and in a long-term study of "genius," focusing largely on his own relations: the Galtons, Darwins, and Wedgewoods. Galton published *Hereditary Genius* in 1869, *English Men of Science: Their Nature and Nurture* in 1874 (an impressionistic and superficial work), *Human Faculty* in 1883, *Natural Inheritance* in 1889, and several works on fingerprints, describing the system of classification he devised. Galton was the first to stress the usefulness of identical twins to differentiate the effects of "nature" from "nurture"; he investigated the capacity for vivid recall; the effects of education on mental ability; and the inheritability of mental traits and ability in families over a period of forty years. He made lasting contributions to statistical theory, using correlational techniques that extended Quetelet's mathematics. His opposition to the idea of the inheritance of acquired characteristics was tied to a program for "eugenics"—a term which he coined. It meant, in effect, selective sterilization of people with inferior characteristics, combined with efforts to stimulate the birthrate of those with superior characteristics. In 1904, he founded the Eugenics Laboratory and endowed a research fellowship in Eugenics at the University of London. His knighthood was conferred in 1909.

Pearson was a close associate of Galton, but did most of his work after the evolutionary paradigm began to break up. He was a mathematician and statistician by training, and held positions in applied mathematics and geometry at the University of London from 1884 to 1911. With Galton he was co-founder of the journal *Biometrika* in 1900, and he served with Galton as joint editor until 1906, when he became managing editor (until 1936). From 1911 to 1933 he also held the chair of Galton Professor of Eugenics (after Galton) at London, and was director of the Galton Laboratory.

Pearson extended Galton's use of correlations, developing the idea of normal deviation within populations in identifying typical or average

features, and he invented the Chi-square test of statistical "significance." His *The Grammar of Science* (1892), borrowing many ideas
from Ernst Mach, developed a specific version of Mill's "empiricism"
that is still actively espoused in the positivistic philosophy of science,
including the ideas that science is a single system of knowledge that
applies to the "whole range of phenomena, mental and physical"
(quoted in Passmore 1962:326); that science supersedes metaphysics
(and therefore that metaphysics is crude science, not concerned with
some other type of problem); that science "ultimately" consists in
mathematically ordered statements that describe correlations among
"facts," reducible to a contingency table (1911:159); and that the entities of science, like "force," are at bottom only arbitrary classifications
of "facts," perceived through the "senses." When science is thus
construed as a set of classifications for correlations and no more, then
statistical generalization can indeed be seen as its ultimate language, and
statistical significance as the only significance of its statements.

The Missing Link

The idea of a "missing link" now seems so simple that it is difficult
to appreciate the full importance it had when it first entered scholarly
concern. It is more than the creature that links human and ape ancestry—it is the link between cultural theory and biological theory, and
between conceptions of human development, biological evolution in general, and absolute chronologies of the earth and its inhabitants. If the
"link" could be established in relatively recent calendrical or geological
time, then human biological development could be closely related to
human cultural, linguistic, and technological development, and the differences between theories stressing individual creative freedom and
those stressing determinism would seem unimportant. But if the link
was far back in time, human biological history, known cultural, linguistic, and technological history would be relatively independent, and
much in the direction and final outcome of history could be attributed to
human creative actions.

The logical possibility of a missing link had been discussed even
before Lamarck, and it must have become a more likely prospect with
the development of linguistics. But up to the time of Darwin's voyage,
no hard evidence was forthcoming. However it began to appear soon

after, and it undoubtedly served as a stimulus to both Darwin and Wallace, as well as their followers and supporters. Credit for the discovery goes to the efforts and vision of Jacques Boucher de Crèvecœur de Perthes (1788–1868), better known simply as Boucher de Perthes. In 1838 he submitted stone hatchets to the Societé Imperiale d'Émulation at Abbeville, France, where he worked as a customs officer. He argued that human craftmanship (and hence human culture and human history in some sense) existed in the Pleistocene epoch. The thesis was rejected—Penniman says "with derision" (p. 53). He argued the point again in *De l'industrie primitive* (1846), which similarly "made no impression on the learned" (Lowie 1937:8) until 1854. Then Jean Rigolet, a former opponent, visited his site, found some remains on his own, and changed his position (Penniman:54–55; Lowie:8). In 1858 Hugh Falconer visited the site and similarly announced his support. He was followed in the next year by Joseph Prestwich, John Evans, and Charles Lyell.

Meanwhile, in 1857, in a limestone cave in the valley of the Neander River near Düsseldorf, Germany, a skeleton was found that was immediately recognized and described as being human, but of a "barbarous and savage race," which could be "regarded as the most ancient memorial of the early inhabitants of Europe" (Leakey, Prost, and Prost:162). The original German paper by D. Shaffhausen was translated into English by George Bush, and appeared in 1863 in Thomas Huxley's influential *Man's Place in Nature*. Huxley considered it "truly the most pithecoid of known human skulls," but, at the same time, he added that it was not "a human being intermediate between Man and Apes" (Leakey, Prost, and Prost:164).

In 1894, a new and more ape-like type was found. In 1898, its discoverer, Eugene Dubois, argued that it

> hardly admits of doubt that this upright-walking ape-man, as I have called him, and as he is really shown to be after the most searching examination, represents a so-called transition form between men and apes, such as paleontology has often taught us to recognize in other families of animals; and I do not hesitate now . . . to regard this *Pithecanthropus erectus* as the immediate progenitor of the human race. (Rpt. in Leakey, Prost, and Prost:175)

A dramatic succession of discoveries of more remains of both these types were made in short order, reinforcing the original identifications and the sense that they represented real past populations.

Finally, in addition to *Pithecanthropus erectus,* there was the "Piltdown man." Its remains were found in gravel pits near Piltdown, En-

gland, in 1912 and 1914, by Charles Dawson and Arthur Smith Wood-
ward. As reconstructed, it had a jaw still more primitive than *erectus,*
though a somewhat more modern cranium. It was accepted as a genuine
linking type, signified by its name *Eoanthropus dawsoni,* by a large
number of scientists until 1955, when it was shown to be a deliberate
hoax (Weiner 1955).

With the exception of the Piltdown remains, the search for the "missing link" has yielded a continuing body of new knowledge, remarkably
little subject to major criticism, that theories in all areas of anthropology
have taken into account and have been assessed against.

The Evolutionary Vision

The vision of a universal natural science based on biological evolution came about when scholars tried to construe biological, linguistic,
and cultural development on the same time scale—necessarily a short
time scale since the chronology of known history was short. Darwin
himself always held for a very long chronology in biology and he obviously felt that he was in agreement in this with Boucher de Perthes.

The preface to *The Descent of Man* (1871) says: "The high antiquity
of man has recently been demonstrated by the labours of a host of emi-
nent men, beginning with M. Boucher de Perthes; and this is the in-
dispensible basis for understanding his origin" (Modern Library ed.,
1936:360). Such a long chronology would militate against accepting a
direct chronological isomorphism or causal connection between biological and linguistic and cultural evolution, although *The Descent of Man*
does note the similarity of pattern. The parallelism between biology and
philology was emphasized more strongly and less cautiously, however,
in an introductory tract written by George J. Romanes, F. R. S., in
1882 (published at Darwin's suggestion). Its underlying reliance on the
linguistic model as well as its implications for a comprehensive evolutionary approach to human history are obvious:

. . . the guiding principle of scientific classification is the comparing of organism with organism, with the view of seeing which of the constituent
organs are of the most invariable occurrence, and therefore of the most typical signification.

Now since the days of Linnaeus this principle has been carefully followed,
and it is by its aid that the tree-like system of classification has been es-

tablished . . . The classification of animal forms, indeed, as Darwin, Lyell, and Haeckel have pointed out, strongly resembles the classification of languages. In the case of languages, as in the case of species, we have generic affinities strongly marked; so that it is possible to some extent to construct a language-tree, the branches of which shall indicate, in a diagrammatic form, the progressive divergence of a large group of languages from a common stock. For instance, Latin may be regarded as a fossil language, which has given rise, by way of genetic descent, to a group of living languages— Italian, Spanish, French, and to a large extent, English. (1882:23–25)

Once the idea of a close fit between linguistic and biological evolution was accepted, a fit between biological history and political and ethnic history was not far behind, and argument could focus on the question of causal directions. In the absence of a clear understanding of the mechanisms of inheritance, or even the physiological basis of bodily form, there was a clear field for conjecture, and all manner of speculation could be advanced—from ideas that psychology influenced physiology to strict biological determinism. For the most part, direct interest in *explaining* the supposed connections between biological and cultural evolution were confined to sociology and psychology, thanks primarily to Spencer and Galton, respectively. Those who styled themselves ethnologists or anthropologists (in the Kantian sense) were generally disinclined to accept the determinism that such a problem brought naturally to mind, as will be described. But their debates could nevertheless hardly avoid being influenced by the immense popularity of the biological arguments, and in many subtle ways were shaped to respond to them.

7.
The Beginnings of Anthropological Theory

The first theoretically defined concepts, subjects, and issues (in addition to linguistics) that directly carried over into the academic anthropology of the twentieth century came under three major heads: 1) kinship and social organization, 2) primitive religion, and 3) psychology. The assumptions in the theories defining these topics were predominantly monistic, and sharply distinguished from the assumptions of contemporary sociology. But there was also the beginning of the dualistic tradition that set the stage for a later radical re-conceptualization of all of these topics.

Kinship and Social Organization

The principal figures in the analysis of kinship and social organization are generally considered to be J. J. Bachofen (1815–87), Lewis Henry Morgan (1818–81), Henry Sumner Maine (1822–88), John F. McLennan (1827–81), and W. H. R. Rivers (1864–1922). Their works were interrelated, and formed a single developing system of argument with a single set of shared assumptions.

Bachofen was born and raised in Basel, Switzerland, where he later served as a magistrate, member of the city council, and Professor of Roman Law in the University. He had studied law at the University of Berlin from 1835 to 1837, and was deeply influenced by Savigny. Most anthropological discussions of Bachofen focus on his *Das Mutterrecht* (*Mother-Right*) (1861), where he advanced the idea that the patrilineal and "patriarchal" social organizations of classical antiquity were themselves reactions to a system of "mother-right," involving descent through women and rule by women, that preceded them; and that "mother-right" was, in fact, the first true organized form of human society, evolved from a reaction against an earlier stage of no family organization. Bachofen's idea amounted to a new version of Hobbes's war of all against all, featuring promiscuous sexual relations and a thoroughly materialistic, nature-bound existence. A recent English translation of a well-rounded selection of his works (Bachofen 1967) has made his ideas much more accessible.

Bachofen's first major work was *Versuch über die Grabersymbolik der Alten* (*Essay on Ancient Grave Symbolism*), published in 1859 and now reprinted in part. Although this followed several papers involving ancient law and the beginning of the investigation of the place of women in ancient society, its main theme was not matriliny but rather the use of mythical allegories in the painted and sculptured materials of ancient tombs. Technically, it was an explication and demonstration of his method of symbolic analysis. Theoretically, it was an influential elaboration of Savigny's idea of symbolism as embodying external, positive law.

The essay proceeds by concrete instances. He first discusses an Italian tomb painting wherein several men are apparently discussing three eggs; he proceeds to discuss the interpretation of three eggs and three dolphins regularly used to signify laps run at the circus and in other contexts; he moves on to discuss a general contrast between *sanctum* and *sacrum*—objects that were untouchable and objects that were consecrated; he adds these conclusions to a further discussion of the concept of love signified in the myth of Amor and Psyche; and, finally, he discusses at some length representations of the myth of Ocnus the rope-plaiter—a mythical figure engaged, like Sisyphus, in unending toil. In this case, Ocnus weaves a rope, and as he weaves it, the rope is eaten by an ass. His method of analysis begins by looking very carefully at recurrent details and the general conceptual oppositions that they appear to signify. In the case of the eggs, for example, he notices that they are always drawn half black and half white, and that the black half is lower, the white half higher. The white is oriented toward the heavens, the black toward the earth (both represented in the painting). The eggs themselves are contrasted with the place in which they are painted—life contrasted with death. And the eggs as feminine representations are contrasted with the men of the painting who are discussing them. Finally, these contrasts are related to the context of the more esoteric symbols included in the painting: a myrtle wreath associated specifically with the Goddess Aphrodite-Venus "the primal mother of all tellurian creation" (Bachofen 1967:29). These contrasts, he argues, reinforce his more "physical" interpretations based on the more objective symbols, and also represent, for those who painted the pictures, later and more abstract elaborations of the earlier meanings of the more material objects:

> The egg is in every respect the (*archai genesius*). It comprises all parts of the material world: heaven and earth, light and darkness, the male and the female potency of nature, the stream of becoming and that of passing away, the germ of all tellurian organisms, of the higher and lower creation, and the whole world of the gods who, of material origin like the entire tellurian world, have one and the same mother as men, animals, and plants—namely, the dark egg. In the Orphic-Bacchic mystery egg the initiate sees not only his own genesis but also that of his god, and the god born of the same egg, and the certainty that tellurian birth can rise to the immortality of the higher luminous world. (Bachofen 1859:29)

Bachofen moves back and forth between physical symbols, the way in which such symbols are employed, and the myths, legends, and cultic information about the symbols at his disposal to build up a sense of the basic assumptions and outlook of those who created them. The process is one of finding a progressively better interpretive fit—fewer, and more elegant, conceptions that will involve more and more of his data. The basic organizing principles are not universal parameters or rules of thought Bachofen himself might share (as, for example, in Lévi-Strauss's conception), nor are they inductive rules known to Bachofen alone. They are, rather, fundamental ideas about society that were shared by those in the society at the time, what we might now call a social "world view," which Bachofen aims to reconstruct.

Das Mutterrecht, like the essay on grave symbolism, is organized around specific cases, and it fills out both his view of the society that generated the original myths and his concept of law. Each case is a place named in myth or legend as having a female-dominated system, or is described in such a way as to make such an interpretation reasonable to Bachofen—Lycia, Lemnos, Lesbos, and so on. Bachofen arranges these cases according to several attributes in what amounts to a general theory of conceptual development. The argument is too subtle to treat here with justice, but the basic ideas are first that each stage begins with a certain set of relationships revolving around survival in nature and focusing on sexual access, child raising, and social authority. Within each stage, defined not as a point in time but rather by a major solution to the basic problems (e.g., no sexual domination, female domination, or male domination), there is a succession of forms beginning with those crudest, most materialistic, and closest to nature, and ending with those most fully rationalized—beginning, that is, with the most crudely physical conceptions of each type of family, and ending with those where the concept of the family was most fully developed into self-consciously refined systems of theology and society as a whole, with its own elaborated system of symbolic expression. The direction of advance, and the motive power behind it, is attributed to a special kind of historical dynamic, recalling at once both Hegel and Montesquieu. Each system carried to its extremes produces abuses, and creates reactions. Those leading the reactions impose their own ideas, and proceed to articulate them, working out the options they provide in turn. The substratum of these changes, the object to which this theory applied, was however not pure social ideation, or strict behavior, but rather "the popular mind" (p. 222). "Matrilineal culture" was "organized by the homogeneity of a dominant idea" (p. 76), and "not restricted to any particular ethnic family" (p. 71).

Hard evidence for Bachofen's stages was never forthcoming from antiquity, if he had wanted it, but his conceptual models seemed to apply with remarkable force to results from ethnology. In fact tribes with matrilineal descent and something much like "matriarchy" had been described as early as 1672 (for a concise summary of these early developments, see Tax, in Eggan 1955), and his ideas gave them renewed theoretical significance. But, as we will see, this turned out to be only one of the many areas where his imprint is evident.

Sir Henry Maine's *Ancient Law,* his work most commonly discussed in histories of anthropology, was published in the same year as Bachofen's *Das Mutterrecht,* 1861. But it followed a line of investigation set down in an 1856 essay later included in *Village Communities in East and West* (1871). Like Bachofen, Maine was a lawyer and legal scholar. He taught law at Cambridge and Oxford, and from 1862 to 1869 served as legal member of the Council of India, then as Vice-Chancellor of the University of Calcutta. (In the Indian system, Vice-Chancellor is the chief administrative officer of a facility, analogous to Chancellor or President in the United States.)

Maine's basic perspective shows some important parallels to Bachofen's, and also some important differences. In several interconnected ways, Maine, like Bachofen, builds an analysis that includes a recognition of the subjective perceptions of those he describes on a par with his own perceptions.

Although *Ancient Law* mentions Savigny, and accepts Savigny's description of the evolution of the law of property, Maine does not trace his own outlook to him. Instead, Maine attributes his basic conceptual apparatus to Montesquieu, Jeremy Bentham, and, especially, John Austin. (Austin, however, had studied jurisprudence in Germany, and had associated with Savigny.) He agrees with these three—and with Savigny—in rejecting attempts to explain the laws people have by reference to universal *a priori* principles or "laws of nature," and he especially seems to single out Montesquieu's historical orientation for praise (1870:85, 115). In addition, he takes from Bentham and Austin a tripartite analysis of the fundamental elements of any law: a *command* that it originates in, an *obligation* imposed by the command, and a *sanction* enforcing the obligation (p. 7). He rejects what he describes as Montesquieu's over-reliance on geography, temperature, and the like as explanatory variables on the grounds he "underrates the stability of human nature. He paid little or no regard to the inherited qualities of the race" (p. 116), and he rejects Bentham's use of the idea of utility as an explanatory principle as "unfruitful"—circular (p. 117).

Maine describes his own "historical method" (p. 91) as being the same as that of "comparative philology" (p. 122), which he describes as analogous to the procedure whereby one does not "contemplate the physical world" as a whole in order to understand it, but rather begins "with the particles which are its simplest ingredients" (p. 119). The particles are "those fragments of ancient institutions which cannot reasonably be supposed to have been tampered with" by later historians or legal chroniclers (p. 121). By arranging these particles according to his method, Maine proposes to deal not only with law itself, but also with concepts about law as they have evolved.

Maine's data and method were quite different from Bachofen's. His data consisted primarily of ancient legal codes—early Roman codes, Islamic laws and legal principles, Jewish law indicated in the Old Testament, ancient Greek legal texts, and quite prominently the so-called "hindoo code" especially the Laws of Manu, even though he recognized that the latter probably never had been law in fact, so much as Brahmanic ideals of what laws ought to be (p. 18). His method is to identify basic principles that are most widely shared in the portions of these bodies of law which appear most ancient, and to ask what type of command, obligation, and sanction they assume. In identifying these features, analogies are freely made between "ancient" laws and "primitive" laws, on the assumption that wherever the same law appears it will involve the same structure of social relations as well. Maine also assumed that social units develop from small to large, by a process of aggregation. Although this last idea may now seem innocuous, it marks Maine as quite distinct from the other major formative figures in this area.

The principal overall trend Maine found was a shift from "status law" to "contract law"—from law based on ascribed social position to law based on agreement and interest (p. 170). The sanctioning basis of the most ancient systems of status law was the *patria potestas*—which Maine translates "paternal power"—which was connected in turn with a specific social organization:

> The points which lie on the surface of the history are these: The eldest male parent—the eldest ascendant—is absolutely supreme in his household. His dominion extends over life and death, and is as unqualified over his children and their houses as over his slaves; indeed the relations of sonship and serfdom appear to differ in little beyond the higher capacity which the child in blood possesses of becoming one day the head of a family himself. . . .
> Men are first seen distributed in perfectly insulated groups, held together by obedience to the parent. Law is the parent's word . . . . (1871:123–24)

From this primal condition, Maine saw the first differentiation of types of law follow from the differentiation of types of relationship within households, based on kinship distance (order of succession) and on the fundamental difference between *cognates* and *agnates*. Cognates are those within the insulated groups related to a common ancestor; agnates are those within the group attached to cognates, such as wives and adopted children (p. 147). Status law of these family groups became status law in states as these groups aggregated, and the authority of the *patria potestas* was generalized into the power of the king, which in turn gave way to constituted oligarchies, then aristocracies, and on into known historical sequences. Contract law developed as the agnates became progressively more emancipated, and their movements between kinship groups became regularized and controlled by higher authorities.

Because Maine was not concerned with pure conceptual systems so much as patterns of conceptualized control over concrete geographical domains that must therefore have existed at a definite time, his conclusions were more completely dependent on the short prehistoric chronology current when he wrote, and were more completely vitiated when it was shown to be in error. Maine could think "primal" conditions existed at perhaps five thousand years before known history. When it became clear that humans, and human culture, were many tens of times that old, his scheme became untenable on that basis alone. Yet many of his ideas persisted, including his view of kinship groups as quasi-legal patterns of command and obligation extending over people in territorial domains, and his view of tribal organization as this type of household organization extended to a larger territory. In these respects, there is a direct line from Maine to the British traditions of kinship analysis following upon the work of Rivers and then A. R. Radcliffe-Brown, discussed below.

John Fergusen McLennan, like Maine and Bachofen, was a lawyer. He was admitted to the Scottish bar in 1857, and appointed Parliamentary draughtsman in 1871. His publications attacked Maine strongly, and his stages agreed with Bachofen. But his underlying explanatory mechanisms differed from both, and mark the beginning of modern approaches to the analysis of marriage systems, as opposed to the analysis of domestic groups (Maine) and to world views utilizing kinship and sexual metaphors (Bachofen).

McLennan's first work, *Primitive Marriage* (1865), carried arguments against a circular letter by L. H. Morgan, as well as Maine. It did not mention Bachofen, as McLennan explained in *Studies in Ancient History,* published in 1886, because he had not read Bachofen until 1866. He considered that they were in fundamental agreement (pp. 319 ff).

McLennan took as his starting point certain aspects of marriage rituals that seemed to him widespread, not only in Europe but around the world, in ancient as well as modern peoples. These revolved around the theme of "marriage by capture"—where the men from one group act out the abduction of a bride of another group. On the philological analogy, McLennan argued against Maine that this custom was a more certain indication of the true ancient condition of mankind because it was spread over many more "races" and regions than the usages that Maine started from, most of which came from relatively advanced Indo-Aryan traditions (1865:115–18n, 208–9).

In place of Maine's conception of increasingly large aggregations of households, McLennan's evolutionary stages involved the idea of increasingly complex progressive divisions within the originally undifferentiated horde. He described this progression in terms of a basic theoretical distinction between two types of marriage rules: rules of *exogamy* ("out-marrriage") and rules of *endogamy* ("in-marriage"). Exogamy was the rule associated with bride-capture. It was the first rule above no rule at all—the rule that one does not take a mate from one's own group. This led to a distinction between wives and mothers on the one hand as against sisters on the other, and eventually led in turn to "po-lyandry," where one's own mother was distinguished from other women from outside but one's own father was not distinguished from other men—"an advance from and modification of promiscuity" (p. 171). Polyandry in turn led to the development of the "levirate"—mar-riage of one wife to a group of brothers (rather than all men of a "tribe"), since brothers could be distinguished as sons of one mother. Gradually (though with absurd directness from a modern perspective), such successive refinements led to a replacement of exogamy with en-dogamy, wherein wives were not taken from groups defined only as other than one's own, but rather from groups defined as subgroups of one's own—from "tribes" related to one's own in a single orderly sys-tem of regular exchanges (pp. 193 f.). Increasing differentiations among classes of kinsmen went along with increasing use of alternative paths of reckoning relations and increasingly precise and orderly rules of mar-riage in an increasingly complex pattern of marriage relations, for which McLennan gave anthropology its current sense of the term "con-nubium" (see pp. 119, 141).

McLennan gave rise to a persistent misunderstanding of Maine when he granted that "the prevalence" of agnation was "most general," but "we have not altogether adopted his view that agnation at one time or other prevailed everywhere in the advancing communities . . . ." (p. 235). But in elaborating this McLennan completely distorted Maine's idea, making agnates a subcategory of cognates: "Those united by ties of blood through descent from the same married pair being called cog-nates; the agnates were those cognates who traced their connection ex-clusively through males" (p. 236).

Lewis Henry Morgan made Maine's distinction between cognates and agnates the basis of his own *Systems of Consanguinity and Affinity of the Human Family,* published in 1871, which followed his *League of the Iroquois* (1851). On the basis of the first work, Morgan had drawn up a schedule of questions for elicitation of kinship systems, which was sent to diplomatic missions of the United States all around the world, under the auspices of the Smithsonian Institute. *Systems of Consanguinity and Affinity* presented the results of the returned questionnaires, arranged in a general theoretical order of development. McLennan attacked Morgan's treatment in an essay "The Classificatory System of Rela-tionships" published in *Studies in Ancient History* (1876; rpt. with

notes, 1886), and this criticism was in turn attacked by Morgan, along
with McLennan's general theses, in a note added to *Ancient Society*
(1877:516–31), which also reprinted the substance of the arguments of
Consanguinity and Affinity, in a still wider theoretical context. The mutual attacks were bitter. McLennan at one point spoke of "Mr.
Morgan's mind" as "antithetical . . . to the historical method"
(1886:250). Morgan repeatedly accused McLennan of "deficiencies in
definitions, un-warranted assumptions, crude speculations, and erroneous conclusions" (1877:518)—and generally poor scholarship. But despite such recriminations, Morgan actually owed a great deal to McLennan, and McLennan's later formulations moved towards those of
Morgan.

Morgan's conceptual borrowings are framed by his distinction between "government" (which held legal power over people and resources) and "the family" (domestic group), with separate, though related,
histories. Morgan first used Maine's distinction between consanguinity
and affinity in the former context, to define such governmental units as
gens, gentes, or tribes. This actually made it distinguish much the same
relationships as McLennan's exogamy-endogamy distinction in relation
to "tribes"—those born to the group as opposed to those attached con-
ventionally. In fact, at one point Morgan said that "exogamy is simply
the rule of a *gens,* and should be stated as such" (1877:517). McLennan
in effect concurred with this observation in his preface to the 1886 edition of *Studies in Ancient History,* saying that exogamy "at its widest
. . . is prohibition of marriage between all persons recognized as being
of the same blood, because of their common blood—whether they form
one community, or part only of a community, or parts of several communities; . . ." (p. viii). With exogamy thus related to consanguinity,
endogamy could have become marriage within the blood group, while
affinity could have become any relationship by marriage, creating one
consistent system of concepts. But the arguments by each scholar to
preserve the primacy of his distinction over the terminology of the other
produced continuing confusion.

For the analysis of the family, rather than government, Morgan added
his own distinction between *classificatory* and *descriptive* systems to the
contrast between consanguinity and affinity:

> Under the first, consanguinei are never described, but are classified into ca-
> tegories irrespective of their nearness or remoteness in degree to *Ego;* and
> the same term of relationship is applied to all the persons in the same cate-
> gory . . . In the second case consanguinei are described either by the pri-
> mary terms of relationship or a combination of these terms, thus making the
> relationship of each person specific. (1877:403–04)

This statement began the distinctive anthropological interest in the analysis of kinship terms. Descriptive systems were taken by Morgan as those of "civilization"—including our own (p. 407)—and our relationships were taken, without any real critical review, as being "consanguineal." More primitive systems were seen as classificatory—because, in effect, they grouped under single terms types of kin we distinguish with multiple terms. Morgan's own native terminology thus became the basis for assessing the relative primitiveness of all others. Morgan's tables of relationships involved the use of a varying but very large number of "descriptions of persons" in English terms—including such ambiguous descriptions as "grandson," "husband," and "wife." Against each of these, the term in the subject language was listed, together with a translation gloss. Terminologies were considered similar if they made the same types of groupings as the English categories, especially those of the nearer kin.

Morgan held that kinship terminologies, which he called systems of consanguinity, "follow" the forms of the family to "record the family relationships" (p. 398), but could persist when the form of the family had subsequently changed. The first form of the family was "consanguine," wherein actual brothers married actual sisters (thus comparing with McLennan's "horde" stage). While no society still had this form, some had the terminology, for example, the Malayan or Hawaiian. The main feature of this terminology was that "under it all consanguinei, near and remote, fall within some one of the following relationships; namely, parent, child, grandparent, grandchild, brother, and sister" (p. 395). Morgan saw this as implying that one's brothers were classed with one's father's sister's children and one's father's brother's children because the father's brothers actually married the father's sisters. By the same token, one's own son was classed with sisters' and brothers' sons because one married one's own sibling.

The next stage was the "Punaluan" family, which gave rise to the "Turanian" system of consanguinity. The characteristic feature of this terminology was that while a man's brother's son was still classed as his son, "because his brother's wife is his wife as well as his brother's" (p. 401), his sister's son is classed as his nephew. Morgan saw this as reflecting the interposition of a clan conception, and the rule that one could not marry within the clan, a concept that corresponded to McLennan's "exogamy." Therefore, one's brother's children could no longer be one's sister's children. Finally, after two variant forms, the third "radical" new form of the family was the "monogamian," wherein one man married one woman and they cohabited exclusively with each other. He called the terminology for this type, among other things, both

"Aryan" and "Semitic." Its characteristic feature was that one's own children were distinguished both from one's brother's children and from one's sister's children. Morgan held that the development of this type of family came with the concept of private, individually held property, an idea which had not existed earlier.

Each broad type of terminology and of form of the family had many intermediate forms, geographical variants, and secondary modifications (as older terminologies outlived their original conditions and were adapted to new ones, for example). But through all the variations, and despite the inconsistencies they introduced, Morgan's constant assumption was that all people a person classed together terminologically had the same social or juridical relation to him, especially in relation to property or to larger social units—a legitimate interpretation of Savigny's conception of custom, but one which turned out to be misleading.

In addition to the stages of government and the family, Morgan's complete scheme in *Ancient Society* involved reconstructions of "The Growth of Intelligence through Inventions and Discoveries," and "Growth of the Idea of Property." The first of these involved Morgan's idea of the leading inventions that radically altered the bases of human subsistence, such as the bow and arrow and writing. The second was concerned with concepts of inheritance and reversionary rights. Each of the "four classes of facts" (Preface, p. vii) formed an "organic series" through time (p. vi). The states of the development of each class, and relations among classes in a stage, were much less important to Morgan than the integrity of the series over time. Morgan did not argue for total integration at each stage, but rather for a movement where an advance in one sequence gradually sets in motion forces which create other advances in other sequences. In addition, Morgan envisioned a much longer chronology than his predecessors. He saw human history as going back before the beginning of the Pleistocene, and saw the end of the Pleistocene as being at least one to two hundred thousand years ago (Preface, p. i). On this scale, it was more important to develop a model that would account for lack of change in the time before known history, than to conform to an assumption of very rapid developments leading to it.

After Morgan, studies of kinship terminologies and "family" organization remained fairly distinct from studies of clan structures and other forms of tribal "government." "Govermental" studies remained concerned largely with juridical relations over people in the territory, while "family" studies have gone in two rather different directions, exemplified by the works of two of the first major academic anthropologists: A. L. Kroeber (1876–1960) and W. H. R. Rivers (1864–1922). Rivers accepted the classificatory-descriptive distinction and developed what he called the "geneological method," a variant of Morgan's questionnaire, as a field technique for obtaining kinship terminologies, marriage rules, inheritance patterns, and a wide variety of other types of information (Rivers 1910). In *The Todas* (1905) and especially *The History of Melanesian Society* (1914) he also tried to develop Morgan's idea of a specific connection between patterns of terminology and patterns of marriage and household composition. Kroeber, by contrast, nominally rejected the classificatory-descriptive distinction and the connection between terminology and household composition. But he stressed Morgan's assumption that terminologies were systems of linguistic categories that could be compared by using a set of universal "discernments," still based implicitly on western kinship concepts (Kroeber 1909, rpt. by Kroeber 1952). The two sets of concerns remain largely separate at the present time. Rivers' contributions were recently reviewed by Raymond Firth and David M. Schneider (Rivers 1968). Kroeber's side in the debate has been reviewed by Steward (1973:36–38) in the context of the rest of Kroeber's work.

The legacy of these three nineteenth-century formulations in modern approaches to social organization is considerable—retaining virtually everything but the idea that organizational differences needed to be given a temporal ordering.

Primitive Religion

Anthropological interest in primitive religion began within the same framework as interest in kinship and social organization, and it used many of the same major types of data, including myth and ritual symbolism. But concepts of what a religion was ultimately came to be associated with quite different fundamental assumptions about human nature, thought, and science. It was especially in this area that dualistic and deterministic theories developed, and it was precisely these theories that later came to be taken as prototypes of general social theory, while the ideas developed by McLennan, Maine, Morgan, Kroeber, Rivers, and others in relation to kinship and social organization were more commonly taken as specialized conceptions of a "subfield."

The point of departure for anthropological concepts of religion is probably best placed with Bachofen, in the works that were discussed above, and also in his *Myth of Tanaquil* (*Die Sage von Tanaquil,* Heidelberg, 1870). Bachofen actually subsumed social organization under religion, as already suggested: "each stage in family organization depended on a religious idea" (1859:113). That is, the core system of ideas that he inferred from myth and ritual, and that defined the family, was in its nature *religious*. Bachofen's description of these ideas as recounted above amounted to a theory of primitive religion.

The elements of Bachofen's conception of primitive religion are not hard to set down. Primitive religion was thought to be *basic* religion, and to exhibit the same internal structure and relation to behavior as all religion, both of ancient and modern societies, and of civilized and uncivilized. Primitive religion was also thought of as being expressed in myths, and myths, conversely, were thought of as religious in this fundamental sense. Rituals were similarly thought of as expressing religion, and as religious in character. Religious ideas were also thought of as defining fundamental relations of society—the behaviors described in myths and rituals were taken as direct models for the behavior of their worshippers in normal life. Finally, religious ideas were thought of as being self-enforcing, in a special way. Bachofen, unlike Maine, was not concerned with developing a theory of the external sanctions that compelled acceptance of the ideas, or of the concrete situations (other than those portrayed in the myths and rituals themselves) within which the ideas would be used. Bachofen argued over and over that the ideas were themselves compelling and powerful, and their modes of expression convincing, once they were understood.

Bachofen's influence on later anthropologists is difficult to separate from that of Adolphe Bastian (1826–1905), Professor in Ethnology at the University of Berlin (the first to hold the title) and founder and Director of the Berlin Ethnological Museum—which initially was devoted primarily to his own collections. He is best known for the conceptions of "folk thought" (*Völkergedanken*), "geographical province" (*geographische Provinzen*) and "elementary ideas" (*Elementargedanken*). To these should be added "folk psychology" (*Völkerpsychologie*), the concept of a "folk" itself (*Völker*), and the concept of "ethnology" itself (*Ethnologie*). While he did not invent these latter terms, he gave them their first systematic theoretical formulations.

Bastian's principal theoretical focus was on folk thought. Ethnology was the study of its development, and Bastian's explanations rejected both racial and geographical determinism. A pattern of folk thought (not race in any sense) was what defined a "folk"—Polynesians, Iroquois, Chinese, or whatever—but there was no attempt to define either such patterns or groups exclusively at a single level of abstraction, so folk also were assignable to regions. The development of folk was (somewhat) restricted by their geographical provinces—for example, South Asia, China, or Europe. But again, there was no effort to divide the world into a single system of such provinces, or to argue for a very rigorous definition of them. They were formed by barriers to migration and communication, and it was understood that different barriers would be important in different circumstances, and at different times. As with Montesquieu's laws, folk thought responded to geography and felt physiological needs, but was fundamentally a product of past ideas and adjustments, creatively adapted to present needs and goals. This is precisely why ethnology had to be a new science in its own right, and not a branch of physiology or geography.

The constituent units of folk thought, as for Bachofen, were specific images or ideas. Fetishism, monism, dualism, heaven, and husband and wife were but a few. These units were not rigidly divided from one another, and it was not Bastian's aim to list them or trace their evolution or diffusion (as some later accounts have suggested). Instead, again recalling Bachofen and others before him, Bastian's concern was with the way these ideas were developed and modified, presumably in accord with universal psychological processes. Accordingly, beginning by rejecting mind-body dualism in favor of the experimental psychology of Gustav Fechner (1801–78), Bastian described his ethnology as incorporating "psychology as natural science." Conversely, he saw himself as offering a "psychological world view" on the basis of this science, meaning that he offered his conclusions, in part, in place of traditional (especially dualistic) modes of philosophical reasoning and their results. This is richly thought out monism, but it goes farther. In many works it is clear that Bastian is not viewing the ideas he discusses only as data, remote and "objective." The way in which he interweaves concepts from folk thought together with ideas and opinions of western philosophers and scholars places them both on an entirely equal footing, part of a single, critical, and evaluative discussion aiming to produce a single synthetic outlook.

Bastian's first major work was *Mankind in History* (*Der Mensche in der Geschichte*) (1860). The book was dedicated to the memory of Alexander von Humbolt. It began with a discussion of the organization of nature, carried through the development of complex organisms and the nervous system, then the emergence and character of thought in general, and finally the development of various basic human intellectual capacities and traits, the concept of the individual, the character of logic in thought and speech and writing. His next major work, *The Folk of East Asia* (1866–1871), reported the results of his first major expedition. Among many later works, *The Civilized Peoples of Ancient America* (1878) reported the results of his second expedition to Ecuador, Colombia, Peru, Guatemala, and the Antilles (1875–76). By contrast, *The Sacred Myth of the Polynesians* (1881) traced a single myth, in various forms, through one area, and attempted to explicate an underlying conception of God and the Universe. In the same year, *The Pre-History of Ethnology* (*Die Forgeschichte der Ethnologie*) (1881), somewhat despite its title, was not historical but rather a theoretical review of ideas leading to his own views on various conceptual and methodological topics, drawing upon folk and scholarly conceptions. Still later works, among the last written, elaborated the ideas of geographical provinces and elementary ideas.

Bastian's scheme was undoubtedly coherent in terms of his own conception of the monistic tradition he espoused. It might also have been so from Kant's point of view, if Kant had been present to view it. But from the point of view of subsequent history, it had a major flaw. The different ''folk'' remained quite general abstractions, whose concerns were rather inferred from their texts and artifacts than observed directly. At the same time, the ideas were not ideas of specific individuals, but of abstract folk—too abstract and too global to be seen in the context of practical action and real interest at the individual level. Nor was the individual-level data on the physiological side actually available, if he had been able to make a place for it in his scheme.

Bastian never found convincing psychological laws of the sort he sought, but his general program was adopted virtually without change by Franz Boas, and thereby became the first theoretical framework for American academic anthropology. In the direction of psychology, the terminological and conceptual resemblances between Bastian's program and Wundt's later folk psychology are far too many and much too complex to be accidental. In the meantime, however, there were still other offshoots, leading in other directions.

Mankind in History and a similar work by Theodore Waitze (1821–64) were singled out as especially important sources by E. B. Tylor in the first edition of *Primitive Culture* (1871), which more than any other work provides the basis for the transition to dualism. It contains Tylor's definition of culture, which is still widely accepted as the one most anthropologists believe to be most generally accepted by their colleagues:

Culture or Civilization, taken in its wide ethnographic sense, is that whole which includes knowledge, belief, art, morals, law, custom, and any other capabilities and habits acquired by man as a member of society. (1871:1)

Compare this, for example, with Lowie's opening lines in his *History:*

Ethnography is the science which deals with the "cultures" of human groups. By culture we understand the sum total of what an individual acquires from his society—those beliefs, customs, artistic norms, food habits, and crafts which come to him not by his own creative activity but as a legacy from the past, conveyed by formal or informal education. (1937:3)

Seven of Tylor's nineteen chapters were devoted to "animism." Among the remaining, three were devoted to mythology, two to language, two to the methodological concept of a "survival," and one to "rites and ceremonies," in addition to introductions and conclusions. Obviously, "animism" must involve many of the aspects of culture Tylor named in his original definition. In fact, precisely because Tylor's scheme is deterministic, it is their source and *cause.* Tylor did not argue explicitly that animism was the first or absolutely the most primitive religion, but he argued that it was near it.

Animism characterizes tribes very low in the scale of humanity, and thence ascends, deeply modified in its transmission, but from first to last preserving an unbroken continuity, into the midst of high modern culture. Animism is, in fact, the ground-work of the Philosophy of Religion, from that of savages up to civilized men. And although it may at first sight seem to afford but a bare and meagre definition of a minimum of religion, it will be found practically sufficient; for where the root is, the branches will generally be produced. (1889:426)

Tylor divided animism into two major subsidiary beliefs: the belief in spirits of persons—souls—and the belief in spiritual beings apart from persons, "upward in rank to powerful deities" (p. 426). He further distinguished both classes of animistic beliefs from a "moral element" of religion, which he considered to be a later development (p. 427). His chapters describe the levels or stages of development in each aspect of the belief, using a wide range of ethnographical source materials mainly from current primitive peoples.

There is a kind of externality to Tylor's descriptions, a tone of deliberately describing other peoples' beliefs from outside their own perspective. No real effort is made to construe animism as a viable and full-fledged conception of the world and man's place in it, such as we find with Bachofen's matriarchy. There is in Tylor no sense that we have to lay aside our own fundamental beliefs in order to understand the beliefs of others. Tylor is not dealing with the problems of cultural differences in the way Bachofen or Bastian was. He is dealing in a much more straightforward sense only with levels, degrees, of cultural development. Tylor was evidently quite conscious of this difference. It is directly related to his opening argument that scientific accounts are those that show continuity of forms from one to another—on the ground that "nature does not act by leaps" (1889: 1:2). This idea in turn was connected to an important attack on the concepts of freedom of the will and purpose which were fundamental to both Bachofen and Bastian.

> The popular notion of free human will involves not only freedom to act in accordance with motive, but also a power of breaking loose from continuity and acting without cause—a combination which may be roughly illustrated by the simile of a balance sometimes acting in the usual way, but also possessed of the faculty of turning by itself without or against its weights. This view of an anomolous action of the will, which it need hardly be said is incompatible with scientific arguments, subsists as an opinion patent or latent in men's minds, and strongly affecting their theoretic views of history, though it is not, as a rule, brought forward in systematic reasoning. Indeed the definition of human will, as strictly according with motive, is the only possible scientific basis in such enquiries. (1:3)

Tylor's further arguments made it clear that "motive" in this case was not private purpose, but rather the inherited beliefs of a community. He equated explanations in terms of such motives with "efficient cause" explanations (1:13), and took pains to argue that such motives could not themselves be explained by their efficacy—they could not be accounted for as necessary responses to natural circumstances:

> Of course the opinions and habits belonging in common to masses of mankind are to a great extent the results of sound judgment and practical wisdom. But to a great extent it is not so. That many numerous societies of men should have believed in the influence of the evil eye and the existence of a firmament, should have sacrificed slaves and goods to the ghosts of the departed, should have handed down traditions of giants slaying monsters and men turning into beasts—all this is ground for holding that such ideas were indeed produced in men's minds by efficient causes, but it is not ground for holding that the rites in question are profitable, the beliefs sound, and the history authentic. (1:13)

Survivals were precisely those aspects of culture that are produced by efficient causes. With free will and invention ruled out, this means that culture comes only from culture, which is what permits inferences of past conditions. The argument stops short of full-fledged cultural determinism, such as we will find in Durkheim, because Tylor is not saying that the inherited beliefs control or preempt the beliefs that are the "results of sound judgment . . ." Such an extreme position would not be necessary for Tylor's purposes—indeed it would be counter-productive, allowing too many routes to the past. But Tylor's position is much closer to determinism than to Kant's type of explanation. Animistic beliefs are not construed in any way as noumenal inventions, created and maintained by people to order their practical affairs as communicative devices.

The source of Tylor's conceptions of science and causality appears to be the same as the source of his concept of animism: Comte's *Cours de philosophie positive,* both directly and by way of Mill. Tylor explicitly equates his own conception of historical explanation with Comte's (1:19), and describes his concept of animism as the direct descendant of Comte's fetishism, which Comte in turn developed from still earlier sources (2:144–45). Tylor even quotes favorably Comte's equation of "the obscure pantheism . . . rife among German metaphysicians" with fetishism "generalized and made systematic" (2:354). And finally, the ultimate goal of Tylor's inquiry into animism is precisely the same as what Comte hoped to realize by tracing the history of thought from fetishism to science:

> Now it is the practical office of ethnography to make known to all whom it may concern the tenure of opinions in the public mind, to show what is received on its own direct evidence, what is ruder ancient doctrine reshaped to answer modern ends, and what is but time-honored superstition in the garb of modern knowledge. (2:445)

And:

> It is a . . . sometimes even painful, office of ethnography to expose the remains of crude old cultures which have passed into harmful superstition, and to mark these out for destruction. Yet this work, if less genial, is not less urgently needful for the good of mankind. Thus, active at once in aiding progress and in removing hindrance, the science of culture is essentially a reformer's science. (2:453)

While Tylor's idea of animism as a primitive religious syndrome long remained viable as a kind of abstract type, it soon gave theoretical pride of place to the concept of "totemism" which had richer implications for social organization.

It is not clear when *totem,* originally an Ojibwa word, became a theoretical concept in anthropology. Sol Tax attributed it to Albert Gallatin, writing in *Archeologia Americana* in 1836 (Tax, in Eggan 1955:447–48). But Andrew Lang, in his article "Totemism" in the 1911 *Encyclopaedia Britannica,* attributed its first use to John Long, in his *Voyages and Travels of an Indian Interpreter* (1791). Whatever may be the history of the concept of the *totem,* the turn-of-the-century arguments that cited one another and that generated the major theoretical formulations that continued to be of interest in the modern period all appear to go back to McLennan's essay "The Worship of Animals and Plants," first printed in the *Fortnightly Review* of 1869 and 1870 and reprinted in *Studies in Ancient History,* series 2 (1896), as an Appendix.

Referring to both Gallatin and Long, McLennan argued that totemism was a system of beliefs that went with a very early general stage of society. These beliefs he described as involving the association of members of social groups, clans or tribes, with specific animals or other natural objects by a principle of relationship, and thus involving their mutual associations with one another as relatives. The totem represented the group, and was inherited by its members through descent; by their relation to it, the members identified their relationship to one another. He saw this set of beliefs as "Fetischism *plus* certain peculiarities" (1896:512), and connected totemism with exogamous kin groups, recognizing only common kinship and not degrees of kinship, that preceded descent through females only (p. 520). McLennan reportedly came to consider totemism an indispensable part of his arguments for matriarchy as the first organized state of society (1896:47).

William Robertson Smith (1846–94), philologist, theologian, mathematician, and Bible scholar, sought the origins of the patriarchial system of Islamic kinship. He found them in a previous matriarchial system that itself presupposed and grew out of a totemic stage of development, precisely in agreement with what McLennan had "hypothesized," in *Kinship and Marriage in Early Arabia* (1885: Preface and 224–27). In recalling McLennan, Smith declined to accept Tylor's conception of science and of historical explanation. Smith's own conceptions remain implicit in *Kinship and Marriage,* but the opening paragraphs of his *Religion of the Semites,* delivered as the Burnett lectures at Aberdeen in 1888–89, describe Judaism, Christianity, and Islam as "positive religions": ". . . they did not grow up like the systems of ancient heathenism, under the action of unconscious forces operating from age to age, but trace their origin to the preaching of great religious innovators, who spoke as the organs of a divine revelation, and deliberately departed from the tradition of the past" (1889:1). Even if we take the idea of divine revelation literally, these ideas of innovation and deliberate direction, recalling Kant's "positive" law, are precisely what Tylor had rejected.

There is very little question that Smith was aware of the larger philosophical implications of his position. A paper, "Theory of Geometrical Reasoning," delivered to the Royal Society in 1869, for example, involved a strenuous and thorough attack on Mill's conceptions of mathematics as developed in his *Logic*, with Smith rejecting the idea that geometry was "inductive" and arguing instead that it was based on "intuition" in Kant's sense (in Smith 1912:8). Other papers criticized Hegel's attacks on aspects of Newton's and Kepler's systems, which were related to current interpretations of Kant's synthetic *a priori*.

Andrew Lang (1844–1912) pressed harder on Smith's idea of innovation and creation. In *Social Origins* (1903), concentrating mainly on Australian examples, he argued that no orderly theory could be constructed involving an idea of the original division of society without "deliberate arrangement" as one explanatory variable—one that could and should be minimized, but which could not be eliminated (pp. 53 ff.). Against Tylor's "survivals," Lang argued (agreeing with an essay by Durkheim) that the Aranta myths did not reflect beliefs from an earlier stage of cultural development, but were rather to be seen as inventions "to explain existing institutions, by attaching them to some mythical beings in the past" (p. 75).

The last person that must be mentioned on the road to modern theories is Sir James Frazer, whose prolix *Totemism and Exogamy*, in four volumes, was first published in 1910. In this, he rejected the position he had taken in an earlier essay (*Totemism*, 1887), where he considered that totemism had not been demonstrated to be universal and doubted the relationship between totemism and exogamy. Now, he took it as more likely that some connection existed, and proposed to find it in the classificatory system of relationship. Basically, Frazer's argument was that the ultimate origin of totemism itself—that is, of the identification of a human group with a *species* of animal and the equation of kinship in the group with kinship to the animal—lay in "ignorance of paternity" as part of a general "haziness" of "mental vision" of primitive people (1910: 4:61). This ignorance of paternity was itself then related to use of the classificatory system of relations to define groups of "fathers," "mothers," and the like within the totemic groups, in an evolutionary sequence based on increasing subdivision that went along with increasing clarification of outlook. The sequence was argued much in the manner of McLennan: the argument was at once structural and psychological, although it lacked the direct sense of voluntarism found in Smith and Lang. In many ways (except for the attribution of low intelligence) Frazer's arguments were very close to the assumptions and goals of Bachofen—an analysis of the evolution of social theories, seen from the point of view of those who believed them.

Emile Durkheim's *Elementary Forms of the Religious Life*, published in French in 1912 and in English in 1915, returned to positivistic conceptions of science going far beyond Tylor, as will be described in the next chapter. It was in many respects the last major study of totemism, and the first theoretical monograph of a modern type.

Psychology

The three great psychological figures of the nineteenth century who have had a most direct and clear influence on the course of anthropology are Wilhelm Wundt (1832–1920), William James (1842–1910), and Sigmund Freud (1856–1939). Wundt and James represent an important and solidly worked out Kantian position. Freud presents a kind of *ad hoc* dualism, loosely compounded of common-sense dichotomies and determinisms.

Wilhelm Wundt is generally described as the founder of experimental psychology (at least after Fechner) and particularly of the first psychological laboratory (at Leipzig in 1879). His ideas place him in a straight line of development from Hume through Kant to Franz Boas and Bronislaw Malinowski, as well as to George Herbert Mead in philosophy and to several major developments in physiological psychology.

Wundt's original training was in physiology, although his interests in psychology were present in his publications from the beginning. He was an assistant and later colleague of Herman von Helmholtz (the great physicist and physiologist who stated the law of conservation of energy and who did important work on nerve impulses and the physiology of the senses) at the University of Heidelberg from 1857 through 1874, before moving permanently to Leipzig (by way of a year in Zurich) to direct his own program, with the title of Professor of Philosophy. Basically, Wundt combined Helmholtz's carefully rationalized experimental approach to nerve function and the physiology of action with a Kantian conception of communication as the locus of noumenal conventions, seeing the thinking individual, in a very strict but rich sense, as a social organism. Thought was not a homogeneous entity, and not separate from other reality. Rather, the "manifold of consciousness" arose in many forms from the interactions of functions within living organisms and, by extension, in the interactions among organisms, as, especially in humans, the internal processes were shaped by that interaction. Thus physical experiments and cultural investigations were two complementary approaches to the same basic phenomena. Wundt's first two works were *Lectures on the Mentality of Animals and Men* (*Vorlesungen über die Menschenseele und Tier-seele*), published in 1863, and *Textbook in Human Physiology*, 1865, followed by *Principles of Physiological Psychology* (*Grundzuge der physiologischen Psychologie*) in 1874.

The *Principles* was primarily concerned with the central nervous system and revolved around a sustained attack on physiological counterparts to associationism and the doctrine of innate ideas. The associationism lay in the idea that nerves were simple conduits that projected sensations from specific receptors onto specific parts of the cerebral cortex, which were in turn organized in other parts into complex ideas. The assumption of innate ideas lay in phrenology, and the more sophisticated "new phrenology" that held the various centers of brain function—speech, sight, hand movement, and the like—to be specific only to those functions and to be strictly limited (Wundt 1969:287–98). His answer was the same to both.

Wundt assembled the new experimental information of such scholars as Golgi, Goltz, Wernicke, and especially, Ramon y Cajal, whose "neurone theory"—that each nerve cell was separate and unconnected to other nerve cells—Wundt made his own major starting point. He argued consistently for complexity and flexibility of function—greater and greater flexibility as organisms became more complex, and greater flexibility at the higher levels of nervous organization within each organism. Within the single nerve, he stressed experiments that showed the interplay of inhibitory and excitory activity. In reflex arcs, he stressed the interaction of inhibitory and stimulatory nerves. In such major structures as the optic nerve, he stressed that there were both motor and sensory functions, and that these were inseparable from each other. And in the central nervous system as a whole, he stressed the "manifold" reflections of sensory impressions as well as centers of control, together with the general capacity for "vicarious function"—now more commonly called transference of function.

In the complex picture that resulted, "consciousness" was not one thing but many things. Consciousness of balance was different from consciousness of visual perception, which in turn was something quite different, both physically and psychically, from consciousness of an idea or concept. The latter case, very carefully and judiciously described, Wundt connected with the prefrontal lobe of the brain, one of its most characteristically human features, and one of the last to evolve. He further connected it specifically with the fact that the nerves of this area are predominantly inhibitory in their function—they do not pass on sensation, or originate impulses, but rather dampen sensations, inhibit the transmissions that come to them; this fact he connected in turn directly with the ability to "concentrate" as a basis of intelligence as we subjectively perceive it (1904:317)—recalling directly both Kant and Herder.

Physiological inference was the required basis of his psychological inference; and occasionally psychological information, where it was subject to experimental control to eliminate contrary interpretations, led to physiological inference where physical evidence itself was unclear, to build up a single vision of mental function as part of the larger range of functions of the total organism.

The *Principles* went through many editions, sometimes but three years apart, as new evidence on the structure and organization of the nervous system continued to come to light. The fifth edition, of 1896, was translated into English by Titchener in 1902, went through a subsequent edition of its own, and has recently been re-issued in facsimile (Wundt 1969). For anthropologists who have recently become again concerned with brain function and intellectual capacity, and who believe their interests and insights are new discoveries, it should be required reading.

Anthropology (or rather folk psychology) was intended to be an extension of precisely the system of analysis based on physiological experiment—providing additional evidence on human capacities and needs that could be related to physiology. The works of principal relevance to social and social psychological theory were: *Logic* (1880–83, three volumes), *Ethics* (1886), and *Völkerpsychologie* (1900–06).

The *Logic* and the *Ethics* formed the basis of an alternative approach to the social issues that occupied Mill and utilitarianism on the one hand, and the continental idealists, related to Hegel, on the other. Like them, Wundt saw logic and ethics as "normative sciences" in contrast with the physical sciences that were "descriptive." This did not mean, however, that logic and ethics involved promulgating rules for others to follow, as both utilitarians and Hegelians had done. It rather meant, for Wundt, that at bottom they involved investigating, empirically, the process of such promulgation. Their *subject matter* was normative, rules, in a way that the subject matter of physics and biology was not.

Wundt's description of "norms" rested directly on Kant's idea of a noumenon as a human imputation to order phenomena, and on the conception that society and religion involved such noumena.

> It is equally true for logic and for ethics, that the laws which govern our apprehensions of objects are always, at the same time, laws of the objects themselves; and that the real relations of this must necessarily be conceived of as in agreement with the principles whereby we systematise and connect them. But this agreement cannot possibly be held to precede the interaction of thought and experience; it can manifest itself only in that interaction. Just as there are no objects of experience without a thinking subject, so there can be no thinking subject without objects of experience. (1897: 1:10–11)

Wundt saw logic as the study of fundamental rules of relationship that people had developed to order their perceiving ("subjective") relations to perceived physical objects, and ethics as the study of fundamental rules of relations that people developed to order their subjective relations to perceived social or cultural objects.

In Wundt's view, both these normative fields presupposed human free will, the capacity for free and voluntary action, either in compliance with norms or in violation of them (p. 8). Ethics, however, was the more fundamental of the two concerns in two main ways. First was the idea that logical laws are applied only under the impetus of an ethical valuation, so that the ethical valuation is prior. Secondly, in Wundt's view, ethics was involved in relating man to all the *objects* of his thought directly while logic applies only to the *subject* of thought, the thinker himself and his thinking operations, when these can be abstracted and treated on the model of objects—a more complex thought procedure that Wundt evidently considered would therefore have developed later in time. Hence *"ethics is the original science of norms."* "Morality is the original source of the normative idea" (1:9). Accordingly, the *Ethics* set out to trace the history of the growth of morality, of ethics and of the concept of ethics. The first volume dealt with the growth of morality, the second with formal theories of ethics from the Pre-Socratics to the present, and the third with principles of morality that Wundt abstracted from the first two.

Wundt's historical treatment of the growth of morality exemplifies his treatment of data from primitive communities. He approaches it in terms of the idea of custom, seen as the primitive substrata out of which religion, ethics, and all other different types of normative systems have developed. Wundt's definition of custom, recalling Savigny, ties it directly to a Kantian conception of thought and of freedom of the will:

In the case of man . . . there are two principle factors at work to make both individual and social life immeasurably richer and more complex. The one is to be found in the freer exercise of the *will;* the other in that comprehensive *prevision,* that consideration of past and future in their bearings upon the present, of which man alone is capable.

It is the presence of these two factors in human life which justifies our speaking of *custom* as a purely human phenomenon. A custom is any norm of *voluntary action that has been developed in a national or tribal community.* (1897:131)

Wundt related custom both to a conception of language (most of his historical evidence was philological) and to a conception of purposes, and both have been historically important for anthropology. ". . . language consists always in a *communication* of ideas, . . . custom, like language, is a mode of common conduct arising from a community of ideas" (p. 161). Custom for humans is the counterpart of instinct for animals, directing action which must occur and must be uniform if the species is to survive.

This idea descends from Grimm and Savigny, and in Wundt's form became the basis of G. H. Mead's conception of a social "symbol," which will be described in chapter 10.

With respect to needs: "Any attempt at a systematization of custom must set out from the consideration of those permanent life-purposes which custom is called upon to subserve, under varying conditions, at the different periods of development" (p. 165). Changing "different periods of development" into different communities is the fundamental idea of Malinowski's theory of needs. Wundt classified customs into four "departments," depending on the way in which they reflected one of four "forms of life." Each form was characterized by the specific types of entities that served the roles of subject and object. *Individual* forms of life involved individuals as subjects and as objects. Forms of *intercourse* involved the individual as subject, but society as the object. *Social* forms involved a group of individuals as the subject, and society as an object. And *humanistic* forms involved either an individual or a group as the subject, and all of humanity as an object. It should be recognized that this treatment parallels the treatment of transcendental ideas in Kant's *Critique* and *Prolegomena,* which take the person as subject, and stipulates three different classes of object: psychological, cosmological, and theological. But it should also be recognized that whatever its abstract basis, the scheme applies very nicely toward sorting out quite different kinds of rituals and usages—birthdays from initiations into office, for example, or military parades from requests that God grant us all long life and happiness in the new year. Customs, for Wundt, were always quite concrete and specific—for example, forms of address, or behaviors like bowing—not a generalized psychic entity like Durkheim's "collective consciousness" or, later, Freud's "group mind."

Wundt often used the term "psychological" to describe his conception of evolution. He doesn't explicitly or simply define the term, but it seems clear that what he means is just this reliance of the interaction of the subjective and objective perspectives on the phenomena of interest (custom) *as those phenomena exist for those who use them.* In this sense, his theory is psychological not only in its basic classifications of phenomena, but also in its evolutionary mechanism, for while Wundt recognized that custom served needs, he did not attribute to these needs any determinative force or completely external reality. Needs merely differ from time to time, but do not evolve or progress. Instead, Wundt considered that progress or development of ethical systems came with what he called the "inwardising of morality"—its progressive detachment from objective states and its attachment instead to inward subjective states, that is, to a growing self-awareness of the individual and of individual values and ideals. This conception is perfectly consistent with his conception of the evolution and function of the nervous system, and was also a fundamental idea for G. H. Mead, although he expressed it in quite different terms.

While the three volumes of the *Ethics* developed these ideas theoretically and philosophically, Wundt's *Völkerpsychologie (Elements of Folk Psychology;* authorized translation by Leroy Schaub, 1916) applied them in a richer range of empirical data, mainly from primitive communities. The main divisions of the argument were historical: "Primitive Man" (including considerable discussion of Bachofen's mother-right), "The Totemic Age" (whose "soul belief" was animism, with fetishism included as a subcategory), "The Age of Heroes and Gods," and "The Development to Humanity" (beginning with a discussion of Herder). Wundt said of folk psychology that:

> Its problem related to those mental products which are created by a community of human life and are, therefore, inexplicable in terms merely of individual consciousness, since they presuppose the reciprocal action of many . . . Thus, then, in the analysis of the higher mental processes, folk psychology is an indispensable supplement to the psychology of individual consciousness. (1916:3)

Wundt's large corpus of works integrated physiology, philosophy, and ethnography in a single system whose power and subtlety of relation to the earlier literatures and of implication for the future cannot be conveyed in a few paragraphs.

William James (1842–1910) is often described by his opposition to Wundt. But it is important to note the larger fact that James, more than anyone else, created "American" psychology by deliberately transplanting the ideas and interests of Helmholtz, Wundt, and their students (see Boring 1950:508ff.; also in Perry 1935 see letter from W. James to Henry James, and letter to Thomas Ward, dated 1867, p. 181).

In many respects James was a German experimental psychologist describing himself in the language of Mill and the English positivists, and his linguistic usages in this connection are at least partly responsible for many terminological confusions current today. He claimed to reject "metaphysics," and considered that the "line of philosophic progress" was "not so much *through* Kant as *round* him" (Perry 1935:162). He explicitly described his own approach as "strictly positivistic" (1890:vi), and he consistently attacked "monism," identifying himself instead with "pluralism." But in context it is clear that by "metaphysical" James means only theories that propose to explain phenomena "as products of deeper lying entities" that amount to Kantian noumena, and that "positivism" in this context means no more than the rejection of such explanations (1890:vi). In other contexts, he saw positivism as it has been described here (and will be described more fully below)—and then rejected it (Perry 1935:128). "Through Kant," in context, meant through Hegelian idealism, the status of which as the main successor to Kant's philosophy James seems not to have challenged. Similarly, monism meant an attempt to see the universe in terms of a single underlying substance or cause—and pluralism meant recognition of many such substances or causes. For James, monism was inherently associated with concepts of determinism, which he rejected, while pluralism was involved with the idea of freedom of the will, and recognition of indeterminacy or chance in nature, which he accepted (Perry:153). In fact, following Wundt, James made the concept of choice, in the context of action, the hallmark not only of human mentality but of *all* mentality, as the first chapters of his *Psychology* make abundantly clear. Following the psychological presumption that "no mental modification ever occurs which is not accompanied or followed by a bodily change" (1890:5), his idea of "functionalism" was that the meaning or import of a statement or idea lay in the behaviors which it reflected and led to, be they proximate or remote. Partly in keeping with this emphasis on will, purpose, and choice, James firmly rejected Mill's associationism in favor of the idea of an unbroken "stream of thought" (1890:ch. 9). This bears an obvious resemblance to Wundt's concept of the "manifold of consciousness," but suggests a unity and direction of flow that Wundt had implicitly rejected (in connection with an attack on Fichte's idealism).

Finally, James's very well known "pragmatic" theory of truth was closely related to his theory of meaning. It was simply that the truth of a statement or proposition lay in the productivity and coherence of the behaviors that were involved in verifying it—a concept only superficially similar to the later positivistic idea of "operational definitions" of scientific terms, which is a type of reductionism. James somewhat unaccountably attributed the term "pragmatism" to his long-time friend C. S. Peirce, a sometime colleague at Harvard, rather than to the post-Kantian German traditions. Yet it is to this tradition, specifically to Kant, that Peirce attributes the concept in turn (Perry:280, n. 4), and it seems quite likely that James would have encountered it there in his own apparently extensive readings of Kant and related scholars in German. James made many trips to Europe and studied at various German universities, including Heidelberg when Helmholtz and Wundt were there (1867), and he read Kant's *Critique, Prolegomena,* and *Anthropology* (which, in a letter to his friend Oliver Wendell Holmes, he said he admired) (Perry:94). Whatever James's reasons for not emphasizing the German origin of this key idea, it is clear that, although his usage appears to differ from Peirce's, it stays largely within the pale of the Kantian concept of "practical reason" as the fundamental action framework for explaining noumenal postulations, rather than using noumena to explain action.

Yet for all the concordance between James and the Kantian tradition, there was one important point at which he differed; and here, apparently without realizing its implications, he leaned sharply toward the British empiricism of Locke and his successors (1890:vol. 2; ch. 28). He tried to construct his psychology predominantly in terms of a single individual human reacting to, and acting in, a physical world, which brought him very close to a new doctrine of innate ideas—in the form of a concept of "natural lines of cleavage in our mental structure" (1890:2:677). He left out the Kantian interest in conventions or custom, considered as a means of communication among groups of people that was as real and concrete for them as smells and sexual stimuli alone were to animals. This difference was to have important implications for the comparative influence of Wundt and James on anthropology.

The ideas of Sigmund Freud (1856–1939) are almost too well-known to need description and will not be reviewed here at length (see Kardiner and Preble 1961; LaBarre 1958). But it is important to point out that they contrast sharply with Wundt and the Kantian tradition generally. Freud's ideas conform instead quite closely to the historical determinism, conception of scientific method, and even substantive doctrines of Tylor and Comte and his tradition, although Freud drew most of his examples, and his treatment of symbols, from Frazer and R. R. Marett.

Of Freud's more ethnological works, one of the best-known and most influential was the set of four essays published together in an authorized translation in English under the title *Totem and Taboo* (1913), which Kroeber reviewed unfavorably in 1920 and re-reviewed almost apologetically in 1939. The sub-title, *Resemblances between the Psychic Lives of Savages and Neurotics,* indicates its major thesis. "Infantile Recurrence of Totemism" argues specifically that as childhood fantasies re-enact early infantile traumas, so totemism re-enacts or recreates early social traumas, and in both cases, the trauma is the same: the pattern of familial alienation, competition, and aggression called by Freud the Oedipus complex. In effect, he seems to argue, the Oedipus complex itself is nothing more than a representation of the first act that formed ordered society, the first religion, and the first system of marriage above the pre-human "primal horde." The horde is a group of females dominated by a single adult male, from which juvenile males are systematically expelled by the dominant male as they mature. (He attributes this description to Darwin, evidently referring to Darwin's description of the gorilla band.) In contrast with this horde, the "most primitive organization we know . . . *is associations of men* . . . of equal rights . . . subject to . . . the totemic system, and founded on matriarchy" (p. 235). Freud's theory is intended to explain how this basic human organization arose out of the prehuman form:

> . . . One day the expelled brothers joined forces, slew and ate the father, and thus put an end to the father horde. Together they dared and accomplished what would have remained impossible for them singly. . . . Now they accomplished their identification with him by devouring him and each acquired a part of his strength. The totem feast . . . perhaps mankind's first celebration, would be the repetition and commemoration of this memorable, criminal act with which so many things began, social organization, moral restrictions and religion. (n.d.:235–36).

Following through the last thought, Freud argued that not only does the Oedipal myth (and hence the psychodynamic of family structure) enact the original uprising, but so do the Christian theogeny and concept of communion as well.

Points in the argument that recall the line from Bachofen to Frazer are the concern with sexual access as the central meaning of ritual and symbolic usages, the identification of ideas pertaining to such access as a general charter for the organization of a social group, the connection of this charter with religion, the interpenetration of social and personal meanings, and, of course, the use of comparative arguments based on a combination of myth, ritual, and private introspection. Superficially, Freud's analysis corresponds to Bachofen's original thesis that the first systems of law and religion arose in a material form, and progressed to a more abstract, codified, intellectual one.

But in another way, and at a deeper level, it was precisely Freud's conception of the interpenetration of the individual and the social, actually more like a conception of the *duplication* of the individual mind in society, which skipped over the Kantian concern with agreement and communication, and that led to the profound dualism and determinism of the theory. Society, when it was not a projective screen or collection of symbols, was described as a kind of simplified individual writ large—complete with an "unconscious" and even mental aberrations, as in his treatment of Fetishism (1927). This, and not Wundt's scheme, is a "group mind." By the same token, the individual became society writ small, though with some additional processes, and this led quite naturally to a new version of the ancient idea of the struggle between the individual and the collective good, introduced by a new application of the planetary analogy:

> Just as a planet revolves around a central body as well as rotating on its own axis, so the human individual takes part in the course of development of mankind at the same time as it pursues his own path in life . . . So . . . the two urges, the one towards personal happiness and the other towards union with other human beings must struggle with each other in every individual; and so, also, the two processes of individual and of cultural development must stand in hostile opposition to each other and mutually dispute the ground. But this struggle . . . is a dispute within the economics of the libido, comparable to the contest concerning the distribution of libido between ego and objects; and it does admit of an eventual accommodation in the individual, as, it may be hoped, it will also do in the future of civilization, however much civilization may oppress the life of the individual today. ["Civilization and Its Discontents" (1930) in Freud 1961:141.]

Despite his evident familiarity with the works of Wundt and Spencer, as well as Marett, Frazer, and others, Freud's social analysis was never more than rudimentary, and was never developed systematically apart from his discussion of individual psychology, as is generally recognized. But it should also be recognized—as his followers sometimes do not—that his psychological analysis itself was in many respects pure mythology, resting on the postulation of deterministic entities whose existence could not only not be proved at the time, but which by definition lay beyond any possible empirical confirmation, and often, in terms of the theory, could be depended upon to produce manifestations that were intended to conceal their postulated "true" character. In Kant's terms, it was an analysis based on quite arbitrary postulated noumena. In James's terms, it was "metaphysical" rather than "positivistic" or demonstrative. Its circularity recalled Hegel in detail, and despite its medical context it was an analysis without any specific basis in physiology. It most resembled Schopenhauer's metaphysic of "will" and "idea," and had much in common with Mill's utilitarianism in making social behavior something the individual was forced to engage in for his own purposes—rather than an inextricable aspect of human cognition, including self-awareness and awareness of purpose *per se*.

The End of the Century

So long as it was possible to think of the whole of evolution, from animal to civilized man, as occurring in a span of something between ten and twenty thousand years, the differences between monistic and dualistic positions in these sets of concerns could have seemed abstract or nitpicking, but this changed when the short chronology became untenable.

In physics, the balance of forces began to shift radically in favor of a longer chronology in 1896, when the discovery of radioactivity made it clear that the earth's uranium and other radioactive materials had been heating it for a very long time—presumably since its formation. This discovery destroyed a basic presumption of the calculations. The new factor counteracted the effect of heat loss to space, so that it had to be conceded by physicists that it could have taken the earth billions of years to cool to its present temperature from a molten state (Asimov, p. 45; see also Barrell et al. 1918:43). Strictly on logical grounds, Tylor's estimates in 1911 were probably too short for the available evidence from this point on, although it seems obvious that neither he nor his audience was aware of it.

As the estimate of the overall age of the earth increased, the absolute value of each geological period increased as well, but not the length of known history, the rates of language change, and the number of generations per century. In geology, Penck and Bruckner published their studies of the European glacial sequences from 1901 to 1909, mapping the climatic and geological changes of the Pleistocene on the basis of the advances and recessions of the Alpine glaciers. In 1910, Baron de Geer placed an absolute upper limit on the period of glacial movement by counting the annual sediment layers laid down since the last recession in the bed of Lake Ragunda, in northern Sweden (Penniman:195). This estimate accords roughly with Tylor's idea of "ancient" noted above—a minimum of 12,000 years. After this, there could be little argument about this period. It was already known that this period was but a very small part of the whole of geological time.

While the absolute value of geological time was thus increasing, a series of additional discoveries of human fossil remains pushed the probable origin of man farther back into geological time. More Neanderthal finds between 1908 and 1927, in all parts of Europe, permitted G. M. Morant in the latter year to consider the biometrics of the Neanderthal population. On the basis of his measurements, he concluded that the population was internally remarkably homogenous, but also that it was far too divergent from modern men to be regarded as a direct ancestral line to them. He concluded that it was outside the main line of human development (Penniman:196), and this of course implied the existence of a much earlier common ancestral stock.

At the same time, and partly reflected in Morant's conclusions, another series of discoveries showed the outlines of the Cro-Magnon population, with its associated tool complexes. These were generally regarded as more likely candidates for ancestors to historic Europeans, and in a sense as a more "recent" racial form though it was clear enough even then that Neanderthal and Cro-Magnon populations had existed contemporaneously and, in some cases, Cro-Magnon had been followed in sites by Neanderthal occupations. Both Neanderthal and Cro-Magnon were placed in the geological time levels of the Upper Pleistocene.

While these excavations were being undertaken in Europe and surrounding parts of the Middle East, a second series of discoveries were being made—often on the basis of careful advance planning and systematic work over many years—that extended knowledge of *Pithecanthropus* and *Homo erectus* still farther back in time. In 1909, on the basis of the judgment that certain "dragons' teeth" found in Chinese apothecary shops were fossils of very ancient human forms, a search was undertaken in China for more complete remains. At Choukoutein, in 1921, quartz tools were found, and in 1926 they were followed by the discovery of more teeth *in situ*. In 1929, an almost complete braincase of very primitive but human form was found, the first of several now classified under the label "Peking man" (Penniman:205). The age of these remains was judged to be Lower Pleistocene, and their morphology and age together fell into a pattern with other discoveries in Java and Germany (the Mauer Mandible, or Heidelberg Man) (Penniman:201–03).

Finally, in 1931 and 1932, L. S. B. Leakey found several skulls at Kanjera and Kanam (site names) in East Africa. These discoveries were the culmination of a pattern of research conceived and undertaken just after the end of the First World War, when Leakey was a student. In 1933, a panel of the Royal Anthropological Institute adjudged the two Kanjera skulls to be of Middle Pleistocene age, while the Kanam Mandible was placed in the Lower Pleistocene. The remarkable thing about these fossils, as compared to those from Java and Peking, was their distinctly modern form coupled with their clearly ancient date. This suggested a very slow rate of change among true ancestral forms, and hence a very early ultimate date for the division between protohumans and other pithecanthropoids. This conclusion lent credibility to earlier finds, such as the Galley Hill jaw found in England in 1888, that had previously been regarded as morphologically too similar to modern man to be as ancient as the geological evidence suggested they were (Penniman:201, 202). Again, the contemporaneous existence of two such different populations pushes the point of divergence from a common ancestor still farther back in time—in this case a great deal farther back.

By the late 1920s, the ultimate biological origin of man was being placed as far back as the Miocene by Elliott Smith and others, and this opinion continued to gain force through the thirties (Penniman:206). On this time scale, known human cultural and social history shrank to near insignificance as a portion of the whole, and the claim that the original condition of mankind could be discovered by the comparative analysis of present languages or of forms of society, even including all known historical forms, became unbelievable for knowledgeable scholars.

Developments in language study, biology, geology, physics, psychology, and history had, for a brief historical moment, appeared to converge in a single natural-historical model of the world, like so many trains that came abreast of one another in their movement along their tracks. Turn-of-the-century anthropologists, and more often sociologists, tried to bridge the gaps between the disciplines, on the idea, voiced by Herder, Comte, Spencer, and many others, that the separation might have been more apparent than real. But the separate disciplines continued their respective movements, driven by internal forces too powerful for any one group to control, and soon drew apart. The bridge-building efforts then fell apart for want of both shore and bottom, and the differences between the Kantian and Hegelian frames of reference, that might have seemed slight as between Tylor and William Robertson Smith, or Freud and Frazen, grew again to major importance as a choice to be made.

8.
The Concept
of the Tribe

Now the question: if the preponderance of opinion in the nineteenth century favored monistic assumptions, why did the transition to the twentieth century involve a shift to dualistic orientations? The answer is too complex and in part too speculative to try to present fully, but one clear component of it turns on the changing status of native populations and the consequent changing role of direct research among them.

At the beginning of the nineteenth century, native populations in major areas were independent and viable, as in previous centuries. "Field work," in the form of exploratory expeditions, recognizing this viability, developed analyses that aimed at understanding the people actually present, and their strategic concerns. Such analyses were consistent with, and supported, monistic, relativistic, theoretical interpretations. But as the century wore on, the viability of the native populations disappeared in significant cases, and field work passed out of the hands of explorers and into the hands of museum collectors and other academics. The framework of orientation shifted correspondingly from the present to the past—from diplomatic and military analysis to historical reconstruction—and the unit of analysis shifted from the actual individuals who lived in an area to the "tribe" and its traditions as a legal and then theoretical abstraction. It was at this point that ideas of cultural determinism provided assurance that what survivors said could be reliably construed as what their predecessors actually did.

Although the changes affected all countries which had an anthropological tradition, and most closely the British Commonwealth and North America, their local circumstances varied greatly. What happened in North America, which was in many respects the leading point of the shift, can illustrate the general process.

Nineteenth-Century Exploration

The assumptions of the Lewis and Clark expedition of 1803 to 1806, sent by President Jefferson (himself a self-conscious student of Montesquieu) to explore the newly acquired Louisiana Purchase as far as the Pacific, can be taken as representative of the large—indeed vast—number of astute accounts by travellers and explorers.

Meriwether Lewis (1774–1809) and William Clark (1770–1838) were both acting as officers in the United States Army. They were charged with informing the Indians of the change of government and of the peaceful intent of the United States. They were to obtain commitments of peace from the Indian tribes and facilitate the negotiation of peace between tribes wherever there were hostile arrangements. They were further charged with assessing the possibilities of trade with the natives, with preparing the way for such trade, and with mapping and conducting a geological survey. They went with a small group prepared for hunting and possible defense, but not for war, and they had therefore to discover, depend upon, and operate within, the established native system. In this sense, they could not afford the speculative isolation of many later theoreticians, or a pose of aloof "objectivity." They had to consider with perfect seriousness the subjective outlooks of the people who were of interest equally with their own outlook, and they had to have a concomitant concern with local interests, varying values, and individual character.

The accounts of personal incidents portrayed native feelings and concerns—as in the dramatic story of the one woman on the expedition, Sacajawea, the wife of the French trapper who served as a guide. Sacajawea literally saved the expedition from failure through her relatives in the first group of Shoshones they reached after crossing the Continental Divide on the way West. A portion of this episode follows:

> We soon drew near the camp, and just as we approached it a woman made her way through the crowd toward Sacajawea; recognizing each other, they

embraced with the most tender affection. The meeting of these two young women had in it something peculiarly touching, not only from the ardent manner in which their feelings were expressed, but also from the real interest of their situation. They had been companions in childhood; in the war with the Minnetarees they had both been taken prisoners in the same battle; they had shared and softened the rigors of their captivity till one of them had escaped from the Minnetarees, with scarce a hope of ever seeing her friend relieved from the hands of her enemies. While Sacajawea was renewing among the women the friendships of former days, Captain Clark went on, and was received by Captain Lewis and the chief, who, after the first embraces and salutations were over, conducted him to a sort of circular tent or shade of willows. Here he was seated on a white robe, and the chief immediately tied in his hair six small shells resembling pearls, an ornament highly valued by these people, who procure them in the course of trade from the sea-coast. The moccasins of the whole party were then taken off, and after much ceremony the smoking began. After this the conference was to be opened. Glad of an opportunity of being able to converse more intelligibly, Sacajawea was sent for; she came into the tent, sat down, and was beginning to interpret, when, in the person of Cameahwait, she recognized her brother. She instantly jumped up, and ran and embraced him, throwing over him her blanket, and weeping profusely. The chief was himself moved though not in the same degree. After some conversation between them she resumed her seat and attempted to interpret for us; but her new situation seemed to overpower her, and she was frequently interrupted by her tears. After the council was finished the unfortunate woman learned that all her family were dead except two brothers, one of whom was absent and a son of her eldest sister, a small boy, who was immediately adopted by her. (Coues, 2:509–10)

Clearly, there was no interest in seeing the Indians as cultural automatons, or their "tribe" as an abstract entity isolated from historical circumstances or from other bases of interpersonal relationships.

The appendix to the journals urged an increase of American trade in the area, in an effort to close out the English companies. But at the same time, it urged a number of direct controls over the trade, including restriction to a few government depots and the outlawing of credit relationships. The measures were calculated to create and maintain a high reputation for Americans by controlling dishonest or destructive practices among the merchants—making them conform to Indian standards of conduct that had obviously impressed Lewis and Clark.

The tone and orientation of Lewis and Clark were largely but not completely replicated by Henry Rowe Schoolcraft (1793–1864), who began his work as an Indian agent among the Chippewa at Sault Marie, between Lake Michigan and Lake Huron, in 1822. While there, he married the daughter of an important chief. He, like his predecessors (and several contemporaries), was a translator of cultures. But it was clear to Schoolcraft that the people he was describing, and their way of life, could not be regarded as permanent. In 1825 Schoolcraft published his *Travels in the Central Portions of the Missippippi Valley*, a descriptive journal of his travels in the region. In 1839, it was followed by *Researches*, which included the "Myth of Hiawatha" and other "Moral Legends" of the Indians, in translation. Subsequent publications included *Notes on the Iroquois* (1846), *Adventures in the Ozark Mountains* (1853), and *Historical and Statistical Information Respecting the Indian Tribes of the United States*, illustrated with 336 plates from original drawings, and issued under the patronage of the Congress in six quarto volumes from 1851 to 1857. His *History of the Indian Tribes of the United States* (1857) summarized the project and presented its conclusions to the President and the Congress, recommending removal of many major groups to new lands west of the Mississippi, where he expected they would be able to remain indefinitely in peace and gradually develop a subsistence base more compatible with the American society in the East. The recommendation was based on the underlying conclusion that Indian character and values reflected their dependence on hunting and were incompatible with the requirements of settled agriculture. But at the same time, the agricultural basis of American society, permitting far higher population densities, gave it crushing power to expand as far as its people wished—regardless of government policy or wishes.

While pursuing his official duties, Schoolcraft also worked through the Algic Society (named after "Algonquin"), which he founded in 1832, to further public appreciation of "the Indian's language, history, traditions, customs, and character" (Hays:9). He much admired the Algonquins, whom he considered the most advanced group in North America, particularly in their character.

Schoolcraft was Lewis Henry Morgan's direct predecessor in many ways. In terms of Schoolcraft's own description of the Indian relations in the Northeast as divided between the spheres of the Algonquin and the Iroquois, the society Morgan founded under the name of the League of the Iroquois was the direct complement to Schoolcraft's earlier Algic Society. The association of "savage" versus "civilized" society with distinctive modes of subsistence is another link, and Morgan's relationship to the United States government was another. Finally and most importantly, Morgan appears to have adopted from Schoolcraft the technique of writing to reconstruct a time immediately before contact—an ethnographic present that represented earlier absolute chronological periods in the east than in the west, but presumably comparable conditions. More than anything else, Schoolcraft's history chronicled the contact of Indian and American governmental and cultural systems, and their mutual relations, as they grew out of the aboriginal systems of politics and land use. But Morgan added to this idea—actually a rather complex one—an important shift toward seeing the reconstructed entities as more monolithic and less personal than Schoolcraft (though not as single organic wholes). This was consistent with his more "scientific" interests and was a major step toward a shift from experimental to speculative theory. The differences reflect a difference between the field situations faced by such men as John Bachman (1790–1897), John Heckewelder (1783–1823), Manasseh Cutler (1742–1823) (see Mead and Bunzel 1960:82–105 for examples of their writings) and George Catlin (1796–1872), on the side of Schoolcraft, as contrasted with those of G. B. Grinnel (1849–1938), Otis Mason (1838–1908), Francis La Flesche (1857–1932), Alice Fletcher (1838–1932), Matilda Stevenson (1850–1930), and many others on the side of Morgan.

The first group worked in cultures still viable and relatively autonomous. Like Schoolcraft, they describe Indian personalities and personal concerns, with a view toward recording and understanding character and avoiding future misunderstanding. The second group worked with cultures, like Morgan's Iroquois, who had lost their autonomy. They speak of Indian cultural traits but not individuals, and do so either in an areal or evolutionary format. Their purpose is not to have Indians understood by whites, or to develop policies by which Indians would respect the Americans, but rather to preserve such knowledge of Indians as they could, and with a view toward better understanding their own (Western or American) societies.

The End of a World

Except for the easternmost tribes who had lost their autonomy long before, the historical pivot point for this broad double shift in the status of Indians and in the interests and orientations of their describers was established about the same time that Schoolcraft started work. Specifically, if a single event must be named as marking the shift, it came in 1830, in a place far from the Western frontiers. That year saw the first steam-powered railroad begin operation in England. The line was the Liverpool and Manchester, and the engine was called the Rocket. It weighed 7.25 tons with its tender, and was capable of drawing a train of forty tons. In the same year, the engine called the Best Friend was made at the West Point Foundry, in New York, and put into service on the South Carolina Railroad. Although this engine was blown up by mishandling after a few months of service, the Baltimore and Ohio railroad, in the next year, offered a prize for a 3.50 ton engine capable of drawing fifteen tons fifteen miles per hour over level rail. Rails would then be able to compete economically against canals in hauling passengers and freight. The prize was won by an engine named the York, built by Davis and Gartner in the following year. Thereafter progress was more than steady—it was explosive. There were 2,816 miles of rail in the United States in 1840; 9,015 in 1850; 30,600 in 1860. The use of railroads in the American Civil War, 1861–65, was one of the principal features that have led military historians to call it the first modern war. By 1880, the railroad mileage had risen to 87,801, and it had nearly doubled from this figure in turn by 1900.

The first transcontinental railroad (Union Pacific) was completed in 1869, seven years after the charter for it was granted. The second transcontinental line was the Southern Pacific, completed in 1881. The Northern Pacific was completed just two years later, crossing the continent approximately along the route of Lewis and Clark (Webber and Garck 1911).

The railroad industry was a major component in the transformation of the United States into an industrial power of worldwide importance, although it was not the beginning of this change. It also consolidated the western advances of the Euro-American culture and productive system that had begun in the politically motivated rush for new states just before the Civil War, and in the western gold rushes to California, Colorado, and Nevada. Directly and indirectly, these movements and the railroads themselves destroyed the ecological and geographical basis of Indian society. The railroad cut across the buffalo trails of the plains, disrupting the annual pattern of migration. Railroad hunters like the famous "Buffalo Bill" Cody killed buffaloes on a new and vast scale, not only to feed the railroad crews but, in greater numbers than this alone would have required, as part of an obvious effort to eliminate the herds as a hazard to rails and telegraph lines and to eliminate the Indians that depended upon them. Lydekker estimated the destruction of bison at 2,500,000 head per year. The last Dakota bison (all that remained of the herd north of the Union Pacific line) were destroyed by Indians in

1883, leaving less than 1,000 animals in all of the United States (1911:12).

While the railroads were moving west, the Homestead Act of 1862 increased pressure on Indian lands directly, encouraging mass migrations of Americans to establish farms. The Morrell Act of the same year increased the pressure still more by providing grants of land to states to aid in the establishment of agricultural ("land grant") colleges. That year also saw the beginning of the wars between the Plains Indians and Federal troops. The Sand Creek massacre, a major defeat of the combined Cheyenne, Arapahoe, Apache, Kiowa, and Commanche forces, followed in 1864. The battle of the Little Big Horn, in 1876, was the last major Indian victory, and was followed by the defeat and destruction of the Sioux tribes as independent communities. The Nez Percé, under Chief Joseph, were defeated in 1877 and forced onto reservations. In 1886 the four-year campaign against Geronimo came to an end in Arizona and New Mexico—the last major war with Indians in what was to become the last continental state. After this time, all major American Indian groups had either been moved into designated Indian Territories or to reservations, as Schoolcraft had recommended (although it should be said he wasn't the author of the scheme). They had become charges of the Bureau of Indian Commissioners, established by Congress in 1869. The new world that Lewis and Clark had explored and extolled in 1804, and Catlin had painted almost in the same condition in the 1830s, had ceased to exist within the proverbial length of one man's life.

The Transition to Reconstruction

Catlin, travelling to the West beginning in 1832, could appreciate that the plains Indians would eventually be doomed by the advancing frontier, but he painted what he saw—people, places, equipment, and scenery, and described it in his letters (1973: rpt. of 1844 ed.). Morgan, working during and after the period of the Civil War, and in the Northeast, had direct and pressing reason to see the Indians as already representative of a past condition. The way of life he described was not that which he literally found on the Iroquois reservations, or even what he fought for in Washington as a lawyer for the Indians' treaty rights. It was rather, even at that time, a reconstruction based on the recollections of informants, and on his own conceptions of what a pure stage of culture would be. This reconstruction is what came to be described with the increasingly important, and deceptively simple-sounding, concept of an ethnographic present.

George Bird Grinnel, whose detailed and dramatic descriptions of the Cheyenne camp circles and the great buffalo hunts have moved generations of subsequent anthropologists and set a model for other monographic studies to follow, began his field work in 1890. What he saw could not possibly have been what he described. Instead, especially by the time his works were published, he too was describing an "ethnographic present" that existed only in his analysis or interpretation of the memories and mementos of his informants. Neither he nor they could ever return to the Cheyenne as he represented them for an experimental approach to field research. This was even more the case for Grinnel's successors who also worked on the Cheyenne. James Mooney (1861–1921) and George Dorsey (who published *The Cheyenne* in 1907) were two of the earlier and more prominent of them, and both figured in the events surrounding Boas and the Boas group as Stocking describes them.

Matilda Coxe Stevenson (1850–1930), a contemporary of Boas, illustrates the last phase of the change in perspective. Even though she worked (in part) among the relatively isolated and undisturbed Zuñi, her safety and continuing presence among them was guaranteed by the power of the United States Government, simply because she was white and American and despite the obvious fact that she showed a singular insensitivity to Zuñi ideas and feelings (see Lurie in Helm 1966:59–63). She selected what she wished to see deliberately, as others selected through necessity. Lurie illustrates this very elegantly by comparing a photograph Stevenson took of a shrine in a kiva with a painting of the same shrine that she later published. In the photograph were two Chinese porcelain dogs; in the painting, they were deleted (plates 4, 5). She failed to learn the language and made no attempt to learn to behave in native terms in general (as her entry into a kiva itself proclaims). She was physically present in a viable community, but the new circumstances enabled her to stand off from the community just as though she were reconstructing it through secondary accounts. Lewis and Clark, or even Cortez, could not have behaved as she did and survived.

As the new technique of placing events in the pre-contact ethnographic present developed from Schoolcraft onward, it came to be assumed, with very little direct argument, that the "unit" that these events referred to was the "tribe"—not individuals, regions, languages, institutions, families, or what-have-you. This idea, of course, was also used by the government in establishing its treaty relationships and in setting up reservations, and it must be relevant that Washington, D.C., was a major center of anthropological interest.

As an ordinary English word, the term "tribe" has had approximately its present sense since at least the seventeenth century, originally derived from the Latin *tribus,* whence also come "tribune" and "tribunal." The Latin term referred to aggregations of families, plebian rather than patrician, with their chiefs, as they formed part of the Roman political constitution. The families were often described as belonging to territorial units, as opposed to being related by descent or some other nonterritorial criteria. In English usage, the term came to have a more racial or subracial sense, carrying the idea that the families were somehow connected by blood—as with the "tribes of Israel." The scholars concerned with comparative law, like Savigny, reminded their peers of the Roman usages, while occasionally suggesting that the tribes pre-dated the empire, and provided its organizational base (this was, in effect, Maine's thesis). At the same time the English term was used to translate the Latin term anew, so the two senses inevitably were conjoined, giving the sense of a distinct biological population and of a legally constituted political entity (of common people).

The concept of a "tribe," accompanied by the concept of the "ethnographic present," made up a new theoretical conception—identical in its use to Hegel's and Comte's concept of the "state." With it, data were to be construed by the ethnologist precisely in the same way that Radcliffe-Brown was later to formally urge in the language of the logical positivists, together with the organic analogy. It came to be assumed that each tribe in the ethnographic present was a single homogeneous entity, a single pattern of institutions and ideas, and that those who were "in" it shared this pattern uniformly and participated in no other pattern. But since by definition any tribe that one could study was being studied after contact, one could by definition never observe the tribe in a pure state. One therefore had to infer or deduce its traditional order from what one could see, by assuming that some sort of uniform pattern existed (whether a pattern of values, or a system of kinship groups, or a set of groups dividing a homogeneous territory among themselves) and by using that assumption in turn to identify foreign elements, attributing them either to contact with European cultures or contact with other traditional cultures. Since historical information was hard to come by, and seldom constructed even when it could have been, the only actual criterion for applying data to both the "tribe" and the time was logical consistency itself. In this exact sense, the tribe in the ethnographic present was a theoretical construct of the analyst—precisely the same as the state-as-reason in one of its historical phases.

As the twentieth century wore on and informants became fewer and older while the "ethnographic present" became chronologically more and more remote, "tribal" constructs relied more and more on theoretical presumptions of the necessary bases of order, and on dualistic metatheory to justify such theory. In the process, the concept of the tribe and of "a culture" came to be more and more closely interdependent.

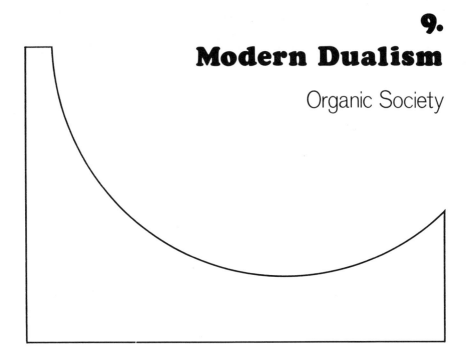

9.
Modern Dualism

Organic Society

The modern dualistic tradition in anthropology coalesced into a single system only after about 1935. Before the coalescence, there were four distinct schools: logical positivism, Durkheim's social positivism, diffusionism, and Radcliffe-Brown's functionalism.

Logical positivism began as a philosophy of science and remained preeminently philosophical. Durkheim's school began in philosophy but soon became almost entirely identified with sociology and anthropology. Diffusionism goes back to the Encyclopedists, but became an anthropological movement in the first decade of the present century, slowly enriching its theoretical tool kit with borrowings first from sociological "Darwinism," then early logical positivism, and finally from Radcliffe-Brown's functionalism. Radcliffe-Brown's functionalism itself began as a part of a reaction to evolutionism and diffusionism, utilizing mainly concepts from Durkheim's tradition. Later, Radcliffe-Brown and his followers added a more modern-seeming meta-theoretical framework from later logical positivism.

What we owe to these developments is an identification of order in society or culture with order in social theory itself—equating "culture" or "society" with the analyst's theoretical construction—in a new, non-historical, version of the comparative method that replaced the earlier monistic assumptions with assumptions from the contemporary dualistic schools.

Logical Positivism

The term "logical positivism" properly applies most narrowly to one particular branch of philosophical "empiricism," a group of men whose backgrounds were in the sciences and who knew one another and worked together, sharing common goals of many sorts. The group's interests were typified by Ernst Mach, who in 1895 was appointed to a newly created professorship in the Philosophy of Inductive Sciences at the University of Vienna. (Robert Lowie credits Mach with "the epistemological purging of natural science," but he links Mach in this to Poincaré [Lowie 1937:77], whose views were in a sense the opposite of Mach's, and distinctly pragmatic. No clarification is provided, although Lowie's own views certainly are more akin to those of Mach. Lowie wrote an extremely appreciative and perceptive obituary of Mach for *The New Republic* in 1916, calling Mach a "scientists' scientist" and commenting especially on the superiority of his psychological theories over James's.)

Mach's conception of science began with a rejection of absolute space and time, and with them of "metaphysics," which he conceived of (following both Mill and Comte) as imperfect or speculative cosmology. Instead, he saw a "science" which consisted of theoretical "pictures" of reality that were ultimately reduceable either to "sensations" or "observations" or both—but not to experiments. He was succeeded in his chair in 1922 by Moritz Schlick, who had become known as an interpreter of Einstein. The "Vienna Circle" formed as a working body corresponding and engaging in related works around Schlick. The group included Max Planck and Niels Bohr, whose interrelated work in physics actually did, in many respects, correspond to the integrative model building that the group advocated. Combining Planck's quantum theory with Rutherford's model of the atom, Bohr in 1913 had developed the modern conception of the atom, as a dynamic system of electrons revolving around a nucleus, that integrated many earlier experimental results. More philosophical members of the group included Rudolph Carnap, Hans Reichenbach, Philipp Franks, and Otto Neurath.

In 1930, the circle took over a journal called *Annalen der Philosophie,* renamed it *Erkenntnis,* and published it under the editorship of Carnap and Reichenbach. In 1934, the journal moved from Vienna to Prague and its name was changed to *The Journal of Unified Science* (see the introduction to *Logical Positivism,* written by A. J. Ayer [1959], for a fuller discussion).

While the Vienna Circle proper was taking form in Austria, W. K. Clifford, Karl Pearson, Bertrand Russell, and G. E. Moore, and then A. J. Ayer argued for almost identical ideas in a parallel sequence in England.

By the late 1930s (Ayer's militant *Language, Truth, and Logic* was published in England in 1936) the distinctive mark of the Vienna Circle positivists ceased to be a unique philosophical view as such and became a specific practical project. When events in Germany, Austria, and Czechoslovakia forced Carnap, Neurath, and others to leave, some came to universities in the United States. Carnap settled at the University of Chicago in 1936, and embodied this aim in what remains the chief and most characteristic work of the movement. They rechristened themselves the "Unity of Science Movement" (Neurath et al. 1938:1), attracted many major scholars in American institutions, and undertook to write an *International Encyclopedia of a Unified Science*. The first two volumes were published in 1938, and it has not yet been completed.

The purpose of the *Encyclopedia* was described in the lead article of volume 1 by Otto Neurath, using a historical format, as a scientifically refined version of the task of earlier encyclopedists, from Diderot through Hegel. Neurath's way of writing history was like Lowie's— which is to say that his essay is not a historical account properly so called so much as a review of previous writers in terms that constitute, themselves, a theoretical argument for his own position. Neurath places a fairly accurate short-term history of his own philosophical movement in the context of a weirdly distorted, and wonderfully self-serving, overall history of the development of Western thought (or, really, of all thought).

Neurath's history used Comte's trichotomy of theological, metaphysical, and scientific periods of thought. Comte, Hegel, and Kant are all described as metaphysicians. But not surprisingly, Hegel was singled out for especially favorable mention. His "comprehensive work can be regarded as substituting philosophico-religious statements for traditional theological statements, and as joining these philosophico-religious statements to metaphysically transformed empirical statements" (p. 6). That is, instead of seeing Hegel (as Hegel did) as attempting to turn from Kant and Deistic Protestantism to Neoplatonism and more orthodox Christian conceptions, Neurath sees him as moving in the opposite direction. He sees Hegel as a precursor of his own efforts, only using a metaphysical language for general empirical satements. He continues: "Hegel's vigor and all embracing enthusiasm stimulated such empirical thinkers as Feuerbach, Marx, and Engels; they received more thoughts that breathe and words that burn from Hegel than from the books in which Helvetius, Holbach, and others wrote about the world in an empirical sense'' (p. 6). This admiration is qualified only by the observation that ''neither Hegel nor Schelling encouraged a scientific attitude'' or ''produced logical analyses or particular theses which could be used directly in the sciences'' (pp. 6, 7). It is his own intent to remedy this deficiency.

Neurath describes, as a further advance, the ''French *Encyclopédie* and its scientific attitude,'' and then pointedly refers to Comte's ''still more constructive ideas,'' remarking also that they are similar to Spencer's (p. 8), but: ''neither the Encyclopedists nor Comte and Spencer nor similar thinkers made an attempt to organize a logical synthesis of science'' (p. 8).

The next section reviews those who have directly anticipated the Unity of Science Movement by engaging, as philosophy, in what he describes as the ''systemization of empirical procedure'' (p. 8). He describes ''modern scientific empiricism'' as having begun with Mill's writings, and as carrying through the work of Stanley Jevons (the economic theorist), and Karl Pearson (whom he describes as a ''seminal linguistic philosopher''). Neurath concludes by indicating the task still left undone:

> But neither Mill nor other thinkers of similar type applied logical analysis consistently to the various sciences, thus attempting to make science a whole on a ''logicalized'' basis. They only achieved a comprehensive understanding of all the arguments which a scientist needs if he makes generalizations and tests scientific hypotheses. This Encyclopedia will show modern attempts to reform generalization, classification, testing, and other scientific activities, and to develop them by means of modern logic. (p. 10)

The next section, ''Logical Analysis of Scientific Statements,'' moves into the task for the future: ''One science after the other separated from the mother-philosophy; scientists became more capable of solving difficult scientific problems than were philosophers occupied by a great many unscientific speculations and the particular problems of their own systems.'' This Comtean view of the growth of science fits perfectly with the positivist goal of replacing metaphysics with logically integrated science—seeing themselves as the natural successors of the ''metaphysicians'' who, one would suppose from Neurath's account, held sway until the first quarter of the nineteenth century.

Historically, it is nonsense to speak of science as an updated and more comprehensive sort of metaphysics. Science developed side by side with metaphysics, and metaphysics, even for Aristotle, was not as Neurath represents it—a rude attempt at absolute comprehensive knowledge of some "objective" world—some totality of facts.

To correct this disintegrative growth of science, the Unity of Science Movement was described by Neurath as the means by which "scientists may now build up systematical bridges from science to science analyzing concepts which are used in different sciences considering all questions dealing with classifications, orders, etc." (p. 18). The basis for believing such axiomatization was possible from what Neurath repeatedly called the "mosaic" of sciences and scientific results was a faith in the ability to develop complex logics that could incorporate all specific concepts. The basis of this faith in turn was the contention that all present scientific languages could be translated into "ordinary" languages: "One can perhaps reduce all scientific terms to one kind of term by means of a special logical technique. The thesis of physicalism which will be discussed in this *Encyclopedia* (see the following article by Carnap) emphasizes that it is possible to reduce all terms to well-known terms of our language of daily life" (p. 19).

It was only a short step from Neurath's "history" to Rudolf Carnap's definition of science in the second essay of the *Encyclopedia*. He saw science as a "body of ordered knowledge" (p. 42) that included "all theoretical knowledge, no matter whether in the field of natural sciences or in the field of the social sciences and the so-called humanities, and no matter whether it is knowledge found in the application of social scientific procedures, or knowledge based on common sense in every day life" (p. 45). To propose to integrate this "body" is to undertake a program similar to Hegel's, Comte's, and Spencer's. But it must be observed by way of contrast that this is not what Kuhn means by science, it is not what Kant meant by science, and it is not a conception of science that recognizes the crucial importance of experiments or demonstrations. Quite the contrary, Carnap's conception of the "body" of science is the idea of science-as-accumulation that Kuhn means to reject with his concept of a "paradigm."

Further expanding his ideas, Carnap developed a key element that has carried into anthropology and persists to the present. He moved from his concept of science as a body of ordered knowledge to the flat statement that: "We mean by results (of science) certain linguistic expressions, viz., the statements asserted by scientists. The task of the theory of science in this sense will be to analyze such statements, study their kinds and relations, and analyze terms as components of those statements and theories as ordered systems of those statements" (p. 43). The idea here, that runs throughout Carnap's writing and most of the others in the Encyclopedia, is that the "generalization" of science is the same as its integration and that it is also the same as the development of more perfect and abstract logical statements, statements of a form that encompasses specific statements of more and more types.

This formulation not only denies the monistic concern with demonstration as the basis of scientific knowledge; at a deeper level it rejects the monistic concern with providing a descriptive characterization of the actual scientific disciplines as they have developed. Carnap is well aware that his characterization includes many bodies of statements—like religion—ordinarily distinguished from the sciences, and it is for this reason that the scheme includes the program for the elimination of subjective or emotive elements. It is, in effect, not really a system for analysis of the sciences as we find them, but for reorganizing all knowledge (or at least all statements) into what Carnap thinks a single total science should be.

The program of the logical positivists accepts without question absolute distinctions between truths *a priori* and synthetic truths, between logic and induction, and between form and matter, and it gains its plausibility from the widespread unwillingness to drop these familiar dichotomies that seem to reinforce each other and promise so much knowledge in return for so little effort.

Logical positivism in the United States, in addition to its major foothold at the University of Chicago, had important representatives at Harvard University and the University of California at Berkeley. At each place, it had a direct and discernible influence on anthropologists and their students. Radcliffe-Brown, Redfield at Chicago, and Kroeber and Lowie at Berkeley show varying degrees of acceptance of the ideas articulated by Carnap, Neurath, Morris, and others. Leonard Bloomfield, also at Chicago, was himself a contributor to the *Encyclopedia*. At Harvard (where C. S. Peirce was eventually succeeded by W. V. O. Quine), the programs of Talcott Parsons and, to a lesser extent of Clyde Kluckhohn and George Homans in the Department of Social Relations, show acceptance of the same beliefs about science and scientific theory. In most of these cases, the influence of the logical positivists was combined with evident influence of the social positivists.

In Britain, the situation was similar. Although the influence of the Unity of Science Movement proper on anthropology was not great, the influence of the closely allied "Oxford analytical" tradition of philosophy has been consistently apparent.

Social Positivism and French Sociology:
Emile Durkheim and His School

The influence of Emile Durkheim and the school of French sociology he built up around himself is even greater than most people imagine. Several ideas, first formulated in this group, have become so deeply ingrained in modern theory and method that they are now hardly noticed as anything for which there might have been a beginning or an alternative, and are not, therefore, attributed at all. This school, more than any other, is the source of the identification of the "tribe" or primitive community with a Comtean "organic" society.

The first work of the school must be considered to be Durkheim's own *On the Social Division of Labor,* submitted as his dissertation in Philosophy at the Ecole Normale Supérieure in Paris in 1882. Starting from the position of Adam Ferguson and Adam Smith, Durkheim argued that the division was not only economic, but preeminently moral and ethical. It did not pertain only to the external activities of individuals, and to society as an aggregate of individual actions, but to the internal mental states of individuals, and (leaving Ferguson and moving toward Hegel) to society as a "mental being." This led Durkheim to equate Ferguson's specialization and separation of one individual from the other, with an alienation of each individual from society as a single entity—an entity like Hegel's "reason" or Rousseau's "general will," interpreted as a Platonic form capable of impressing itself on individuals as matter. At one point, Durkheim even argued that the division of labor impressed itself on the physical form of members of the society—saying that people in very simple societies, with nearly no division of labor, are nearly indistinguishable from one another physically, in contrast to great diversity of physical form among modern members of advanced societies (1893:309, 310).

In this framework, the problem for Durkheim's new version of Comte's sociology was to reconcile increasing individuality with the persistent need for unity in the more diversified states—to counter a tendency toward social disorganization or disruption that appeared in his scheme to be determined by the development of society itself. Durkheim's succeeding works aimed at carrying out his program and developing his argument. *Rules of the Sociological Method* (published in 1895) attempted to spell out what was involved in giving a truly "objective" and warranted "sociological" interpretation of specific observations—that is, in interpreting them as true expressions of society.

Suicide (published in 1897) was concerned with demonstrating the application of these rules in the most dramatic possible illustration of the subordination of individual mentality to society. Comparing rates of suicide in different social categories, and during different historical periods in certain places, he argued that there were three basic types, arising from three different disturbances in social order. Egoistic suicide arose from incomplete integration of the individual into society, especially from the breakdown of the family in industrial society. Altruistic suicide was in a sense its opposite, arising from very high integration of the individual into the group, so that a person would sacrifice himself to avoid a disturbance to it—as he felt often happened in primitive societies. Finally, anomic suicide occurs where individuals are caught between conflicting or inconsistent norms, as between the conflicting implications of European roles for women and men in sexual affairs. Eventually, Durkheim directly attacked the problem of explaining how society itself originated and developed in *The Elementary Forms of the Religious Life,* published first in 1912, and in an authorized English translation in 1915. But between Durkheim's first work and this last major one, his work gained support and significance from efforts of the members of his increasingly large and influential school.

One of the most important intervening works was Lucien Lévy-Bruhl's *La Morale y la science des moeurs* (*Morality and the Science of Mores*), published in 1903. Lévy-Bruhl was older than Durkheim, and had published works in philosophy before Durkheim's *Division of Labor* was printed (Lévy-Bruhl 1890). But Lévy-Bruhl himself described his later work as "fully in accord with the spirit" of Durkheim's *Rules* (1903:13n.). It is to this work that Evans-Pritchard was apparently referring in his obituary of Lévy-Bruhl when he wrote: "In his treatment of moral philosophy, Lévy-Bruhl exposed, devastatingly but charmingly, the futility of ethical theories which set out to provide a basis for conduct, and he laid the foundations for an inductive study of morals" (1940a:24).

Although Lévy-Bruhl's argument wasn't quite what Evans-Pritchard's formulation might now suggest, it did in fact attack the idea that the aim of the science of morals was to set norms for action, and in this connection quite erroneously attacked Wundt's concept of a "normative science" as a contradiction in terms. What was normative (legislative and/or deductive) could not be theoretical (inductive)—as if Wundt had himself attempted to direct behavior (1903:11). But at the same time, Lévy-Bruhl adopted a formulation rather like Wundt's in some major respects, revolving around the theme of the difference between "practical morality" (*la morale pratique*) and "moral theory" (or theoretical morality: *morale théorique*) (all translations are my own): "theoretical morality and practical morality do not differ among themselves as pure mathematics, for example, and applied mathematics. In reality, both together, theoretical morality and practical morality, have for their object *the regulation of action*" (pp. 12,13). The difference is that practical morality, "has for its object, not to know *that which is,* but to determine *that which ought to be*" (p. 15).

Theoretical morality involves explicating and integrating the underlying principles of practical morality, of action and its goals. Extending the implementation of this in one direction, Lévy-Bruhl held, again *contra* Wundt, that there: "could not exist any theoretical morality that employed the same method as the physical and natural sciences" (p. 15). The subject of the latter, of course, was precisely "that which is," while: "a moral order . . . is conceived as superior to the natural order, is represented as an ideal, is sensed as the obligatory object of our efforts" (pp. 15–16).

Thus moral facts, which apparently are precisely these ideals or goals, are a special class of social facts, with their own "function," summarized under their own "laws" (p. 18). The goal of moral theory is to "reduce to a single principle, if that is possible, the rules that direct action" (p. 11). In this sense, it is a matter of "the abstract formulation of the rules of an art, [like the] theory of naval architecture" (p. 11). While this program of investigation is indeed not what physical scientists do, it is precisely what the logical positivists were to propose as a way of integrating the results of science.

The body of Lévy-Bruhl's argument develops these basic ideas in the form of a critique and synthesis of the preceding philosophical literature, focussing mainly on Kant, Locke, Leibnitz, Hegel, Spencer, and—most closely allied to his own position—Comte and Durkheim. He argues that practical moralities had to reflect the usages of their times, and that moral facts had real existence apart from reason (referring to Kant's arguments) and could only be related to reason through a sociological theory (saying Kant, lacking such a theory, had failed to show the "rapport" between them) (ch. 2). He argued that since human nature is always and everywhere the same, the contents of the moral consciousness everywhere formed a harmonious and organic entity (ch. 3). Extending the idea that the object of the theoretical science of morality was to study the moral reality that was given, he argued that the historical study of society in this connection could have an integrating role in moral development analogous to the role of mathematics in the sciences of nature (ch. 4). Recalling Durkheim's rules, he argued that the morality of a society had to be seen from both a static and dynamic point of view, that this required a comparative method, and that with application of this method the form of the morality would be seen to reflect its function with respect to other "series of social phenomena" (ch. 7:208). This is followed by an extremely important argument connecting the idea of "sentiments" with the idea of "representations." This formulation is still in many respects the major modern alternative to the concepts of "custom" in relation to individual psychology in Wundt's tradition. A fairly long passage is worth quoting:

> To tell the truth . . . one doesn't easily see what "sentiment" can be if one isolates it from representations, beliefs, and customs. If one sets aside purely physiological needs, like eating and drinking, and the fundamental and obscure instinct of the "will to live," common to all organisms, man living in society (and above all in primitive societies) is determined in his action, not by sentiments as distinct from ideas and from representations, but by complex physiological states, dominated by energetic and imperative representations. That imperative force manifests itself for him by the very lively awareness that he *must do* some action, that he *must abstain* from some other, and, if he commits it nevertheless, even involuntarily, by repentance, remorse, and by a religious horror which can go so far as to cause death. (ch. 7, pp. 225–26)

The argument is engaging, plausible, and seemingly complete. But we should note that the whole force of the work of Helmholtz, Wundt, James, and the physiologists was that one could *not* simply dismiss hunger, drinking, and the will to live as if they were common to all animals and *therefore* were not intimately related to the way humans function as thinking and civilized creatures. In effect, Lévy-Bruhl dismisses physiology offhand, by a subtle invocation of the old idea that humans were essentially different from animals. This clears the way for a purely social analysis of psychology, and for identifying internal states on the basis of social *forms,* not even requiring actual individual behavior. Its importance has been inestimable. The work closes with a return to Comte's concerns, in a review of the practical consequences of the theoretical apparatus described.

Lévy-Bruhl's scheme fully articulated the framework of the group associated with the *Année Sociologique* (papers published in volumes from 1898 to 1913). There was no interest in physiology, no interest in language or interactive modes of communication. Instead, there were several major attempts to discuss society as an organic system of social principles and a relatively large number of studies of specific institutional complexes, customs, or symbolic "representations." The titles tell a large part of the story: *Mental Functions in Inferior Societies* (Lévy-Bruhl, 1910); *Primitive Mentality* (Lévy-Bruhl, 1922); *Primitive Mythology* (Lévy-Bruhl, 1935); *Sacrifice: Its Nature and Function* (Hubert and Mauss, 1898): *Primitive Classification* (Durkheim and Mauss, 1903); *Dissertation on a General Theory of Magic* (Hubert and Mauss, 1904); *The Gift: Form and Function of Exchange in Primitive Societies* (Mauss, 1925); *The Collective-Representation of Death* (Hertz, 1907); *Techniques of the Body* (Mauss, 1936); and *Divisions and Proportions of the Divisions of Sociology* (Mauss, 1927), to name but a few. Each study purported to focus on a pattern widely current in primitive societies or in all societies, arrive at its fundamental character by comparisons that point up the common and general symbolic or representational features, describe that pattern in terms of obligations and proscriptions of action and of sentiment and show its form and function in relation to other series of social phenomena more or less clearly. The conclusion of each study was a universal substantive model of the thing it took as its subject—a universal model of the meaning and elements of sacrifice, gift exchange, mythology, and so forth. This, it soon came to be recognized, raised the classic functionalist problem of "reification"—taking analytical categories for real entities.

Durkheim's *Elementary Forms* follows precisely the pattern of the other studies in this series. It is, in fact, a study of totemism as a system of representations on a par with gift exchange and the rest. Durkheim begins with an observation recalling both Comte and Lévy-Bruhl, proposing to replace metaphysics with the historical study of the development of thought:

> At the roots of all our judgments there are a certain number of essential ideas which dominate all our intellectual life; they are what philosophers since Aristotle have called the categories of the understanding; ideas, time, space, class, number, cause, substance, personality, etc. They correspond to the most universal properties of things. They are the solid frame which encloses all thought. (1915:9)

Durkheim identified such categories as "born in religion and of religion" (p. 9), and undertook to study them in their "elemental" form by studying the most primitive religion of the most primitive group he could find—the "totemic" religion of Australian natives.

Durkheim's description was based largely on the account of Australian totemism and social organization provided by Baldwin Spencer and F. J. Gillen in *The Native Tribes of Central Australia,* first published in

1899. Spencer and Gillen in turn attribute their own major intellectual debt to Tylor and Frazer. Spencer's and Gillen's account is lopsided in precisely the way that would bias its users toward supporting a theory of ritually dominated society with a single basis of organization: its data come almost entirely from one set of annual rituals, and their myths, performed in one place. It does not take into account the full round of rituals or the range of non-ritual concerns the natives might have had, and is therefore analogous to an analysis of British organization and mentality abstracted from Christmas festivities, without looking at coronations, cricket matches, or union hall activities.

Durkheim saw previous philosophers as providing partial and inadequate answers to his questions, and saw them in strictly dualistic terms,

> Up to the present there have been only two doctrines in the field. For some, the categories cannot be derived from experience; they are logically prior to it and condition it. They are represented as so many simple and irreducible data, imminent in the human mind by virtue of its inborn constitution. For this reason they are said to be *a priori*. Others, however, hold that they are constructed and made up of pieces and bits, and that the individual is the artisan of this construction. (1815:11)

The second position, which he calls the "material theses," corresponds to Locke's empiricism, and he holds it to be inadequate on the ground that it could not account either for the universality or necessity of such general concepts, or for the fact that they "are not attached to any particular object" and are therefore "independent of any particular subject" (p. 13). He felt that "the *a priorists* have more respect for the facts," recognizing the universality and generality of the ideas, but that their position still could "give neither explanation nor justification" for the power of individual minds "of transcending experience and of adding to that which is given to it directly"—of adding the universal categories to its immediate experience. He considered the concept of "divine reason" as a "superior and perfect reason from which the others emanate by a sort of mystic participation" (p. 15) to be a partial explanation, but felt it did not explain individual variability and temporal mutability of basic conceptions. This was apparently a reference to Hegel, and perhaps the rationalists, although no one was specifically named in either connection.

In the same discussion, Durkheim considered and rejected the position of Kant—evidently taking him as a major reference point (as did Lévy-Bruhl) and also evidently recognizing that he was in fact neither an "*a priorist*" nor a "materialist." The points he specifically men-

tioned were Kant's conception of space and his "categorical imperative." The first he dismissed as though it were an erroneous description
of space itself, offering instead the view that "spatial representation
consists in a coordination of the data of sensuous experience" (p. 11).
This apparently attributes to Kant the same view Spencer assigned to
him, while it offers as an alternative a close idealistic paraphrase of
what Kant actually said. The categorical imperative he dismissed as a
"game of concepts," attributing to Kant the view that any action at all
was moral if it could be "universalized" (p. 12). Both criticisms merely
rephrase Kant in terms of dualistic assumptions, and both fail to come to
grips with the alternative Kant was actually offering. Durkheim's own
position remained dualistic.

In place of the two opposed dualistic "theories," Durkheim offered
his "sociological theory of knowledge" that "the categories originally
only translate social states" (p. 18).

> From the fact that the ideas of time, space, class, cause or personality are
> constructed out of social elements, it is not necessary to conclude that they
> are devoid of all objective value. On the contrary, their social origin rather
> leads to the belief that they are not without foundation in the nature of
> things. Thus renovated, the theory of knowledge seems destined to unite the
> opposing advantages of the two rival theories, without incurring their incon-
> veniences. It keeps all the essential principles of the *a priorists;* but at the
> same time it is inspired by that positive spirit which the empiricists have
> striven to satisfy. (p. 19)

The plan is identical in conception to the logical positivists', both in
the scope of knowledge that Durkheim hopes to systematize—all shared
conceptions—and in the structure of his problem. Like them he sets up
his entire program on the basis of the radical dichotomy between *a
priori* forms and empirical particulars, between concepts and what are
conceptualized. The two schools of thought Durkheim proposes to reconcile correspond to the complementary groups of dualistic philosophers
that the logical positivists drew upon.

Combining Hegel's concept of the state as reason, representing or
analogous to divine reason, with Comte's concept of the state as an
"organic" whole, Durkheim argued that society was an organic integrated whole, a "unity" (1915:23) "conscious of itself" (p. 231) de-
scribable with the term "collective consciousness" (p. 444): ". . . im-
personal reason is only another name given to collective thought" (p.
446). The social entity is "outside and above individual and local con-
tingencies" (p. 444), and constitutes a "reality *sui generis*" (p. 16),

whose representation was the basis of religion. The nature of such a collective consciousness was inferable as natural law, the result of scientific investigation, from the study of its "collective representations" (p. 233) such as rituals, social behaviors, organizational rules, and even physical characteristics (see esp. pp. 309–28). As a concomitant of this view of society, it was Durkheim's contention that "man is double." "There are two beings in him: an individual being which has its foundation in the organism and whose activities are therefore strictly limited, and a social being which represents the highest reality in the intellectual and moral order that we can know by observation—I mean society" (p. 17). He continues: "This duality of our nature has as its consequence . . . , in the order of thought, the irreducibility of reason to individual experience" (p. 17). For Durkheim, literally all concepts, all regularity in cognition and experience, were imposed from without "by the authority of society" (p. 17). The relationship between the individual and society corresponds to the relationship between "the whole and the part, and the complex and the simple" (p. 16). Finally, in the closing paragraphs of the *Elementary Forms of the Religious Life,* Durkheim suggested that the Kantian antinomies expressed this same gulf between the individual and society.

The most apparent problem in his approach was resolved by Durkheim to his own satisfaction, and probably to the satisfaction of many others at that time, by an evolutionism closely related to Tylor's. If we see society as plural, as numerous unconnected and distinct societies, we might at first be inclined to feel that Durkheim had avoided the one classical dualistic problem of deriving the "general" thought from "particular" individuals only at the cost of many new problems of deriving each society from each group of individuals and having each such society nonetheless exhibit the necessary constant features uniformly. The greatest portion of the discussion of the *Elementary Forms* was devoted to articulating the ways in which social morphologies would be identified at different levels of development, and with arguing that a single original "reality *sui generis*" represented by Australian totemism evolved into all present social forms in accordance with fixed quasi-physical laws, increasing in "volume" and complexity and, in effect, pulling human mentality along with it.

In effect, the perspective of Durkheim and his associates embodied a new transformation of the historical solipsism associated with previous dualistic social analysis. Durkheim identifies natural law as his own discovery, beneath the surface of those things which the members of society do and believe. He contends that such laws—his laws—direct and control all behavior, or rather all social behavior. But the sole criterion for whether some piece of information reflects any given society rather than the "particular and local circumstances" of its individuals, is whether it fits Durkheim's own model of social morphology. If something fits his model, it qualifies as social and proves the rule; if it does not, it is assignable to particulars, that is individuals, and is considered as sociologically insignificant. There is thus no way of identifying data except by determining that they confirm one's analysis, and there is, accordingly, no data that can disconfirm an analysis.

It was only a short step from Durkheim's sociology to Radcliffe-Brown's functionalism, and in 1915, when the *Elementary Forms* was published, social and intellectual movements leading to that step were already underway. Part of the movement consisted in the diffusionists' attacks on "totemism" and their raising of the problem of reification under the heading of "convergence."

Diffusionism

Just as the idea of evolution referred to a genuine core phenomenon of progressive development, which occurred sometime in some places but not at all times in all places, so the idea of diffusion referred to the equally real transmission of cultural artifacts and other "traits" from one region or community to another. No one would deny such transmission occurs sometime. But when this was then blown up as an "ism," into a supposed universal and exclusive historical process, it raised basic issues by requiring that an investigator always be able to identify "the same" item in multiple contexts.

Within academic anthropology, the principal diffusionists were a group associated closely with Boas: Clark Wissler, A. L. Kroeber, Roland B. Dixon, Robert Lowie, Paul Radin, and in some respects Alexander Goldenweiser, among others. Wissler appears to be the major formulator of the "ism" as a theory. Lowie is one of its most forceful proponents, and is apparently largely responsible for the idea that Boas shared his views. While Lowie is generally known as a student of Boas, he began to work for Wissler during his graduate years, and continued as assistant curator in the American Museum after he obtained his doctorate in 1908—and after Boas' estrangement from Wissler and the museum. Wissler looms much larger than Boas in Lowie's autobiography (Lowie 1959).

The idea of diffusion was closely tied to the idea of a "culture area"—roughly convergent, in North American ethnography, with the older idea of the area exclusively associated with a tribe or related group of tribes. The term itself is a rough translation of the German geographical term *Kulturkreise*. Individual interpretations of the idea varied, but it was agreed that somehow the culture occupying a region amounted to a single integrated system or pattern. Wissler used the idea of a "culture climax" to define the areas by centers of particularly intensive development, such as a more urbanized region, with progressively fewer and more attenuated elements fading out toward the peripheries. This made diffusion a principle of organization *within* a tribal area, as well as an explanation of the movement of traits from one region to another.

Major studies of "diffusion" included Mooney's fine study of the development and spread of the Ghost Dance Religion, which he himself witnessed directly and in a sense even took part in (Bureau of American Ethnology, Annual Report no. 14, 1896); Wissler's reconstruction of the movement of the horse through western and central North America, and its impact on Indian culture (1914); Wissler's influential text, *An Introduction to Social Anthropology* (1926); Radin's many studies of myth, demonstrating the recurrence of thematic elements across linguistic and cultural boundaries; and Lowie's *Primitive Society* (1920) (at least in its express intent). Kroeber's most important *Cultural and Natural Areas of Native North America* (1939) was constructed in terms of the culture-area concept and the notion of a pre-contact ethnographic present (although it did note migration patterns), and had an underlying diffusionist purpose, but did not argue for diffusionism *per se*. The same also applies to the many Culture-Element Surveys that were a hallmark of ethnology directed by the Department of Anthropology at the University of California at Berkeley while Kroeber's and Lowie's influence there was decisive.

But in the long run probably the most influential work of this group and period was Lowie's *History of Ethnological Theory* itself. This took as its starting point the view of the lineage of modern anthropology that Wissler had presented in passing in his *Introduction,* as beginning in Morgan and being developed mainly by Tylor and the diffusionist *Kulturkreise* geographers. Wissler had entirely ignored Bastian (even in his section on the history of museums), and barely mentioned Boas. Lowie redressed this imbalance somewhat by devoting considerable space to both scholars, but he did not part notably from Wissler's assessment of their ultimate influence. If anything, Lowie strengthened the impression Wissler offered, by draping the diffusion-versus-evolution argument over his entire discussion, as if the whole history of anthropology had been devoted to a choice between two deterministic theories—and as if Bastian, Boas, and others had not been opposed to determinism of any sort. It was in this work that Lowie argued for a new version of Tylor's concept of an "efficient cause" explanation in the form of his own concept of "contact diffusion," a kind of cultural osmosis. The idea that contact diffusion was itself explanatory of cultural forms required that Lowie rule out purpose or choice of the members of the community exposed to the new trait in question. He argued for this under the heading of the "non-intellectual motives" of peoples in primitive communities. Lowie specifically and explicitly rejected the view of the "savage primarily as a reasoner" (1937:108), attributing it to Tylor. Evidently, Lowie did not consider that Tylor went far enough, for he is in fact doing nothing so much as applying Tylor's conception of "survivals" that persisted from one stage of culture to another without regard to truth or utility, by their own force, to all culture traits whatsoever.

Lowie's arguments were buried in what he praised and condemned in others. For example, in a chapter titled "Progress" he recognized "two principal contributions" of Gabrielle de Tarde (1843–1904): "A detached view of modern civilization, and a psychology of social man that did justice to nonintellectual motives of behavior" (p. 108). The main such "motive" cited was imitation, but even invention was implicitly defined as something that would come about largely automatically, when traits came together:

> Invention is the fusion of two or more preexisting ideas into a new synthesis; its laws belong essentially to individual logic, while the laws of imitation are in part social, largely extralogical. Since such creative synthesis is not calculable, Tarde assigns a role to historic accident. He accurately recognizes, however, the logical interrelation of ideas, whence the irreversability of intellectual process. (p. 109)

Edward Hahn (1856–1928) is similarly commended by Lowie for making the same type of psychological points in relation to comparative economics, especially the relationship of economic tasks with the sexual and social divisions of labor, the uninventiveness of man, and the complexity of economic activities and their many unforeseeable consequences.

This conception of human uninventiveness was applied in turn to argue for one or "at best a few, centers of diffusion" for domestication and for each other major complex of techniques. For example, the geographer Friedrich Ratzel (1844–1904), as Lowie describes him, contributed to progress by taking as principles man's "limited inventiveness" and "the force of past history" to preclude that even similar traits can be attributed to "an automatic response to environment" (p. 120): "Accepting psychic unity, Ratzel will have none of it as an interpretation of similarities. The uninventive human beings that were constantly migrating hither and yon simply transported what they had picked up as their cultural inventory" (p. 123). Lowie ends the chapter thus:

> Ratzel shares with Hahn the fruitful distinction between hoe and plough farming. But his chief contribution lies in certain more general ideas—the conception of humanity as a unit, the tempering of environmentalism with a historical perspective, the demand for a conversion of space into time relations, the deprecations of spectacular migrations in place of slow, continuous infiltration, the postulation of marginal peoples. (p. 127)

The improved type of study toward which these were "progressing" were, of course, the works of Lowie's own group. Lowie went on in the history to see fundamental compatibilities between his perspective and the assumptions of Durkheim and Radcliffe-Brown—and to attack bitterly the functionalism of Malinowski.

The unity of the principal diffusionists with others associated with Boas, and with Boas himself, under the common anti-evolutionary banner was a very weak sort of unity, since evolutionary schemes based on the short chronology (and lack of knowledge of the physical basis of inheritance) were defunct in any case. Serious problems were recognized within the diffusionists' theoretical framework almost from the beginning—not only by Boas, who never accepted either Lowie's idea of uninventiveness or the idea of "totalitarian" culture Lowie attributed to him (1937:256; see Boas' "The Aims of Anthropological Research" 1932). The differences turned on the question of cultural integration, and by implication on the important question of cultural boundaries and cultural "traits" themselves. It was evident that horses, seeds, and literary symbols could move across cultural boundaries and have implications of far-reaching and subtle sorts. But was this really evidence that culture traits of a more complex sort could so move? And more basically what could such a trait be, and how would one find it moving—detached in some sense from the rest of what it was coming from or going to?

The most elaborate cultural "trait" whosed diffusion was traced in an American study was probably Mooney's Ghost Dance movement. But this hardly would have served Lowie's purpose. Its inception and history were closely tied to the creative activity of one man; it was most difficult to say *where* it came from (since it borrowed many American

religious and political notions, as well as indigenous Indian ideas); and
it never really became integrated in any Indian "cultural whole."

Failing to say what cultures were as totalities separated from individuals, caused by mechanical processes, or what traits were, the main theoretical discussion focussed on a related issue—generally called the
"principle of the limitation of possibilities," a phrase that referred both
to cultural form and to possibilities for development. The main discussions were presented in a remarkably important series of papers by
Alexander Goldenweiser.

According to his own account, Goldenweiser first discussed the idea
of a "principle" of limited possibilities in a paper read before the Pearson circle in New York in 1910 (1913:259). It was first published in the
paper "The Principle of Limited Possibilities of the Development of
Culture" in the *Journal of American Folklore* in 1913. In the interval,
the idea had already been adopted and developed by Boas, Radin, and
Lowie, as Goldenweiser acknowledged. It remained a topic of occasional theoretical papers from then on (Gibson 1948; Erasmus 1950;
Harris 1966).

Goldenweiser's essay was concerned with "convergence," by which
he referred to the appearance of similar traits from dissimilar origins in
unconnected cultures. The concept was obviously borrowed from biology, but the phenomenon posed a crucial problem to the emerging
debate between deterministic social evolutionism and deterministic diffusionism. Goldenweiser traced its anthropological usage back through
Boas to a presentation by "Professor Ehrenreich" before the German
anthropological society in 1902, wherein Ehrenreich traced it still farther back to "Thilenius and von Lucian," but giving no reference (Goldenweiser 1913:259). Goldenweiser's own treatment begins by criticizing a 1912 article by Lowie titled "On the Principle of Convergence in
Ethnology" (published in the *Journal of American Folklore*). Goldenweiser says he will reject Lowie's position in that article that absolute identity of cultural traits between two cultures was "inexplicable"
(p. 262). The argument, following Lowie, distinguished "genuine convergence" from "false convergence." Genuine convergence is "the independent development of psychologically similar cultural traits from
dissimilar or less similar sources, in two or more cultural complexes."
The second type of convergence occurred "when the similarities between the cultural traits are not psychological, but merely objective or
classificatory . . ." (p. 269).

Beginning with "false convergence," which he also calls "objective" convergence, Goldenweiser introduced the "Limitation of Possi-

bilities'' as a series of principles that tend to limit the form traits can take when they combine into progressively larger cultural features (p. 207). The significant and important aspect of this part of the paper is the broad range of problems or observations he saw as reflecting convergence of this type: those "certain definite features," the "sum of which constitute the individuality of the culture''; the "fundamental cultural traits" that "are not specific in each culture, but show marked similarities and are found again and again in different cultures" (p. 274). These include the general finding that "social organization consists of social units (in the limited sense) of families, or of local groups, or of various combinations of these units; that an art consists of carving, or drawing, or painting . . . ; that the form of it is realistic or semiconventionalized, or purely geometrical; . . .'' (p. 273). All these patterns were "convergent" in the sense that they arose from a multiplicity of divergent historical roots, had possibly dissimilar meanings in each culture, and were recurrent patterns that encompassed nonrecurrent, diverse, and multiform elements in a purely conceptual sense. In a significant footnote, Goldenweiser considered the possible critique that this convergence was due to the imposition of our own limited cultural forms on the observations of other behaviors and objects. He rejected this as an objection to his argument not on the grounds that our cultural concepts were not the basis of such classification, but rather by saying that even if they were not, some other set of concepts or categories would act in the same way, so that this type of convergence would exist anyway (p. 273, n.1).

True or psychological convergence was a phenomenon over and above objective or false convergence. For example, after describing similar classes with different social functions as an instance of "false convergence,'' he adds:

Similarly with taboos, animal taboos of heterogeneous origin and development may also differ in their psychological connotations; the one may emanate at a given time from the conscious prescription of a chief, the other may be based on the totemic character of the animal. Again, the convergence would be purely objective. But if, in these or similar instances, the cultural features, while of different derivation, acquire similar psychological content, or, in the cases of official divisions, similar functions, the case is one of genuine convergence. (p. 277)

Despite the original objection to Lowie's position, the rest of the paper was not devoted to showing that objective convergence was any kind of direct evidence for psychological convergence, but rather only that "genuine convergences are more likely to arise than would at first sight appear'' (p. 277). He specifically adduced *rites de passage* as an example, and used the same structure of argument as in the case of "objective'' (false) convergence to argue that there are in fact a limited number of psychological aspects of culture into which diverse elements can be formed, regardless of "the multiplicity of their possible psychological historical origins'' (p. 228).

The article concluded with the introduction of a new concept to explain the last point, the idea of an "assimilation'' as a psychological consolidation of several disparate elements into a cultural "complex'' that represents a psychological convergence. These types of limitations were merely classified, not analyzed in detail or explained.

It is important to notice the special version of metaphysical dualism that Goldenweiser imbeds in this argument, which appears to have neo-Kantian roots. Like Kant, Goldenweiser thinks of what is "psychologically real'' as that which is "subjective.'' Also like Kant, but in a peculiar and limited way, he further thinks of that which is merely or only "objective'' as Kant wrote of an imputed noumenon—a "hyperbolical entity.'' But, he speaks of both sorts of patterns, subjective (genuine) and objective (false), as if they were radically separate from each other—in principle distinct, even though they might coincide in fact. The two patterns are thus mutually exclusive dichotomous categories, where for Kant all perceptions were subjective, and "objective'' perceptions were constructed upon them by organizing consensus under appropriate sets of categories. Further, Goldenweiser identified "subjective'' only with the native viewpoint, and "objective'' only with his own—another dichotomy thus formed on the basis of "self'' versus "other'' and "perceives'' versus "perceived.'' But it is a paradoxical formulation, like the sound of one hand clapping. It makes what is subjective inaccessible by assigning it to others in a way that suggests it is private to them, and it makes what is objective inaccessible by bidding us to see it from our own perspective but without subjectivity. Such things can't be found, by definition. It is quite as confusing as Hegel's speaking of reason as something he could observe in nature, as an active causal force.

The effect of Goldenweiser's kind of adaptation, like those of Hegel and other neo-Kantians, is twofold. First, insofar as one takes it as a Kantian perspective it misinforms one on the Kantian position. It shuts one off from using Kant's real ideas as an alternative to dualistic schemes and their built-in and time-tested problems. Secondly, it presents a particularly discouraging dualism in its own right. In equating true convergence with subjective convergence and with historically genuine convergence, and contrasting them with objective, historically false and psychologically false convergence, Goldenweiser definitely says there is no necessary relation between the two types, a statement that was taken by many as suggesting that a choice had to be made between them. Especially because the concept of a "convergence" as Goldenweiser used it meant virtually any identifiable phenomenon or pattern that emerged from the flux of individual events; the suggestion was that any analyst had to choose between descriptions that were subjectively and historically real but lacked "objectivity," and descriptions that were "objective" but lacked historical depth and psychological reality for the natives. Coupling the dualistic distinctions between "subject" and "object" in this way with "genuine" and "false" and with the new contrast between historical and, by implication, nonhistorical (Radcliffe-Brown would later use the term "synchronic"), Goldenweiser thus converted the simple and undeniable observation that one may "see" things in a culture that the natives did not recognize or acknowledge, and one may not see things they do believe to exist, into a major theoretical dilemma that involved in part a choice between history and "objectivity," and where objectivity in this sense necessarily involved imposing one's own categories on the data and rejecting the categories of the native viewers of the data. This is the first articulate and conscious expression in the modern literature of this important anti-historical version of Hegel's solipsism, and it marked a major dualistic reconstruction of the nature and goals of anthropology.

A. R. Radcliffe-Brown

Lowie was quite right in grouping Radcliffe-Brown with Durkheim in his history. Radcliffe-Brown's "social anthropology" (his term) by the 1930s consisted of Durkheim's sociology generalized into "comparative sociology" without the cry for reform and without evolution. However, Durkheim's ideas were combined in a most original way with the constellation of dichotomies aligned with the contrast between "objective" and "subjective" that had been developing in the debates over convergence, and that borrowed heavily from British empiricism and, later, logical positivism.

Radcliffe-Brown (1881–1955) was born in Birmingham, England,

and educated at Trinity College, Cambridge. He began reading for his
A. B. in "Mental and Moral Science," with W. H. R. Rivers, and
went to work with Rivers, Haddon, and others when Rivers shifted his
interests to anthropology. In the years 1906–08, he undertook field
research in the Andaman Islands, working mainly through interpreters at
the British penal colony on Big Andaman. The results were presented as
his doctoral thesis, then rewritten in 1913–14, and finally published in
1922, and republished with a new Preface in 1933—his only large-scale
work. For the most part, the work was a potboiler, following the earlier
On The Aboriginal Inhabitants of the Andaman Islands by E. H. Man,
in an attempt to reconstruct pre-contact, traditional, Andaman culture.
Radcliffe-Brown borrows most of Man's topics and even illustrations,
merely qualifying, correcting, or elaborating the earlier descriptions.

Radcliffe-Brown travelled widely in his early career, not unlike Boas.
He formed a new department of social anthropology at Capetown
(1921–26). He held the first Chair in Social Anthropology at the
Australian National University at Sidney (1926–31), with support from
the Rockefeller Foundation. He visited the United States and taught at
the University of Chicago from 1931 to 1937, again with support from
the Rockefeller Foundation. He then returned to England, where he became the first Professor of Social Anthropology at Oxford, in 1937,
again founding a department. He retired from Oxford in 1946, then
went on to take a chair in Sociology in the Farouk I University, at Alex-
andria. He also held visiting professorships at Yenching, China
(1935–36) and São Paulo, Brazil (1942–44). Elkin, speaking especially
of his experience at Sydney, describes him as one who always "stirred
things up," but intimates that he was not very good at keeping them
going (1956, p. 245).

Radcliffe-Brown's chief arguments appear in bits and pieces, either in
relatively short articles, or in the introductory remarks to such articles,
or later in introductions to collections of works of his students and followers. His basic assumptions evolved slowly through his thirty-odd
years of active writing, and the shifts reflect his location.

The most obvious points at which *The Andaman Islanders* fore-
shadows Radcliffe-Brown's later theoretical views come in his treatment
of customs, ceremonials, and beliefs. His aim is to remove all sense that
his theories are "psychological" (p. 233). To do this, he argued that he
was concerned with the "social function" of the "ceremonial (i.e., collective) expression of any sentiment," wherein "social function" in
turn meant "the effects of an institution (custom or belief) insofar as
they concern the society and its solidarity or cohesion" (p. 234). This
led to the formulation that the function of a set of beliefs was "to main-

tain in the mind of the individual the feeling of his dependence on society'' (p. 264)—a view that recalls at once the passive mind of Locke's
empiricism and the primitive uninventiveness of the diffusionists. The
argument is unconvincing because of its obvious circularity and lack of
definite relevance to any specific usage it purports to explain. Radcliffe-
Brown tried to restate the argument in the 1932 Preface to the second
impression (signed at the University of Chicago). The Preface begins
with a discussion of the relationship between his work and Man's, and
moves quickly to a statement of Hubert, to the effect that myths have to
be understood not only as the ideas they contain, but also in relation to
all the circumstances in which they are regularly told. Similar views are
expressed on the study of rituals, and on religious phenomena in general. This, he says, was the "method" he attempted to apply "to the
beliefs and customs of the Andaman Islanders in the fifth and sixth
chapters of this book. These chapters deal with what I have called the
meaning and the function of rites and myths, but no definitions of those
terms are given. It seems desirable to supply them" (p. viii). As he does
so, he moves consistently away from individual psychology and from
Rivers' physiologically-derived sense of observational procedures to
Durkheim's conception of an *a priori* interpretive device.

The discussion begins with the observation that: "Just in the sense
that words have meanings, so do some other things in culture—customary gestures, ritual actions and abstentions, symbolic objects,
myths—they are expressive signs . . . There is a danger that the ethnologist may interpret the beliefs of a native people not by a reference to
their mental life but by reference to his own" (pp. viii–ix). He thinks
that this is what Man did, in some cases. "It therefore seemed to me
necessary for ethnology to provide itself with a method of determining
meanings as effective and free from personal equation as the methods by
which a linguist determines the meanings of words or morphemes in a
newly studied language" (p. ix).

Up to this point, the words could have been written by Boas, except
for the use of the concept of "expressive signs" and the significant call
for freedom from (rather than control of) the personal equation. The
linguistic methods he apparently refers to could be those described in
Bloomfield's *Language* (which had been developing since 1914, and
was published in 1933).

The basic dualism of Radcliffe-Brown's perspective begins to surface
in the next paragraph, discussing "function":

The notion of function in ethnology rests on the conception of culture as an
adaptive mechanism by which a certain number of human beings are enabled

to live a social life as an ordered community in a given environment. Adaptation has two aspects, external and internal. The external aspect is seen in the relation of the society to its geographical environment. The internal aspect is seen in the controlled relations of individuals within the social unity. It is convenient to use the term "social integration" to cover all the phenomena of internal adaptation. One of the fundamental problems of a science of culture or of human society is therefore the problem of the nature of social integration. This problem can only be approached by the study of a number of different cultures from this specific point of view, by an intensive investigation of each culture as an adaptive and integrative mechanism and a comparison one with another of as many variant types as possible.

The discovery of the integrative function of an institution, usage, or belief is to be made through the observation of its effects, and these are obviously in the first place effects on individuals, or their life, their thoughts, their emotions. Not all such effects are significant, or at least equally so. Nor is it the immediate effects with which we are finally concerned, but the more remote effects upon the social cohesion and continuity. (pp. ix, x)

The point, which echoes Goldenweiser's distinction between psychological and objective convergence, is stated clearly by Radcliffe-Brown himself: "Thus 'meaning' and 'function' are two different but related things" (p. x). Implicitly, he is also suggesting that the integration of society as such refers to the latter (which is based on comparative analysis by the outside observer) and not the former (which is based on the mental categories of the native), and this is the point he tried to make in the text itself.

In the roughly concurrent article "The Sociological Theory of Totemism" (1929, in 1952), the idea of function in this sense was extended to account for the "ritual attitude" associated with totem rituals—in place of Durkheim's concept of "the sacred." In the 1939 article "Taboo," function was further used to explain both "ritual value" and the "ritual objects." Ritual objects were any objects represented in ritual, from health to animal species. Values, positive and negative, were equated with interests in the objects. Rituals were seen to harmonize those interests, and thereby to create an ordered system of interpersonal relations. Radcliffe-Brown's arguments are obscured by many side issues and incomplete discussions. Not the least of these is the favorable invocation of R. B. Perry's *General Theory of Value* (1926), and adaptation of Perry's terminology, without commenting on Perry's clear declaration that such harmonization was created only by individuals acting reflectively, not by "society" as an extra-individual entity and certainly not by rituals as such. Nevertheless, despite the contradictions and obscurity, it is quite clear that Radcliffe-Brown intended "function" to explain at least part of what is ordinarily called the "meaning" of rituals, conveying specific attitudes and ideas.

Function was one half of Radcliffe-Brown's major theoretical explanatory conception. "Structure" was the other—the entity that it was the "function" of each ritual, institution, and concept to preserve. Structure, like function, was purely an analytic construct. Accordingly, it was no fault in terms of his assumptions that Radcliffe-Brown never actually described a complete structure for any specific society. What was important was that he provide a justification for the construct in terms of general principles. The main arguments are in "On Social Structure" (1940, republished in 1952) and in the Introduction to *Structure and Function in Primitive Society* (1952). The latter arguments, though they come a bit late in the period, are the clearer and easier to use to illustrate the position.

The Introduction begins with the remark that the essays have "a measure of unity as being written from a particular theoretical point of view." The second paragraph then defines "theory" in an elaboration of the earlier idea of an "hypothesis": "What is meant by a theory is a scheme of integration which is applied, or is thought to be applicable, to the understanding of phenomena of a certain class. A theory consists in a set of analytical concepts which should be clearly defined in their reference to concrete reality, and which should be logically connected" (1952:1). Accordingly, the rest of the Introduction is written as a set of "definitions" of the "terms" Radcliffe-Brown regards as his theory.

The first terms are paired—"History and Theory"—and both reflect and codify a set of issues widely discussed in the 1930s and '40s. He proposes to "explain the difference between historical study of social institutions and the theoretical study" of them "by using the recognized terms of logic and methodology and distinguishing between *idiographic* and *nomothetic* inquiries" (p. 1): "In an idiographic inquiry the purpose is to establish as acceptable certain particular factual propositions or statements. A nomothetic inquiry, on the contrary, has for its purpose to arrive at acceptable general propositions" (p. 1). This application of the general versus particular dichotomy had first been used (and quickly repudiated) by the neo-Kantian historian-philosopher Wilhelm Windelband in 1894, arguing to protect history from evolutionary "scientific" demands, and he in turn evidently obtained the concepts, but not the terms, from Schopenhauer (Collingwood 1946:166–67).

By verbal substitution, but no real argument, Radcliffe-Brown then identified theoretical understanding with nomothetic understanding, and both historical studies and descriptive ethnography with idiographic. He concluded with a new and influential dichotomy: "Comparative sociology, of which social anthropology is a branch, is here conceived as a theoretical or nomothetic study of which the aim is to provide acceptable generalization. The theoretical understanding of a particular institution is its interpretation in the light of such generalizations" (1952:3). History, by implication, is not a part of comparative sociology, and theory cannot pertain to history.

This radical split between history and theory is an indirect but logical consequence of rejecting Durkheim's mentalistic orientation. Although Durkheim did not make an explicit point of saying so, his view of society as a mental object was precisely what enabled him to see it as both organic and as evolving and dividing in time, because there is ground for seeing ideas themselves as "timeless," existing without an inherent time dimension. But when Radcliffe-Brown slipped over from Durkheim's view of the units of society as mental objects to the idea that social relations were "concrete" objects (a word he uses often), time became an inherent and inflexible dimension of the analysis because it is a dimension of such units. With this shift, organic unity could not be reconciled with historical integrity, and this is what required Radcliffe-Brown's theoretical distinction. But the distinction in turn further obscured the possibility of saying what data were to be involved in social analysis—for it is as difficult to find data lacking a time dimension as it is to find informants' conversations or social relations that exist apart from "meanings." The difficulty is elaborated, but hardly resolved, in what follows: "A first question that must be asked if we are to formulate a systematic theory of comparative sociology is: What is the concrete, observable, phenomenal reality with which the theory is to be concerned" (p. 3). His answer is: "that the concrete reality with which the social anthropologist is concerned in observation, description, comparison, and classification, is not any sort of entity but a process, the process of social life. The unit of investigation is the social life of some particular region of the earth during a certain period of time" (p. 4).

The sense this conveys is consonant with his earlier image of an organism's "external" adaptation to its environment, but it sets the impossible problem of distinguishing between "history" and a "period of time." He continues after emphasizing the complexity of the process:

> Amidst the diversity of the particular events there are discoverable regularities, so that it is possible to give statements or descriptions of certain *general features* of social life of the selected region. A statement of such significant general features . . . constitutes a description of what may be called a *form*

of social life. My conception of social anthropology is as the comparative theoretical study of forms of social life amongst primitive peoples. (p. 4)

This removes theory, and comparison as well, yet another step from data, interposing "form" (the analyst's form) between that which is observable (insofar as "process" in this sense is observable) and theory itself.

Radcliffe-Brown continues that in the context of this overall system, "culture and cultural tradition are names for certain recognizable aspects of the social process." Social systems such as kinship systems are things which "in a given society we can isolate conceptually, if not in reality"; they are "a certain set of actions and interactions amongst persons which are determined by the relationships by kinship or marriage, and that in any particular society . . . are connected in such a way that we can give a general analytical description of them as constituting a system" (p. 6). Note that he does not give an independent definition of "relationships of kinship and marriage." They are to be defined by the analyst in his "theory," as is the "system" they "constitute."

The definitions of forms of both social life and social systems present important paradoxes—in fact, two-way paradoxes—that are further aspects of the transformed solipsism that many anthropologists were to be unable to escape for at least the next twenty-five years. The first paradox is that what is supposed to be only the product of the observation and classification for theoretical study of the analyst is learned and passed on by natives; and that such pure analytic entities, defined only as "aspects" or general tendencies discernible in the process under study in a region, nevertheless "determine" actions and interactions. In addition to the problem of locating the information that would conform to such a formulation—the problem of determining what observable data would be pertinent—there is the problem of explaining how native behavior can be influenced by matters that the natives are not conscious of in any way at all. It makes a muddle not only of the relationship between data and theory, but also of the relationships between motivation and action, prediction and behavior, and the whole problem of assessing choice and communication in human communities.

A final point deserves special stress, although it is implicit in what has already been said. In "On Social Structure" Radcliffe-Brown had repeated Durkheim's claim that every person had a dual nature, social and biological. This was restated yet again in the Introduction: "The components of units of social structure are persons, and a person is a human being considered not as an organism but as occupying a position in a social structure'' (pp. 9–10). This further complicates all the problems of validation, data selection, and prediction previously pointed out. It makes even the individual person recognizable only as a product of social structural analysis and bids us to ignore from the start two of the most obvious facts of human existence—the biological integrity of individuals and the interplay within them of multiple goals, desires, and roles.

These formulations allowed Radcliffe-Brown to reject evolution—and race if that was still necessary—while adopting Durkheim's basic, and historically important, fourfold concept of society as 1) a theoretical entity that 2) contained individuals as its parts in some way and 3) determined their action, while 4) moving by its own laws. At the same time, and equally basically, he retained the paradoxical but popular idea that the general model of society he proposed was at once the equivalent of "natural law" in the natural sciences, and an entity whose existence had yet to be proved—an abstract logical schema to be filled out in use in the interpretation of ethnographic data. But the modifications also carried forward the methodological solipsism that goes directly back through Comte to Hegel. There are still no methods apart from interpretation, and no recognizable criteria for deciding what is to be investigated apart from the model to be established.

Conclusion

In practice, Radcliffe-Brown's scheme had led him to seek to explain certain mother's-brother kinship relations as "extensions" in some mechanical way of behaviors associated with nuclear family relationships (1924, in 1952:25, 26), joking relationships as determined by "conjunctive and disjunctive components" (1949, in 1952:110, 111), and kinship systems as structured by relationships of kinship and affinity (1941, in 1952:51). As explanations, these are no more satisfying than the "soporific principle" that explained why opium worked, in the example Comte used to ridicule metaphysics. They are also of the same order as Lowie's "diffusion," "culture," and "contact metamorphosis." They are reifications, and the mechanism that produces them is the assumption that an analytic principle of classification can determine phenomena. The assumption demands reification, and provides no safeguard against it, for reification is nothing more than attributing real force to an arbitrary concept made up for convenience.

There are three obvious historical reasons for the rapid and almost universal adoption of Radcliffe-Brown's position in the 1940s. The first, which cannot be dealt with here, is that he spoke for a broad movement cross-cutting many disciplines, promising much, that many took very seriously. The second is his own special articulateness in speaking for this movement in ways that seemed convincing, and the third is that every basic point he made was consistent with what was already believed, but had not been fully articulated. His position fit closely, as suggested already, with Lowie's own type of deterministic and comparative formulations that preserved basic assumptions of evolutionary anthropology and, more strongly, sociology, without the chronological presumptions that had proved to be unwarranted. The problems of function and comparison restated, and in that sense co-opted, Goldenweiser's conception of the problems of identifying a cultural form. Radcliffe-Brown "led" where others were already going as part of a reaction against evolution that was itself conditioned by ideas of determinism and of method-as-interpretation that certain evolutionists—notably Spencer, Comte, Tylor, and Durkheim—had themselves developed.

10.
Foundations of the Modern Monistic Tradition

The Organic Individual

While mutual criticisms among those who accepted dualistic assumptions were often forcefully phrased, criticism from those who rejected such assumptions was more fundamental—and more difficult to assimilate. The two principal proponents of the monistic alternative to the dualistic assumptions of the positivists, of Radcliffe-Brown's functionalism and of diffusionism (as an ''ism''), were Bronislaw Malinowski and Franz Boas. Boas and Malinowski were strongly influenced by Wundt, and the monistic tradition more generally. Both had close ties with the pragmatic philosophy of William James, John Dewey, and G. H. Mead, and its related psychological theories. Boas in addition tied himself directly to Kant. Their views of human nature and human mentality were as a consequence rather more similar than their surface arguments suggested, as will be described at some length. (Malinowski evidently accepted the common view that Boas was a diffusionist, along with Lowie, Wissler, and the rest, and appears not to have looked at Boas' own work very closely.) In addition, both avoided deductive frameworks in argument, and concentrated instead on developing a sense of a replicable experiment or demonstration that others could follow in practice. For Malinowski, the experiment lay in tracking down information in its natural context, and the task of the ethnographic description was to represent faithfully the circumstances under which the information was obtained. Boas took the comparative method of monistic philology as his model, and in consequence constructed a more complex literature consisting of a graded series of materials, from highly circumstantial field interview records (or material collections) to increasingly general and abstract historical and comparative analyses— often seeking general aspects of the development of human mentality as it was embodied in cultural symbols and artifacts.

At the heart of the theory, method, and practice of both Malinowski and Boas was a concept of the focus of analysis as being not an organic society or culture, or any theoretical abstraction of the analyst, but the organic individual—actual living human beings, quite like the analyst, in all their complexity, as they are found in the world. Further, their interest in the individual lay not in developing universal substantive typologies of behavior or relations so much as general understandings of the processes through which order in thought and behavior is generated. For Malinowski, this centered on the idea of individuals using conventional symbols and concepts to define and order ''needs''; for Boas the generative basis of culture lay in something like Bastian's ''elementary ideas.''

Bronislaw Malinowski and Pragmatism

Bronislaw Malinowski (1884–1942) was born in Kraków, Poland. He took a Ph.D. in mathematics and physics there in 1908, but was (reportedly) prevented from going on in this area because of ill health. He enrolled at the University of Leipzig from 1908 to 1910, and in this period, much of it devoted to recuperation, he came across and read Sir James Frazer's *The Golden Bough* (Richards 1943:1). This, he later wrote on several occasions, was a turning point in his life and interests. In 1910, he entered the London School of Economics to study anthropology, and continued until 1914, working under the guidance and influence of Frazer (who was at Oxford), and, especially, of C. G. Seligman (see Richards, p. 1; Firth 1957:3) and Edward Westermark (Firth, p. 5). He also associated closely with Leonard Hobhouse and W. H. R. Rivers.

In 1914, Malinowski left for the South Pacific with fellowship support, obtained largely through Seligman, from both the London School of Economics and the University of London. While there, England and

Poland became involved in hostilities in the First World War, and Malinowski technically became an enemy alien. He was, accordingly, interned for the duration in the field, where he remained, with the support of the government of Australia (in part), until the war ended (Kardiner and Preble 1961:163). He had met Radcliffe-Brown on the way to Australia, where he and others were to attend the meetings of the British Association at Melbourne that year (see Firth 1957:3 for a fuller account). He left the Trobriands in October of 1918 to return to Melbourne, where he met and married Elsie Masson, the daughter of a Professor of Chemistry at Melbourne University. After a few years in Melbourne and the Canary Islands, he returned to England and took the post of occasional lecturer at the London School of Economics in 1921–22. In 1924 he was appointed to a Readership in Social Anthropology at the University of London, and in 1927 this position developed into the first professorial chair in anthropology at that university, a position which he held until 1939.

Malinowski and Radcliffe-Brown are often discussed together. There is in fact an extensive, if scattered, literature comparing their views on almost every conceivable topic in social anthropology. The comparisons indicate a shared interest in social theory, conceived with an emphasis on seeing social facts in their social and "functional" contexts, a common dissatisfaction with evolutionary schemes as well as with diffusionism, and a common responsiveness to many of their mutual associates. But despite the similarities, there are two obvious and clear points of difference. The first and most pervasive is that Malinowski forcefully and explicitly retained the idea that the organic human being was inseparable from the social actor, and social theory had to be constructed accordingly. "Function" for Malinowski, as opposed to Radcliffe-Brown, involved the relation of the institution or object to the people who used or were in it. With this was a persistent interest in such straightforward social-psychological questions as "whether the primitive mind differs from our own or is essentially similar; whether the savage lives constantly in a world of supernatural powers and perils, or on the contrary, has his lucid intervals as often as any one of us; whether clan solidarity is such an overwhelming and universal force, or whether the heathen can be as self-seeking and self-interested as any Christian." (From the Preface to *Crime and Custom in Savage Society,* 1926 [1959:ix].)

The second major point, related to the first in practice, is that Malinowski did not share Radcliffe-Brown's views of theory as a set of logically integrated statements into which data could be classified, that is, a hypothetical descriptive schema. His view was that explanation, rather than classification, was the goal of inquiries, and that it was to be obtained by control of field observations of individuals in relation to their social settings. The purpose of a monographic description was to arrange the observations in such a way as to indicate clearly the procedures by which they could be obtained. These themes were reflected systematically in every one of his major publications.

Malinowski's first and most direct treatment of psychological issues was in *Sex and Repression in Savage Society,* which is, in part, an inquiry into the utility of Freud's idea of the Oedipus complex, which Malinowski sees as "essentially a theory of the influence of a family life on the human mind" (p. 2). But he interprets Freud's theory by reference to the quite different conception of human psychology of Alexander F. Shand, especially to Shand's idea of "sentiments." Sentiments were institutionalized aspects of "character," which was itself seen as composed of emotional-behavioral drives organized into systems and subsystems on the model of physiological complexes. Shand argued for the existence of a rather long list of "instincts," from "flight" to "characteristic modes" of exercise, as the "primary emotions" out of which the "greater systems" were constructed (Shand 1914:28). His acknowledged historical lineage combined a bit of James with British associationism, from Mill to Galton. He shows no systematic interest either in the physiological or communicative orientations of Wundt, although there is a resemblance in the concepts of emotions as such.

In addition to Shand, Malinowski discusses "animal psychology" and acknowledges debts to a mixture of British psychologists, Americans associated with "functional psychology" at Columbia and Chicago, and the closely related gestalt tradition. Here, a persistent interest in the problems of Wundt is clear, but the connection is indirect. Attributions include "Lloyd Morgan" and "Thorndike," as well as "Herrick" and "Köhler," among others (p. xi). Morgan and Thorndike are unquestionably C. Lloyd Morgan (1852–1936) and E. L. Thorndike (1874–1949), two of the founders of what is called "comparative psychology." Broadly speaking, these men were oriented toward studying what was called the "mental evolution" of man, and did so by trying to base theory of mentality on a theory of "instinct" and physiological function of the organism. Herrick in this connection must be the anatomist Charles Judson Herrick (b. 1895), who was then at the University of Chicago, and engaged in what was called "comparative neurology" oriented in the same general direction as the work of Thorndike and Morgan. Köhler is, of course, the gestaltist (Wolfgang Köhler,

1887–1967), who had just published the *Mentality of Apes* (1925) based on studies of learning among chimpanzees, that built upon Wundt's initial concept of the emergence of intelligence in concentration. Köhler had been a student of Carl Stumpf at Frankfort, and Stumpf in turn was one of the most important figures in German experimental psychology apart from Wundt (with whom he engaged in some bitter arguments).

Malinowski prefaces the first section of his argument with a long quotation from John Dewey's *Human Nature and Conduct* concerning the way "social conditions" have "educated original activities" (instincts). Malinowski refers again to Dewey when he discusses and rejects the "group mind" idea he finds in Freud—along with Durkheim's views, which, he believes, verge upon Freud's (p. 157). Malinowski describes Dewey's approach as an alternative, which he accepted (see especially p. 157, fn.). At this stage in his thinking, Malinowski appears to have envisioned the development of social mentality on the basis of individual problem-solving behavior, a view that closely corresponded to the contemporary work of G. H. Mead. Later, following developments in psychology, Malinowski moved toward his better understood theory of "needs." It is significant that Malinowski first began using the term "functionalism" (much before Radcliffe-Brown) after it had come to name one aspect of this developing psychological tradition, closely related to the work of Thorndike and others. William James's influence on Thorndike, as well as on Dewey, was directly acknowledged and widely known.

Sex and Repression deals with the same substantive problem as Radcliffe-Brown's "The Mother's Brother in South Africa," published three years before—the relation of the mother's brother to sister's son in certain societies with matrilineal descent, in contrast to similar relations in our own societies. Radcliffe-Brown's arguments had been based on Morgan's idea that people classed together terminologically had similar juridical properties, and that therefore this relation to mother's brother was an "extension" of the relation to mother. Malinowski's counterpositions were developed, however, in the context of a larger attack on Freud's conception of the origin of the incest taboo (in *Totem and Taboo*). One major point was that the "repressed part of a man's attitude toward a person" cannot be cut off and "treated separately from nonrepressed elements" (p. 174). For Malinowski, following Shand, "the various emotions which constitute the attitude towards a person are so closely connected and intertwined that they form a closely knit organic indissoluble system" (p. 174). And further: "The attitudes or sentiments towards father, mother, sister and brother do not grow up isolated, detached from one another. The organic, indissoluble unit of the family welds also the psychological sentiments towards its members into one connected system'' (1927:178). On this basis, Malinowski argues that the truly general pattern of relations organized around the incest prohibition was not the Oedipus complex but the ''nuclear family complex.''

With this concept of a system of sentiments corresponding to a basic pattern of social organization, he proceeded to reconstruct Freud's analysis of the origin of incest without Freud's concept of a primal traumatic event and without the concept of a ''collective unconscious'' that preserved the memory of that event. He referred instead to learning, habit formation and memory through life, and a need for organization at an individual level. The interesting and rather subtle argument was based on the ''plasticity of instincts'' progressively modified and expanded through training emotions and creating patterns of sentiments wherein such expansion was controlled by a kind of principle of internal order or balance, rather like what is currently designated with the phrase ''cognitive dissonance.'' (Here again the ideas of Shand played a major role.) He applied this developmental model in two units, separating the explanation of incest from the explanation of male authority. A concept of incest, he argued, does not arise from a concern for the child so much as for the near-adult male who begins courting, seeking a mate on his own. At this point, some aspects of previously cultivated affections for the mother have to be repressed to avoid confusion of new emotions with old, and new social roles with old: to permit ordered separation of sentiments and relations, and, thereby, ordered creation of new families beside old ones.

> In any type of civilization in which custom, morals, and law would allow incest, the family could not continue to exist. At maturity, we would witness the breaking up of the family, hence complete social chaos and an impossibility of continuing cultural tradition. Incest would mean the upsetting of age distinctions, the mixing up of generations, the disorganization of sentiments and a violent exchange of roles at a time when the family is the most important educational medium. No society could exist under such conditions. The alternative type of culture under which incest is excluded, is the only one consistent with the existence of social organization and culture. (p. 251)

His treatment of the male role was similar, arguing that at different times, an adult male must exercise different roles—protector and helper of the mother when the infant is being gestated and then is nursing, and authority figure when the child is being introduced to the necessary lore and the obligations and responsibilities of the community. Malinowski sees it as a matter of choice whether both these functions are combined in one person or separated in two. Both possibilities can produce viable orderly systems of roles and sentiments, but each fits more reasonably with a certain set of rules of inheritance and group membership. The co-occurrence of both male roles in father is most efficient or harmonious if inheritance is through the father. The separation of roles is most harmonious if the inheritance is from the mother. In the latter case, the reasoning is that the group the child will belong to is the one that will have to control his instruction, and that if this is not the father's group it would be easiest and most orderly not to have the father exercise authority at all, but rather to adhere only to the role of protector and supporter of both mother and child.

This explanation could hardly differ more from Radcliffe-Brown's, which had provided no reasoned cognitive or psychological underpinnings, no recourse to concepts of purpose or learning, and no overriding principles such as the division of labor by sex outside the family context.

In "The Epistemological Background to Malinowski's Empiricism," E. R. Leach has argued flatly for the influence of William James—partly on the basis of his own personal knowledge of Malinowski and partly on textual grounds. He also says that Malinowski met and studied under Wundt, but he observes that Malinowski rejected the "group-mind" implications of Wundt's historical theories, although he "approved of Wundt's empiricism" (Firth 1957:121). There can be no doubt that this latter point is correct, although the former point misstates Wundt's position, as previously noted. It should be clear that in broad outlines the present analysis agrees with Leach, although the influences appear to derive at least as much—probably more—from the successors of James and Wundt than from the two men directly, and apparently Malinowski's pragmatism developed rather later in life than earlier. It is certainly clearest and most thoroughly worked out in his later works, notably in *A Scientific Theory of Culture and Other Essays,* published posthumously in 1944, and evidently never completed to Malinowski's satisfaction. It contained Malinowski's well-known and not very successful theory of "needs" as a basis for social analysis, and especially for cross-cultural comparison. But at a more fundamental level, it involves a major reworking of cultural theory, relying on concepts and terms from the pragmatic tradition, as Radcliffe-Brown relied on concepts and terms from positivism.

The points where Malinowski uses the word "pragmatism" itself in these essays are critical to the difference between his position and Radcliffe-Brown's, and his usages are correct in terms of the technical literature of the pragmatists themselves. One important example is his discussion of the empirical status of ideas and other "psychological" objects. He begins by endorsing the pragmatically stimulated "behaviorism" of Clark L. Hull and others, following then-current theoretical usages, wherein descriptive behaviorism (as opposed to the "atheoretical" and materialistic behaviorism of B. F. Skinner) had replaced the earlier "functional" psychology of James and Dewey, generally retaining a concern with learning, motivation, and biologically-based "needs." Note especially the way the terms "behavior," "function," and "pragmatic" are interrelated:

> The problem as to whether we do or do not admit the existence of "consciousness," "spiritual realities," "thoughts," "ideas," "beliefs," and "values" as subjective realities in other people's minds, is essentially metaphysical. I still see no reason why such expressions referring directly to my own experience should not be introduced, provided that in each case they are fully defined in terms of overt, observable, physically ascertainable behavior. Indeed, the whole theory of symbolism which will be briefly outlined here, consists in the definition of a symbol or idea as something which can be physically recorded, described, or defined. Ideas, thoughts, and emotions have to be treated with all the other aspects of culture, both functionally and formally. The functional approach allows us to determine the pragmatic context of a symbol and to prove that in cultural reality a verbal and other symbolic act becomes real only through the effect which it produces. The formal approach is the basis for our conviction and proof thereof, that in sociological or ethnographic fieldwork it is possible to define the ideas, the beliefs, the emotional crystallizations of a completely different culture with a high degree of precision and objectivity. (1944:23–24)

Among other things, this argument is very close to being a paraphrase of Wundt's description of experimentation in experimental psychology: "that it makes an exact introspection possible"—in the introduction to his *Principles* (1904:11).

A second major use of the term "pragmatism," also associated with learning, motivation, and behavior, occurs in Malinowski's treatment of knowledge itself, which is closely related to his concept of science:

> . . . I think that we will have to admit that from the beginning of culture its transmission by means of symbolically framed general principles was a necessity. Knowledge, partly embodied in manual skills, but also formulated and centered in certain principles and definitions referring to material technological processes, has, too, an early pragmatic or instrumental causality, a

factor which could not be absent even in the earliest cultural manifestations (1944:173).

The historical process that these references reflect is complex. Although each of the men Malinowski names reflects influences other than that of James and Dewey—for example Hull's interest in positivisim—the way in which Malinowski selects and combines them, and applies their ideas, reemphasizes their pragmatic aspects to the exclusion of other orientations. Malinowski's theory of needs was one attempt among many to put the pragmatic conceptions of behavior-as-adaption on a more "scientific" footing.

We should remember that by the 1930s and '40s James and Wundt themselves were hardly news, and Malinowski was always fashionable in his explicit references and choice of issues, which makes Boas' position, formed much earlier, the more interesting.

Franz Boas and George Herbert Mead: The Linkages

The modern philosophical context of Franz Boas is basically the same as that of Malinowski: experimental psychology and philosophical pragmatism. However, where Malinowski drew mainly from these traditions, Boas drew directly from Kant and Wundt and contributed to pragmatism. And where Malinowski's pragmatism most closely resembles James's in its individualism, Boas' has its closest parallels in the more interactional pragmatisms of Dewey and, especially, G. H. Mead. Direct relations between Boas and Mead are less conspicuous than indirect ones. Together the two men define almost a single intellectual position, which was evidently recognized by numerous scholars who followed them both, and who moved between them.

Mead was a mainstay of "Chicago pragmatism," and was the major pragmatic philosopher most directly concerned with social-psychological theory as such. He went to Chicago in 1896 and remained until he died in 1931, whereupon the "school" of Chicago pragmatism rapidly dissolved.

Among the personal links between Boas and Mead, the most prominent was John Dewey himself. In 1904 Dewey left Chicago for Columbia, where he remained and where, apparently, he associated with Boas. Dewey evidently agreed with Boas' psychology—see, for example, the references to Boas' *The Mind of Primitive Man* in *Experience and Nature* (1926:168, 211n.). At the same time, Dewey maintained close working relations with Mead and Chicago.

In addition to Dewey, particular mention should be made of W. I. Thomas and Ellsworth Faris, both of whom were influential in the Chicago school and eventually had roles in the early history of anthropology there. Thomas' connections to Mead and Boas were explicit and far-reaching, although superficial in the sense that his deepest sympathy lay not with Boas, but with social evolutionism, as will be described in connection with Redfield below. He took his degree at Chicago in sociology in 1896, but came to claim special indebtedness both to Mead and Dewey in philosophy, and to Boas (as reported by his student and colleague Robert Burgess [see Rucker 1969:135]). Thomas taught at Chicago in ranks from instructor to professor from 1894 to 1918, then held a number of posts at different institutions in the northeast, including the New School for Social Research and Harvard University. He wrote on various aspects of the evolution of society in the mode of social Darwinism represented by W. G. Sumner, but he tempered it with recognition of diffusion and relied heavily on data from the ethnological diffusionists associated with Boas in so doing, mainly Wissler, Lowie, Kroeber, Dixon, Goldenweiser, and Herskovitz. At the same time he elaborated (and reified) the pragmatic ideas of practical action into four definite categories of goals or motivations, sometimes called the four universal "wishes." (This line of interpretation leads toward Talcott Parsons' universal "need dispositions," and enabled Parsons to adapt many of Mead's terms and ideas to a thoroughly dualistic set of fundamental assumptions, thus encouraging the belief that pragmatism and positivism had been closely related at the outset.)

Ellsworth Faris was in more fundamental sympathy with Boas as distinct from the diffusionists, and he made his view of relationships between Boas and Mead more tangible than Thomas had. Faris took his doctorate in psychology at Chicago in 1914, and was "an avowed follower of Mead" (Rucker:136, see also Faris 1967:32–33). He succeeded Albion Small as head of the Department of Sociology at Chicago in 1925, and was involved in the appointments to the department of Edward Sapir (1925), Fay-Cooper Cole (1924), and Robert Redfield (1927). Sapir and Cole were Redfield's seniors at the time, and both had been trained at least in part by Boas. While Sapir was at Chicago, he was an extremely popular undergraduate lecturer, and acknowledged as one of the leading figures on the campus (personal communication from Harry Hoijer). He also, reportedly, like Faris among others, directed his students to Mead, just as Mead did the reverse. At Columbia there apparently were similar interactions between pragmatism and Boas' anthropology involving students and colleagues of Dewey, although these relations are less well documented.

Franz Boas

As has already been suggested, Boas came of the same intellectual background as pragmatism, and especially as the pragmatism of Mead. Boas had attended school through Gymnasium in Minden, Westphalia. He spent four years at the Universities of Heidelberg, Bonn, and finally Kiel, where he obtained the Ph.D. under Theobald Fischer in 1881. His dissertation was titled *Contributions to the Perception of the Color of Water (Beiträge zur Erkenntniss der Farbe des Wassers)*.

Boas spent the year after receiving his doctorate in the army in the reserve officer training program, and in 1883 he travelled to Baffin Island for a field study of Eskimos and Eskimo society (see Stocking 1968:140). It was on the way back from this trip that he first visited the United States (Kardiner and Preble 1961:137). On his return to Germany he became an assistant in Bastian's Museum für Völkerkunde.

The relation of Boas' field trip to his earlier work has become a matter of some historical dispute. Those who have argued that Boas did not bring his earlier training to anthropology, and that he was essentially an atheoretical gatherer of facts who stressed painstaking care in the field, have construed his field work as representing a radical break with the past. For example, Lowie calls the field trip "a decisive factor in determining Boas' lifework" (1937:129). Kardiner and Preble use almost the same words in their description, after first making the even stronger remark that "in 1883, he began his anthropological career with a trip to Baffinland; . . ." (p. 137). Both descriptions (and these are not the only ones) suggest that the subsequent appointment at the Museum was a consequence of the trip to Baffin Island, the first step in the new career, and not part of an ongoing development of a train of thought in an established tradition.

George Stocking, in his essay "From Physics to Ethnology" (in 1968:133–60), presents a quite different view, based on much fuller evidence:

there was no sharp break, no conversion experience, no sudden realization of "the significance of culture". On the contrary, his viewpoint developed slowly out of his family background, his work in physics and psychophysics, his geographical interests, his contact with the German Romantic idealist and historicist traditions, and his work with Bastian, all in the context of his field experience. In short, it flowed from his total life experience. (1968:157)

More specifically, Stocking argues that Boas' initial dissertation on the perception of color led him to the problem of minimal perceivable differences in colors in general, which in turn involved him in Gustav Fechner's psychophysics—that focused on "just noticeable differences" as the basis of what was intended to be an experimental resolution of the mind-body problem. Psychophysics, and especially his realization that some parameters influencing perception are not physiological but situational (Stocking:142), in turn led him to larger problems of perception and these in turn involved him in the geography of Karl Ritter. In a solidly Kantian frame of reference (beginning immediately in Humbolt and actually going back directly to Montesquieu), Ritter had considered geography to be "man centered," and had insisted that geographical provinces could not be defined absolutely but only relative to the perceptions of those people who lived in the area, with the significant features being subject to changes as these human populations themselves developed and changed. This set of ideas, which was already very close to the ethnology of Bastian, provided the framework for the trip to Baffin Island, as Stocking makes clear with a number of excerpts from letters written by Boas at the time. A portion of one, written in 1882 (before the expedition), will illustrate the point:

The objectives of my studies shifted quite a bit during my university years . . . In the course of time I became convinced that my previous materialistic *Weltanschauung*—for a physicist a very understandable one—was untenable, and I gained thus a new standpoint which revealed to me the importance of studying the interaction between the organic and the inorganic, above all between the life of people and their physical environment. Thus arose my plan to regard as my life's task the [following] investigation: how far may we consider the phenomena of organic life, and especially those of the psychic life, from a mechanistic point of view, and what conclusions can be drawn from such a consideration? . . . I have for the present given up psychophysical work as there was no time to make experiments during my military training . . . At present I am studying the dependence of the migration of the present-day eskimo on the configuration and physical condition of the land. . . . (Stocking 1968:138–39)

It is especially important to note in this letter that "the interaction between organic and inorganic" is not thought of as the interaction between mind and body. "Organic life" *includes* "psychic life." "Inorganic" means non-animate "physical" nature. The perspective is thus akin to Bastian's and Wundt's, and does not involve a mind-body dualism. In addition, the stated aim to "see how far may we consider the phenomena . . . of psychic life from a mechanistic point of view" must be taken strictly literally. The aim was to "see how far," and assess the value of such consideration; it was not to go ahead and consider these phenomena from this viewpoint only. There was no sense of reductionism, but rather of putting the mechanistic considerations in a larger context. That larger context, as other letters indicate, was "history," specifically the historical development of a social psychological perspective of the sort that had been of interest to the tradition going back to Montesqueiu. History encompassed the results of an indefinite series of past creative acts, arranged in what we would now call a stochastic sequence. Each act was only partially constrained by what went before, and only partly constrains what follows, so that the whole is in a Kantian sense the legacy of the progressive development of creative human thought. In this context, Boas' project was to assess the relative weight of free choice as against necessary response to immediate physical circumstance, and it was evidently precisely the result of his consideration that led him to shift from geography to ethnology. In doing so, he directly replicated the original course of Bastian's reasoning for the independence of the two fields—which had, as noted, also begun with an invocation of Fechner (Bastian 1860:Preface).

Boas completed his military service on October 1, 1881, and went to Berlin (Stocking 1968:139). At the time the quoted letter was written, he was actively associated with several important Kantian scholars in an important revival of interest in Kant's thinking (as opposed to the idealism, often called neo-Kantianism, that had often been passed off in Kant's name in the mid-century period). Among the scholars were Bastian and Virchoff, as well as the historian Dilthey, to whom he refers often, and Benno Erdmann, who published editions of the *Critique* and *Prolegomena* and compiled *Kant's Reflections on Anthropology* (*Reflexionen Kants zur Anthropology*, 1882), based on Kant's handwritten manuscripts used in his courses before 1752, among other works, by the time Boas went on his expedition. Erdmann's *Reflexionen* is especially pertinent, for it not only covers much of Kant's earlier thinking in social psychology and national character, but in the introduction Erdmann also describes the general development of Kant's anthropological thinking, including his projections for a "handbook of anthropology," which apparently would have brought together many of Kant's lines of thought. Perhaps it was one of these that Boas was describing when he wrote of spending "long evenings" with a "a copy of Kant . . . which I am studying so that I shall not be so completely uneducated when I return" (Stocking:143). Both Dilthey and Erdmann were especially explicit in articulating the differences between Kant and the idealistic "neo-Kantians" in the tradition of Hegel, including especially Edmund Husserl, and in their rejections of dualism and determinism. In addition to his direct interest in Kant's anthropology, Erdmann shared Dilthey's interest in philosophical history. He also argued for a "psychological" theory of logic—which was opposed by Frege (Bynum 1972:34–36).

To further underline the continuity of Boas' efforts, it should be borne in mind that in the Germany of Boas' time (and now, for that matter), the Ph.D. itself was essentially a library problem, calling for the marshalling of evidence on the basis of existing sources. One's own original research was generally organized and—with support and luck— accomplished after receiving the doctorate. Boas' field project would be a perfectly feasible research project following upon his dissertation in this system. It should be remembered that there were no programs in ethnology as such in Germany when Boas began his work. Once he entered geography (and his thesis under Fischer can as easily be called "physical geography" as "physics"), he was about as close as he could get to anthropology in an institutional sense. When Boas returned from Baffin Island, he reentered this milieu when he became an assistant in Bastian's museum and Docent of Physical Geography at the University of Berlin. His next position, at Clark University in the United States, was to carry the label "anthropology."

Boas' conception of the relationship between geography and ethnology after the Baffin Island trip is represented by two essays: "The Study of Geography," published in *Science* in 1887, and "The Aims of Ethnology," presented as a public lecture in New York in 1888. In the first he argued that "anthropo-geography—the life of man as far as it depends on the country he lives in—is the true domain of geography" (1966:640). He argued that geography in this sense was interested in "understanding," rather than subsuming phenomena under laws, and as such was a historical study.

Boas expected geography to draw upon ethnology and psychology just as it drew upon geology and meteorology. That is, he saw ethnology and geology rather in the same way we now describe the "disciplines," such as social and cultural anthropology, in relation to "area studies.'' It is hard to avoid seeing this conception as an autobiographical statement on Boas' part, as an indication that he saw his own interests as having settled on ethnology as one aspect, one set of problems, that he encountered in geography.

"The Aims of Ethnology'' filled out Boas' conception of ethnology itself: ''. . . the first aim of ethnological inquiry must be critical analysis of the characteristics of each people. This is the only way of attaining a satisfactory understanding of the cultures found in wider areas'' (Boas 1939:629).

Then he describes how this study will yield "laws," and adds a quite clear indication of the way his earlier work in geography appeared to him to be mistaken:

> The frequent occurrence of similar phenomena in cultural areas that have no historical contact suggests that important results may be derived from their study, for it shows that the human mind develops everywhere according to the same laws.
>
> The discovery of these is the greatest aim of our science. To attain it many methods of inquiry and the assistance of many other sciences will be needed. Up to this time the number of investigations is small, but the foundations have been laid by the labors of men like Tylor, Bastian, Morgan and Bachofen . . . As in other new branches of science there is no lack of hasty theorizing that does not contribute to healthy growth. Far-reaching theories have been built on weak foundations. Here belongs the attempt to explain history as determined by the nature of the country in which the people live. A relation between soil and history cannot be denied, but we are not in a position to explain social and mental behavior on this basis and anthropogeographical "laws" are valid only as vague, empty generalities.

Boas had apparently concluded that the answer to "how far we may consider . . . psychic life from a mechanistic point of view'' was not very far, and he took this next, and last, step along the Kantian path he had already started. He came to consider that the immediate environmental influences were both obvious and trivial, inadequate to account for the basic forces that "mold behavior,'' and he turned from this approach as "shallow'' (Stocking:151).

The similarity to Wundt's, as well as Bastian's, reasons for engaging in folk psychology is precise. The resemblance between Boas' conception of "critical analysis" and Grimm's idea of a "critical" method is directly mentioned by Boas, and obviously influenced Boas' own research practices. He refers to the Grimm brothers affirmatively, accepting Grimm's idea that the tales he had collected manifest such psychological traits, rejecting only Grimm's unilinear evolution in favor of a broad framework wherein different levels and types of culture contact had to be seen as influencing later patterns of "customs and traditions" (Boas 1939:625). Since all the customs and traditions that had been brought into the pattern, exemplifying life and culture, had historical depth, there could be no possibility that such analysis would be nonhistorical. But it is equally obvious that Boas is not equating history with explanation, not favoring diffusion as against history, and certainly not rejecting "laws" of science.

Boas discussed the method and expanded his conception of the way one sought the "laws which govern the growth of human culture" in "The Limitations of the Comparative Methods of Anthropology," in 1896 (rpt. in Boas 1939:270–80). The essay begins with something like the idea of "convergence": "Modern anthropology has discovered the fact that human society has grown and developed everywhere in such a manner that its forms, its opinions and its actions have many fundamental traits in common" (Boas 1939:270).

He mentions the fact that some anthropologists consider such similarities as evidence of common historic connections, but then describes the "new school of Bastian and others, including Brinton in this country, who took the alternative view that such similarities were 'results of the uniform working of the human mind' " (p. 270). And finally, "others while not denying the occurrence of historical connections, regard them as insignificant in results and in theoretical importance as compared to the working of the uniform laws governing the human mind" (pp. 270–71). This combined or compromise position he says is the view of "by far the greater number of living anthropologists" (p. 271). He evidently means his own as well.

Twenty-eight years before, Tylor had set aside interest in most common cultural features in order to focus on historical connections. Here Boas is reversing Tylor's emphasis. Ironically, he does so in part by attributing to the authority of Bastian almost exactly the same general remark Tylor had attributed to Samuel Johnson. Boas says: "The modern view is founded on the observation that the same ethnical phenomena occur among the most diverse peoples, or, as Bastian says, on the appalling monotony of the fundamental ideas of mankind all over the globe" (p. 271). As illustration Boas refers to metaphysical ideas, "curious and complex customs," ideas of future life, shamanism, inventions, and certain elementary features of grammatical structure. He then continues: "But discovery of these universal ideas is only the beginning of the work of the anthropologist. Scientific inquiry must answer two questions in regard to them: first, what is their origin? And second, how do they assert themselves in various cultures'' (p. 271).

Remarking that the second question was the easier to deal with, he briefly reviewed various studies that showed different factors affecting variation within or between cultures, ranging from geography to psychological predictions to studies to see why some traits are easier to assimilate than others. Then he turned to the first question:

> Many attempts have been made to discover the causes which have led to the formation of ideas "that develop with iron necessity wherever man lives" . . . They may be indigenous, they may be imported, they may have arisen from a variety of sources, but they are there. The human mind is so formed that it invents them spontaneously or accepts them whenever they are offered to it. This is the much misunderstood elementary idea of Bastian.
>
> To a certain extent a clear enunciation of the elementary idea gives us the psychological reason for its existence. To exemplify: the fact that the land of the shadows is so often placed in the west suggests the endeavor to localize it at the place where the sun and the stars vanish. The mere statement that primitive men consider animals as gifted with all the qualities of man shows that the analogy between many of the qualities of animals and of human beings has led to the generalization that all the qualities of animals are human. . . . (pp. 272, 273)

After several examples he did not consider so obvious, including "totemism" (which he changed his mind about later) and clan organizations, Boas restated his point with some remarks on the way historical study can reveal environmental and psychological factors affecting the "growth of culture." The underlying idea is that history provides an *internal* comparative analysis, which brings out the components of a culture without the difficulties of arbitrary comparisons between unrelated groups:

> A detailed study of customs in their relation to the total culture of the tribe practicing them, in connection with an investigation of their geographical distributions among neighboring tribes, affords almost always a means of determining with considerable accuracy the historical causes that led to the formation of the customs in question and to the psychological processes that were at work in their development. The results of inquiries conducted by this method may be threefold. They may reveal the environmental conditions which have created or modified cultural elements; they may clear up psychological factors which are at work in shaping the culture; or they may bring before our eyes the effects that historical connections have had upon the growth of culture. (p. 276)

For Boas historical explanations stood as complementary to psychology, culture contact, or environmental adaptation. One did not explain a custom in some abstracted world of social forms, but in some community at some point in time, and to argue for any one of these types of explanation one had to take the others into account. Each "explains," ultimately, by using one cultural phenomenon to account for others; and such explanatory phenomena are neither logically related sets of analysts' propositions nor derived in any important sense from the comparative study of "forms" in Durkheim's, the diffusionists', or Radcliffe-Brown's sense. Nor, equally importantly, is the data of the analysis radically separate from the results of analysis. For Boas, the data of psychology are the psychological elements one finds by careful field analysis; the data of historical analysis are the historical orderings one finds in the field, and so forth. One does not collect undifferentiated data, and then later turn it to different problems by applying different verbal categories to it. Boas was no less opposed than Radcliffe-Brown to using short field trips and superficial cultural resemblances as a basis for elaborate conjectural historical reconstructions. But he acted on this objection by advocating and carrying out longer field trips and repeated field trips, as well as utilizing carefully controlled systems of comparative analyses of the field material in a graded series of publications, from a limited analysis of the design of Eskimo needle cases to his broadly comparative *Primitive Art* (1927), that were intended to show the historical processes at work. The publications, as a corpus, clearly laid out both the data selection process and its situational origin as well as all the manipulations Boas used to process it in a form anyone else could replicate. This, obviously, was Boas' implementation of the Kantian notion of the importance of demonstration in the only appropriate form—as a demonstration in its own right.

Since these three essays were all written before diffusion became diffusionism, before Kroeber, Lowie, and Radin took their degrees from Boas and began to speak for him and link him to their movement, before Wissler was associated with him and with them, and before Malinowski and others began to accept the idea that Boas was a diffusionist, perhaps he later changed his views? Boas himself took up on the question and was quite clear about his answer, in a 1936 essay "History and Science in Anthropology: A Reply" (rpt. in Boas 1939:305–15). Boas' primary purpose in the article was to refute Kroeber's "explanation" of his (Boas') conception of history. Boas also took the opportunity to attack the characterization of his position on the same issues that Robert Redfield had included in the "Introduction" to the *Social Anthropology of North American Tribes* (Eggan 1937), which had been written expressly as a "hail and farewell" to Radcliffe-Brown when he left Chicago. Lowie's rather similar interpretation of Boas' works in his *History* had not yet appeared.

After arguing that Kroeber had used the word "history" as if it meant functional analysis of process, Boas rejected the usage as one no historian would agree to. Boas then extended his remarks:

> Robert Redfield, in the introduction to "Social Anthropology of North American Tribes" (Chicago 1937), takes up Kroeber's argument. He accepts Kroeber's definition of history; "a historian is he who confines himself to 'functional' ethnographic accounts—definitions of unique societies, without comparison, but each presented as an organic whole composed of functionally interrelated and integrating organs." Others would call this a good ethnographic description and I do not believe that any historian would accept it as history.

(Evidently this last sentence means that Boas himself would not consider this either good ethnography or good history.) He continues:

> Redfield's criticism of my work is summed up in the words: "he does not write histories, and he does not prepare scientific systems." The latter point agrees fully with my views. The history of any selected group or of mankind—history taken both in the ordinary sense of the term and in the abnormal sense given to it by Kroeber—including biological, and general cultural phenomena, is so complex that all systems that can be devised will be subjective and unrevealing. Classification, which is a necessary element of every system, is misleading, as I tried to illustrate in the discussion of totemism . . . What Kroeber and Redfield call the "history" of a tribe appears to me as a penetrating analysis of an unique culture describing its form, the dynamic reactions of the individual to the culture and of the culture to the individual. It obtains its full meaning only when the historical development of the present form is known. Unfortunately, we are compelled to reconstruct the historical development of the primitive cultures from very inadequate material, but part at least can be inferred. I think that Radcliffe-Brown's indifference to these reconstructions is based on an overestimation of the certainty of documentary history, particularly of history of culture. Some of our results obtained by means of archeological or distributional studies are no less certain than those obtained by documentary history. The difficulties encountered in the attempts to give an adequate picture of the dynamism and integration of culture have often been pointed out. To introduce the analogy between the organism and society—one of the earliest speculative theories—as Radcliffe-Brown seems to do in his emphasis on function—is no help.

Redfield objects to what he calls ambiguity of my methodological approach, that is to say "a reluctance to classify the historical and social anthropological ('scientific') approach.'' This seems to indicate that he considers these approaches as mutually exclusive. An unbiased investigator will utilize every method that can be devised to contribute to the solution of his problem. In my opinion a system of social anthropology and "laws" of cultural development as rigid as those of physics are supposed to be are unattainable in the present stage of our knowledge, and more important than this: on account of the uniqueness of cultural phenomena and their complexity nothing will ever be found that deserves the name of a law excepting those psychological, biologically determined characteristics which are common to all cultures and appear in the multitude of forms according to the particular culture in which they manifest themselves. (p. 311)

Although no detail of this statement is unimportant, note in particular that Boas chides Redfield and the others for empirical ignorance of other fields—history and physics—that they appear to refer to in their arguments regarding the differences between the "laws" and history. Note too that Boas, like Kuhn (and Kant), sees physics itself as dynamic and, in part, consensual. Those he criticizes (whom I think he represents accurately), by contrast, see it as static and fixed, and thus follow the philosophical "empiricists" (positivists) in adopting the necessarily static view of science as generalization from "facts" that are given in experience.

Boas reviews the ways others view him:

The confusion in regard to my own point of view is perhaps largely due to the fact that in my early teaching, when I fought "the old speculative theories," as I am now fighting the new speculative theories based on the imposition of categories derived from our culture upon foreign cultures, I stressed the necessity of the study of acculturation (1895) and dissemination. When I thought that these historical methods were firmly established, I began to stress, about 1910, the problems of cultural dynamics, of integration of culture and of the interaction between individual and society. (pp. 310–11)

By this he obviously means to say that he did not, as Kroeber suggested, forgo history for functional studies, but rather that he had one consistent view all along that included history and cultural dynamics together. He stressed historical aspects of culture at an early time when there was a public focus on such matters, and when it was logical to do so in terms of his own research program. Later, when concerns shifted, he stressed the internal and psychological aspects of culture. But that is all. He did not at any time want to be associated either with the view that the two types of studies could be disassociated from each other, or that one was more "scientific" than the other. Nor, in a larger frame of reference, did he wish to be identified with the ideas Kroeber, Redfield, and Radcliffe-Brown were advancing about the characteristics of a "scientific" theory that cultural theories could conform to. Boas was, by contrast with them, a methodological opportunist, thinking always in terms of field research and seeking methods that worked as part of seeking the phenomena that existed there. Like Malinowski, he felt free to seek what was useful in whatever disciplines existed, or in any new techniques that could be invented.

Although Boas did not restate his early interest in elementary ideas with equal force in his later writing, this early concept is perfectly consistent with his later critiques of the organic position. The "absolute" system of categories for culture for which he criticized Kroeber and Radcliffe-Brown is obviously quite the opposite of his own idea of a generative beginning of culture in individuals that varied as it was developed in particular historical and geographical settings.

Boas' work in physical anthropology and linguistics was consistent with, and helped develop, this core of psychological ideas. His studies of racial form of immigrants does indeed embody what Stocking calls a "critique of racial formalism" (1968:161–94)—that is, a criticism and rejection of the idea that the kind of physical features that Galton and Pearson were concerned with were direct indicators of genetic constitution. His studies came to the overall conclusion that immigrants and their descendants, in the United States, changed form from their national type in a way not predictable from that type alone, but rather in a way that was predictable from that type in relation to United States' norms. That is, they became more like "Americans"—and progressively more like them in proportion to their residential status. Those brought over young were more like the American norms than those who were older when they came, those born and raised in the United States were more like the Unites States' norms than those brought over young. In some cases, Boas noted, the difference between descendants and their exact parent populations was great enough to warrant their being classed in different races by some current standards ("New Evidence in Regard to the Instability of Human Types," 1916; in Boas 1939:77). But while this could imply a kind of *reductio ad absurdum* of the racial studies *per se,* it was not what Boas said in conclusion—he said only that his results showed that one could not understand the effects of "nature" without first studying the obviously greater effects of "nurture" (in "Changes in the Bodily Form of Descendants of Immigrants," 1912; in Boas 1939:74–75). For Boas, it was a demonstration of human physiological plasticity, and plasticity was an important positive feature of human physiology as it was for Wundt and the entire tradition he represented, one that would have, eventually, to be thoroughly understood.

Similarly with linguistics. Boas' paper on systematic "spelling" errors in recording Indian languages was relativistic, as Stocking says (1968:157–58). However, it was not supportive of, or based upon, the idea of a total cultural whole so much as on the idea of differences in sounds that are close to minimal perceivable differences (Fechner's just-noticeable differences), and which thus call for cultural cues to discriminate them.

In the introduction to the *Handbook of American Indian Languages* (1911), Boas argued that people could not be "classified" in the same way by physical type, language, or culture: people who have the same physical type need not have the same language or culture, those with the same language need not have the same culture or physical type, and those with the same culture need not have the same language or physical type. Not only is language separate from race, but also language, specifically spoken language, is distinct from the ideas it conveys and the objects it refers to. "A" culture was not one "thing," so much as a group of people using a number of cultural systems. To argue for seeing things in their contexts is one thing. To argue that all contexts boil down to only one absolute context, and that a total cultural unity, is quite another.

The other differences between Boas and his opponents and interpreters arrange themselves quite neatly around the difference between the analyst's organic model and Boas' conception of the developing native mentality-in-culture. It need hardly be stressed that in referring to Bastian, as to Grimm, Boas was referring to a tradition wherein "Psychology" was highly social. This is even clearer when he links his views of primitive art to Fechner's recognition of the "direct" effect of the "form" of a work of art as well as the force of the ideas associated with it. He also links his views to Wundt, although he criticized Wundt for being "one-sided" in stressing only the ideas and leaving aside form (1927:13–14). Psychology was not only an aspect of individual mentality but at least equally a matter of the social forms of mentality. The tradition focused on emotions and ideas, both conceived as inherently "shared," and bound up with communicative processes. An elementary idea was therefore an element of social process, conception, and communication.

George Herbert Mead

The pragmatic social philosophy of George Herbert Mead is the anti-thesis of positivism, the descendant of Wundt's experimental psychology and the logical complement of Boas' ethnology. Mead was five years younger than Boas and twenty-one years younger than William James, whom he studied under and later worked with on cooperative publications.

Mead's philosophical ideas are preserved chiefly in posthumous publications of his lecture notes, which he had been constantly revising, and in notes taken by his students. They had anticipated that his ideas might otherwise be lost, since he was manifestly not a prolific writer of the sort that Dewey became very early in his career. But the basic conceptions of Mead's system are so often repeated and so closely interwoven with all facets of his interests that there can be no real doubt about what they were.

Mead's central concept, which links his concepts of society and of mind, is often designated "emergent evolutionism," a term that reveals its nineteenth-century roots on its face. What is "emerging" in Mead's scheme is the individual mind of the individual person. He is concerned with how actual individuals, in the course of their individual activity in the context of other human actors similarly acting, evolve for themselves a perception of their own personal "mind" and, at the same time, of a "perceived" world of stable forms that mind is set off against.

Mead takes as his starting point, both for philosophy of science and social theory, the Kantian position that the actual individual is the basis of both social and rational order. In this context, he describes "the problem of society" as the problem of providing for individual order in a social context that was constantly undergoing evolutionary change (in Strauss 1964:20–21). He saw language as an evolutionary device to meet this problem, and "the field of mind" as emerging from language (p. 195). (The time span for this "emergence" was unstated, but his manner of argument suggests he means the process to be seen on a long time-scale for social evolution and a much shorter one as the development of each individual recapitulates the larger process.)

As one aspect of his view of language and of mind, it was Mead's position that "you cannot say anything that is absolutely particular; anything you say that has meaning at all is universal." This position, of course, is completely at variance with that of the logical positivists and other philosophical "empiricists." But his purpose is not merely to disagree. It is, like Boas' purpose in attacking Kroeber's view, to assert an alternative frame of reference. Mead is not saying that all words are "general" rather than "particular," as he would if he accepted the positivists' basic assumptions. Instead, he was saying that they are not "particular," but *shared*. He was recalling Kant's point about the necessary relationship between the "objectivity" and "universality" of a judgment. His point is that language, *as an evolved means of communication,* is inherently both shared and classificatory. When one uses language, "You are saying something that calls out a specific response in anybody else provided that the symbol exists for him in his experience as it does for you" (Strauss:211). It is not hard to see this as the other side of the same coin we encounter in Boas' view that everything cultural is a locus of mind, and of the importance of language as an indispensable tool in its study. Mead goes on:

> Mind, as constructive or reflective or problem-solving thinking, is the socially acquired means or mechanism or apparatus whereby the human individual solves the various problems of environmental adjustment which arise to confront him in the course of his experience and which prevent his conduct from proceeding harmoniously on its way until they have thus been dealt with. (Strauss:268)

But: "The locus of mind is not in the individual. Mental processes are fragments of the complex conduct of the individual in and on his environment" (p. 100).

"Self" and "Society" are entities that appear as aspects of mind, and they are also the basis of actions whereby mind, as conscious problem-solving behavior, perpetuates and orders its activities in a kind of feedback loop, or cycle of reinforcement (Mead's derivation of these concepts from general behavioral psychology is explicit and obvious). And:

> A self can arise only where there is a social process within which this self has had its initiation. It arises within that process. For that process, the communication and participation to which I have referred is essential. (p. 42)

And again:

> After all, what we mean by self-consciousness is an awakening in ourselves of the group of attitudes which we are arousing in others, especially when it is an important set of responses which go to make up the members of the community. It is unfortunate to fuse or mix up consciousness, as we ordinarily use that term, and self-consciousness. (p. 227)

Mead's concept of society was less well developed than the concepts of mind and self. Society itself was not treated as an entity but rather as a locus or general setting for social institutions. Institutions, in turn, were described as "organized forms of group or social activities—forms so organized that the individual members of society can act adequately and socially by taking the attitudes of others towards these activities" (p. 250). The idea of institutions as patterns of interchangeable perspectives is not unique to Mead, although he has to be given credit for this clear formulation of the idea of defining the limits upon institutions (their "boundaries") by the ease with which one person can take the place or position of another. This seemingly innocuous idea provides a way to avoid the kind of circularity that plagued Malinowski and others after him who recognized the ephemeral character of institutions but who have felt that they had to infer from it that the only way to set institutional limits was by introducing an element of arbitrary fiat of the analyst. Mead's concept provides another approach, a way to clearly describe boundaries that were in fact "fuzzy" while keeping sight of the fuzziness as an empirical aspect of the phenomenon.

Institutional Aspects of the Debate

If one would ever wish to debate the possibility of historical "causes," he might very well consider the alternative answers to the questions that are posed by the logical similarity between Mead's perspective and that of Boas. What if Boas had not been edged out of a position at the Field Museum in 1895 by the changes at the Bureau of American Ethnology? Surely, there can be no doubt that Boas' loss of this opportunity was circumstantial and not structural or in any way foreordained. Yet we can easily imagine its consequences on the basis of the many similarities between the situation in Chicago and that in New York. In New York, Boas came to influence many aspects of Columbia University through his position there. Would he have had a similar influence in Chicago? If he had, might he have replaced Frederick Starr, a rather mild man, as the representative of anthropology in the Department of Sociology? If he had replaced Starr, would he have rejected the social Darwinism of Albion Small? And if he did, might Boas not have had his way? Would Redfield and Radcliffe-Brown then eventually have appeared and said what they did? And finally, the big question, would Boas and Mead have cooperated and influenced each other directly? If they had, there is no doubt in my mind that anthropology would be very different today in almost every respect—covering roughly the same phenomenal ground, to be sure, but for different reasons, with different tools, and in the context of different relationships with other social and natural sciences. As it happened, what cross-fertilization there was, occurring indirectly, was probably too late to influence major trends. Anthropology remained static at Chicago under Starr until he retired in 1924. By then, Mead had neared the end of his time at Chicago and Boas was completely established at Columbia. The misconceptions of Boas' position were already being promulgated, and those students he came to disagree with had established independent careers of their own. In fact, they had established departments and programs of their own (notably at the University of California, Berkeley). By 1924, therefore, the trends toward submergence of the ideas of Boas and of the pragmatists seem to have been so far underway as to have been irreversible.

Although I personally do not see in Sapir's writings a clear-cut understanding of the difference between Mead's and Boas' position and the positions they opposed, the last possibility for the development of a pragmatically oriented school of anthropological theory in this country must have ended when Sapir left Chicago for Yale. Sapir accepted the Sterling Professorship in Anthropology at Yale in 1931, the same year in which Mead died (after having accepted a one-year appointment at Columbia). As noted, this is also the year in which it is generally agreed that the Chicago pragmatic school, as a school, effectively broke up. The Department of Anthropology had split off from Sociology in 1929. When Sapir left the new department it fell effectively into the hands of Fay-Cooper Cole and Redfield, over whom Redfield exercised the predominant intellectual leadership. At that point, new appointments were arranged that included Radcliffe-Brown, although not all the reasons for this were intellectual. As noted above, he had been previously supported in Australia by a grant of the Rockefeller Foundation and was therefore already in a sense connected to the University of Chicago, John D. Rockefeller was the largest single backer of the University, and had been since the Board of Directors had taken over the assets and records of the "Old University of Chicago" that had been Baptist-oriented and associated with the Baptist Union Theological Seminary (see Levi 1972). By 1910, the University had received some $35,000,000 in support from Rockefeller as contributions to its direct endowment (Rucker

1969:6). Several other appointments were made at the same time, including those of Harry Hoijer, who had started as a student of Sapir in 1928, and Wilton Krogman.

By 1934, Redfield was full professor and dean of the Division of Social Science, and he remained a dominating administrative influence in this position and in the position of Chairman of the department throughout the better part of the next twenty-four years, until his death in 1958 while serving as R. M. Hutchinson Distinguished Service Professor of the University. Hoijer left Chicago to go to the University of California at Los Angeles in 1940. After this, the only major student of Sapir at Chicago was Norman McQuown (who had been trained at Yale). Otherwise, the next generation of prominent faculty at Chicago, principally Sol Tax, Fred Eggan, and Milton Singer, were, in general, followers of Redfield and Radcliffe-Brown; although Singer did work with Charles Morris, who was a student of Mead and who stayed on at Chicago and brought out major editions of Mead's works. In effect, this meant that from 1931 until after 1958 the assumptions of Radcliffe-Brown and Redfield served as a taken-for-granted factual description of the nature of social science at Chicago. Their assumptions served as the accepted bases against which the competence of students and faculty and the adequacy of training programs were to be measured. The situation at the University of California at Berkeley, dominated by Kroeber and Lowie, was the same for a similar period.

At Harvard, William James's academic base, pragmatic ideas failed to gain a foothold in anthropology, probably because the Anthropology Department continued to follow the division of labor that had been developed between Harvard and Columbia by Putnam and Boas. The Harvard Department, located in the Peabody Museum, specialized in archeology, a field in which issues of social psychology were not sharply defined. When activity in social and cultural anthropology increased—especially beginning in the 1940s, it was centered in the separate Department of Social Relations. Its leading figures were Clyde Kluckhohn, George Homans, and Talcott Parsons; its orientation was dogmatically that of Durkheim, Weber, and positivistic social theory, together with a positivistic and (Hegelian) idealistic philosophy of science. W. V. O. Quine, certainly one of the principal modernizers of this type of philosophical empiricism, exercised a prominent influence in the Department of Social Relations, and on Harvard philosophy, for several decades up to the present.

The one principal anthropology department after about 1930 able to see a viable choice between positivist and pragmatic approaches to social science was Columbia, to which Dewey had gone from Chicago. But continuity was aborted by Boas himself, who failed to build a cohesive departmental organization to carry on his vision. When a department was created, after his death, there was in its rationale a strong sense of repudiation of Boas' theories as a concomitant of rejecting his institutional policies.

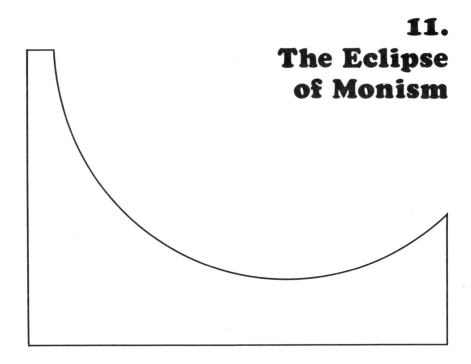

11.
The Eclipse
of Monism

The most critical element in the shift to dualistic assumptions between 1935 and 1955 was the masking of the earlier monistic orientations, wherein the topics, issues, and (some) theoretical ideas originally framed in monistic concerns were recast to extend and support dualism. The complete process was quite complex, and in some respects is still underway. A few major steps will indicate how it was carried out.

It was consistent with their commitment to experimental clarity that neither Boas nor Malinowski attempted to attack positivistic assumptions at a purely speculative level, although they certainly made their opposition plain on an individual and case-by-case basis. But this consistency itself allowed their students, who played increasingly important roles after the mid-1920s in both the North American and British traditions, to reframe their practices in positivistic terms. One part of this reformulation was the description of Boas and Malinowski as field workers *rather than* theoreticians (which was said of Boas by Lowie [1937:131] and Kroeber [1935], and of Malinowski by Fortes [1945:xiv] and Richards [1943], among others). This suggested, of course, that they failed to accept the positivist conceptions of society and language out of disinterest in theory in general rather than out of opposition to positivistic theory as such. The second part of the argument was to explain the failure of field work following the pragmatic example to support positivistic social or linguistic conceptions by invoking the positivistic conception of the inherent gap between "general" theory and "particular" observation.

Undoubtedly, one reason that this rather hasty reconciliation of monism with dualism was accepted was the war-time limitation on field-work opportunities. After the war, when field work could again begin in earnest, the monistic assumptions implicit in the field-work examples set by Malinowski and Boas rose again to the surface, and a new generation of anthropologists began the painful process of discovering that what they were trying to bring together were not theory and data at all but two quite incompatible theories, each containing quite different concepts of what "data" could be.

Reinterpreting Malinowski

As with Boas, the most important voices leading to the reinterpretation of Malinowski's assumptions were those of his students, especially those who claimed to speak for him and who were taken by others as doing so in fact. British anthropologists after Malinowski, including his close students, seem quite generally to have failed to see the most fundamental differences between his own "functionalism" and that of Radcliffe-Brown—in their conceptions of native mentality, the nature of field work, or the relationships between the analysts' models and the realities of those being described. Most importantly, they failed to see in his rejection of determinism an alternative framework. At best, Malinowski appears to have been remembered as an inspiring teacher, an example to be followed in his use of the monograph as a vehicle for systematic social description, and a fount of scattered insights. At worst, he was an exhibitionist or a vulgarian (see Beidleman 1974:558).

Among Malinowski's students, Audrey Richards represents a kind of middle ground between self-conscious loyalty and a self-conscious rejection. She followed patterns Malinowski laid out, but construed them in a deterministic conception of theory that was out of keeping with everything he argued for, and she seems always to have stopped short, in description, of a real analogue to the crucial experiment—of devising a way to obtain data that was absolutely decisive, rather than merely relevant, to a problem she posed. For example, in *Hunger and Work in a Savage Tribe: A Functional Study of Nutrition among the Southern*

Bantu (1948), she appeared on the surface to be following Malinowski's *kula* trade analysis (1920) in trying to show the subordination of considerations of utility to other "values." But it is an oddly divided work. Each of the main chapters carries a close description of the indigenous productive system, detailing the care spent on the gardens, the different techniques for each crop and the reasons for them, and the obvious flexibility and resourcefulness of the people in using their system. Yet each chapter concludes with an attempt to summarize the same description in such a way that it indicates the overriding domination of productive behavior by social constraints, and ritual and magical considerations—elaborating the argument Malinowski tried to make about *kula* voyages. A major point was that after all the work and preparation, despite their self-interest, people succumbed to social demands and gave away their stored grain, mainly millet, on the basis of kinship or lineage connections, out of fear of being accused of witchcraft or of being victims of witchcraft if they refused, even though this led to a regular period of hunger before the next harvest. Yet as with the *kula,* the key evidence was missing. Millet is known for its poor storage qualities. If one's surplus millet under local conditions would not in any case last until the next harvest, why not give it away, especially since the kin one gives it to are those one will have to rely on as a casual labor force for sowing, weeding, and harvesting the next crop? To hold it would gain nothing; to "give" it returns a kind of credit. The information needed to decide the case are the returns in labor from the people who take the millet, the storage properties of the grains under local conditions, and the actual amounts involved. None of this is provided, so the case was not made.

Meyer Fortes' still greater concern with determinism, which led him to reject Malinowski's tutelage and align himself explicitly with Radcliffe-Brown, is more efficiently described in the next chapter. On the other end of the continuum, when consensus on the desirability of deterministic theory began once again to break up, at least three of Malinowski's students were in the forefront of the efforts to find a new perspective. There, their arguments showed the clear imprint of their early backgrounds. These are Raymond Firth, E. R. Leach, and S. F. Nadel, who will be discussed in chapter 13.

Reinterpreting Boas

The first set of issues wherein the assumptions of Franz Boas were replaced by the dualistic assumptions of his students revolved around diffusionism, as already discussed. When diffusionism ceased to be an issue, the reinterpretive process continued into newer areas. The main points of continuity between Boas and those who reinterpreted his ideas are the interest in general developmental laws coupled to a rejection of strict progressive evolutionism, a rejection of "totemism," an at least nominal interest in psychological reality, and the claim to be using a "comparative method," bringing together data from many areas or cultures, rather than attempting intensive theoretical analyses of single communities. One major line of development in this tradition, of considerable historical importance, begins with Robert Lowie's *Primitive Society* (1920), and carries through George P. Murdock's *Social Structure* and Claude Lévi-Strauss's *Elementary Structures of Kinship* (both 1949). This particular development takes the nineteenth-century monistic approaches to social organization and appears to assimilate them to Boas' comparative and "scientific" treatment; but in fact it rephrases them in terms of the concepts of human nature, human mentality, and scientific explanation that began with the religious treatments of Tylor and Durkheim. A second major line, exemplified by Ruth Benedict, leads into modern culture and personality theory.

Lowie's *Primitive Society* describes itself as applying a more critical method to the data and problems of L. H. Morgan, and it bears a surface resemblance to Boas' generalizing monographs such as *The Mind of Primitive Man* (1911) and *Primitive Art* (1927). Like Boas' works, the argument aims at historical patterns from which to infer "laws." Also like Boas, Lowie argues for multiple trends and a kind of pluralism. But unlike Boas' works, the laws are sought by "induction"—a general impression in spite of negative evidence—rather than by demonstration. Further unlike both Morgan and Boas, Lowie predicates that individuals in themselves are passive—uninventive—and tries to combine his historicism with "efficient cause" determinism and the claim that he is dealing with totally integrated cultural wholes. Lowie's main theme is the rejection of "unilinear" evolution, in favor of convergence and independent evolution resulting from "diffusion" as the major—ultimately the only—causal explanation.

The chapter headings of *Primitive Society* show Lowie's cross-cultural comparative categories, the features he thought to find in some form in every primitive society: "Marriage" (including a discussion of cross- and parallel-cousin marriage and a unilineal model of the connection between cross-cousin marriage and dual organization that comes from Tylor and reappears directly in Lévi-Strauss, preparing the ground for his more general two-line model), "Polygamy," "The Family" (arguing that the bilateral family is universal), "Kinship Usages" (discussing stereotypic patterns such as avoidance and joking relationships), "The Sib" (arguing for "multiple origins" [p. 162] and rejecting the idea that Sib organization was uniformly associated with "Dakota terminology"), "History of the Sib," "The Position of Woman" (discussing "matriarchate" and related issues and again arguing for diversity of origins of seemingly similar usages), "Property," "Associations," "Theory of Associations," "Rank," "Government" and "Justice."

The "Conclusion" confirms the overall impression: "Primitive Society wears a character rather different from that popularized by Morgan's school. Instead of dull uniformity, there is mottled diversity; instead of the single sib pattern multiplied in fulsome profusion we detect a variety of social units, now associated with the sib, now taking its place" (1947:427).

He expands the point after a Crow biographical example to show how people become associated with a variety of groups in normal life, not at all based on uniform principles, which Morgan in fact probably would not have disagreed with (e.g., some relations in terms of kinship groups, some friendships formed in part by chance associations). But note the problems he presents for the idea of cultural wholes he otherwise held to be the hallmark of modern theory:

> The multiplicity of social relations could be as strikingly illustrated by other examples. Multiplicity by itself would not be fatal to a generalized scheme of social evolution, for abstractly it is conceivable that at a certain definite stage in the history of the sib organization status groups would supervene, at another age-classes, and so forth. But empirically it turns out that the several types of social unit are combined in a purely capricious fashion. In one region we find secret societies with sibs; in another sibs but no secret societies; in a third a secret society without sibs; a fourth tribe has either or both features in combination with all sorts of associations; a fifth lacks both. (p. 430)

The Conclusion ends with the famous phrase that civilization, seen in the context of the "facts of culture history," was a "thing of shreds and patches" (p. 441). Radcliffe-Brown later said flatly that this was "in conflict" with the "functionalist hypothesis" ("On the Concept of Function in Social Science," first published in the *American Anthropol-*

ogist 1935:concluding paragraphs). In the preface to the second edition, Lowie rather lamely denied this, but without suggesting how the positions were reconcilable:

> Finally . . . concerning the final paragraph of *Primitive Society,* which has been rather generally misinterpreted. The sentence in which civilization is called "that thing of shreds and patches" had no bearing on anthropological theory. It was written in a mood of disillusionment after World War I . . . I was casting about for something derogatory to say about *our* civilization, and as an admirer of Gilbert and Sullivan I naturally bethought myself of the phrase in question. It is true that I not believe, nor do now, that *all* the elements of a culture are necessarily related by some organic bond; on the other hand, ever since 1915 my treatment of kinship ought to have absolved me from the charge of viewing culture as *only* a fabric of shreds and patches. (pp. xii, xxii)

One of the most interesting points about this reply is that it does not argue that the culture might be "shreds and patches" historically and yet still have unity from the point of view of those within it. A probable reason is that it would directly imply that the perceived unity of a culture was an *a*-historical phenomenon of some sort, and therefore that Lowie's type of trait-by-trait history cannot account for at least some of the most important aspects of cultural organization. It would, by the same token, make Lowie concede much greater importance to what he would regard as "subjective" perceptions than would be consistent with his conceptions of scientific, "objective," "efficient cause" explanations. In short, Lowie's dilemma—history *or* integration—comes about precisely because he accepts the same ideas of objectivity, causality, and structural unity as Radcliffe-Brown, not because he differs. Radcliffe-Brown in turn obviously was not convinced, and had Lowie's arguments in mind, along with related views of Kroeber and Redfield, among others, when he phrased his 1952 discussion of history *versus* theory, noted previously.

In the same new preface, Lowie rejected the criticism that his work was too "negative." His reply was, in part, that he would like to update the argument taking into account the great amount of new material available since the first publication, in an area-by-area attempt at historical reconstruction, and: "By way of supplementing this historical line of inquiry I should like to resume Tylor's statistical approach" (p. xxi). He noted that this is what Murdock was then attempting, but that "to date not enough has been published to permit an assessment of the results" (p. xxi). This was soon to change. George Peter Murdock (b. 1897) took Lowie's comparative method based on inductive generalization from data arranged in substantive categories, gave it a statistical form in the manner of Pearson, and applied it to "prove" a rather literal Radcliffe-Brownian (and Spencerian) functional view of society, rather than a diffusionist view.

Murdock took his doctorate at Yale in 1925 in Sociology under Albert G. Keller (Murdock 1949:xii). Keller's *Societal Evolution,* first published in 1915, remains a landmark of social Darwinism—adopting Spencer's general ideas of social evolution to what he considered Darwin's more scientific attitude and method. After two years at the University of Maryland, Murdock returned to a teaching position in sociology at Yale, moving to anthropology in 1943. He remained at Yale until 1960 when he left to become the first Andrew Mellon Professor of Social Anthropology at the University of Pittsburgh.

The foundation for Murdock's *Social Structure* was laid in 1937, when he was a founder and then director of the Cross Cultural Survey at Yale. During the war, he became director of the Oceania committee of the Ethnogeographic Board, and made the material available in that context. This committee in turn became a prototype for other area committees of the board (Bennett 1947:7), and the information they collected in turn was apparently fed back into the Survey (see Murdock 1949:xi). After the war, the Survey grew into the Human Relations Area Files, a systematic classification of features of known societies intended for cross-cultural quantitative analysis.

When Malefijt says that in *Social Structure* "historical, functional, psychological, and statistical methods are brought together to form a harmonious synthesis of cross cultural comparisons" (1974:245), she is crediting it with having accomplished its declared aims. Many anthropologists undoubtedly agree, enough to make Murdock a major formulator of modern approaches to social organization, and even of "scientific" comparative analysis in general. But many others do not share this assessment. The side one takes largely turns on whether one accepts the underlying dualistic assumptions, and the statistical methods based upon them. Because they are still accepted widely, these assumptions and methods deserve rather close scrutiny.

The argument of *Social Structure* begins directly with the first chapter, "The Nuclear Family." The remaining ten chapters proceed through: "Composite Forms of the Family," "Consanguineal Kin Groups," "The Clan," "The Community," "Analysis of Kinship," "Determinants of Kinship Terminology," "Evolution of Social Organization," "The Regulations of Sex," "Incest Taboos and Their Extensions," and "Social Law of Sexual Choice." There is no Conclusion.

The best description of the overall approach is given in the Preface, but much must be inferred from the acknowledgments—as from the dedication to Kroeber, Ralph Linton, Lowie, Morgan, Radcliffe-Brown, and Rivers, "and to" John Dollard, Sigmund Freud, Clark Hull, and A. G. Keller. The Preface also describes the way the 250 societies of the sample were selected. It does not describe the selection of categories into which the data were coded, nor does Murdock here or any place deal with the issue of comparability of reported usages for different areas. Instead, he expressed his admiration for a number of younger scholars demonstrating "catholicity" of approach (p. xvi), and described his own conceptions of multiple causality, requiring blending perspectives from different fields.

The first chapter sets out the major premise:

> The nuclear family is a universal human social grouping. Either as the sole prevailing form of the family or as the basic unit from which more complex familial forms are compounded, it exists as a distinct and strongly functional group in every known society. No exception, at least, has come to light in the 250 representative cultures surveyed for the present study, which corroborates the conclusion of Lowie: 'It does not matter whether marital relations are permanent or temporary; whether there is polygamy or polyandry or sexual license; whether conditions are complicated by the addition of members not included in *our* family circle: the one fact stands out beyond all others that everywhere the husband, wife, and immature children constitute a unit apart from the remainder of the community.' (pp. 2, 3)

As in many ethnographic generalities, what is important here is not so much the truth or falsity of the statement, but the meaning given to it in making it true or false. Construed one way, it means only that where there are children, there are two parents, and by and large it is known who they are. Nearly all anthropologists would accept this. But is it also true in the stronger sense suggested by "distinct and strongly functional"?

Murdock began the chapter by describing the family in general as "a social group characterized by common residence, economic cooperation . . ." and as "consisting of a married man and woman with their offspring" (p. 2). But if he is saying that this group is everywhere recognized as a co-residential, economic, and reproductive unit, he would be wrong, and evidently knows it. The bet is hedged, and the assertion saved, by the device of construing other forms of the family as compositions of nuclear families. For example, "A *polygamous family* consists of two or more nuclear families affiliated by plural marriages, i.e., by having one married parent in common" (p. 3). Once this sort of interpretation is allowed, of course, then any case can be interpreted as involving some combination of nuclear families. This will make the nuclear family universal indeed, but it gives "distinct" a very weak sense. Moreover, the argument also becomes circular, and the meaning of the assertion really does come to rest on the fact that children require parents, perhaps coupled with the idea that the parents, if alive, must live somewhere in some arrangement. For this kind of statement, statistical proof is irrelevant.

After espousing this weak conception of the nuclear family to prove its universality, he quickly shifts to a much stronger sense to build the next stage of the argument: the idea of a universal set of reciprocal kin behaviors:

> A social group arises when a series of interpersonal relationships, which may be defined as sets of reciprocally adjusted habitual responses, binds a number of participant individuals collectively to one another. In the nuclear family, for example, the clustered relationships are eight in number: husband-wife, father-son, father-daughter, mother-son, mother-daughter, brother-brother, sister-sister, and brother-sister. The members of each interacting pair are linked to one another both directly through reciprocally reinforcing behavior and indirectly through the relationships of each to every other member of the family. (pp. 3, 4)

From this point on, the argument for the rest of social structure is built on the "extension" of these initial relationships. He argues that since incest is always prohibited within the nuclear family, each person in his life is involved in two families: his family of orientation (of his own birth) and his family of procreation (which he founds and into which his children are born). In each family, he has "primary" relatives, "his parents and siblings in his family of orientation and his spouse and children in his family of procreation" (p. 14), and "secondary" relatives—primary relatives of his primary relatives who are not his own primary relatives in their own right (i.e., mother's mother), and so on.

The argument through the chapter on "The Community" extended the discussion outward from the family, classifying the new configuration on the basis of permutations of ideas already discussed, with each classification a set of logically exhaustive categories. The system of distinctions thus elaborated is the same as the coding system for the survey data, and the basis for the analysis of kinship terminologies and systems that follows. Although most of the individual terms used, and their general meanings, had been present in the literature before 1949—some long before—this was, and remains, their most comprehensive and systematic exposition.

At the point where the analysis finally turns to kinship terminologies, the obvious question that arises is: how can something as complex and variable as kinship terminologies be classified into a few exclusive categories like the categories of residence rules, inheritance, family types, and the rest? Murdock's answer is to invoke "the criterion of limited possibilities," recalling Goldenweiser, so that: "While kinship terms themselves show unlimited variability, the methods of classifying them do not" (p. 115). He refers this in turn to limited possibilities in manifesting nine universal criteria of kinship relation, building on both Rivers' genealogical method and Kroeber's 1909 "discernments": generation, sex, relative age, and so on (pp. 103–07). On the basis of these categories Murdock offers his extremely important idea of a "kin type," defined as "a class of relatives defined by all six major criteria, i.e., consisting exclusively of relatives between whom no inherent distinction exists" (p. 133). Examples, in the notation he bases on the primary relationships previously defined, are Mo (mother) and MoSi (mother's sister). Kin types in turn become his universal code for testing propositions about kinship organization.

To complete the method these ideas in turn were finally combined with positivistic ideas (from several sources) of the use of statistics to validate theory, in what he calls the "postulational method of scientific inquiry." This involves setting out a list of "assumptions" as explicitly as possible, then stating a major "postulate" to be investigated, and finally proceeding to the investigation by specific correlational tests of "theorems" deduced from or consistent with these postulates in turn. His major first postulate and the first theorem supporting it will suffice for examples. The postulate is:

> The relatives of any two kin-types tend to be called by the same kinship terms, rather than by different terms, in inverse proportion to the number and relative efficacy of (a) the inherent distinctions between them and (b) the social differentials affecting them, and in direct proportion to the number and relative efficacy of the social equalizers affecting them. (p. 138)

The first theorem, to which he assigns special importance, is:

> When secondary or tertiary relatives of any kin-type are called by a kinship term used to denote a primary relative, the daughters of such secondary or tertiary relatives tend to be called by the same kinship term as the daughters of the primary relative. (p. 139)

For example if you call your mother's sister "mother," you will tend to call her daughter "sister." Table 15, in which he claims the theorem "is decisively and positively validated," is in part:

Pairs of Relatives	Parent Called "Mother"		Parent Called Otherwise		Statistical Indices	
	Child called "sister"	Child called otherwise	Child called "sister"	Child called otherwise	Q	X^2
FaSi-FaSiDa	18	22	42	156	+50	1000
MoSi-MoSiDa	110	16	62	34	+58	1000
FaBrWi-FaBrDa	85	9	50	24	+64	1000
MoBrWi-MoBrDa	17	10	29	113	+74	1000

This means that for the relationship father's sister–father's sister's daughter, for example, in 18 societies the parent is called "mother" and the child "sister," in 22 the parent is called "mother" but the child is not "sister" (to ego) and so forth.

There are serious conceptual weaknesses in Murdock's interpretation. Both the Q coefficient and the X^2 statistics are designed to measure the deviation of the values in each cell of a two-by-two matrix from the values expected from their row and column totals. For example, the standard form of this matrix for the last row of the table would be:

Relation: MoBrWi-MoBrDa*

	Child called "sister"	Child called otherwise	Totals
Parent called "Mother"	17 (7.4)	10 (19.7)	27
Parent called Otherwise	29 (38.6)	113 (103.3)	142
Totals	46	123	169

*Expected values are in parentheses.

The X^2 measures the likelihood for the total deviation to represent a chance outcome of drawing a sample this size from an indefinitely large population whose mean values on the two parameters of interest (which *should* be independent) corresponded to the mean values of the sample. The Q coefficient of correlation measures the tendency of the distribution of the 2x2 matrix to follow a linear relationship; that is, for values of one variable to go up or down in direct proportion to changes in the other, across the full range of its values. Both these measures are highly sensitive to categories of analysis that create automatic inverse relationships, or that inflate one square while leaving the others relatively unchanged, and Murdock has both in the intersection "parent called otherwise/child called otherwise." Basically, this is a double null class of two dichotomous variables. The large number of cases it contains is purely the product of the fact that the positively defined variable is so narrowly construed as to make it very rare in Murdock's sample. By inflating such a null category in this way, one can jack up a statistical correlation and significance level on any measurement as high as one likes. The correlation and X^2 score would decrease if the theorem involved more options, such as looking for a child term of either sex, or if the null cases were deleted as irrelevant.

A variant of this problem that appears in tests of other postulates is analogous to the phenomenon of "genetic drift." As a trait becomes more rare, the chance that it will appear more concentrated in fewer segments of the sample automatically increases. If there are but five cases of feature A_1, for example, and ten classes of feature B to associate them with, it is automatically the case that at least five of the B classes will show no association with the cases of A_1. If further, one of the classes of B is far more frequent than the others, the chances increase that all the cases of A_1 will be associated only with that one class of B, and this will appear statistically as a high positive correlation (but at a low significance level). Hence, again, one can make one's correlations almost as high as one wishes by defining the independent variables so narrowly that they occur only rarely, and then assessing them against a large number of options. If one or two of these options is further defined so as to be more frequent than the rest, the likelihood that the rare variable will show high positive correlations with them in particular is increased still further. To infer a causal relationship in such a situation is totally unjustified (unless, following Pearson, one believes that there are no such things as causes apart from correlations).

Murdock's high correlations and/or significance levels uniformly involve either one or the other of these errors. In the row of Table 15 just noted, only 17 usages for MoBrDa out of 250 actually conform to Murdock's prediction, and in 29 cases the same kin type is called "sister" even though the parent is not called "mother." By any experimental (rather than statistical) standards, this could never be taken as confirmation of the hypothesis.

This use of statistical inference prejudges Murdock's eventual rejection of diffusion, evolution, and functionalism in favor of a multicausal use of Keller's idea of "adaptive" processes tending toward equilibrium (pp. 196, 197).

There still remains the underlying problem of the variables themselves, which continue to bedevil kinship theory: Is a "kin term" any term partially definable in terms of a kin type? If so, is "child" an American kin term on a par with "son"? How does one deal with parameters of kinship that are important in some societies (like status relations, or whether the person in question is dead or alive) that are not allowed for in the kin types? How, more generally, can one get a sense of the overall meaning of terms that cannot be reduced to lists of kin types? And how, after all, can the pattern of terminology be reduced to lists of kin types and the terms used to label them? How does one distinguish the "behavior" due different kinsmen from among the other behaviors that are in fact never identical on two occasions between any people? Does one classify a society as "matrilocal" only 1) if (some or all?) new couples actually live with the wife's mother, 2) if they live *near* the wife's mother, or 3) if they live in the wife's mother's group's area, or what? The general definitions Murdock uses for his parameters do not apply clearly to hosts of actual cases, and the questions remain unanswered.

Similar problems attach to the classifications of kinship terminologies. Murdock is willing to characterize an entire terminology by a few terminological equations that appear only in contrast to our own system, such as: "*Eskimo*-FaSiDa and MoBrDa called by the same term as parallel cousins but terminologically differentiated from sisters; the terms for the two cross cousins are usually but not always the same" (p. 223). Are all terminologies with these features in common the same in all other respects, or somehow *fundamentally* the same? There is no reason to think so, and to rest with this kind of categorization and not seek some other means for representing the systems and displaying their properties for comparison would be destructive in the extreme.

In 1956, Ward Goodenough, initially a student of Murdock, attacked some of the problems Murdock raised in a way that preserved his underlying dualistic assumptions. This produced the extremely influential system of "componential analysis," discussed in the next chapter, as a technique for characterizing the overall pattern of kinship terminologies. The tradition that has followed componential analysis has in part blended with that following Lévi-Strauss and, more especially, Noam Chomsky, and greatly stimulated the current widening of debate.

A second response to Murdock (perhaps in some respects a parallel to him) is represented by Julian Steward's *A Theory of Culture Change* (1955). Steward, an early student of Kroeber at Berkeley, used the same underlying idea of the limitation of possibilities to identify general cultural features that would appear from cross-cultural comparison as "objective," and to argue that correlations among such features showed causal connections. However, in contrast to Murdock, he concentrated only on material culture, treating kinship as ephemera of the material "core," and qualifying the cross-cultural associations with the idea of evolutionary levels. He attempts to "resolve" Murdock's problems by setting them aside.

While Murdock blends Boas' conception of history as a component of ethnographic explanation into precisely the kind of universalistic scheme that Boas rejected (using statistical methods Boas surely would never endorse), Ruth Benedict (1887–1948) represents a similar distortion of Boas' idea that culture was in some fundamental sense an elaboration of basic ideas, and of his interest in psychological laws.

Benedict took her doctorate at Columbia under Boas in 1923, and of all Boas' students was the closest to being his direct institutional successor. She was the only person appointed as a full-time anthropologist of professorial rank at Columbia during Boas' tenure there. In addition to Boas, she was also, throughout her life, a close associate of Edward Sapir and Margaret Mead, among others. Her work reflected these associations and a sophisticated interest in art, style, humanism, and psychoanalytic psychology that formed a major component of their mutual relationships (see Mead 1959).

In Benedict's early career, she closely followed Boas and joined in his criticism of the organic analogy and deterministic theories generally—as Redfield once observed (1955:19). Then, rather suddenly in the early 1930s, she seemed to reverse her position. *Patterns of Culture* (1934) revolves around a comparison of Zuñi, Dobuans, and the Kwakiutl. The main theme was a three-way analogy among cultures, aesthetic styles, and personalities, all conceived of as totally integrated wholes. As for Freud there is a strict parallelism between the characteristics of these wholes and the characteristics of the personalities of the people within them.

A culture, like an individual, is a more or less consistent pattern of thought and action. Within each culture there come into being characteristic purposes

not necessarily shared by other types of society. In obedience to these purposes, each people further and further consolidates its experience, and in
proportion to the urgency of these drives the heterogeneous items of behavior
take more and more congruous shape. Taken up by a well-integrated culture,
the most ill assorted acts become characteristic of its peculiar goals, often by
the most unlikely metamorphoses. The form that acts take we can understand
only by understanding first the emotional and intellectual mainsprings of that
society. (1934:46)

This is tied to an awareness of the difficulties of diffusionism:

Cultures . . . are more than the sum of their traits. We may know all about
the distribution of a tribe's form of marriage, ritual dances, and puberty initiations, and yet understand nothing of the culture as a whole which has used
these elements to its own purpose. (p. 47)

So that:

What has happened in the great art-styles happens also in cultures as a
whole. All the miscellaneous behavior directed toward getting a living . . .
is made over into consistent patterns in accordance with unconscious canons
of choice that develop within the culture. (p. 48)

In view of Boas' and his students' great interest in myth, poetry, dec-
orative art, and language (and a growing interest in psychoanalysis), this
formulation promises a great deal. If the unconscious canons of choice
can be explicated in such a way as to pertain to all these materials,
Benedict could have done what Boas did not do: show how all these
diverse materials can be interpreted psychologically, subjectively, by a
single scheme. Yet in the end, Benedict did not develop the idea of
"canons of choice" in any strict sense, or even look at the kind of data
that would have been appropriate for doing so. Instead, she simply asserted that people in the different cultures had generalized attitudes or
values: "Behind a show of friendship, behind the evidence of co-opera-
tion, in every field of life, the Dobuan believes that he has only treach-
ery to expect. Everyone else's best endeavors, according to their institutions, are directed toward bringing his own plans to confusion and ruin"
(p. 171). Comparing such Dobuan attitudes to the contrasting attitudes
of the Kwakiutl and Zuñi, the work ends with a plea for the recognition
of the importance of "cultural relativity."

Patterns of Culture is a forceful but anecdotal rejection of Lowie's
diffusionist suggestion that a culture is integrated at the level of its
several traits—that its overall pattern is the sum of the linkages between
its customs and usages and no more. It argues for a return to the idea

that order exists in the mind of the native beholder. But where to go from there? If the styles are imposed or expressed by individuals, how do the individuals share them uniformly? If the styles are imposed *on* the individuals, by what are they imposed? There is a hint of some pan-human psychological mechanism producing a universal range of possible character types, in the mode popularized by Margaret Mead and many others, but this can't be pushed too far without itself interfering with the importance of culture, and in any case it will only raise once again the question: who or what *chooses* the traits to be treated as valuable in any given culture?

Benedict's wartime service in the Bureau of Overseas Intelligence, Office of War Information, provided the material for a more complex restatement of her ideas. Using ethnographic accounts together with interviews with Japanese immigrants to the United States and indigenous "primary" material of all sorts, from myths to propaganda, she wrote *The Chrysanthemum and the Sword: Patterns of Japanese Culture* (1946). Here, Benedict recognized that no one attitude could be attributed to all Japanese at all times—indeed no single "personality" could be attributed to them. For every attitude some evidence supported, one could with equal evidence find its opposite. Therefore she saw Japanese attitudes as divided among separate "provinces," types of situations. This did not, however, lead her to join Wundt or Malinowski in questioning whether "a personality," a uniform set of attitudes, independent of situations, was characteristic of herself, or her fellow Occidentals in general. Instead, she simply assumed that such uniformity, or wholeness of personality, did exist in the West, and that this in itself represented a major contrast with what she then called the "situational ethic" of the Japanese. Westerners had integrated personalities, but Japanese did not. The conclusion reviewed the typical Japanese life cycle to show how training induced them to accept the separate disciplines of their several situations, suppressing the desire for personal expression or individual freedom in a Western sense.

Historically, one of the most important features of the work lay in Benedict's selection of evidence to exemplify the "cultural" pattern. At each juncture where the argument had to move to a wider viewpoint, and relate one or a few usages to others, it referred to the social organization. The divisions of the pattern of Japanese culture are the divisions between the Imperial office and the Samurai/military, between state and household, between male and female, father, mother, and children. It is in many respects a standard social structural monograph, blending American and British traditions—except for the extremely important point that no field work had actually been done. Where, then, had social structure been observed? Obviously, it had appeared in the textual materials that made up the main part of Benedict's data. In some sense, the structural pattern really was implicit in the individual creative choices that produced these materials and that the materials described, even though such structure was not at all the sort of aesthetic style that Benedict had originally argued for (and that she had reduced to near vacuity in her interpretation of all American Indian cultures as either passionately Dionysian, like the Kwakiutl, or cerebrally "Apollonian," like the Zuñi). This point became quite significant in the late 1950s, when social anthropologists began to reject the distinction between structure and culture they had initially accepted from Radcliffe-Brown, and began to see society "symbolically."

For the short term, *The Chrysanthemum and the Sword* moved Benedict more toward the social end of a continuum of American positions that took individuals and culture/society as its major variables—positions that differed mainly in the explanatory weight assigned to each of these entities as the main locus of the sought-for patterns. Near the other end of the continuum one might place A. I. Hallowell (b. 1892), who took his doctorate in 1924 at Pennsylvania. Hallowell stressed the interaction between personality characteristics and typical cultural situations. Ralph Linton stands near a balance point, with equal weight assigned to culture and the individual. But in all cases, no matter how much the positions differed from one another, none crossed the intellectual Rubicon from dualistic into monistic orientations that would have been marked by abandoning the quest for determinism and recognizing the problem of consensus, viewing it as something that individuals create. When variation among individuals was noted, it was seen as the distinction between conformance, or normalcy, and deviance, which has quite different implications than the distinction between consensus and disagreement. The result was that one way or another, every version of the position came around to a version of Benedict's dilemma: if individuals imposed the pattern, their agreement could not be explained; if they did not, none could say what did (at least in anything but mystical terms that reified society itself into a willful being).

Physical Anthropology

As dualistic theories were adopted in ethnology, the relationship between ethnology and physical anthropology had to change, and physical anthropology itself changed in consequence. This was especially true in relation to the arguments for radical cultural determinism that, under the banner of rejecting "racism," tacitly denied the relevance of any sort of study of human physiology and physiological development. Even for physical anthropologists who did not themselves accept this idea, it raised a barrier between their interests and cultural and social theory and placed them in a poor position to attack. Conversely, the cultural and social analyses produced under the deterministic aegis simply did not approach data or theory with a view toward asking what kind of rules the human organism was capable of following or how memory or training actually worked, and therefore failed to provide data that was in fact necessary for leading physiological research into fruitful areas of general interest. The gap between the "organic" and the "superorganic" levels, as it was so often described, became increasingly influential over the period of the Second World War, even though it was, in fact, artificial and hastily conceived.

Within physical anthropology, the two broad lines that had been present in the beginning of the century persisted throughout the period. The monistic tradition represented by Wundt's physiological psychology and Boas' related emphasis on inherent human plasticity and variability within genetic stocks received an immensely popular updating in George Dorsey's *Why We Behave Like Human Beings* (1st ed., 1925), and continued to be represented by Theodosius Dobzhansky (b. 1900) and Ashley Montagu (b. 1905). Montagu is principally identified with anthropometry, but not at all with Galton's idea of its significance. He was responsible for drafting the UNESCO statement on race (1949–50), subsequently endorsed by the American Anthropological Association, which rejected all ideas of inherent racial differences in intelligence, character, or moral worth; and he followed this more pointedly with the widely read *Man's Most Dangerous Myth: The Fallacy of Race* (1952), whose content and aim are clear from its title. Dobzhansky received his initial training in Russia, came to the United States in 1927, and began teaching at Columbia in 1936. He is primarily a geneticist, concerned with the genetic basis of evolution. A sometime collaborator with Montagu, his own conception of the importance of evolving human plasticity is clearly presented in *The Biological Basis of Human Freedom* (1956).

This has been the dominant general theoretical orientation of physical anthropology proper, and one could easily add many other well-known names to the list.

On the other hand, Galton's interests were continued into the 1930s by Charles Davenport. Davenport began an argument that still persists, with his work measuring the intelligence of American soldiers in the First World War, finding significant differences between Negroes and Whites. He directed the Eugenics Record Office of the Carnegie Foundation, as well as the related Station for Experimental Research at Cold Spring Harbor, until 1934. Davenport's interest in genetic determinism of fine details of behavior, but not his eugenics, was echoed in the work of Earnest Hooton (1887–1954), whose *Why Men Behave Like Apes and Vice Versa* (1940) carries in its title the difference between its author's orientation and Dorsey's. The same deterministic spirit continues into Stanley Garn's and Carleton Coon's classification of world populations into numerous races and subraces, with exceptions being attributed to various admixtures or hybridization. In a 1955 article, Garn and Coon suggested there might be seven "major" races and from thirty to sixty "local" races. Obviously, the more one postulates that morphological differences are inherited and that they are related to behavior, the closer one is to racial determinism of behavior.

In the course of the early decades of this century, partly in response to the criticism by Boas and others, the claims of anthropometry to be able to distinguish races or other fine genealogical divisions were firmly rejected by most anthropologists, recognizing that in gross physiology "nature" and "nurture" were inextricable, and their relative weighting was far from knowable. But anthropometric measurements and description had to be retained in dealing with fossil material at least, and in the course of their application they underwent considerable reconceptualization and some refinement (see the review in Penniman 1965:285–315). At the same time, however, complementary interest was focused on genetics, which was initially not felt to be associated with racism and which was, in biology, an area of spectacular research progress, epitomized by Thomas Hunt Morgan's description of mutation rates using fruit flies that brought him the Nobel prize for physiology and medicine in 1933. Concurrently, the mechanism of the ABO blood group system (discovered by Landsteiner in 1900) was being worked out. The Rh factor, of obvious relevance to pre-natal selection as a new and potentially very powerful evolutionary force, was reported in 1939.

The first holders of anthropological degrees who were interested in human genetics were Joseph Birdsell, Alice Brues, and James Spuhler, all graduate students together at Harvard just before the Second World War. Birdsell attributed their interest mainly to Clyde Kluckhohn's encouragement and vision of what the research would lead to (personal conversation, 1975). Kluckhohn arranged Birdsell's introduction to William Clouser Boyd (b. 1903), who had himself worked in Rh. Boyd and Dobzhansky were both helpful, but Birdsell stresses that the students were nevertheless largely self-directed. Their interests were, in various ways, to demonstrate that the human blood groups had adaptive value. The issues and methods were largely ambiguous with respect to the major opposed views of man, mind, and science: they identified themselves as being in opposition to racism on the one hand, but on the other hand showed an interest in building some sort of deterministic theory that would parallel the contemporary "functionalism" of Radcliffe-Brown. But under all interpretations, the work was far removed from experimental psychology, and remained so. According to Birdsell's recollections, the main psychological interests within the purview of physical anthropologists in the 1940s revolved around William Sheldon's attempts to directly associate bodily form with personality characteristics, which made a major impression on Hooton. This lacked any genetic basis and would have been, from the point of view of experimental psychology, hopelessly imprecise in both its physiology and its psychology.

Conclusion

While monistic positions did not cease to exist in an absolute sense in the period between about 1935 and 1955, as will be noted shortly, they dropped from the view of most anthropologists—especially those just entering the field. Continuations of Wundt's work, leading eventually to the studies of language behavior in apes, language acquisition in humans, and human intellectual maturation, were all under way. But they were deemed to be psychology and not anthropology. Similarly, several traditions of linguistic analysis that used meanings and concepts as part of the basis of order were considered to be something apart from anthropological linguistics. And even within ethnology, though Boas had clearly set out a prototype of his view of the future of the field in *General Anthropology* (1938), which drew together a number of his students with different specializations into a remarkably unified view focusing on human variability, no one emerged who was accorded Boas' leadership status. Nor, in Britain, did any monist attain the status of Malinowski. In this sense, the monistic tradition in modern academic anthropology declined with the powers of its major founders, and it died when they themselves passed from the scene. Yet such is the nature of ideas that the death was only temporary.

12.
The Proliferation of Dualistic Traditions

Alongside dualistic sub-traditions that claimed to subsume the interests of Boas, Malinowski, and their nineteenth-century monistic predecessors, were a number of additional lines of thought that claimed other historical bases, more clearly and explicitly dualistic at the outset. Four of these that merit a detailed look are American descriptive linguistics, British social anthropology, French sociology after Durkheim, and the various adaptations of ideas from German sociology, revolving especially around Robert Redfield at Chicago and Talcott Parsons and other scholars in the Department of Social Relations at Harvard. These new traditions abetted the separation of ethnology from archeology and from physical anthropology, and led, especially in ethnology, to a characteristic pattern of debate involving the continuous creation of conflicting deductive or logical theoretical frameworks, each defining its own essential basis of society or behavior in its own universe of discourse, with no common factual or experimental foci.

Linguistics: Bloomfield to Chomsky

Descriptive linguistics as a distinctively dualistic American tradition dates from the publication of Leonard Bloomfield's *Language*, in 1933. The first major aspect of Bloomfield's *Language* of general theoretical interest was the adoption of positivist conceptions of theory as deductively ordered logical classes, to which data was to be reduced. The second was his behavioristic stimulus-response theory of meaning, indicating how the reduction was to be conceived, which was phrased entirely in individualistic terms (leaving out any form of consensus or conventional agreement) and explicitly intended as a rejection of Wundt's *Völkerpsychologie* (Bloch 1949:89). And the third aspect was a special conception of "language" as spoken language only, apart from what the language conveyed, from bodies of texts and from systems of writing. Together, these three ideas enabled Bloomfield to achieve his powerful initial simplification over the systems of the new grammarians, seeing language strictly as a sequence of recurrent sounds, although the argument was not without contradictions. His conception of the hierarchical order of language, and language theory, with higher forms that can incorporate lower units but not the reverse, follows directly from this.

Bloomfield's main levels were phonology, the lexicon, and grammar, with many sublevels. Phonology began with "laboratory phonetics," the study of the actual physical production of speech sound, hence was more a branch of physics (acoustics) than linguistics. The second level was "practical phonetics," a hazy area concerned with the methods of articulation of main recurrent forms of the spoken sounds, a distinction of principal importance in field analysis and language teaching, but not in theoretical analysis. Above this was phonemics—the delineation of *phonemes*, defined as "the smallest units which make a difference in meaning" (p. 136). His argument for separating phonemics from phonetics was that the former units were purely "functional." Describing their roles did not require knowledge of the actual sounds by which they were articulated. We can know that the English words spelled *bow, toe, tow,* and *dough* all end with the same element without knowing the mechanics of how that element is pronounced.

As phonology is (implicitly) defined in reference to morphology, so morphology in turn is defined with reference to the level above it, a *morpheme* is the minimal unit of language that can have a grammatical function. *Bound* morphemes exercise this function only in combination with other morphemes. *Unbound* forms can exercise it standing alone.

The catalogue of morphemes for a language is its *lexicon,* in Bloomfield's scheme.

Since construction of the lexicon involved describing the functions of the morphemes and their rules of combination, it also involved the articulation of the grammar or *syntax* of the language—the delineation of basic functional classes that are combined in forming phrases and sentences, together with the rules for their combination. Analytic interest ceased at the level of the sentence.

After Bloomfield, the subsequent theoretical efforts of such men as Bernard Bloch, George Trager, Martin Joos, Eugene Nida, H. A. Gleason, C. F. Hockett, and Joseph Greenberg mainly involved the progressively clearer separation of the levels of analysis, and the articulation of the methodological procedures appropriate to each. The success of these efforts in producing consistently clearer and more powerful frameworks in turn appeared to confirm the basic scientific value of the positivistic conceptions Bloomfield had designated as his underlying assumptions. So, in no small degree, did the success of these same men in developing whole new systems of language teaching, applied with great success in missionary work connected, for example, with the Hartford Seminary Foundation, and, most especially, during the Second World War, in the United States Government, the army, and the civilian language-training programs.

Two works of the mid-1950s represent the culmination of the tradition of analysis Bloomfield set in motion, together with a shift toward a more moderate position on the amenability of meaning to scientific analysis, and a series of internal criticisms of his dualistic perspective. The two are Kenneth Pike's *Language in Relation to a Unified Theory of the Structure of Human Behavior* (1954) and Noam Chomsky's *Syntactic Structures* (1957).

Pike took Bloomfield's implicit distinction between "etic" objective sounds as against their "emic" subjective meanings, elevated it into a major explicit dichotomy between types of approaches and subject matters, and used it to organize a general theory of social analysis based on a generalized version of the linguistic methods for segmenting the flow of speech. Within the larger hierarchies of segments of behaviors isolated by objective, "etic" techniques, from church services to football games, Pike would seek subjective "emic" significance by direct inquiry of native informants, or participants, insofar as such inquiries could be relied upon. The interpretive opinion of the analyst was thus set off against the opinion of the participant, and meaning was thus a property—a rather mysterious one—of the event. It was not, for example, something conveyed by one person to another *through* the event. There was no notion of meaning as shared interpretation, and of course no notion of meaning as an imputed or created aspect of the activities. But the fact that Pike directly attacked the issue of meaning was itself a significant step, for it signalled a rejection of Bloomfield's implicit contention that meaning could be reduced to purely "etic" phenomena and their formal orderings alone.

Pike's work was widely discussed among social and cultural anthropologists, as well as among linguists. His version of "emic" and "etic" as both types of approaches and types of phenomena are now almost universally accepted as part of the anthropological vocabulary. Concomitantly, no one has made a serious effort to resurrect Bloomfield's rejection of meaning as an independent subject matter. But this is not to say that the more fundamental assumptions that Bloomfield drew from both the dualistic tradition and the specific tradition of logical positivism were themselves rejected. Quite the contrary. The principal attacks on Bloomfield's system, namely those originating with Chomsky, while vociferous, have been comparatively superficial. Instead of being based on a different major intellectual tradition and advocating a radically different approach to the problem of meaning, the opposition has been based on a slightly different version of the dualistic tradition, and still sees meaning as an inherent property of the communication, exactly like the ancient essences, recognized by its single native receiver or perceiver.

Chomsky's *Syntactic Structures* was mainly a systematic attack on Bloomfield (although not by name), and only secondarily an argument for "generative-transformational grammar"—extending Zellig Harris's conception of "transformational" grammar.

Chomsky has denied a direct relationship to Bloomfield, and was in fact a student of Harris, who affiliated himself most closely with Sapir (Hymes 1971:230). Nevertheless, this denial cannot be accepted uncritically. Chomsky's basic conception of the phonological and morphological elements of language, as it has appeared consistently since 1957, is the same as Bloomfield's. His conception of grammar is of the rules by which such elements (alone) are combined into grammatical sentences, regardless of sense or meaning, and his overall framework is no less solidly oriented to the positivistic tradition than Bloomfield's. In an important sense, Chomsky completed Bloomfield's program by bringing the analysis of grammar up to the same level of explicitness as the analysis of phonology and morphology by Bloomfield's associates. The major difference between them is that Chomsky sees his approach to the problem of relating the structure of language to broader issues not in behavioristic reductionism on the ''inductive'' side of the language-referent dichotomy, but rather in logical constructions on the ''deductive'' side, which he calls a ''philosophical'' approach to grammar.

Chomsky's argument follows the style that descends from Carnap and the *International Encyclopedia*. Formally it is phrased only as a discussion of the proper definition of the term ''grammar'':

> 2.1 From now on I will consider a *language* to be a set (finite or infinite) of sentences, each finite in length and constructed out of a finite set of elements.
>
> . . . The fundamental aim in the linguistic analysis of a language L is to separate the *grammatical* sequences which are the sentences of L from the *ungrammatical* sequences which are not sentences. The grammar of L will thus be a device that generates all of the grammatical sequences of L and none of the ungrammatical ones. One way to test the adequacy of a grammar proposed for L is to determine whether or not the sequences that it generates are actually grammatical, i.e., acceptable to a native speaker, etc. We can take certain steps towards providing a behavioral criterion for grammaticalness so that this test of adequacy can be carried out. For the purposes of this discussion, however, suppose that we assume intuitive knowledge of the grammatical sentences of English and ask what sort of grammar will be able to do the job of producing these in some effective and illuminating way. We thus face a familiar task of explication of some intuitive concept—in this case, the concept ''grammatical in English'' and more generally, the concept ''grammatical.''

The analysis of ''L'' then consists of a set of premises that define L, and an associated logical apparatus that fulfills the requirements he sets out at the outset, of generating all grammatical (which merely means ''generated'') sentences of L and no ungrammatical sentences. There is no attempt to work systematically through a corpus of data. (In this connection, it should be noted that Chomsky's ''native speaker'' who makes the judgment that a sentence is grammatical is not an actual person or group, but an ''ideal speaker-hearer.'')

On the basis of his examples that resolve ''ambiguous'' sentences by formal grammatical analysis, most or all linguists would probably now be prepared to agree with Chomsky's modest explicit conclusion that ''the notion of understanding a sentence must be partially analyzed in grammatical terms'' (1957:107)—if indeed any had doubted it before his arguments. But his implied or suggested claims went far beyond this. By repeatedly remarking that one must understand the generative structure of a language, Chomsky leaves no real doubt that he would have us believe that real languages do have such single, monolithic systems of rules operating "within" them in some way. Further, the very formalism Chomsky employs in setting up his problem itself implies that the resolution fits *any language whatever*—or at least any grammatical language. Given this, it is also easy to see the implication that the sequence from phrase structure to transformational structure to surface structure represents not only the order in which a grammatical utterance is generated analytically but that it also somehow corresponds to, or controls, the responses of the informant who recognizes the sentence as grammatical or ungrammatical. This, of course, is what had led Chomsky, and some interpreters even more, to the idea of a universal grammar. Finally, the connection between grammar and thought (and really to meaning in at least some sense—in relation to "ambiguity"— despite his disavowal) has suggested to many the idea of universal categories expressed in speech that are somehow based on universal rules of logic or on universal ideas.

These implications of the 1957 arguments were stated more explicitly and fully in *Aspects of a Theory of Syntax* (1964). Here he explicitly aligns himself with the rationalism of Saussure and the Port Royal grammarians, although he does not abandon his reliance on logical positivism. The argument relies on elaborate recourse to a panoply of related dichotomies from both traditions.

Among the many distinctions that reflect the positivistic tradition is the crucial dichotomy between "deep structure" and "surface structure." This corresponds directly to the logical analyst's distinction between a spoken or written sentence and the "propositions" that underlie it. The organization of deep structure, in turn, is based on the related philosophical distinction between the proposition's subject and predicate. Classically, of course, subject and predicate were equated with substance and form, respectively. Chomsky does use the form versus substance dichotomy, but not in this way. He argues that "linguistic universals" (using the dichotomy universal versus particular) must be either formal or substantive, and then that: "Substantive universals . . . concern the vocabulary for the description of language; formal universals involve rather the character of the rules that appear in grammars and the ways in which they can be interconnected" (p. 29). This must be taken to mean that the entire propositional structure of a sentence (deep structure) is composed of both formal universals and substantive universals in different aspects (see p. 40). In the manner of Neurath, Carnap, and many others, Chomsky then argues that the reduction of features of actual languages to the "universal properties of language" (i.e., his formal phrase structure) is the basis of "progress" (p. 35). And finally, he gives an important place in his argument to the idea that his grammar "assigns" structure to sentences, presumably as opposed to finding it within them, or recognizing it as something the ordinary users assign or establish. Meanings are also described as "assigned to" sentences (p. 21) on the same assumptions.

Two additional dichotomies important to the argument do not derive from the positivistic literature, but are made to act like the dichotomies that do—the dichotomy speaker versus hearer (p. 9 and following) (as if these exhaust the possible foci of theory, and thus his concern with the ideal speaker-hearer is the most comprehensive alternative), and the dichotomy descriptive versus generative (obviously on the pattern of inductive-deductive) as applied to possible grammars—again as if they exhaust the possible universe, and as if one is necessarily the negation of the other (p. 8). A further important distinction between performance and competence is treated partly like a dichotomy, in that one or the other is taken as the object of explanation. But the main relation between them is seen as one of class inclusion. Chomsky maintains that performance depends upon competence but (by implication) not the reverse (p. 10).

All these distinctions came together in Chomsky's widely accepted review of the argument between "rationalist" and "empiricist" theories of "language acquisition" (Ch. 1, Sec. 8). By "rationalist" he means primarily Descartes and Leibnitz, and under "empiricist" he refers mainly to W. V. O. Quine's and to B. F. Skinner's ideas of reinforcement systems (carrying on his critique of Bloomfield's stimulus-response behaviorism that began in *Syntactic Structures*). He focuses on the explicit issue of the status of the possibility of "innate" (versus learned) ideas, which he sees as being directly involved with the status of the kinds of ideas he wants to make the basis of his phrase structure, and the basis of his claims for the universality of his analysis at this level. He quotes with evident sympathy Descartes's contention that such ideas "are those arising from the faculty of thinking rather than from external objects" (his summary), and that "such notions as that things equal to the same things are equal to each other are innate, since they cannot arise as necessary principles from 'particular movements' " (p. 48). He concludes that the approach of "modern linguistics" is "an empiricist view that contrasts with the essentially rationalist alternative proposed in recent theories of transformational grammar" (p. 52)—apparently including his own work as well as the ideas and theories of J. J. Katz, P. M. Postal, and a few others named in his references (pp. 52–54).

Logically, the most fundamental basis of the argument is the concept of the "ideal speaker-hearer," Chomsky's new version of the Cartesian "I." *If* one is dealing with the problem of explaining how a single, isolated, individual obtains his general ideas, then it probably is evident that he cannot get them from his "own" (isolated) experiences. If, further, the only alternative one is allowed to consider is that the ideas must be innate, then it follows that this explanation holds. But there is no real or good reason for not considering people in communities, rather than in isolation, and no real reason to assume that one either has to chose between immediate experience or innate ideas as the only possible explanation for the existence of general conceptions that are taken to be self-evident and universal *by those who hold them*. There is no reason, that is, except the historical one of Chomsky's own submergence in the dualistic tradition that structures its problems in terms of these options, and denies the existence of others.

A final point that ought to be mentioned about *Aspects* is the idea of "recursiveness" as a fundamental property of the phrase structure of grammar. This is now considered a major theoretical insight, and its incorporation in Chomsky's theory is for many a major point in its favor, seeming to ensure or demonstrate its overall value. Recursiveness is literally a "turning back." In general, it means that a generated compound element of the system, such as a sentence, can be re-classified according to definite rules, and function as a subordinate element in a still larger structure. This adds great power to the rules, saying in effect there are certain points in a generative process where, having gone through all the rules once, one can begin again and go through them all again. Chomsky evidently considers that this idea was a major theoretical addition to his earlier scheme, and conveys this impression in his lectures. But the word itself is not indexed in *Aspects,* nor is the concept either stressed or defined there. Further, the only major place a recursive device appears is in the treatment of phrases, where, for example, the symbol "S" (indicating a sentence) is given among the alternative components in "VP"—a verb phrase (p. 107). In fact, recursiveness is not necessarily tied to the dualistic apparatus.

Aside from the logical power it adds to the scheme, recursiveness adds an aura of scientific relevance because of other associations it had at the time Chomsky began to use it. It is used in computer programming, to describe what is otherwise known as a "loop" in a series of operations. By the mid-sixties, such features of programs had been focused on as especially important in computer simulations of human intelligence (along with the concepts of branching choices that one sees in Chomsky's conceptions of lexical definitions). If it all reminded one of a bit of science fiction, perhaps it was so much the better. Chomsky has attracted an unusually wide following for a linguistic theorist, extending well beyond linguistics, and beyond anthropology as well. (See the recent review of the overall 'movement' by Searle [1972], whose assessment of the weakness of Chomsky's theory in dealing with semantics concurs with the present view.)

Since *Aspects* was published, many linguists, especially in the United States, have devoted themselves to extending and codifying Chomsky's ideas, without substantial criticism. In this sense, dualistic traditions in linguistic theory are not part of the past. But the scope of Chomsky's interests, the range of topics he finally embraced within this tradition, has had a profound effect on those who are less than wholly devoted to his assumptions. It is quite possible to accept Chomsky's technical accomplishments—the system of transformational phrase-structure analysis—without his dualistic theory of meaning or mentality. This has been done by a wide range of younger scholars who are now making progress on old questions—the questions abandoned by Bloomfield—with wholly new techniques. One aspect of this change, which will be described shortly, involves new approaches to what was called the "Whorf-Sapir hypothesis."

Social Anthropology

Social anthropology through the mid-1950s consisted largely of a series of arguments that differed with Radcliffe-Brown in detail, but drew upon the same sources and showed all of his fundamental conceptions of human nature, human thought, and the nature of scientific theory.

The first major dualistic school to form in opposition to Radcliffe-Brown begins with Edward Evans-Pritchard (1902–73), who followed Radcliffe-Brown as Professor of Anthropology at Oxford University after the latter's retirement in 1946. Under his leadership, Oxford formed one of the most cohesive and respected traditions of anthropology anywhere.

Evans-Pritchard's first major work was *Witchcraft, Oracles, and Magic among the Azande* (1937), followed by *The Nuer* in 1940. Both were based on extended original field work, and both involved surprisingly mature formulations of the viewpoint he was to continue to develop throughout his life, using monographic expositions of theory much more on the pattern of Malinowski's work than Radcliffe-Brown's.

There were many points of explicit disagreement between Evans-Pritchard and Radcliffe-Brown, most of which have recently been reviewed by Thomas Beidleman (1974). Most notable are his explicit interest in the coherence of "primitive thought" in direct relation to questions of the nature and function of social structure, and his continuing concern with cultural translation. But in the end, the differences are differences within a school, and the problems of the school arose for Evans-Pritchard just as they had for Radcliffe-Brown.

The Nuer is probably Evans-Pritchard's best-known work, and his fullest attempt at a coherent description of an entire social system. In a 1965 review of the alliance-descent controversy David Schneider identified one part of the difficulty of this work when he said that Evans-Pritchard failed "clearly to distinguish" the Nuer lineage segment "as a conceptual entity from its concrete counterpart as a group" (1965:75). But this criticism is itself based on the limits of a form-substance way of thinking, and does not go nearly far enough. A deeper problem is that Evans-Pritchard's own reliance on dualistic (mainly French positivist) assumptions allows him to avoid seeing the problem of the relationship between a people's ideas and their behavior as truly researchable, in experimental terms.

The argument of *The Nuer* makes consistent use of certain very simple versions of the organic imagery one finds in both Radcliffe-Brown and the French sociological tradition in the form of a combination of geographical determinism, social determinism, and an argument for an organic structure in "dynamic equilibrium." But as Evans-Pritchard applies this imagery to more phenomena in more ways, the whole becomes not more but less consistent and clear.

The intent is to argue that all the social systems are related in one single social structure, which "determines" individual behavior, in many senses (pp. 149, 151, 220, etc.). After some preliminary distinctions, the main argument starts with a description of Nuer cattle rearing, and of the importance of the "values" associated with cattle, meaning both the sense of importance vested in cattle, and such concepts as the virtues of a warrior as a person who defends his own cattle and steals cattle from others—especially the neighboring Dinka. Then, taking the cattle as a focus, he proceeds to describe the ecological system in terms of the annual cycle of group movements, especially the patterns of aggregation and separation, in response to water, forage, pests, and other resources in relation to human needs.

One of the principal links between the ecology and the social structure is through the concepts of space and time, which are not absolute but cultural and relative. The Nuer have unique concepts of "structural time," of "ecological time," of "structural distance" and of "ecological distance," which are contrastive, although social distance is "always influenced and, in its political dimensions, to a large extent determined by ecological conditions" (p. 109). Structural distance is associated with the segmentary lineages, clans, and tribal groups of Nuer society; ecological distance with the patterns of persons one interacts with in the course of an annual cycle of activities. Structural time "is a reflection of structural distance" (p. 108), and the "perception" of this time "is no more than the movement of persons, often as groups, through the structure" (p. 107).

Values come together with time and space in the overall conception of the organization of the Nuer as a system of "balanced antagonisms," "expressed" through warfare (p. 134) between Nuer and Dinka and through feuds between Nuer segments. "The function of the feud, viewed in this way, is therefore to maintain the structural equilibrium between opposed tribal segments which are, nevertheless, politically fused in relation to larger units" (p. 159). Thus individuals are forced into warfare for cattle and territory, and such conflict in turn involves balanced opposed groups that are progressively larger, with the hostility more intense and long-lasting, as the numbers of cattle and the areas of land involved increase. In this context, it is argued that warfare against the Dinka was incessant and protracted, while Nuer were more peaceful among themselves:

> The predatory tendencies, which Nuer share with other nomads, find an easy outlet against the Dinka, and this may account not only for the few wars between Nuer tribes but also in consequence, be one of the explanations of the remarkable size of many Nuer tribes, for they could not maintain what unity they have were their sections raiding one another with the persistence with which they attack the Dinka. (p. 132)

The pattern of reciprocal hostility provides a consistent picture of Nuer tribal organization, from the smallest segment to the tribe. It is in fact too consistent. It leaves no place for other groups Evans-Pritchard knows to exist and cannot ignore, such as age sets and domestic groups.

Accordingly, Evans-Pritchard brings in the idea of classes of social situations to limit the application of the segmentary model:

> A tribe very rarely engages in corporate activities, and furthermore, the tribal value determines behavior in a definite and restricted field of social relations and is only one of a series of political values, some of which are in conflict with it . . . We would, therefore, suggest that Nuer political groups be defined, in terms of values, by the relations between their segments and their interrelations as segments of a larger system in an organization of society in certain social situations, and not as parts of a kind of fixed framework within which people live. (p. 149)

At this point the argument begins to unravel. If the tribal organization is not a "framework within which people live," what is the force of the arguments deriving social time and distance from ecological time and distance, or of his description of cattle raiding and territorial expansion as a determinant of the segmentary organization as a system of balanced hostilities? It also soon develops that Evans-Pritchard provides a long list of causes of fighting among the Nuer that belies the idea of relative peace within local communities, as compared to relations between larger segments (p. 151). He goes on, in describing the adoption of Dinka captives and immigrants, to seriously undermine the main thesis of Nuer-Dinka hostility as creating the boundary of the system, as well as the entire territorial analogy. It turns out that the large groups are not in distinct sectors at all, but are "mixed" locally. It is further often unclear who is of what lineage in local communities, or even who is a Dinka (pp. 218, 219). But he consistently avoids seeing the groups as native concepts or ideals. In the course of this particular discussion, he describes the differences between his own theoretical model of branching lineages in vertical hierarchies and a quite different native conception picturing lineages as coming together at a point on a plane, like a sliced pie seen from above—to which he assigned no explanatory importance (p. 202).

What, then, controls values in social situations—if not actual distributions of peoples or their conceptions of such distributions? The answer, apparently, is to return to the idea that values, situations, and structure are all Evans-Pritchard's own abstractions from observations—without saying which observations were applied to what abstraction, or by what reasoning: "We have . . . tried to describe Nuer social organization on a more abstract plane of analysis than is usual, . . . but in case it be said that we have only described the facts in relation to a theory of them and as exemplifications of it and have subordinated description to analysis, we reply that this was our intention" (p. 261).

This leads him to reiterate his basic abstract definition of social structure, and comes to the startling formulation that families, domestic
groups, are not structural:

> By social structure we mean relations between groups which have a high
> degree of consistency and constancy. The groups remain the same irrespec-
> tive of their specific content of individuals at any particular moment, so that
> generation after generation of people pass through them . . . In this defini-
> tion . . . the family is not considered a structural group, because families
> have no consistent and constant interrelations as groups and they disappear
> with the death of their members. (p. 262)

The only plausible reason for seeing the tribe as less dependent on the
lives of individuals than families in this way is the adherence to the
physical imagery of the organic analogy, and the idea that tribal positions (occupied by lineages and clans) are in some physical sense bigger
or more encompassing than families—containing more individuals of
more types, and less dependent on any one or any few of them.

Finally, he takes structure as at once his model and as actual groups
of people together, when he makes his final claim for the overriding
unity of the entire structure, and attempts to dismiss various inconsistencies or contradictions, by attributing them to the process of abstraction
itself (see also p. 136): "To avoid misunderstanding . . . we would
remark that the contradiction we have alluded to is on the abstract plane
of structural relations and emerges from a systematization of values by
sociological analysis . . . There may sometimes be conflict of values in
the consciousness of an individual, but it is structural tension to which
we refer" (p. 266).

Why Evans-Pritchard would go to such mind-twisting lengths is unclear, unless it is that contradictions in society would be incompatible
with the concept of systematization of analysis, based on unifying the
implicit goals of action, that is recommended by Lévy-Bruhl and others.
Evans-Pritchard obviously considers social structure, as his abstraction,
to be based on native groups, perceived situations, and native models
when it suits him; and he denies that it consists in each of these things
when it further suits him. The end of it all is precisely what it was for
Radcliffe-Brown and for Durkheim and the long line of his predecessors
going back to Hegel: social theory does not involve the delineation of
specific ranges of phenomena, nor the specification of methods for their
description. It rather involves, first and foremost, the promulgation of
the analyst's own organic conception of society as a single integrated
entity that controls behavior, conceived in some orderly way. Then
whatever information conforms to the model assumes the status of data,

while information that does not conform—being recognized as such—is dismissed as non-data. Social structure is not so much the phenomenon to be described as the description itself.

Evans-Pritchard's later works were of a piece with the early ones. His interest in primitive thought, in seeing it as a complete, coherent system, involved seeing it as a system of "values" described precisely as in *The Nuer:* as determined by the social structure of the people in question, uniform for all members of the community. His later declarations in favor of history, in disagreement with Radcliffe-Brown, were tied only to a sketchy description of the features of his tradition of social theory that made such ignorance possible (i.e., the reliance on arbitrary categories to organize data), and were not tied at all to a reconstruction of social theory that would make history a necessary (rather than merely desirable) component of any analysis—as he recognized it was for Malinowski (see "Anthropology and History" [1961], rpt. 1962:184). This did not entail any real departure from his fundamental theoretical position, even though he did at times commend history as a guarantee of native conceptual reality, in the manner of Boas.

Evans-Pritchard's conceptions of primitive mentality have attracted the interest of a number of philosophers (almost philosopher/anthropologists) associated with logical positivist traditions. Notable among them are Alasdair MacIntyre, I. C. Jarvie, and Ernest Gellner. Converging toward anthropologists also developing Evans-Pritchard's two ideas that: 1) primitive thought constitutes coherent systems based on premises reflecting primitive social organization and 2) such social organization can only be seen with respect to the abstract categories of the analyst, these scholars have developed sophisticated re-examinations of the nature and possibility of cross-cultural explanation. Their re-examinations are also about the most intensive study of the problem of primitive mentality in the modern literature, even though their conclusions are somewhat foreordained—namely that primitive mentality may not be orderly or rational in its own right (see Wilson 1970).

The second important line of development in explicit but limited opposition to Radcliffe-Brown begins with two works of Meyer Fortes. Fortes used Evans-Pritchard's conception of a segmentary society, but returned to Radcliffe-Brown in attempting to demonstrate the direct coherence of political organization and social structure as such, rather than the coherence of native systems of values and sentiments.

Fortes was born in South Africa in 1906, took his B.A. and M.A. at the University of Capetown, and then his Ph.D. in 1930 at London, as a student of Malinowski (see Fortes' essay "Malinowski and the Study of

Kinship'' in Firth 1960). In 1934 he began field studies among the Tallensi, in the trans-Volta region in West Africa. The first resulting publication was with Evans-Pritchard: *African Political Systems* (1940), with a preface by Radcliffe-Brown. Fortes and Evans-Pritchard jointly wrote the Introduction (Fortes evidently was senior author), which set out the general division of African systems into centralized and segmentary systems, and described the approach to the description of both types of systems, through the distribution, in a "territorial framework" (1940:10), of the pattern of "balance between power and authority on the one side, and obligation and responsibility on the other" (p. 12). These balances were described as "constituted arrangements, not . . . how they work in practice" (p. 12).

Fortes' first major publication as sole author was *The Dynamics of Clanship among the Tallensi* (1945), followed by *The Web of Kinship among the Tallensi* (1949), which were described as two parts of a single analysis. While the Preface to *Clanship* acknowledges a general debt to Malinowski and to the seemingly ubiquitous influence of the Seligmans, Fortes explicitly goes on to note that the last draft was written while he was at Oxford, and that "every significant statement in it" was discussed at that time with Radcliffe-Brown: "The results are obvious in every chapter. My approach to the study of social structure in primitive society is basically derived from him" (p. xiv).

The next most specific acknowledgement is to Evans-Pritchard:

> I look upon him as my older brother in anthropological studies. I have, in this book, followed where he has led. His preliminary reports on the Nuer gave me the clue to the lineage system among the Tallensi. He was working on his Nuer book at the same time as I was struggling with my Tale material, and there is very little in this book that does not owe much to discussion with him. (p. xiv)

Fortes would later say that "Malinowski had no sense for social organization" ("The Structure of Unilineal Descent Groups" [1953], rpt. in Fortes 1970). Evidently he did not see in Malinowski an alternative framework so much as no framework at all, even though he went on to note that "paradoxically enough, his most valuable specific hypotheses fall within the frame of reference of social organization" (p. 71).

The argument of *The Dynamics of Clanship* is that the Tale patrilineal clans are major "corporate" units in a segmentary system, in an equilibrium (see p. xi) of balanced opposition. Each clan is set off against others as their internal segments are set off against one another down through maximal to minimal lineages. Each holds, or represents, a unit of territory, and each represents a community of "interests" among its members, precisely on the model of Evans-Pritchard's Nuer.

A fundamental problem in this type of analysis stems from the fact of clan exogamy. A woman does not marry into her own clan, but rather into another. Such exchanges make up, in Fortes opinion, "linkages" that hold the system together. But at the same time, they mean that *in the nature of the case* no local group can have only members of one lineage. Even if all the men in a local area are patrilineally related, their wives and mothers will surely not be. And if there is any pattern of visitation or residential exchange between sisters and brothers (as there is in this case), local situations will be further complicated. This was in part the problem Evans-Pritchard's idea of "situations" was intended to rationalize, and what generated his "mixed" local groups. Fortes takes a different approach, relying exclusively on the idea that the social structure is a theoretical abstraction. His exposition is justly famous for its careful and explicit development.

Although both monographs are theoretically low-key, Fortes' arguments rest squarely on the use of the form:matter dichotomy. Social structure was the form, or "social morphology." Content, following Radcliffe-Brown, was identified as "culture," at least in part (p. ix). Culture in turn included both concepts of social categories—like the concepts of clan, clansman, and lineage—and religious and ritual usages. The main part of Fortes' method of argument is to accumulate such "cultural" usages from all over the Tallensi area, and stitch them together into one pattern of social relationships. For example, in the discussion of "ritual institutions": "We have considered only the two major ritual institutions through the medium of which the clans of the Talis are articulated into interdependent sets, and these again serially interlocked into a single system" (p. 114).

But Fortes, like Evans-Pritchard, recognized that the conceptions of social relations between groups expressed in one ritual may not be in accord with relations involving some of those same groups in another, and that individuals may not be related in fact in the way they should be according to the expressed clan rules (p. 115). Also like Evans-Pritchard, his response is to accept the ideas when they fit his "larger" conceptions and reject them when they do not, on the idea that social structure is something they "perceive," like platonic forms or essences, only imperfectly:

> In the social philosophy of the Tallensi, . . . kinship is the model of all social ties between individuals and groups. The ties of clanship, ritual collaboration, or local contiguity are visualized as so many different extensions

and transformations of the fundamental patterns of kinship. For the individual this is accurate to a very large extent. There is a kinship element in all his social relations; for him they are all contained within a single frame of social reference, determined, at bottom, by his parentage. He cannot connect the rules and conditions that govern his own social behavior with the general principles of Tale social structure. He has no means of ascertaining these, since the Tallensi do not make a systematic study of their own society. Every native knows only a limited sector of the social system, and the picture he has of it is built up out of his direct experience of the way in which it acts upon the day to day conduct of his life. (p. 116)

Social structure is arbitrarily defined as that which encompasses all Tale and not just what is visible for each; therefore, all Tale do not know what it is because they see only their own local settings, and not the social structure as a whole.

The idea of social structure as purely a generalized analyst's model was developed further in the remainder of the monograph. Domestic group organization, left for the second book, was not dealt with directly. But related issues were, including lineage control over land. The argument involves choosing from among alternative facts those that support or illustrate the analysis. For example, in connection with lineage corporateness, it is noted that women live in the area of their husbands, but stressed that "When a woman's funeral is celebrated by her husband's people the last act is 'to send her home (*kulh*)' to her father's house" (p. 148). Numerous rituals that indicate the membership of sisters in the brother's and father's lineage are related to this, as if to suggest that the residence with husband was therefore insignificant.

Land tenure is treated similarly. It is noted that the boundaries that are supposed to exist between lineage territories are frequently adjusted to changes in social relationships, and that individuals are extremely reluctant to point out actual physical features that mark them. Yet they are still spoken of by Fortes as if they were "really" on the earth. They are "shaped by social relationships" but are not conventional means by which individuals *create* relationships. Lineages are connected with a lineage "home," defined by reference to ancestors' graves and "ancestral land," "even if many of their members are permanently or temporarily away" from it (p. 208).

The argument for the "reality" of clans and lineages as corporate landholding groups is strengthened by a second argument for the reality of descent itself, the relationship upon which they are based: "Since the tie of descent is indestructible, women members of the lineage and clan have definite rights and duties in all those practical and ritual institutions which bring out most precisely the solidarity and corporate identity of the lineage through the passage of time and the mutability of generations'' (p. 153).

Clanship concluded with a postscript that began: ''This book has dealt with the constitution and interrelations of the corporate groupings found in the Tale society'' (p. 259). But the argument, in the end, was unconvincing; or at least it gave a very strange meaning to the word ''corporate.'' So the issues had to come up again and again in later works.

The Web of Kinship extends Fortes' general tribal model into the composition of the domestic group, its activities, and the ''domestic cycle'' in which it develops as the husband acquires wives, as his children mature, and as they eventually found smaller households that will start the cycle again in turn. The consistent argument is that the small is determined by the large: the domestic group organization and interpersonal roles reflect the lineages, which in turn reflect the total social structure, and not the reverse. The lineage is viewed as real in fact, not as a kind of noumenon that natives use to impute or create order in their local settings. And since the lineages are real in fact, a person's place in society is not a function of his abilities, skills, or accomplishments, but simply determined by the fact of his birth:

> It is clear from Chapter II that *dɔyam,* the fact of birth, the event that fixes one's descent immutably, takes precedence of all other conditions governing the social relations and the social roles of a Talan. This principle comes out in all departments of life, and nowhere so plainly as in the organization of domestic life. (p. 78)

With descent fixing a person's kinship relations (taking his or her sex as a given) the foundation is laid for a deterministic analysis of the domestic group as a system of complementary rights, vested in their respective lineages:

> A man has exclusive sexual rights over his wife, as we have said. If any other man has relations with her this is either incestuous or adulterous, and a serious wrong against the husband himself and his effective minimal lineage, section, or clan, according to the structural relations of the husband's and the seducer's effective minimal lineage, section, or clan.
>
> To appreciate the significance of this we must recollect that a woman marries an individual, but marries *into* a lineage and clan. Men, and even women and children, of a clan or lineage speak of the wives of its members as 'our wives' . . . . If a man sees the wife of a clansman trying to sneak away in flight from her husband, he will take it on himself to bring her back home by force if necessary . . . There were many fights in the old days, as we have

learnt, between clans because the wife of one clan was abducted by a member of the other.

This corporate interest of the husband's lineage and clan in his wife, implying, on the surface, a diffused 'ownership' of the women, is most precisely shown in the joint levirative rights of clansmen (reference to *Dynamics of Clanship*). (pp. 109–10)

Subsequently Fortes and others developed these ideas of domestic group organization into a rather elaborate general theory of kinship systems, called "descent theory." As Roy Wagner recently put it, these formulations ultimately cast the native subjects "in the unseemly roles of barristers and bewigged judges and made their collective existence a droll parody of the Bank of England" (1974:97). Bride price became the "impartial jural instrument . . . for the adjustment of . . . rival claims on the woman" (Fortes 1943 in Fortes 1970:53). "Descent" that linked each individual juridically only to his "own" group (in a unilineal system) was contrasted with biological "filiation" that linked him bilaterally to the groups of both his parents, and these linkages were further divided into "overt" and "submerged" lines (p. 61). Filiation eventually was distinguished from "complementary filiation" (in "The Structure of Unilineal Descent Groups," rpt. in Fortes 1970:87). The direct rights of membership in one's own group were supplemented by "shadowy claims," "submerged rights," and rights of various degrees (like usufructuary as opposed to rights of alienation). Yet all the deterministic power of the corporate groups that were taken as the principal explanatory devices in this scheme remained tied to the idea of the reality of physical descent.

Specific developments under the rubric of descent theory included Daryll Forde's and Jack Goody's continuing attempts to delineate a kind of deterministic relationship, or at least interaction, between corporate group structure and the specific ecological and technological settings of local groups—from tool inventories to land-holding requirements. And at a quite different extreme, the same set of debates produced Max Gluckman's important elaboration of the analysis of ritual.

While all descent theorists used ritual as social structural data, and most had at least an implicit theory of its relation to social structure, Gluckman's formulations, especially of the concept or category of "rituals of rebellion," were notable in two major respects: they appeared to provide increased support for Fortes' and Evans-Pritchard's idea that conflict or opposition was itself a structural principle, and they provided an interesting reformulation of Durkheim's conception of the force of ritual without recourse to the idea of a collective consciousness as an intervening variable. Gluckman himself evidently considered this reformulation "Marxist," at least in some degree.

Although Gluckman has on many occasions described himself as a "strict Durkheimian," he attributed the idea of rituals of rebellion to Frazer's *Golden Bough* (*Rituals of Rebellion in South-East Africa,* first delivered as the Frazer Lecture, 1952; first pub. 1954; and rpt. in Gluckman 1963:110–36). Rituals of rebellion were ceremonies, often connected with first fruits or annual changes of seasons, which: ". . . openly express social tensions: women have to assert license and dominance as against their formal subordination to men, princes have to behave to the king as if they covet the throne, and subjects openly state their resentment of authority" (p. 112). His contention is that ". . . these rebellions proceed within an established and sacred traditional system, in which there is dispute about particular distributions of power, and not about the structure of the system itself. This allows for instituted protest, and in complex ways renews the unity of the system itself " (p. 112).

Of Gluckman's several examples, the most extensive and convincing was based on Hilda Kuper's description of an annual Swazi first-fruits ritual, in which the Swazi king was a most prominent participant. The ceremony proceeds through several days of feasting (with bulls "stolen" by the king) and whole systems of ritual insults and threats, and builds up to a "Great Ceremony" wherein, among other things, the king "bites the new crops" (p. 123) and goes naked except for a "glowing ivory prupice cover" while the people chant "songs of hate and rejection" (p. 123). Gluckman summarized the complex description:

> This ceremony is not a simple mass assertion of unity, but a stressing of conflict, a statement of rebellion and rivalry against the king with periodical affirmations of unity with the king, and the drawing of power from the king. The political structure, as the source of property and strength which safeguards the nation internally and externally, is made sacred in the person of the king. He is associated with his ancestors, for the political structure endures through the generations though kings and people are born and die. The queen-mother links him with past kings, his queens with future kings. Many other elements are present, but again we see that the dramatic, symbolic acting of social relations in their ambivalence is believed to achieve unity and prosperity. (p. 126)

Comparing the Swazi ceremonies to others, including both Zulu and ancient Egyptian, Gluckman extends the conclusions:

The acceptance of the established order as right and good, and even sacred, seems to allow unbridled excess, hence to act the conflicts, whether directly or by inversion or in other symbolical form, emphasizes the social cohesion within which the conflicts exist. (pp. 128–29)

And finally:

The great ceremony which was believed by the Swazi to strengthen and unite their nation achieved these ends not only by massed dances and songs, abstentions and festivities, but also by emphasizing potential rebellion. If this emphasis on potential rebellion in practice made the nation feel united, is it not possible that civil rebellion itself was a source of strength to these systems? (p. 130)

While the last point may be inconsistent with the idea that ritual rebellion precludes actual rebellion, it does move Gluckman's treatment to a clear alternative to the idea that social structure involves concrete groups based on actual descent, and very close to the idea that it consists in general organizing principles. Social stability becomes simply the maintenance of the principles, the concepts of the constituent classes of society and their relationships, but not the personnel of actual groups or even the configuration of groups. Social change could then be the modification or rejection of such principles.

But it should be noted that Gluckman's treatment is still silent on the most basic points that would take him out of the dualistic tradition and into the tradition of Wundt, or Malinowski. His variables are rituals and society, each explained only by the other. Individual attitudes are treated only as a reflection of these, or as a source of disruption that has to be controlled. There is no real consideration of the possibility that the meaning of the ritual is not inherent in it, but rather attributed to it by its sponsors and participants, or that it does not represent objective social order *per se* but rather a local view or theory of social order that quite specific individuals want to promulgate for ordering a distinct range of circumstances. The ideas that the society exists as a whole, and is stable, and that it "corresponds" to the ritual representation, are taken at face value. These ideas are neither viewed critically nor substantiated, to say nothing of the idea that a ritual could provide a "catharsis" that would in fact stop a rebellion.

Gluckman's work with other types of rituals, most notably rites of passage following the ideas of Arnold Van Gennep, further expanded the scope and power of descent theory as one major successor to the concepts of the French sociologists, and mounted a limited critique of some key substantive assumptions within it. The methods of interpretation of data, concepts of theory, and concepts of the mentality of those being studied remained substantially unchanged. It should hardly need to be added that his interpretation of rituals of rebellion is not the only possible one. It would, for example, be difficult to find a type of ritual that provides more dramatic evidence of an indigenous awareness that social order requires maintenance of arbitrary conventions for mutual survival—in effect a dramatization of a version of Kant's more formal exposition.

In the United States, the central figure in the tradition associated with Radcliffe-Brown has been Fred Eggan, both intellectually and institutionally. Eggan took his doctorate at Chicago in 1933, and stayed on at Chicago for his entire career, retiring in 1972 as Harold H. Swift Distinguished Service Professor (a position he held from 1963).

Eggan took over Fay-Cooper Cole's projects in Philippine studies at Chicago after Cole retired, but is best known for his work on American Indian materials. His doctoral dissertation was "The Social Organization of the Western Pueblos with Especial Reference to the Hopi" (1933). The field work was carried out jointly with Mischa Titiev (a graduate student at Harvard at the time) (Eggan 1950:337). Data from both studies were used in *Social Organization of the Western Pueblos,* 1950, probably his best-known work. Eggan recently described this initial research interest by noting that when he began it, Radcliffe-Brown was at Chicago and had just recently completed his *Social Organization of Australian Tribes* (1931). In this he had emphasized that "the kinship system was composed of *both* the terminology and the patterns of social behavior between relatives and that the kinship system was an integral part of the total social structure" (Eggan 1966:16). As Eggan saw it, this was quite at variance with the approach that had dominated American ethnology since Boas, which radically separated kinship terminologies from "sociological" phenomena, and considered them more a part of language than of social organization (pp. 15–16).

Partly because of ethnographic peculiarities of the Hopi, the application of Radcliffe-Brown's organic model to the new material did not show the same apparent success it had in Africa. In the African cases, despite the difficulties, the idea of a correspondence between native models and "objective" groups had some general validity: there were lineage territories and shrines corresponding to conceptions of lineages, household compounds corresponding to conceptions of households manifested in rituals, and so forth. But for the Hopi, the clear conceptual entities had no clear concrete counterparts, and the clearly most important "objective" grouping had no formal conceptual recognition. The principal conceptual group was the clan. As Eggan put it: "The clan is the outstanding feature of social life, in Hopi eyes" (1950:62). Clans were named; the kinship terminology divided according to clan membership and clan relations; and clans sponsored, and were represented in, the principal annual cycles of rituals. Eggan described the clans as divided into "lineages" and grouped into "phratries." Theoretically, clans own the land, and pass it on through matrilineal succession. But clans were not residential units, their territories were not consolidated, and it was not clear either what lineages were grouped into what clans and phratries, or what households went into what lineages or clans. On the other hand, the households were discrete and clear "objective" groupings, despite the idea that Hopi men had no actual rights in their wives' households, and marriage was what many anthropologists characterized as "brittle monogamy." Actual farming was done by households; households contributed to the ceremonies; and grain and goods were stored and controlled by households, not clans. But the household as such had no ritual recognition, and: "There is no native term for the household, nor is it considered an independent unit by the Hopi" (p. 30).

But unlike Evans-Pritchard, Eggan was not disposed to dismiss it from the total social structure:

> But, despite being an ethnological abstraction, the household group is important in many contexts. Its correlation with the lineage has been noted; in terms of the lineage diagrams above we can see it overlapping the lineage groupings, uniting blood and affinal kin in a domestic group. A Hopi born into such a household finds there representatives of practically all his kin, and here he receives his basic orientation with regard to kinship which serves as a pattern for later extension and elaboration . . . A Hopi is thus linked to a set of households which parallel the lineages and clans . . . but which provide a somewhat different and more concrete orientation. (pp. 30–31)

The explanation is troubled. That the household "parallels" a lineage contradicts the idea that it "overlaps" lineages—presumably meaning it contains members of many lineages, as it must. The idea that Hopi are "born into" households rests only uneasily beside the idea that it is an "ethnological abstraction." Why *this* abstraction? And how, in any case, can Hopi children be born into an anthropologist's intellectual construction—and receive training there? Obviously, clans and households were different types of phenomena, but equally obviously both were real for the Hopi in some sense. The idea of an ethnological abstraction was of little real help in saying what the differences were. In the long run, it offered more of a question than an answer.

A second line of work, more unusual in the context of the British tradition, consisted in a series of analyses of terminological systems, mainly in the American Southeast, that showed historical changes under pressure of acculturation at a surprisingly rapid rate and with surprising appropriateness to the social and political circumstances into which the tribes who used the terminologies were moving. The interest began with Eggan's article "Historical Changes in the Choctaw Kinship System," which appeared in the *American Anthropologist* in 1937, and continued through *The American Indian: Perspectives for the Study of Social Change* (1964). Adhering in all other respects to Radcliffe-Brown's program, the early paper quietly made a very convincing argument against the theoretical dichotomy between scientific and historical studies. The article blended Eggan's interests with a number of other well-established American interests, both in historical analysis and culture change.

These formulations indicate the quite general reliance in social anthropology between 1935 and 1955 on certain simple images and ideas—and the not-so-simple reliance on a common conception of the relationship among theory, social organization, and behavior. Despite their simplicity, the images and ideas obviously had very definite consequences for any argument that relied upon them, however lightly or seriously their users may have regarded the philosophical sources in which they first appeared.

Durkheim to Lévi-Strauss

The developments in French sociology following Durkheim closely paralleled the developments related to Radcliffe-Brown, as the intellectual borrowings already noted would suggest. Ultimately, one outcome of this parallelism was "alliance theory" as a proposed alternative for "descent theory."

Over the first part of the period from 1935 to 1955, the principal representative of Durkheim's tradition was unquestionably Marcel Mauss (1872–1950), his nephew and colleague. Mauss taught until 1939 (see Steven Lukes's excellent biographical article in the *Encyclopedia of the Social Sciences*).

While Mauss continued publishing throughout his life, his principal work in general estimation will probably continue to be the *Essay on the Gift* (1927). The essay combines McLennan's idea of social organization as based on a "connubium," involving exchange of women as part of a legal or contractual system, with Durkheim's idea of society as a determinant of cognitive categories and attitudes. The argument was that the gift (and counter-gift) was the universal basis of primitive systems of contract and social order, expressed in such institutions as marriage, potlatch, and blood feud. Gifts both recognized and, apparently, created a basic sentiment or predisposition to feel an obligation in exchange for a benefit, a principle of reciprocity, out of which all laws and morality unfolded. Systems of gifts, or prestations, are "total social facts": "These are thus more than themes, more than elements of institutions, more than institutional complexes, more even than systems of institutions divided, for example, into religion, law, economics, etc. . . . These are 'totalities,' entire social systems whose functioning we have tried to describe" (from the Conclusion, rpt. in Mauss 1950:275; my translation).

The study of "social facts" in this sense

> . . . has a double advantage. First, an advantage of generality, because these facts of general function have a chance of being more universal than the diverse institutions or the diverse theses of these institutions, always more or less accidentally tinted by a local color. But above all, it has the advantage of reality. One comes thus to see social things themselves, in the concrete, as they are. In societies, one knows there is more than ideas or rules, one knows there are people, groups, and their comportments. One sees them move as in a machine one sees masses and systems, or as in the sea we see octopi and anemones. We perceive numbers of men, moving forces, and that which floats among them and in their sentiments. (p. 276; my translation)

The analogy between men and anemones puts Mauss's social determinism succinctly.

Succession to Mauss's intellectual position was unclear during the war, as leading French thinkers were scattered or otherwise involved. But by 1949 it became clear in Britain, and shortly after that in the United States, that Mauss's place had been taken by Claude Lévi-Strauss (born in 1908).

Lévi-Strauss took a degree in law and passed the *Agrégation* (State examination to qualify to teach in secondary schools) in philosophy at the University of Paris (1927–32). He taught in a *lycée* from 1932 to 1934, then obtained a post as Professor of Sociology at the University of São Paulo, Brazil. In 1938–39, he took part in a small expedition into central Brazil, the nearest he ever came to doing fieldwork (see Leach's chronology and estimation of the experience [Leach 1970:x]). The following year, he was back in France on military service, but fled after the French surrender in 1941. Eventually he arrived in New York (see the impressions in *Tristes Tropique,* part 1; Leach 1970:1–13). Partly through the good offices of Robert Lowie (whose *Primitive Society* he says he read in 1934 as his first anthropological work), he obtained a teaching position at the New School for Social Research, which he held through 1945. After a year as cultural counsellor to the French Embassy in Washington, he finally returned to a position as curator in the Musée de l'Homme, Paris, in 1948. In 1950, he was appointed Professor in the Ecole des Hautes Etudes, where he has remained.

Les Structures élémentaires de la parenté (1949) was Lévi-Strauss's first anthropological work of major scope, and clearly sets out his basic assumptions. A revised French edition was published in 1967, and an English translation was prepared by Rodney Needham and others in 1969. Although Lévi-Strauss has refused to endorse the translation, it is in most respects excellent. What difficulties there are can be readily attributed to the original text, which was by no means crystal clear. The work is dedicated to Lewis Henry Morgan, and the title suggests its intent to provide a kinship version of *Elementary Forms of the Religious Life.* But the main intellectual debt appears to be the American comparative traditions represented by Lowie, and to Mauss. There is also an overlay of ideas reflecting Lévi-Strauss's New York association with Roman Jakobson, which has loomed larger in his more recent works.

The main concern of *Elementary Structures* is described in three different ways: to "show that marriage, rules, nomenclature, and the system of rights and prohibitions are indissociable aspects of one and the same reality, viz., the structure of the system under consideration" (1969:xxiii); to provide "an introduction to the general theory of kinship systems" (p. xxiv); and to answer the question "where does nature end and culture begin?" (p. 4). Although these questions are not logically related, the structure of the argument depends upon the way the assumptions they involve are intertwined.

The arguments develop slowly and obliquely, beginning by building up a discussion of cross-cousin marriage and "dual organization"—a division of a group into two descent units, each of which takes its wives from the daughters of the other. With dual organization, given unilineal descent, cross-cousins would always be in the opposite moiety, while parallel cousins would be in one's own. He proceeds in this context from the position that the incest prohibition "alone among all the social rules, possesses at the same time a universal character'' (1969:8), to the view that ''incest prohibitions express the transition from the natural fact of consanguinity to the cultural fact of alliance'' (p. 30). He then connects incest prohibitions, as allocation of women, to food and food allocation as a second such area of transition, suggesting that it is always involved in the exchanges for women (p. 36). This gives him a new formulation of Mauss's gift, and the position that ''exchange . . . is from the first a total exchange'' (p. 61). He finally gives the key to his own view of kinship systems in Chapter 8, ''L'Alliance et la filiation'' (translated by Needham et al. as ''Alliance and Descent''):

> Dual organization accounts for the dichotomy of cousins into cross-cousins and parallel cousins, and explains why cross cousins are possible spouses, and why parallel cousins are prohibited. But it does not make it clear why, as is often the case, the cross cousins are preferred to all other individuals who, like them, belong to the opposite moiety to Ego. A man finds women in the opposite moiety to his own not only with the status of cross ''cousins'' but also . . . of cross ''aunts'' and cross ''nieces.'' All these women have the same quality of being exogamous. Why then are cross cousins privileged spouses?
> Suppose now that a second unilateral dichotomy of the dual organization is added to the first unilateral dichotomy, but follows the other line; e.g., let there be a system of matrilineal moieties, A and B, and second division, this time patrilineal, between two groups, X and Y. Each individual will hold a status A or B from his mother, and a status X or Y from his father. Hence each will be defined by two indices: AX, AY, BY, BX. If the marriage rule is that the possible spouses shall differ as to both the maternal index and the paternal index, it can easily be established that only cross-cousins satisfy this requirement, while uncles or aunts, and cross-nephews or nieces, differ in one index only. (1969:106–07)

This pattern is precisely what Lévi-Strauss wants to call a ''structure.'' Its logic is such that marriages following the rule will preserve the same basic groups and relations without change in every generation.

Variations on the basic abstract model could be seen to apply to specific categories of known societies, each preserving their consistency and stability through time. There are three such variations, and these are the ''elementary structures'' to which the title of the work refers. When the basic model is interpreted as involving a rule that one must marry one's ''bilateral cross-cousin,'' that is either father's sister's daughter or mother's brother's daughter, then the stable outcome is that there is no cycle of exchange of goods for women, and the marriage pattern is that two groups simply exchange wives between themselves. When marriage is "patrilateral," that is, when one marries one's father's sister's daughter, then that pattern was one of exchange between descent groups in alternative generations, and gifts in exchange for women move in a "short cycle." Finally, when marriage was "matrilateral," that is with mother's brother's daughter, there was a general pattern of "circulating connubium," with A giving wives to B, B to C, and so on through the group, with a long cycle of gifts flowing in exchange throughout the entire society.

The elementary systems are related to one another as a single set of logical possibilities, which Lévi-Strauss represents graphically with the shape of an inverted "T." Patrilateral and matrilateral systems are at opposite ends of the base, differing from each other in all respects. Bilateral systems are a mediating type at the top of the perpendicular, differing from both yet also sharing some characteristics of both. In all such systems, one's choice of a mate—and hence place in the total system of prestations—is supposed to be completely determined by one's social group.

Numerous ethnographic cases are treated as if they either correspond directly to one or the other of these elementary structures or to direct elaborations of them. "Complex structures," defined as structures that do not "involve positive determination of the type of the preferred spouse" and evidently intended to include all remaining societies (p. 465), "can all be reduced to the three elementary forms, independently transformed or intercombined" (pp. 464–65).

None of Lévi-Strauss's critics have questioned the internal logic of his models, and many anthropologists have found his reduction of seemingly complex structures to applications of the fundamental abstract idea of dichotomous characteristics both fascinating and stimulating. Most especially, recognizing that the dichotomy was fundamentally an intellectual or psychological principle, many saw Lévi-Strauss as providing a timely reentry of "subjective" considerations in place of the oddly external and mechanistic formulation exemplified by Fortes and Forde. At one level, with these models, Lévi-Strauss obviously succeeded where Durkheim and Mauss could not: in connecting a conception of social structure viable in its own right with a convincing set of subjective categories that could be seen as constituting a consistent cosmological outlook, but that was not simply acceptance of the social structural model as such. But at the level of a theory of society as a whole, even Lévi-Strauss's strongest defenders (most notably Rodney Needham) have not accepted all of his claims, and most anthropologists have been quite skeptical indeed.

The obscure and difficult character of the debates that have grown up around Lévi-Strauss's analysis reflect fundamental conceptual problems that his position carries to extreme forms, and which have been shared and spread by many of his nominal critics as well as by his defenders. Four of these problems should be especially mentioned.

First, Lévi-Strauss's terminological usage is remarkably inconsistent, even in the most important parts of his argument. Sometimes, for example, he speaks of groups as abstract Durkheimian collectivities: "By establishing a general rule of obedience . . . the group asserts its jural authority over what it legitimately considers an essential valuable" (meaning women: p. 42). At other times, he argues as though a group has to be a named, conceptualized, ethnographic division, and that stating what such named groups were was sufficient evidence of their presence (p. 107). Yet again he describes Weil's mathematical division of an Australian system into sixteen categories as "surely justified" even though "one can be sure . . . the aboriginal mind never has recourse to these sixteen categories" (p. 109). And finally, he often—and at crucial points—speaks of the group as its male members only, whom he insists exchange women and are not exchanged by them (p. 115). Similarly, "incest" is sometimes treated as if it were a prohibition of actual sexual relations between actual parents and children and among siblings, sometimes as if it were a prohibition of marriage in the same actual group, and sometimes as if it were a prohibition of either sexual relations or marriage simply between conceptually recognized categories. Kinship terms are often represented in charts as designating several distinct positions, but treated in the text as if they had a unitary meaning in order to argue for conceptual identification of several types of relations under one head, and there is no systematic attempt to distinguish terms that might be analogous to "clansman" from terms like "father" or "uncle." Patrilineality is sometimes spoken of as a principle of inheritance of goods or characteristics, sometimes of group membership, and sometimes as an unconscious identification of some sort: especially as the three elementary structures are described as always "present in the human mind" (p. 464). Even such an important concept as "cross-cousin" remains unclear. It is important to his argument to show that female cross-cousins are consistently distinguished from parallel cousins and from aunts and nieces, as noted. Yet he does not always do so. Sometimes he appears to be dealing with a native kin term that is distinct from a term analogous to "parallel cousin" and other relations, but sometimes he is obviously dealing with terms designating clan relations or section relations, which may or may not be strictly like kin terms, and may or may not supplant kin terms in a stricter sense. The ethnographic literature in 1948, as now, was full of examples of kinship terms that made distinctions not found in clan rules or clan terminologies, and vice versa. Lévi-Strauss, for the most part, used the terms as he found them in the literature. But what was clear enough within the context of an extended ethnography of a single community was often quite unclear taken out of that context and used in his own free-ranging comparisons.

A second problem was his implicit evolutionism. Even though he explicitly claimed to be describing only a "logical" and not a historical order, his argument actually makes sense only in the context of the obsolete short chronology. This includes the idea of searching for a single innovation that marked the end of "nature" and the start of "culture," and the idea that this had to involve the prohibition of incest within the group—the prohibition that "initiates" organization (p. 43)—as if organization came about with a modern type of human form living in some sort of already dense and interactive pattern. The idea that food distribution was involved fundamentally with exchange of women "from the first" (p. 61) similarly makes no sense in view of currently accepted developmental chronologies. Equally to the point, unless one implicitly accepts evolutionary assumptions like Durkheim's, the argument that Lévi-Strauss's structures are "elementary," "total," and recurrent everywhere is a vague and circular recourse to a fundamental proclivity for the human mind to organize itself by means of dichotomies in a dialectic process (the argument he subsequently came to stress almost entirely).

The third major problem, and the one most widely shared, is in taking the characteristic of a part for the characteristic of the whole. To show that one marries one's cross-cousin, and that one's cross-cousin is in another lineage, is not to show that one's lineage members all marry members of one's cross-cousin's clan or even, strictly speaking, that one's lineage *as such* has marriage relationships with one's cross-cousin's lineage. To show that some gifts are given at a wedding is not to show that all goods in a society are given in exchange for women (in fact, of course, it is not to show that *any* of the gifts are being exchanged for women—but that is a problem of misreading data, rather than a fallacy of composition). To show that a ritual of a society embodies one principle is not to show that the principle is uniformly applied to all acts in that society by all people at all times. Even if one could show that a society used a system of clans, that all the women of the clans married into other clans in a regular pattern corresponding to a matrilateral connubium, and that there were countergifts moving in the opposite direction, this would still not show that yet other goods were not exchanged on other bases, and that other social systems did not exist side by side dividing the population into quite different patterns of association. Finally and most importantly, to show that a community sees a contrast between two ideas is not to show that they see the ideas as a dichotomy—as underlying essences exclusively defining and exhausting some conceptual universe (or all possible universes). Again, the literature in Lévi-Strauss's time, especially the American literature, was full of examples of contradictory values and principles, and crosscutting patterns of organization. The contributions to Boas' *General Anthropology* (1938), for example, laid major stress on the idea that variation within cultures was or could be as great as variation between cultures.

The final problem is his treatment of conscious native conceptions. He is willing to concede, after noting several clear cases of native models similar to his own, that "Primitive thought, therefore, is not incapable of conceiving of complex structures and apprehending relationships" (p. 127). But his more basic position appears to be:

> The fact that classes exist elsewhere than in the mind of the sociologist has the same value as the fact that syllogisms exist for others than the logician, but no more than this. The existence of both forms must be acknowledged when attested to by experiment and observation. It does not follow from this that they are always the *raison d'être* for phenomena analogous to those produced when they are attested to. (1949:110)

In practice, as noted above, he goes from this to saying that he can then ignore native conceptions when they do not give the results he feels are required. The position that social structures might be native conceptions in use is implicitly rejected, although it is never explicitly discussed.

This view of native thought might be reasonable for Fortes or Forde, but it makes little sense in a work constantly referring to "primitive thought," and whose main aim is to establish the existence of three "mental structures": ". . . the exigency of the rule as a rule; the notion of reciprocity regarded as the most immediate for the integrating of the opposition between the self and others; and finally, the synthetic nature of the gift. . . ." (p. 84). Lévi-Strauss does at several points invoke the distinction between "conscious" and "unconscious" thought (as if it were a clear and simple dichotomy), but while this may fend off criticism, it does not remove the Hegelian solipsism. Apart from agreement with Lévi-Strauss's own conceptions of society as systems of generalized or restricted exchange, there is no way to identify what he will count as data. How can one claim to be establishing the exigency of a rule as a rule without being interested in asking if it is in fact known as a rule for those who should follow it?

In June of 1952, Lévi-Strauss was invited to a major conference at the Wenner-Gren Foundation in New York City. His paper on "Social Structure" appeared with the other conference papers in *Anthropology Today*, edited by A. L. Kroeber (who had served as conference president). It was selected to be reprinted ten years later when Sol Tax republished a selection of original papers that had appeared to wear best. The essay argues for an abstract difference between "mechanical models" of social structure and "statistical models." The former model involved "elements on the same scale as the phenomena themselves," while statistical models were "on a different scale" (1962:325). Such "a structural model may be conscious or unconscious without this difference affecting its nature" (p. 324), and Lévi-Strauss repeated the main arguments from *Elementary Structures* on the irrelevance of native ideas, construing them as "models already constructed by the culture to interpret" what he considers "raw behavior" (p. 324). He had already indicated that mechanical models correspond to his elementary structures, while statistical models correspond to complex structures (1949:xxv).

In 1955, the major outline of Lévi-Strauss's conceptions was completed by the publication of "The Structural Study of Myth" in the *Journal of American Folklore*. Rejecting as "facile" attempts to analyze myths by showing the social roles and values they represent, he argued that myth was part of language, but at a higher level of organization. Given this, he proposed a method of analysis which began by breaking a myth into its constituent minimum elements—sentences. These were then arranged according to similarity of form and content, grouping like elements together. The groups of like elements were then related to one another by construing them as representing pairs of dichotomously opposed ideas. The two principal myths used to illustrate the method were the Oedipus myth and what he described as "the" Zuñi origin myth (actual text not indicated). Only the first is described in detail. Two of the lowest level groups of the Oedipus myth were contrasted as representing "over-emphasis of blood relations" and "under-emphasis of blood relations"; the two remaining groups were held to represent affirmation and denial, respectively, of "the autochthonous origin of man." The meaning of the myth as a whole was held to lie in the contrast between the contrasts—the similarity and differences among the groups. For the Oedipus myth, the contrast was between over- and under-emphasis of blood relations, on the one hand, and affirmation and denial of the autochthonous origin of man, on the other. The meaning of the Oedipus myth as a whole was held to be a solution to the "problem" of the origin of man—that he is somehow at once born from unlike (man and women) and from like. Finally, comparing both myths, Lévi-Strauss introduced the view that "mythical thought always works from the awareness of oppositions towards their progressive mediation . . ." (1955:437).

Since it is clear from the article that Lévi-Strauss did not systematically apply the method he advocated, there is nothing to obscure the fact that Lévi-Strauss's conclusions follow only from the dichotomies he used to group the elements he offers in evidence. It is not mythic thought but Lévi-Strauss's article that proceeds by developing and reconciling either-or contrasts. The resemblance between the conclusions in regard to myth and those of his kinship analysis further follow from the fact that the method is basically the same in the two cases, as in fact are many of the specific dichotomous parameters it invokes: nature and culture, male and female, life and death, part and whole, dominant and dominated.

Since "The Structural Study of Myth," Lévi-Strauss has produced several longer works on cosmology, symbolism, and thought, but still none that systematically applied his ideas to a clearly delineated body of data. The arguments remain highly suggestive, impressionistic, and programmatic. Many have taken up the program; many others, after careful consideration, have not. (For a sympathetic overview of Lévi-Strauss's later work, see Leach 1970.)

Lévi-Strauss is obviously in the same broad dualistic tradition as Radcliffe-Brown and those he has come in most direct conflict with. His differences from them, however, were still great enough to extend the previous range of discussions. At the same time, his use of dualistic devices as virtually the only support of his conclusions and the clear circularity of his defense of their use have been a major reason for the dualistic assumptions themselves to have come into focus among the debated issues.

Influences from German Sociology

Beginning in the mid-1930s and continuing through the early 1950s, anthropologists came to borrow ideas from a second major sociological tradition—the German sociology whose best-known representatives are

Ferdinand Tönnies (1855–1936), Georg Simmel (1858–1918), and Max Weber (1864–1920). The tradition differed from its French counterpart in two major respects: it concentrated much more explicitly on western society, and it was far more sensitive to the Kantian frame of reference. To be precise, it drew heavily on Schopenhauer's neo-Kantian idealism, using it as a framework to interpret the more truly Kantian ideas of ethnology and folk psychology.

Tönnies' first major work was *Gemeinschaft and Gesellschaft (Community and Society)*, in 1887. Each term indicates a polar type of social order. Community corresponded to Durkheim's organic solidarity; society to mechanical solidarity. Community was, further, associated with "natural will" as a principle of motivation (*Wesenwille*) which submerged the individual's interests and volitions in the requirements of the group, or society as a whole—to custom and tradition. Society was associated with "rational will" (*Kürwille*), which distinguished the individual's own goals from those of the society, and was represented by their calculated pursuit. In 1889, this was followed by an edition of Hobbes's *Behemoth, or the Long Parliament.* The two works marked the two major threads that were interwoven throughout the rest of Tönnies' work: sociology and social contract theory.

Despite Tönnies' earlier publications, Simmel is generally considered the tradition's major formulator. His major publications began with *The Problem of Historical Philosophy* (1892) and *Conceptual Foundations* (2 volumes, 1892–93). They were rather quickly followed by a number of shorter but still important works, including *Philosophy of Money* (1900), *Kant* (1903), *Religion* (1906), and *Sociology* (1908), along with a number of important essays.

Simmel's system was built on three major ideas. One was clearly dualistic, one clearly Kantian, and one ambiguously assignable to either tradition. The clearly Kantian idea was that sociology itself arose in the course of the development of society, and is part of that development, creating new levels of order and providing new bases for freedom. (This in one sense avoids the dualistic claim for a privileged position outside the flow of activity one tries to describe). The clearly dualistic idea was that society consisted, universally, in social relations, built of specific general types of *transactions* that formed networks, and that such relations were the "forms" of behavior impressing themselves on individuals as their "substance." The linking concept, beautiful in its elegance and power, began with the idea that mind developed out of action, first closely tied to nature and then progressively more abstract, independent, and complex—as for Bachofen, Bastian, and Wundt. Then, however,

Simmel argued that society finally broke free entirely from material nature, a completely abstract and ideal (formal) entity, asserting its own identity, and continuing thenceforth by its own logic—as for Hegel. The development of the "metropolis," with its commercialism, complexity, extreme division of labor, and necessity for common reference to a precise framework of abstract temporal and spatial concepts, was essential to the final phase of this process, the final source of complete "intellectualization" of relations.

Whether the scheme as a whole is dualistic or monistic, given these linkages, would depend upon which elements were assigned logical priority. In fact, in the system of argument as a whole, the developmental ideas were invoked when convenient, but the dualistic dichotomies and the idea that society was an abstraction of the analyst to be imposed on those he described, were relied on at all key points.

After Simmel's groundwork was laid and after Tönnies had cooperated with Simmel in a series of monographs edited by Martin Buber, Tönnies wrote his influential *Custom: An Essay on Social Codes* (1909). The title invokes two of the most distinctive topics of folk psychology and ethnology: "custom" (*Sitte*) and communicative interaction. Like Simmel's works, it thereby suggests that sociology has overcome the gap between the traditions, or has been reformulated on Kantian lines. The argument does in fact begin with the Kantian observation that a custom is a rule. But the meaning of this idea is transformed by a series of dualistic dichotomies, going back directly to Hobbes, that are subtly invoked as Tönnies equates a rule (something one must follow or obey) with the idea of "will." From this point in turn he leaps to the idea that there is a totality of all customs, and that this embodies the totality of will, or the "general will," also called the "social will": "I maintain . . . that the sociologist must in the first place study and isolate custom as a highly important form of *social will*. He must perceive and analyse social will on analogy to individual will. The same meaning which 'will' in the ordinary individual sense has for individual men, 'social will' has for every community or society" . . . (1909:37).

Implicitly, here again are the radical dichotomies between will and reason and the single individual and the cultural whole, along with the idea that both are essences to be sought behind the appearances of things. From here, Tönnies went on to argue that customary society corresponded to his *Gesellschaft,* and that in it the individual will that followed custom (the "natural will" of his earlier work) was truly free insofar as it acted from its own free choice—directly recalling Hegel's twist on Kant's conception of freedom in obeying the state, in what was to become a powerful theoretical portrait of primitive and peasant behavior blindly conforming to tradition rather than rational perceptions of self-interest.

Max Weber's training was in law, and his academic positions were formally in economics, rather than sociology. His professional activity began in the 1890s, but his major publications began to appear only in 1920–21 with *Collected Essays on the Sociology of Religions (Gesammelte Aufsatze zur Religionssoziologie,* in three volumes: 1920–21); followed in 1922 by *Collected Essays on the Theory of Knowledge (Gesammelte Aufsatze zur Wissenshaftlehre),* and *Economy and Community (Wirtschaft und Gesellschaft).* Much of this soon began to appear in English translation. *The Protestant Ethic and the Spirit of Capitalism* was Talcott Parsons' 1930 translation of Volume I of the *Sociology of Religions.*

Weber's aim was to provide an anti-Marxist synthesis of sociology and neo-classical economics. He described his theoretical focus as "action," individual and collective, that was meaningful to those who engaged in it. His approach to this action was based on two dominant ideas: religious determinism and the concept of the "ideal type." The determinism began with the idea that religious creeds engendered an "ethic" or general outlook toward one's self, others, and the world that in turn shaped the economic activities and institutions of the believers. Calvin's theology generated a "Protestant ethic" that in turn generated a rational, self-reliant, and disciplined attitude that Weber considered "the spirit of capitalism." Catholicism, by contrast, generated only "anticipatory" capitalism; while Judaism produced "pariah capitalism."

The arguments integrated a mass of factual material, but often by assigning inconsistent meanings to such key terms as "rationality." There were also numerous counter-factual or simply ungrounded assertions (Weber's conception of Calvin's theology itself, for example, was never justified textually). However, all such difficulties in detail were set aside in the larger view by the claim that what was being described was not this or that actual institution, but rather a set of "ideal types." Like so many other key ideas, this had several meanings. Minimally, it meant (1) that the pattern of individual or collective action was the analyst's own abstract construct; (2) that it was a goal or pattern which reality attempted or tended to approximate; and (3) that it was a pattern that underlay and determined the behavior of the people associated with it.

Despite the great differences in subject matter, the concept of the "ideal type" gave Weber's scheme the same logical structure that the concept of a "collective consciousness" gave to Durkheim's, and the "Protestant ethic" assumed the same status as Durkheim's "totemism."

The first important anthropologist to adopt the framework of German sociology was Robert Redfield. Redfield's long career at the University of Chicago began as a graduate student in the Department of Sociology and Anthropology under Robert E. Park, W. I. Thomas, and Albion Small. Park, who was also Redfield's father-in-law, was the principal theoretical influence.

Park's career was extraordinary. He did undergraduate work at Wisconsin under Dewey, worked as a reporter, taught at Howard University, and in 1899–1900 travelled to Berlin to study under Simmel for a year. In the following year he wrote his dissertation, largely based on Simmel's ideas, under Windelband at Strasbourg. Park acknowledged that it was from Simmel that he "finally gained a point of view for the study of the newspaper and society" (Levine 1971:1), but he obviously considered himself as representing a synthesis of both traditions—as indeed did Simmel. Park included numerous selections from Simmel in the famous text he edited with Robert Burgess. Thomas also evidently considered himself (and was, to some extent) a representative of both traditions—and saw them as coming together especially in the ethnology of Lowie, Kroeber, Wissler, and others associated with them, as already suggested. Small was a major proponent of Simmel's ideas, and of the German sociological tradition more generally, blending it with the Anglo-American social Darwinism stemming from W. G. Sumner.

Redfield's dissertation was a plan for the study of Tepoztlan based on a preliminary visit. The bibliography was drawn entirely from ethnology and social anthropology—apparently reflecting the interests and preferences of Thomas. There was no mention of any sociologist. The Introduction began with a quotation from Boas describing anthropology as "the science that endeavors to reconstruct the early history of mankind, and . . . to express in the form of laws ever-recurring modes of historical happening" (Redfield 1928:1). Redfield then commented that "in this single sentence he simultaneously embraced for anthropology the method of history and the method of explanatory science" (p. 1). The rest of the Introduction was devoted to separating the two methods, rejecting history, and taking the side of pure science—which he construed as the search for "uniformities independent of the time factor" (p. 2). He cited especially Kroeber and Malinowski, for "an interest in culture process as distinct from culture history" (p. 4), in addition to Tylor's evolutionism and diffusionism, all of which he saw as moving toward this more scientific goal. By name, in addition to Kroeber and Malinowski, he also commended repeatedly Lowie, Wissler, and Radcliffe-Brown—thus already foreshadowing the position which would later be attacked by Boas, as noted.

After receiving his degree, Redfield conducted the proposed study. The results were published in 1930 as *Tepoztlan: A Mexican Village*. No explicit reference was yet made either to Simmel or any other German sociologist, but Redfield nevertheless used their ideas to provide the overall framework of his argument. To them, he added an important series of modifications intended to incorporate ethnology as a theory that pertained to just part of the larger sociological totality—to define the "folk" in what would become the "folk-urban continuum."

Redfield takes Mexico as a "society," qualitatively more advanced and more complex than the isolated "primitive" communities anthropologists normally dealt with. He construed Mexico City as its metropolis, with all the attributes Simmel assigned, and construed all else as a "folk society"—specifically rejecting the idea that the "folk" were primarily Indian as such. The argument of the book then concerned the "diffusion" of rational, modern, secular, urban attitudes outward, and the gradual modernization of the "folk" in the process. A key, and original, part of the argument was the idea that the urban attitudes were not limited to residents of the metropolis; and that by the same token all residents of rural areas were not folk. Within Tepoztlan, the sociological characteristics of the folk were assigned to a group Redfield designated as *"los tontos,"* while the urban attitudes were represented by *"los correctos."* Each chapter emphasized the differences between them; in material culture, organization, calendars of activities, rituals, occupations, and ceremonies. Each chapter concluded with a statement to the effect that the traits or characteristics of *los tontos* were slowly giving way to those of *los correctos*. The conclusion, recalling at once the imagery of Wissler and Simmel, portrayed the diffusion of urban attitudes and ideas outward from the town plaza to the surrounding progressively more distant barrios.

In 1934 (Redfield and Villa-Rojas), Redfield had added the ideas of a "world view," of "holistic" theory, and of "ideal types" to his theoretical vocabulary (although the first two had been used more casually before). In 1950 *A Village That Chose Progress* incorporated most of Weber's conceptions of the relationship between religion and cultural change—aligning village Protestanism with the urban, rational, commercial segment of the population, and Catholicism with the more backward, conservative folk. Still later works developed the ideas even more, never departing significantly from the German sources (and Park's conception of their relation to pragmatism) in basic ideas.

Despite the nominal incorporation of ethnology, Redfield's work never did present, in an orderly way, most of the "ethnographic" detail that one finds even in contemporary works of the same general tradition—like Evans-Pritchard's. The descriptions always retain a thin, abstract, and distant quality—suggested by the use of the term *los tontos* ("the fools") itself. It is highly unlikely that such a term was used by those it named for themselves, but no description of its incidence was actually provided. Without the support of closely analyzed data, Redfield's framework remained only programmatic, although it was the program most widely followed by anthropologists who were less interested in the reconstruction of "tribal isolates" than in modern complex societies, in both the old and new worlds.

After 1945, a second major center for theory deriving directly from German sociology in North America was the Harvard Department of Social Relations (founded in 1946), and its principal representative was Talcott Parsons (b. 1902). Parsons attributes his own shift of interest from economics to sociology to his initial, almost accidental, acquaintance with Weber. However, there are also obvious debts to Durkheim, Pareto, American common-sense social intuitions, and the philosophy of science of the logical positivists, especially of W. V. O. Quine.

Parsons' conception of scientific theory is succinctly given in "The Present Position and Prospects of Systematic Theory in Sociology," first published in 1945 and republished in *Essays in Sociological Theory Pure and Applied* (1949):

> "Theory" is a term which covers a wide variety of different things which have in common only the element of generalized conceptualization . . . A theoretical system in the present sense is a body of logically interdependent generalized concepts of empirical reference. Such a system tends, ideally, to become "logically closed," to reach such a state of logical integration that every logical implication of any combination of propositions in the system is explicitly stated in some other proposition in the same system. (1949:17, 18)

This corresponds directly to Radcliffe-Brown's idea that theory was a logically integrated body of statements. As a description, it may apply to science in a rough way, although it leaves out precisely the open-ended generative power of scientific theory that is its most valued feature. But it applies much better to theology, and perhaps political ideologies. It completely ignores the ideas of experiment and demonstration.

Parsons' theory conformed to his conception of science: it is a generalized set of statements, tautologically interrelated, with no clear empirical relevance. His stated focus is not on society as such but, like Weber's, on "action," or rather "social action." His conceptions of society and of social roles are brought in as means to this end: "In the nature of the case, within the frame of reference of action, such a conceptual scheme must focus on the delineation of the system of institutionalized roles and the motivational processes organized around them" (*The Social System*, 1951:vii).

In *Toward a General Theory of Action,* written with Edward Shils, the social system is conversely said to consist "in actions of individuals" (1951:190). But action is not individual activity, and not organized around the physical individual but rather around the social role in a way reminiscent of Radcliffe-Brown's formulation: with the role in turn defined as the "conceptual unit of the social system" (p. 190), and as "a complementary set of expectations and the actions to be performed in accordance with these expectations" (p. 199). The values attached to roles were the same as those attached to collectivities: in effect, collectivities were defined only as coordinated roles, more than one actor with shared function (p. 203): ". . . the primary integration of the social system is based on an integrated system of generalized patterns of value orientation" (pp. 202–03).

Since value orientations and role actions were in turn closely tied to the idea of shared collective "goals," it was obviously impossible to see collectivities as corresponding to such durable social units as clans, religious organizations, and the like, conceived as persistent concrete bodies. Instead, as for Evans-Pritchard, the collectivity and roles were related to situations:

> The concept of boundary is of crucial significance in the definition of a collectivity. The boundary of a collectivity is that criterion whereby some persons are included as members and others excluded as non-members . . . (it) depends on whether or not he has a membership role in the collectivity. . . . Thus the boundary is defined in terms of membership roles. (p. 192)

The psychoanalytic distinction between latent and manifest symptoms was invoked to account for the existence of collectivities when their goals were not actually being sought: "The solidarity of a collectivity may, therefore, be latent as long as certain types of situations which would activate them fail to arise" (p. 193).

A very large part of the theoretical effort involved in popularizing this scheme went into developing terminologies for separating different types of collectivities, types of functions within them, and "levels" of analysis along which they were seen to be hierarchically related, from individuals through small groups to large societies, conceived of as increasingly larger collectivities with increasingly more general and encompassing goals.

Although Parsons reportedly views his system as incorporating the contributions of Kant and Mead, as well as Durkheim and Weber, it should be obvious that the work remains subject to the Kantian and pragmatic critiques. Even though the ideas that roles involve mutuality of expectations and actions, and that collectivities are sets of roles, resemble Mead's conception of the "generalized other" and the idea that institutions involve the sense that one can take another's place, and even though the idea of "latency" of situations recalls Mead's idea that self-consciousness existed only when it was called up for the solution of a life problem, the emphasis on the relation of the concepts to the actors is reversed between Parsons and Mead. For Mead, motivations, roles, and collectivities are categories of the actors, imputed by them to action to create a *sense* of situation. For Parsons as for Hegel, the situations are real beyond the perceptions of the actors, the motivations are inherent in the collectivity, and the goals are actual. They are categories of the analyst, not the actor, and are proposed as being universal and logical, prior to verification, rather than phenomenal and contingent, dependent on the situation by their very nature. Where Mead was proposing a theory about the creation of a sense of order, Parsons, Shils, and their colleagues were offering a theory about how social order is manifested, and how theory should be framed to show it. At bottom, for Parsons, society is separate from the actual individual; theory is separate from data; conceptual generalities are separate from concrete particulars; and the behavior of actual individuals is determined by the collectivities they take part in insofar as it is theoretically recognized or recognizable at all.

On the face of it, since Parsons' theory purports to be complete before empirical observations are made, and is tautological, it leaves nothing for a field analyst to do but show that phenomena in the field can be found to correspond to the elements of theory. And since actual phenomena cannot themselves be described fully by the terms of the theory (since the terms are stipulated as vacuous at the outset), this in practice means that "research" boils down to writing monographs or articles that describe one thing in two different sets of terminology—one ordinary, the other Parsons'—exactly corresponding to the data, or description, and abstract theory of the dualistic ethnologists. Interest in this has been understandably limited, and there are few anthropological "Parsonians" in this sense.

But many of what might be called Parsons' basic intuitions or suggestions have been taken up by a wide range of leading anthropologists, mainly trained at Social Relations in the 1950s. One was a revival of the dualistic view of motivation as a social fact, and a necessary component of social theory; another was a responsiveness to the idea of the ''situation.'' (The idea seems to be generally accepted that Parsons' treatment incorporated and developed G. H. Mead's formulations.) A third was a sense of the importance of ''values'' in an intellectual or cognitive sense as a determinant of action (here Parsons' own influence cannot be divorced from that of Weber as Parsons described him). And finally, Parsons restated the importance of *some* type of general theory (though not necessarily ''pure'' theory in his sense): and the consequent conflict between this conviction and that of the importance of recognizing ''cultural relativity'' has been a major contribution to the new character of anthropological debate.

Parsons' influence on anthropology cannot be disentangled from that of his colleague and associate, Clyde Kluckhohn (1905–70). Kluckhohn was not a sociologist but an anthropologist, by choice of professional label and general recognition. He did field work among the Navaho, and wrote ethnographic monographs. But his ideas show little continuity with previous anthropological tradition. On the surface, they are an amalgam of logical positivist conceptions of scientific methods with large amounts of psychoanalytic terminology and ways of conceptualizing relevant variables. More subtly, he appears to have accepted Parsons' conceptions of ''general'' theory, and to have seen his own work as either a more particular version of it, or an anthropological parallel to it. For example, Kluckhohn commonly would lecture by writing an aphorism from the *International Encyclopedia for a Unified Science* on the blackboard, and then attempt to relate it to the topic of the day, his own work, or whatever else had taken his interest at the time (personal reports, Harold Garfinkel and Roy D'Andrade).

Although Kluckhohn's writings obviously do not account for the affection and respect he is accorded by many very able anthropologists who knew him, they do indicate why there are few direct ''followers'' of Kluckhohn, as of Parsons. Most of his publications were aimed at non-professional readers, of which *Mirror for Man* (1949) was perhaps most important. One of the fullest of his few attempts to implement his theoretical ideas technically was *Navaho Witchcraft* (1944). This purports to explain the content and persistence of beliefs in witches and their supernatural powers among the Navaho, despite the fact that no one will admit to being a witch (to do so would be to risk severe sanctions). The argument is divided into two parts, the first purportedly giving the data, the second the theoretical "interpretations." Yet, in fact, the first part has highly selected description, coming almost entirely from structured interviews, and the second part has more of the same. The final conclusion is simply that Navahos believe in witches because it is psychologically reassuring to do so, displacing aggression against those they are in close contact with and expressing aggression toward others more distant. But since the primary evidence for the existence of the aggression thus used to "explain" the beliefs consisted in the beliefs themselves, the argument was circular. There was, for example, no systematic effort to see who was in fact accused of witchcraft; and the possibility that the beliefs were invoked in contexts completely unrelated to accusations was not even considered. In structure, the argument was precisely like those of the sociological traditions. A general substantive model is offered that is supposed to underlie and account for behavior. Cultural materials of diverse types—in this case mainly de-contextualized informants' accounts—that seem relevant to the model then are interpreted in its light, and the behaviors the accounts represent are inferred accordingly. Non-conforming material is either not indicated or noted and set aside, and nothing like the crucial test in an experiment is sought. The principal difference between Kluckhohn and the sociological analysts is that in this case the substantive model concerns supposedly universal psychological characteristics and their symbolic expressions, rather than universal models of society and its symbolic expressions. As a scientific analysis, the monograph is generally conceded to be a failure, but it set a pattern for many other workers to refine by stricter interpretive methods, aimed partly at making a clearer distinction between theory and interpretation.

Archeology

As linguists, cultural anthropologists, and social anthropologists became progressively more involved in their various searches for deterministic laws, divorcing history from "science," archeology became progressively less important to them, and vice versa; and the subfields drew increasingly apart.

Within archeology, the period from 1935 to 1955 falls into a larger period which Willey and Sabloff, in their recent history (1974), delineate as from 1914 to 1960, and call the "classificatory-historical period,'' subdivided into "the Concern with Chronology," extending to 1940, and into a period marked by a "concern with context and function." Basically, the first period involved seeking type-objects or features, mainly in sequences of like features, such as pottery-design motifs. Once sequences had been built up in many regions, and many series of objects were coordinated in the framework the sequences provided, it became possible to think in terms of the context and pattern. Concern then naturally shifted to complexes of unlike objects associated together rather than individual types of objects seen only through time.

In the first period, theory often took the form of proposed universal design or stylistic sequences, which had little relevance to major issues concerning man, mind, or science. In the later period, there was increasing inclination to see a "culture" not as represented by one or a few typical forms, or a single style, but rather as a set of frequencies of artifact (and style) occurrence. Willey himself provided an early and important version of this in his attempt to characterize the internal structure of settlements in the Viru Valley of Peru (1953). Robert M. Adams provides a very early attempt at seeing overall pattern in his schematic review of the ecological bases of the first "civilizations" (1950), and, at about the same time François Bordes applied statistical summation and analysis to the problem of describing paleolithic tool kits in a way that would suggest the ecological and industrial adaptations of their original users (see Bordes 1968:22–31 for a brief review and the relevance of his experimental reconstruction of manufacturing techniques that formed the basis of the typologies that the statistics quantified).

The shift to a contextual orientation was greatly aided by the simplification of chronological problems produced by radiocarbon dating, which could be used within the time range from 50,000 b.p. to very near the present. The theory of the technique had been developed in the 1930s by Willard Libby (b. 1908) at the Lawrence Radiation Laboratory at the University of California, Berkeley. It was adapted to archeological use in a series of experiments during 1948, 1949, and 1950, in a joint project with a committee of archeologists representing the American Anthropological Association, and sponsored by the Wenner-Gren Foundation and the University of Chicago. The experiments yielded dates for a wide range of archeological materials, from sites distributed worldwide and ranging in age from over 20,000 years to 538 ± 200 years (Libby 1952).

Occasionally, even before the functional period, archeologists did couch their theories and larger-scale reconstructions in terms that bore upon the theoretical arguments of cultural and social anthropology. The most important of these reconstructions were generally not favorable toward either the idea of cultural determinism or the lack of inventiveness and creativity in "primitive thought" (insofar as ancient civilizations might be regarded as primitive). Lowie, Murdock, and Lévi-Strauss would find scant comfort in V. Gordon Childe's *Man Makes Himself* (1941), or Henri Frankfort's *The Birth of Civilization in the Near East* (1950), both of which portrayed people as working to the limits of their capacities and as constantly producing innovations in doing so—and both of which in consequence stressed the contribution of individual creativity, rather than accident or diffusion, as long-term causes of culture change. But most archeologists were slow to accept the full implications of Childe's ideas in their field methods, and cultural and social anthropologists have largely ignored Childe, Frankfort, and the broad and highly sophisticated tradition of archeologically informed reconstructive history that they represent, which continues rather directly from the nineteenth-century historical tradition coming from Kant and, ultimately, Montesquieu. About the only major exception is Redfield, who explicitly framed his *Primitive World and Its Transformations* in terms of Childe's notion of an "urban revolution" as part of his restatement of Simmel's argument (somewhat distorting Childe) for a radical distinction between urban and "precivilized" society, with distinct moral orders and world views.

By the late 1950s, archeologists had reconstructed at least reasonably coherent, and often remarkably detailed, histories of the Near East, North India, most of the classical world, the American Southeast and Southwest, the great civilizations of Central and South America, and parts of Central Asia, going back to the apparent beginnings of settled agricultural life and its antecedents, and coming up in almost all cases to recorded history. There was found to be a great deal more pattern than the explanations for disregarding history in cultural and social anthropology would have suggested, and the patterns themselves suggested a richer, more complex, and more creative conception of human psychology than the dualistic determinisms appeared to be prepared to allow. Many thoughtful ethnologists soon found it rather difficult to ignore them.

Institutional Changes

The shift to dualism was abetted by a shift of the geographical center of anthropological activity to the English-speaking countries, particularly to the United States, and by the rapid increase in the numbers of new anthropologists. There was, for example, a sharp increase in both the absolute membership of the American Anthropological Association and in its rate of growth. By 1911, the original 87 members of the Association had grown to 217. Between 1911 and 1935, the average increase in membership was just 1.75 percent a year. In 1935, there were 735 members of all types (including institutional members). In 1943, the number had increased to 875. But in 1947, there were 1,271 members—raising the average rate of increase to 11 percent a year. This rate continued to accelerate to 18 percent a year from 1951 to 1955. In 1951, there were 1,555 members, and in 1955 there were about 2,688; or thirty for every one member of 1889, and 3.7 for every one member of 1935.

The Association was reorganized in 1947, adopting a new constitution drawn up by a committee headed by Julian Steward. The constitution provided for a distinction between "members" and "fellows," with the right to vote and hold office vested only in the latter. Fellows made up about 40 percent of the total in the first few years after the reform, and thereafter declined to about 20 percent. Candidates for election as a fellow had to hold the Ph.D. in anthropology or its equivalent.

Immediately before World War II there were still only four major graduate programs: at Chicago, Columbia, California at Berkeley, and Harvard (Archeology). Within a fairly short time after the war, there were large graduate programs at Harvard in the Department of Social Relations and at the University of Arizona, Cornell, Indiana University, the University of Michigan, the University of Pennsylvania, and the University of Wisconsin. At the same time, the size of departments increased sharply. Berkeley, for example, had seven full-time faculty members in 1935, nine in 1945, but fourteen in 1955. Columbia had only two regular full-time faculty members in the last years of Boas' life (he and Ruth Benedict), and fourteen in 1950.

New programs produced new anthropologists in turn. Adkins estimates the total "stock" of holders of the doctorate in anthropology in 1930 at 62. For 1935 it was 139. By 1945 it was 246, and in 1955 it was 600. The "stock" of holders of the Master's degree was about 20 percent larger at each point, so that the total stock in 1935 of some 466 persons with the M.A. had increased by 1955 to 1,431. The total number of persons actually employed in anthropological positions was consistently equal to about half the "stock" (see Adkins n.d.:27A).

Paralleling the increases in anthropological population and the amount of teaching activity was a rapid postwar increase in anthropological funding. Before the war, apart from individual departments, museums, and the Bureau of American Ethnology, funding came mainly from the Social Science Research Council, founded in 1923, with the American Anthropological Association as one of the constituent organizations that sent delegates to its governing board. The Council was the only funding agency concerned mainly with theoretical issues and raising scholarly standards, as opposed to sponsoring research in specific substantive areas. Prewar funding for the Council itself came mainly from two Rockefeller foundations (which also supported anthropologists directly through several programs). After the War, this support was over-shadowed by contributions to the Council from the Ford Foundation. The National Science Foundation and the National Institutes of Mental Health also began to provide funding to the Council, along with several other Government agencies and programs (see Sibley 1974:3). Concurrently, apart from the SSRC, the Ford Foundation also began direct sponsorship of anthropological research and institutional development through several programs. The NIMH also began its own direct sponsorship, and the NSF expanded its support from archeology and physical anthropology to ethnology and linguistics as well. The Viking Fund, devoted exclusively to anthropology, was incorporated in 1941—to be renamed the Wenner-Gren Foundation in 1951.

These changes reflect increasing public interest in and awareness of anthropology, attributable at least in part to increased commitments in world affairs and a postwar sense of world leadership responsibility that stood in sharp contrast to the predominant prewar isolationism, as well as new accessibility to American scholars of previously more or less closed colonial areas. More specifically, they can be attributed to the direct participation of anthropologists in wartime activities with the Government, and the relative success of those efforts. In 1943, according to a report prepared for informal circulation to anthropologists at the time (Setzler 1943), approximately 50 percent of all anthropologists were engaged full-time in war-related activities, and another 25 percent were engaged part-time. The total number employed was over 170, with about 125 in intelligence-related work, 40 in "action" programs (like the Office of the Coordinator of Interamerican Affairs and the War Relocation Authority), and the rest in teaching topics of special interest to the war effort and in other miscellaneous activities.

Anthropologists in war activity were associated with the Social Science Research Council, the Office of Indian Affairs, the Smithsonian Institution, and, very importantly, the Ethnogeographic Board, which acted as the central clearing house for anthropologists generally (see

Bennett 1947). They were also involved in a number of area-oriented programs related to intelligence that carried directly over into academic area and language programs after the war was over, among which were Clyde Kluckhohn's Russian Studies Project and Ruth Benedict's project on Japan.

British and Commonwealth anthropology also expanded after the Second World War, but not so sharply or with such dramatic organizational shifts as in North America. The British system had already been more strictly professional and had been more closely involved with Government interests and Government funding in the prewar colonial period. There was, for example, no category analogous to the American "members" in the prewar Royal Anthropological Institute of Great Britain and Ireland, only "fellows": minimally, holders of the Ph.D. or its equivalent. In 1935, there were 564 Fellows of the Institute. In 1945 there were 581, and in 1955 there were 1,010 (about the same as the number of Fellows in the *AAA*). The academic organization was different as well, and remained so. Many anthropologists were employed singly as fellows of colleges, linked to other anthropologists only through crosscutting boards and committees. The strictly anthropological bodies that did exist, like the Institute for Social Anthropology at Oxford and the Department of Anthropology at the London School of Economics, were rather more specialized than their American counterparts. They generally did not attempt to incorporate physical anthropology, and often excluded archeology, although the journals showed about the same range of interests as did those in the United States (the main exception being less emphasis on theoretical linguistics).

Anthropology in the Commonwealth outside Britain proper sometimes developed along lines that combined elements of both the British and American patterns. Canada in particular showed a blend of the two systems, since some of the American funding support was available to Canadians, and there was widespread conscious commitment to a unified North American anthropology, with free movement of scholars between positions in the two countries.

French anthropology retained its prewar character with remarkably little change. Many scholars had been forced into exile or into the Resistance, but after the war they reassembled the prewar patterns, with little acceleration in growth or change of direction. As before, French anthropology remained much more closely linked to explicit philosophy and political movements than did either the North American or British traditions.

German anthropology had been virtually wiped out by a series of internal developments, beginning in many respects with anti-Semitic movements in the universities in the 1890s. Nazi suppression after Hitler came to power in 1933 finished the process, so that all branches but physical anthropology and some extreme diffusionisms were defunct by about 1937 and could not be reconstituted after the war. The Kantian tradition, associated as it was with academic and political liberalism, had been an especially marked victim.

There had been a sophisticated Italian tradition up to about 1930, dominated by Kantian conceptions with a Hegelian positivist opposition. But with the rise of Fascism the former tradition was suppressed and the latter suborned, with stultifying effects. Anthropology has been of only minor interest in Italy since, and remains heavily politicized.

These world-wide institutional changes had the net effect of concentrating more scholars in settings that were not only dominated by dualisms, but more importantly, in settings where issues framed dualistically were no longer in explicit conflict with issues framed monistically. In leading North American, British, and French universities, it was an easy matter for a student to come to believe that the assumptions of the dualistic tradition were basic properties of knowledge itself. This all worked to support the impression that the dualistic subtraditions represented a greater portion of the spectrum of all possible theories than was in fact the case.

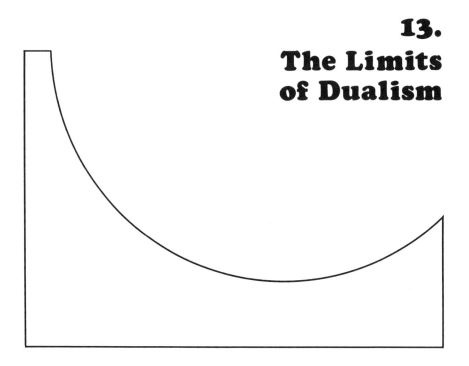

13.
The Limits
of Dualism

The continuation of the pre- and postwar dualistic schools after 1955 was itself a major cause of the transformation from the postwar sense of optimism to a sense of crisis. Murdock, Redfield, Lévi-Strauss, Evans-Pritchard, Kroeber, Fortes, Kluckhohn, Parsons, Steward, and most of the others continued to attract followers who made only minor amendments to their ideas without defending or even questioning the dualistic assumptions they all shared. Indeed Redfield, in 1955, went so far as to explicitly describe a number of the British and American interests as virtually different phraseologies for the same kind of analysis—what he called the "methodological resemblances of social structure, total cultural pattern, and typical biographical development" (1955:23). This description was precisely correct, in just the sense that has been argued here. But it was hardly conducive to a sense that the debates over the previous twenty-odd years had been progressive or that the issues were real. Redfield was equally correct, and equally discouraging, when in the same essay he observed that the "scientific" character of these anthropological theories consisted primarily in the use, in writing, of certain metaphors, the "evocation of images" of a mechanistic or scientific type—such as the concept of "networks" or the organic analogy itself.

A second component of the change of outlook derived from a second set of debates developing partly in reaction to the first. They aimed at finding ways to decide definitively among the claims of alternative dualistic formulations on more than stylistic or literary grounds, and at more clearly delineating the many ranges of phenomena that were slowly being distinguished from one another as field-work practice was progressively refined. To do this, this second group of scholars not only began once again to evaluate the dualistic assumptions themselves, but in most cases they engaged either in a limited effort to reject them or to restrict their application, or at least to prepare the way for such a challenge. In this, they explored and delineated the limits of dualism in a way their predecessors had not done, and in several notable cases they recreated major elements of the monistic orientations and contexts of Malinowski and Boas. Five of these debates can serve to indicate the overall range of topics and approaches that were encompassed. Roughly in the order in which they came to general notice, the five are: the discussion of the relationship between social structure and social organization (aggregated behavior), componential analysis, the alliance-descent controversy, cultural ecology, and economic anthropology.

Social Structure, Social Organization, and Individual Behavior

The first and in most respects the clearest and broadest of the explorations of the limits of dualism was a specific series of changes in the conceptualization of social structures and social organization, which eventually resurrected much of the critical outlook, if not the positive theory or background, of Malinowski. The line can be dated from about 1951, when Nadel published his *The Foundations of Social Anthropology* and Raymond Firth published *Elements of Social Structure. Foundations* is a critical review of most of the major concepts and topics then in use in ethnology, from ideas of "groupings," explanation, and experimental method, through meaning and symbolism, to psychology, and "function and pattern." The conclusion, which does not by any means summarize all the points made on the way to it, was equally skeptical of "functional," "structural," "cultural," and culture and personality theory,

Culture and society exhibit three pattern formations—purposive, psychological, and logical. None can be absent, and there is some overlapping and "fit" between them; yet equally, there is the latitude of alternative solutions and some measure of independent variability. In brief, we have, not a conspicuous coherent configuration, but a composite picture with blurred contours and many gaps. We can speak only of pattern trends extending a certain way, and only of an incipient wholeness. Nor are the pattern trends ready-made or unequivocal in the manner of a perceptual *gestalt*. The integration of purposes must be constructed from calculations of means and ends; and the existence of the psychological "pattern," from our knowledge of level mechanisms, that is, of some "hidden machine" intervening between diverse impulses and attitudes. In either construction we may err. (1951:403)

Nadel proposed no real solutions, and the many types of patterns he described and separated from one another still remain largely unaccounted for, but at least someone had said it: the emperor was not fully clothed.

Firth's *Elements* was a textbook rather than a theoretical *tour de force*, but it did step squarely into one of Nadel's "gaps" with a very important empirical distinction. The gap was that between social structure and behavior, and the distinction was between social structure and social organization:

In studying a field of social relations, whether we are using the notions of society, of culture, or of community, we can distinguish their structure, their function, and their organization. These are separable but related aspects. All are necessary for the full consideration of social process. Briefly, by the structural aspect of social relations we mean the principles on which their form depends; by the functional aspect we mean the way in which they serve given ends; by the organizational aspect we mean the directional activity which maintains their form and serves their ends. (1951:28)

The assumptions here descend directly from Malinowski and are quite different from those of the strongly deterministic and organically oriented theories. All these "aspects" are equally empirical and analytic or both. One is not the form of the other, nor does one determine the other.

Also in 1951, E. R. Leach published "Structural Implications of Matrilateral Cross-Cousin Marriage," primarily as a reply to Lévi-Strauss' *Elementary Structures*. It dealt with the same societies that were later to be reviewed as part of the alliance-descent debate and was, therefore, squarely in the middle of the arguments for the various determinisms—between Lévi-Strauss's Hegelian arguments and Radcliffe-Brown's positivistic inductivism. Leach did not reject determinism to the extent Firth did, but neither did he cleave to one deterministic position or the other. Instead, he attempted to construct a blend of all three options. He moved in the direction of recognizing individual voluntarism and the status of social structures as conceptual models used by natives on what he considered an empirical level, but he tried to retain a deterministic conception of what to say about such facts at what, he argued, was a theoretical level.

The general topic is marriage, which Leach says at the outset, is of "two kinds": "The first results from the whims of two persons acting as private individuals; the second is a systematically organized affair which forms part of a series of contractual obligations between groups" (1951, rpt. in 1961:56). Thus associating systematic organization only with groups *rather than* individuals, he goes on to say what kinds of groups especially concern him: "I am concerned with only systems of unilateral (and double unilateral) descent," about which he argued that:

> In a unilaterally defined descent system where a clan, or large scale lineage, ceases, for one reason or another, to be a localized group, then, in general, it ceases to be a corporate unit for the purposes of arranging a marriage. The corporate group which does arrange a marriage is, in such circumstances, always a group of males who, besides being members of the same lineage or clan, share a common place of residence. (1951, rpt. in 1961:56)

Leach went on to set up a major analytical distinction between "descent lines" and "local lines." "Descent lines have nothing whatever to do with local grouping, they are merely a diagrammatic device for displaying the categories of a kinship system in relation to a central individual called Ego" (1951, rpt. in 1961:57).

While he seems to agree with Lévi-Strauss that descent lines are analytic models, as discussion proceeds Leach shifts more and more to the view that they are also aspects of native categorical systems:

> Kachin society as described in the standard ethnographic accounts and by Lévi-Strauss is made up of 5 exogamous patricians which marry in a circle in the manner already discussed. In a paper published in 1950 . . . I showed that this circular marriage system does not represent empirical fact but is simply a kind of verbal model which the Kachins themselves use to explain the general pattern of their system. (1961:81)

One aspect of the counter-analysis concerned the presence, among the Kachin, of rules of marriage between social classes, and of patterns of bride wealth given to the groups from which wives are taken. According to Lévi-Strauss, the Kachin rule of matrilateral cross-cousin marriage should have produced a system of equal groups on the same level, and equality of exchange, because the last wife-giver was the first wife-taker. If there were invidious comparisons, if wife-takers were lower in status than wife-givers, then this would produce the anomolous situation where the first wife-giver was of the highest status and the last wife-taker of the lowest, although they were in fact the same group. Similar reasoning precludes complicated and non-uniform bride-wealth systems. Since everyone in the circle should send bride wealth in one direction and brides in another, it seemed that there ought to be a general simplicity or equality of bride wealth throughout the system, to avoid a destructive accumulation of brides in one area and wealth in another. But in fact, as Lévi-Strauss had himself recognized, the system was not egalitarian, nor was bride wealth uniform, nor were there some groups that accumulated brides while others accumulated wealth.

Leach argues that the only way the logic of the model could be recognized alongside the complexity of the data was by dropping the idea that the model directly corresponded to, or represented the overall pattern of, actual intergroup relations. Rather, it described only part of the pattern, or rather was used in only part of the pattern, and when this usage was put in the context of the other, related patterns, it would be seen to be "neither contradictory or self-destructive" (p. 88). His summary of this portion of the article is worth quoting in full:

(1) From a political aspect, chief is to headman as feudal Lord of the Manor is to customary free-holder.

(2) From a kinship aspect, chief is to headman as *mayu* to *dama,* that is as father-in-law to son-in-law.

(3) From a territorial aspect, the kinship status of the headman's lineage in respect to that of the chief is held to validate the tenure of land.

(4) From an economic aspect the effect of matrilateral cross-cousin marriage is that, on balance, the headman's lineage constantly pays wealth to the chief's lineage in the form of bridewealth. The payment can also, from the analytical point of view, be regarded as a rent paid to the senior landlord by the tenant. The most important part of this payment is in the form of consumer goods—namely cattle. The chief converts this perishable wealth into imperishable prestige through the medium of spectacular feasting. The ultimate consumers of the goods are in this way the original producers, namely, the commoners who attend the feast. (1961:88–89)

At this point, Leach had an option. He could have recognized that this argument did not in fact depend on the initial association of structural relations with groups rather than individuals, or his associated deterministic conception of theory. He could even have concluded that it leads to an abandonment of a primary concern with such cross-cultural systems, and instead encourages a concern with the way individuals build up their contexts out of diverse but systematic conceptual elements and out of responses to constraints of a more concrete kind. This would have dove-tailed neatly and in a very interesting way with Firth's ideas in many respects, and it would have made individual choice and relativity of perspective major aspects of theory. Yet in the end, he would not abandon the dualistic assumptions: "My own argument, in which to a great extent I follow Lévi-Strauss, is that the comparison of models rather than of 'whole cultures' is a necessary and valid method—indeed I would go much further in such abstraction than has usually been the case with the followers of Radcliffe-Brown" (1961:104).

In several subsequent works Leach's conception of comparative theory that sets aside individual action and volition was still more sharply juxtaposed to his contrasting conceptions of the way individuals utilize social structures as culturally established mental constructs in a practical setting. *Political Systems of Highland Burma* (1954) extended his description of Kachin society. Kachin social organization was seen as involving an alternation between an aristocratic and an anarchic form of Kachin society, wherein there was a tendency for power to accumulate in fewer and stronger hands in local areas, up to the point that organization approached that of the Shan (Chinese) communities in some areas. But then, for a combination of ecological and structural reasons, the organization did not go over to the Shan type but became unstable and generated a rebellion of sorts that returned it to the Kachin anarchic form. While the overall structure of the analysis preserved determinism in the face of change and variation, Leach went on to provide all the evidence needed for a strong anti-deterministic case. It wasn't clear who actually was Kachin and who was Shan; in given local areas there were often competing versions of the social organization; and it was clear that individuals and groups were using rituals to promulgate the views they wanted, self-consciously and creatively.

Leach recognized the two aspects of his account—deterministic and anti-deterministic—and tried to reconcile them with the general distinction between analysts' "ideal" models as opposed to ethnographic "reality":

My conclusion is that while conceptual models of society are necessarily models of equilibrium systems, real societies can never be in equilibrium. The discrepancy is related to the fact that when social structures are expressed in cultural form, the representation is imprecise compared with that given by the exact categories which the sociologist, qua scientist, would like to employ. I hold that these inconsistencies in the logic of ritual expression are always necessary for the proper functioning of any social system.
Most of my book is a development of this theme. I hold that social structure in practical situations (as contrasted with the sociologist's abstract model) consists of a set of ideas about the distribution of power between persons and groups of persons. Individuals can and do hold contradictory and inconsistent

ideas about this system. They are able to do this without embarrassment because of the form in which their ideas are expressed. The form is cultural form; the expression is ritual expression. The latter part of this introductory chapter is an elaboration of this portentous remark. (1954:4)

In subsequent works, Leach expanded and refined still further the ideas of "Structural Implications" and *Political Systems,* retaining the critical stance toward Lévi-Strauss at an empirical level, bringing in a fuller sense of the force of ecological and economic constraints, but remaining unable or unwilling to break away from dualistic (deterministic and organic) assumptions about theory as such.

In 1960, F. G. Bailey added an important new dimension to Leach's type of critique. Bailey was a student of Gluckman, and reflected the then-current concern with "conflict" as a basic social structure. *Tribe, Caste, and Nation,* focusing mainly on the social organization of a village in the Kond tribal area in Orissa State, India, carried the idea of conflict into new areas by describing not one social structure but three "incompatible with one another, existing in the same field" (1960:10). The structures were those named in the title, and the term "incompatible" was explicitly given theoretical weight to make it the relation that existed between unrelated structures, rather than between parts of a single structure or possible conflicts arising from roles within a structure:

It is helpful to make a distinction between conflict and contradiction. 'Conflict,' as I use it, is contained and 'sealed off' within a structure. 'Contradiction'—between roles or institutions—is not, and is symptomatic of social change. Contradictions of this kind are most readily apparent at the level of 'structure' rather than 'substructure.' It was, for instance, very obvious in Bisipara that the ritual substructure in which the WARRIORS and the untouchables interacted was in many respects inconsistent with their political and economic relationships. There was an irresolvable contradiction between these two substructures, and taken together they did not add up to one consistent structure. There were neither rules nor institutions nor roles within the caste system designed to cope with such a situation. The same was true in Baderi (. . .). The presence in any situation of irresolvable contradiction between different roles indicates that the total situation cannot be understood within the framework of a single omnicompetent structure. If this is to be continued within the framework of one structure, then one or the other side of the contradiction must be ignored. This is not satisfactory since it removes the analysis further from reality. Alternatively it may be assumed that there is not one structure to be analyzed, but there are two or more structures operating in a single social field. (p. 8)

Recognition of multiple structures more than any other point in the literature stands against the idea of determinism, for it inherently raises the necessity for a choice of roles for any individual at any time, and eliminates any external mechanism whereby that choice might be preordained or determined. Bailey recognized this and stated it clearly:

> In a field of activity as complicated as that of the Kond hills we need to emphasize complexity, and to look not for one political system, but for several. Secondly, we need to see individuals not as passive creatures exhibiting for our benefit regularities in behavior, but as actors who may not only choose between systems but may attempt to twist and amend these systems to their own advantage.
>
> In this book I have largely been content to show that people do behave in this way: that there are several political systems: and that the actors pick and choose between them. (p. 271)

But despite these clear statements, and a clear empirical argument in support of them, Bailey did not press his argument to the full theoretical conclusions. Instead, like Leach, he summarized his argument by treating the description of multiple structures, of choice, and of manipulation, as description *rather than* theory. The reason given was that such description applies to "dynamics," but that structure (and hence theory in general) is inherently "static" (pp. 14, 238–39).

In effect, Bailey recognized the shortcomings of the assumptions of organic social theory, rejected its claim to provide determinate accounts of behavior, but then turned around and considered it good "theory" precisely because of these shortcomings, refusing thereby to grant the status of theory to what was obviously and acknowledgedly a better account of the same actual data:

> A social structure can be described without any reference whatever to particular individuals and without the use of specific cases. A description of this kind, if well done, makes a strong appeal to the intellect: it is elegant, sparing in detail, rounded and complete, and has a sharp, tidy, thoroughly 'scientific' exactness. It is a work of logic: the various parts of the structure agree with one another and all fit together to make a neat whole. On the other hand, the more exact is the structure the more difficult it becomes to fit it to reality. The presentation of the material at a high level of abstraction makes it impossible for the reader to measure its adequacy as a description of the society which it is supposed to explain, and to see whether this is the only possible interpretation. Indeed, it would be unfair to question the interpretation in this way, for the only accepted criticism is one which shows an internal inconsistency in the structure. (p. 14)

The intent is to involve the dichotomy between abstract and particular, but the actual sense given the term "abstraction" in this defense of theory is much more precisely that which at other places and times might be assigned the word "fictitious" as opposed to "accurate." The explanation temporarily rescues dualistic organic theory from total rejection, but it also provides license for developing descriptive models of society in relation to behavior that are quite out of keeping with the dualistic tradition that organic theory represents. Against Evans-Pritchard and Lévi-Strauss, it removes determinism as a feature to be sought in actual descriptions, introduces individual relativity of perspective and individual purpose as possible explanatory variables, and, perhaps most importantly, rejects out of hand the traditional dualistic solipsism. If structures are what natives choose and manipulate, they must be what natives "see," construe, or impute. They therefore cannot be inventions of the analyst alone, and the analyst is therefore not free to reject data that do not fit his conceptions on the ground they are not theoretically significant.

While Bailey's *Tribe, Caste, and Nation* does not appear to have been as widely read as the originality of its arguments should have merited, and his later works did not restate the same points so clearly, similar changes in theoretical outlook were argued for in a more scattered way by a number of other scholars. Frederick Barth's "Segmentary Opposition and the Theory of Games" (1959) had argued that Pathans obviously switched their allegiance to "lineal" segments, and that the strategy for joining such segments—whether stronger or weaker—that were in conflict over land and other resources could be described in terms of the idea of a zero sum game. This made an explanatory variable of a very specific type of choice, one which was both public and competitive, and it suggested very strongly that the form of the social structure was itself a response to that competitive situation, and was maintained by the same choices that it helped organize. Later, Barth added another dimension to the picture by arguing that social structure itself should be seen not as a system of categories that encompassed ordered behavior, but rather as core forms or relations that generated it (1966).

Clifford Geertz's *Agricultural Involution* (1963a), describing the course of population movement and agricultural development in Indonesia under the impact of Dutch colonial policies, made a point very similar to Barth's game theory analysis by arguing that considerations of personal need and gain determined the actual outcome, unwanted though it was, of the Dutch policies under the given ecological and cultural circumstances. And he made a point similar to Bailey's, though broader, by arguing for the separation not only of social organization and value systems from each other but also from the regimes of "cultural ecology" and from economic mechanisms and forces (p. 9). However, Geertz, too, declined to follow out the implications of these cleavages in the data as he recombined the various cultural and economic elements to argue for two distinct and separate sectors or "spheres" of a "dual economy"—one Indonesian, the other Dutch, and each virtually an organic cultural whole, dominated by its distinctive values, in its own right.

In other important and very widely appreciated monographs and essays Geertz has invoked both phenomenological and pragmatic concepts of symbols and their relation to perception and behavior, treating both culture and social organization alike as fundamentally "textual," a network of meaningful symbols. He has implicitly advocated the application of interpretive techniques from philosophical and literary criticism with great success, as against the techniques of psychological or social determinism. He has explicitly invoked both the ideas of Ludwig Wittgenstein and Alfred Schutz in arguing for the independent observability of ideas within social situations, in opposition to both "Hegelian or the Marxist forms of reductionism" (1966a:3). His work has stressed that culture and social organization alike do not exist apart from individuals but rather in and through individuals' interpretations of events and objects around them, and he has thereby reasserted the idea that social order was both subjective and objective, a matter of individuals' values and motivations, yet bound up in public symbols and communication. He has in the process restated and clarified for many anthropologists the fundamental issues that had generated the technical debates, but had often been obscured by the very arguments they generated.

Yet Geertz's main orientation remained rooted in Harvard Social Relations, where he received his early training. His explications of the concepts of personal inter-relations implicit in social symbolism concentrated on the relationship between symbols—from funerals to cockfights—and their audience, on the flow of interpretation "outward," in a sense, from message to receiver, and thence by implication from receiver to some final application. But the major differences between phenomenology and pragmatism, or rather between dualistic phenomenology and pragmatism, come from the other side of the relation—not the way in which the symbol gives up its meaning but in the way it obtains its meaning. The pragmatic view, consistent with the larger monistic tradition, is that the meanings are *assigned* to the symbols by their users, and the central theoretical effort focuses less on interpretation than on the way this assignment is made. On this crucial point Geertz most often returns to the formulations of Max Weber, arguing finally that culture simply *is* an integrated system of values that individuals enact and that in itself determines their behavior or perceptions—a view that ultimately minimizes the theoretical significance of the ability of individuals to create such values in turn (cf. "Ritual and Social Change, A Javanese Example" [1957]; *Peddlers and Princes* [1963b]; "Religion as a Cultural System" [1966b]). Even when, in several important recent essays, he avoids postulating such extra-phenomenal entities as "social organization," "culture" or unified systems of values, his position remains at bottom cultural determinism: "Our ideas, our values, our acts, even our emotions, are like our nervous system itself, cultural products—manufactured, indeed, out of tendencies, capacities, and dispositions with which we were born, but manufactured nevertheless ("The Impact of the Concept of Man," in Geertz 1973:50).

Geertz, like Lévy-Bruhl, takes the dualistic conceptions of the study of society close enough to the border of monism to incorporate much of the material usually better dealt with in the monistic framework, and close enough to avoid many of the more forceful critiques. But he does not cross over.

Componential Analysis

The empirical and theoretical scope of componential analysis was far narrower than that of the debate over the relationship between social structure and social organization; and its original conceptions of man, mind, and science were far more wholly and consistently dualistic. But in part for these very reasons, it succeeded in defining an area of inquiry—kinship terminologies and similar taxonomies—where the case for an alternative monism could be more clearly and concisely stated.

Componential analysis began in the middle 1950s, in an effort to reconstitute Murdock's universalistic analysis of kinship on a narrower basis. Ward Goodenough, its originator, retained Murdock's approach through kin types, but dropped the statistical methods and rejected the claim to connect terminological meaning to larger domestic group and social organizational patterns. To do this, Goodenough combined two distinctions from very diverse sources. The first was Kroeber's idea that kinship terminologies were "psychological" and not "social," as noted. The second was a dichotomy between the "denotation" of a term and its "connotation" that was invented by Gottlob Frege (according to T. W. Bynum 1972:45), and is still widely current in the literature of logical positivism. In this literature, "denotation" is roughly equated with referential meaning (subject to qualifications that arise from the difficulty of actually specifying referents in many cases), while "connotation" is roughly what a term may suggest to the user but not signify objectively. Goodenough's seminal 1956 paper (following usages in Murdock's *Social Structure*) put the dichotomy to work by formally equating the kin-type gloss of a term with its "denotation," considering all other aspects of its meaning as connotation, and defining his analysis as concerned with denotative meaning only.

Analysis was performed on kinship terminologies as *sets* of terms. It began by substituting kin-type sets for each of the actual terms of a terminology and then sought, mainly by trial and error, the minimal contrasts that would discriminate the groups of glosses, like differences in sex, relative age, and so on. In 1960, Wallace and Atkins elaborated Goodenough's method, stressing that it gave meanings that were "psychologically real" but not "sociologically real," and recorded more fully the history of the development. By the mid-1960s the techniques had been extended to the analyses of several types of taxonomic systems, and to law, and had been connected to a series of techniques to corroborate the "psychological reality" of the components discovered by the analyst through his formal manipulations (see Romney and D'Andrade 1964). This extended version was called "ethnosemantics," "ethnoscience," and even "the new ethnology." Partly because of the association with the positivistic philosophy of science, these techniques seemed to many to promise very general applicability, once they could be sufficiently refined and convincingly applied to a wider range of phenomena. Work to refine and extend them overlapped with work undertaken in pursuit of Chomsky's rather closely related program in linguistics. For example, "kernel" meanings in terminologies have been delineated and described as analogous to "kernel" sentences out of which more elaborate syntactic structures were generated.

Through a complicated series of arguments and counterarguments within the basic framework, Goodenough's original program has given way to a quite diverse and sophisticated set of arguments. Most scholars concerned with them still adhere to a basically positivistic program, but some have begun to see their concern as a more empirical and pragmatic effort to explicate the formal properties of various types of restricted but real cultural systems. In addition to Goodenough and Wallace and At-kins, major contributions have been made by Roy D'Andrade, A. K. Romney, Floyd Lounsbury, Harold Scheffler, Paul Kay, Eugene Ham-mel, William Sturtevant, Fred Strodbeck, Dell Hymes, Harold Conklin, and Charles Frake (the last three being especially noted for their disin-clination to accept the positivistic theory of meaning and framework of argument).

Componential analysis in the broad sense made three major contribu-tions to the formation of a non-dualistic reorientation. It provided a major critique (in the classroom more than in print) of the established "functional" practice of explicating the meaning of kinship terminol-ogies (and other classifications), by taking the terms one at a time or in small sets and placing them not among other terms but rather in "insti-tutions," marriage rules, ritual usages, and the rest. Secondly, even though the method is contaminated by the use of Anglo-American ideas of the biological basis of kinship to define the "denotata" (and non-kinship applications have some related problems), the analyses did show how an important set of anthropological data could be organized and analyzed without *any recourse whatever* to a "total" cultural analysis, total structure, or the like, seeing the data only as embodying a re-stricted set of contrasting classificatory categories. Thirdly, the tena-cious concern for making the basis of the analysis explicit struck many anthropologists as a great improvement in rigor over the often com-pletely unstated observational basis of traditional theorizing, even though componential analysis was not in fact a system for the field elici-tation of data but rather for the organization of data already obtained (by the usual very unclear means).

Once componential analysts had set up the problems, it was natural that more skeptical anthropologists would seek to apply the same basic type of contrastive, pattern-fitting methods to produce logically com-plete terminologies directly in the process of field elicitation, offering the results as more naturalistic counterparts to the componential analy-sis, without relying on the positivistic metatheoretical overlay (Burling 1970; D'Andrade 1970; Leaf 1971). In a slightly different vein others used the methodological concepts to describe techniques for the field elicitation of native "events," "behaviors," and significant objects, by allowing those who enacted them to say what were contrastive elements and features, and what were not (see Frake's 1964 analysis of "religious behavior"). However, before this counter-current developed strongly, in the early 1960s an important running argument developed between Good-enough and Scheffler (mainly) representing the componential analysts on the one hand, and David Schneider, primarily representing concerns reflected in the alliance-descent debate on the other (see Schneider 1965a, 1965c, 1969). This argument came to be a significant stimulus to the subsequent development of "symbolic anthropology."

The Alliance-Descent Argument

The alliance-descent debate began with Lévi-Strauss's *Elementary Structures,* although it was formally named and identified only in retrospect by Louis Dumont in 1961 (Dumont 1961, see Schneider 1965b:25). Thereafter, it was discussed mainly by those taking the "alliance" side intermittently until 1965, when Schneider's pivotal and widely discussed summary of the debate reminded most participants that the positions were very largely two sides of one coin (1965b), and raised problems common to both. Although Schneider did not provide an alternative formulation, the critique helped to clear the ground for a wide range of work that ultimately departed quite sharply from both "functionalism" and "structuralism."

Schneider describes the conflict wholly in dualistic terms, in large part as a conflict between "positivist" and "idealist" assumptions:

> Alliance theory, with roots clearly in Durkheim and Mauss, has specifically arisen out of Lévi-Strauss, Dumont, Leach, and Needham. Descent theory also has its roots in Durkheim and Mauss, but its development has been through Radcliffe-Brown to Fortes, Goody, Gough, Gluckman, and, in certain respects, Firth. . . . It would also be useful to point out, that where Durkheim tried to bridge the gap between positivism and idealism and ended up as an idealist in the remnants of some positivist clothing, Needham's version of alliance theory is, if anything, squarely on the side of the idealists. Lévi-Strauss and Dumont, on the other hand, go with Hegel (Murphy, 1963). Descent theory has moved in the direction of positivism; some of its misunderstandings stem from its positivist premises; and the direction which the younger descent theory people (Goody, Gough) have taken seems to me to be consistent with this view.
>
> . . . both alliance and descent theory are concerned with social structure. But for descent theory, social structure is considered one or another variant of the concept of (a) concrete relations or groupings, socially defined, which (b) endure over time. To Radcliffe-Brown, social structure is the network of 'actual social relations'; for Evans-Pritchard in discussing the Nuer (Evans-Pritchard, 1940) it is the enduring social groups, the concrete lineages. For

alliance theory, the problem is not what the concrete patterns of social relations actually are, although these are not neglected; it is not the actual organization of any specific group like a lineage. It is, instead, that construct or
model which is fabricated by the anthropologist and which is presumed to
have, as its concrete expression, the norms for social relations and the rules
governing the constitution of social groups and their inter-relations (Lévi-
Strauss, 1953). (Schneider 1965b:26)

"Positivism" and "idealism" are being given meanings here that
overstate the actual differences between them. Evidently on the basis of
recourse to the form-matter dichotomy itself, positivism is being treated
as a kind of crude materialism, and idealism as the contention that mentality alone was the locus of social order. In fact, neither Evans-
Pritchard nor Radcliffe-Brown is as far from Lévi-Strauss as Schneider
suggests. Yet not withstanding this exaggerated characterization,
Schneider concludes only that:

Instead of typologies we need a series of relevant elements, like descent,
classification, exchange, residence, filiation, marriage, and so on; these need
to be rigorously defined as analytic categories and then combined and recombined into various combinations and permutations, in different sizes, shapes,
constellations.
The model of defined parts can be constructed with, or without, Lévi-
Strauss's kind of intellectualist or Hegelian assumptions, or the kind of positivism which Fortes requires.
Finally, there is one point which needs stressing and which I only touched
on. Alliance theory as a theory is capable of dealing with the symbol system
as a system apart from, yet related to, the network of social relations. . . .
Where Radcliffe-Brown rejected culture in favor of what he was pleased to
call structure, and where Leach in an earlier work separated out cultural or-
naments, alliance theorists have brought culture and social structure into an
ordered relationship which even Needham's gross manipulations of the
Purum data cannot obscure. (1965b:78–79)

Since the mid-1960s social structural theory has very largely followed
the lines Schneider suggests here. There has been a sharp decrease in
explicit concern with total societies, and much more concern with specific social entities and processes, especially "symbolic" process
(variously conceived).

It might seem that a concern with culture as symbolic process, or cultural symbolism, would be inherently incompatible with a tradition of
theory that ignores individual relativity of perspective, imposes the analyst's own categories, and seeks eternal objects of knowledge based on
imagined universals of logic or fact. But a very large portion of the

work in recent symbolic anthropology has been based on precisely these ideas—in a word, on the dualistic tradition in yet another transformation. These have mainly involved a search for some kind of universal substantive symbolism, or symbolic relations, with invariant meanings or uses independent of cultural context. But a few writers, most notably Mary Douglas and Victor Turner, have seen the inconsistency in this, and have striven to reformulate the assumptions upon which such a search for symbolic order is to be based. Douglas has moved definitely toward phenomenology (in a way, however, that does not at all preclude the idea of universal symbols or continued reliance on the mind-matter dichotomy). Turner, starting from a position rather like Gluckman's (Turner 1957), has moved to a more critical stance (in the philosophical sense), and to explicit recourse to "information theory." In the reflective introduction to *The Drums of Affliction,* written some time after the main text (personal communication), he summarized his view:

> . . . I have long considered that the symbols of ritual are so to speak 'storage units,' into which are packed the maximum amount of information. They can also be regarded as multi-faceted mnemonics, each facet corresponding to a specific cluster of values, norms, beliefs, sentiments, social roles, and relationships within the total cultural system of the community performing the ritual. In different situations, different facets or parts of facets tend to be prominent, though the others are always felt to be penumbrally present. The total 'significance' of a symbol may be obtained only from consideration of how it is interpreted in every one of the ritual contexts in which it appears, i.e., with regard to its role in the total ritual system. (1968:12)

To have gone on to say that the "packing" of meaning in such symbols was done by the users would have broken completely with the dualistic tradition. Turner would then, by implication, have left the analyst only the task of describing the way others construct and convey the information that defines their realities, perhaps going on to describe general features of the packing process itself. This in fact became the concern of Turner's next work, discussed in the following chapter.

Cultural Ecology

Compared to the changing conceptions of social structure, and despite an active following, developments in cultural ecology added few new themes to the general widening of debate, mainly several important dimensions to the revival of interest in cultural variability and competition. Several widely circulated arguments for cultural ecology, perhaps most notably Harris' persuasive history (1968), have attributed this lack of influence to a kind of conspiracy of neglect among other ethnologists, based on political (anti-Marxist and anti-materialist) or anti-scientific prejudice.

In fact, however, the reason is that while their formulations address some general interest in comparative theory, they have tended to repeat old generalities about society as a whole, or evolutions as a whole, and have because of this had little new to say about the most pressing and direct problem of most anthropologists—making sense out of the fine details of direct field research experience. Moreover, the generalities have relied on basic assumptions that were already being challenged as noted. Steward, for example, identified the material "culture core" to be found in different societies with the most constant features that would be revealed by comparative study. But there is no guarantee that the most constant features will not simply be those that correspond to the most vague and least empirical categories of the analyst, and further no guarantee that such constant features will be ecologically significant—as a consideration of the difficulties of Murdock's comparative method (or Tylor's [1889]) should have made clear.

Sahlins and Service abandoned Steward's overt comparative method in their *Evolution and Culture* (1960) as they argued, mainly, for two "laws" of evolution, the law of cultural dominance and the law of evolutionary potential:

> A culture is an integrated organization of technology, social structure, and philosophy adjusted to the life problems posed by its natural habitat and by nearby and often competing cultures. (1960:53)

The law of cultural dominance is:

> . . . that cultural system which more effectively exploits the energy resources of a given environment will tend to spread in that environment at the expense of less effective systems. . . . (1960:75)

And the law of evolutionary potential is:

> The more specialized and adapted a form in a given evolutionary stage, the smaller is its potential for passing to the next stage. Another way of putting it which is more succinct and more in conformity with preceding chapters is: Specific evolutionary progress is inversely related to general evolutionary potential. (1960:97)

Yet their discussion still rests squarely on *prior* acceptance of the idea of culture or society as a organic whole, and by 1960 at least, this key idea was no longer exciting or even particularly meaningful. Harris did not remedy this inadequacy when he used his history (1968) to extend the claims of a kind of persecution by a dominant theoretical persuasion of "historical particularism," and to generalize the ideas of cultural ecology by rephrasing them as "cultural materialism."

The formulations were welcome and useful insofar as they reminded some anthropologists—especially *contra* Lévi-Strauss—that kinship structures did not exist in a vacuum, and that a people's tools, crops, and systems of production were as much a part of their "culture" or society as their kinship and ritual symbols—which is the sense of "cultural ecology" Geertz stressed in *Agricultural Involution,* as noted. But they were quite unacceptable insofar as they asked anthropologists to give up the growing feeling for several quite different kinds of social order—symbolic, linguistic, and organizational—as the price of this recognition.

Economic Anthropology

Since economic anthropology was not a specialization in the way that cultural ecology or cultural materialism was, it was not restricted in its impact for the same kind of reasons. It was not a single theoretically defined area or camp, but a more or less clear common focus of several quite different theoretical lines. One line has already been indicated—a portion of the main body of structural studies that included discussions of economic decision-making or economic behavior as an aspect of the increasing recognition of manipulative, creative, and calculating orientations of natives to their social structures. Geertz's *Agricultural Involution,* Leach's *Pul Eliya* (1968), Bailey's *Caste and the Economic Frontier* (1957), several major works by Firth, and, it should be added, Scarlett Epstein's widely discussed and influential study of differing responses to economic development in two South Indian villages (Epstein 1967), all represent this theoretical concern but still fall easily and properly under the heading of economic anthropology. In these studies the economic arguments were but an aspect of the larger arguments.

Several other lines of thought coalesced under the rubric of the "for-

malist-substantivist'' controversy, which carries in its title the mark of
the dualist framework within which it has been argued (see Kaplan 1968
for a clear résumé). Although it borrowed some of the ideas and literature of the economic historian Karl Polanyi (whose position in economics is more commonly called "institutionalist" than "substan-
tivist''), the anthropological version of these ideas assimilated them to
the old concerns with the applicability of "western" economic theory to
primitive societies, and/or the "rationality" of the people in such societies. Substantivists were associated with the view that such theory did
not apply, formalists with the view that it did. None of the arguments
were conclusive, and most involved fairly conspicuous problems with
inadequate data, misunderstandings of economic theory, and misunderstandings of the views of Polanyi himself. As with the cultural eco-
logists, the either-or positions in the debate rested on the assumption
that societies had to reflect one and only one type of motivation, and the
assumption that all motivations operated at the same level in relation to
behavior. When the debate finally came to a head around 1968 (see
LeClair and Schneider 1968), leading anthropological theorists were no
longer interested in such simple assumptions unless they could be given
radically new significance. In consequence, the impact of the debate
was limited to those with direct personal interest either in economics or
economic theory as such. Probably the most important general contribution of the debate was to add to the awareness of the need to recognize,
somehow, both "traditional" and "rational" aspects of behavior everywhere.

Conclusion

   As a result of the increasingly explicit and self-conscious defences of
dualistic assumptions in these arguments, many anthropologists laid increasing stress on a sharp distinction between "description" and
"theory," and confined dualism more and more narrowly to the latter.
At the same time, however, direct descriptions of social and cultural
phenomena were increasingly diversified, and increasingly recognized
as being supportable by a range of new operational techniques and observational examples that were crowding into the literature: for example,
the much clearer conceptions of what a kinship terminology was as opposed to a domestic group, of social structural models (be they native's

or analyst's) as opposed to local groups, and of economic rules and models as opposed to social relational rules and moral norms. "Theory," on the other hand, increasingly consisted of highly abstract general substantive models of cultural or social elements, relations, or processes—from marriage patterns through "networks," to supposedly universal symbolic meanings. In the nature of the case, as the field continued to be divided, each of these general models came to have less and less to do with more and more data.

In all probability, the pattern of increasing generation of new specializations or theoretical camps as the difficulties in old ones became apparent, but before they could be fully examined, was abetted by the continuing rapid numerical growth in the field. The approximately 2,688 members of the American Anthropological Association as of 1955 had grown to 9,382 members of all kinds by 1971, and to 10,166 members of all kinds by 1973—including 8,345 private persons (excluding institutional members). Over the same period, the Royal Anthropological Institute of Great Britain and Ireland had increased from 1,010 fellows to about 1,500 fellows. According to Adkins, the total "stock" of holders of the doctorate in anthropology in the United States rose from 600 in 1955 to 1,795 in 1970, and would more than double by 1975; by the same time the stock of M.A. holders would be 7,000—847% of the 1955 level. Under the best of circumstances, conditions of such rapid expansion would mean that a very large proportion of the people in the discipline would be relatively new to it, and would in all probability simply not have had the time to examine their assumptions fully, regardless of intent.

But sooner or later, interest had to turn to the obvious question: how do we know the division between theory and data is absolute? Why, indeed, should we not rather view it as a difference between two kinds of theory, one without clear relation to observation, grounded in speculation, and resting on criteria of consistency; the other grounded in field method, inherently tied to observation, and resting on criteria of replicability and experimental adequacy?

14.
The Re-Emergence of Monistic Alternatives

As the last major theoretical dimension of current debates, the monistic perspectives that began to reappear after 1955 were in some cases direct continuations of the work that had never been interrupted, but had merely dropped over the anthropological horizon for a time. In other cases they were logical extensions of the dualistic analyses that had been pressed to their limit—such as Geertz's treatment of culture as a text, that again raised the monist's questions: "Who writes it?" "How is it written?" "Why is it accepted?" And in some cases they were intuitive reformulations based more on mutual recognitions of the problems of dualism than conscious identification of a coherent alternative tradition.

By about 1970 the body of discussion had been built up to the point where it re-created and even refined the broad theoretical outlooks of Malinowski, Boas, and Wundt. In place of the idea of science as a system of logically related statements, there was again a conception of science as based fundamentally on empirical demonstration and description; instead of "objectivity" of subject matter, there was again a stress on replicability of observation in a controlled situation that included the analyst; instead of an assertion of privileged perspective of the analyst, there was again a concern with the fundamental equality and relativity of all perspectives; and in place of attempting to arrive at explanatory entities that were inherently unlike what was directly perceived, there was a concentration on the detailed analysis of the process of perception, and its direct contents.

As for Wundt, Malinowski, and Boas, this perspective did not involve its proponents in a series of theoretically bounded and separate specializations but rather in a network of empirically interconnected problems, from the relationship between human physiology and the processing of sensory information, through the production of gestures under voluntary control, to the use of symbols to promulgate ideas, and the relationships between symbols and meanings. Indeed, the crystallization of the new perspective grows very largely from the rather belated realization by ethnologists of continuing relevant developments in other areas, including philosophy and psychology, as well as linguistics, archeology, and physical anthropology; and from their consequent efforts to break out of isolated specializations and reformulate ethnological theory to fit it to the central place it must occupy in any complete view of human nature, human thought, and human science.

Developments outside Anthropology

In the 1950s, there were several major intellectual developments that provided powerful new technical tools and formulations for monism. The first to take effect was the development of the mathematical theory of information by Shannon and Weaver at the Bell Laboratories.

Two key papers in information theory were published in journals in 1948 and 1949, and republished together as a book in the latter year (Shannon and Weaver 1949). The theory treated information potential as an aspect of a communication system, consisting of a linear transmission of a selected set of symbols by a transmitter through a channel (which had an input of "noise") to a receiver, in which it effects a change. Within this frame of reference, information could be defined without reference to dualistic ideas of meaning as an inherent property of a symbol. It was defined with reference to the ability of a transmission to bring about a desired action or state in the receiver—such as to direct a person to do some act. Specifically, the information value of a transmission was directly related to the probability of its occurrence, which was itself seen as the sum of the separate probabilities of the transmitter choosing each of its constituent components. The lower the probability of any specific combination of signals, the greater was its ability to evoke any specific action in the receiver. For example, a single undifferentiated tone always produced by a machine (or person) would have the probability of occurrence of 1.0, and could direct no response at all in a receiver. An on-or-off option, where each possibility might have the probability of .5, could be keyed to produce a choice of two options in a receiver—do something or not, or do just one thing or just another. A message representing a probability of .001, or one in a thousand, could by the same token produce one response out of a thousand. The single response out of a thousand could be far more specific than one response out of just two, or than no response, and in that precise sense could reasonably be construed as reflecting more "information," or potential information, in the transmission.

The theory assumes that actual communications involve prior consensus between participants in the communicative action, and it assumes that communications are oriented toward practical actions or decisions. It also, at the same time, assumes creative freedom on the part of the communicators. According to Weaver, "information is the measure of one's freedom of choice when one selects a message" (1964:9). The theory, with the closely related "cybernetics" of Norbert Weiner (1948), had diverse origins, prominent among which were gestalt psychology and the behaviorism of Clark Hull. There is no way to derive it solely from monism (or dualism). But its net effect was to provide a new and powerful formulation of the action and effect not only of the uses of communicative symbols in overt behavior, but also of the human nervous system itself—in the way that Wundt and his successors had described it.

The second intellectual development was philosophical: the publication of Ludwig Wittgenstein's *Philosophical Investigations,* in 1953. In it, Wittgenstein repudiated his *Tractatus Logico Philosophicus* (1922), an obscure work that had been construed by many logical positivists as providing the reasoned and consistent proof of their conception of language and meaning. The *Investigations* was bitterly attacked by logical positivists. Bertrand Russell, Wittgenstein's early patron and teacher, said that in it he had abandoned philosophy. But in fact, he had abandoned only dualistic philosophy. He abandoned the analytic-synthetic distinction and the concomitant idea that language had an inherent logical order, and he abandoned the search for meaning as a direct relation between linguistic forms and their referents. He replaced all this with two key concepts: the idea of a "language game" and the idea that most of the seemingly insoluble problems that concerned philosophers (obviously mainly positivists) involved unwarranted extrapolations from the way words were used in the language game. The first idea is strongly pragmatic and also perfectly consistent with the assumptions of communication theory. The second reverts directly to Kant's conception of the generation of noumena in the *Critique of Pure Reason*.

The idea of the language game is basically very simple. It is that words appear not only in the context of other words and linguistic forms, but also in the context of patterned behaviors of various sorts. One learns words by learning to connect them properly to such expected patterns. For example, one does not know the meaning of the formula for generating the series of all odd numbers by somehow having all odd numbers present in one's mind, but rather by knowing how to write down some representative string of odd numbers in an appropriate way. One does not know the meaning of the word "pain" by knowing some essence of pain that one shares with others from time to time, but rather one knows when it is appropriate to use the term and related gestures to indicate and adjust to some event like hitting one's thumb. Words have "grammars" in Wittgenstein's treatments, and a grammar is a set of habitual understandings of when and how to use them. He applies this treatment prevasively not only to ideas of mathematical formulae and terms of aesthetics, ethics, and cognition, but to such terms as "idea" and "truth" as well, so that the idea of the game itself alone remains basic, the encompassing framework. And it is at once empirical and logical, subjective and objective. It is, in the richest sense of the word, a thoroughly pragmatic concept. It is also, in a strict sense, a monistic one. There is a great deal of resemblance between Wittgenstein's analysis of truth and meaning in the language game and traditional Hindu concepts of truth and meaning in the world of "illusion," as well as to pragmatic epistemology.

Wittgenstein's change of position has gradually attracted major scholarly interest and an exegetical tradition of its own. More importantly for anthropology, his emphasis on learning and practical demonstration as aspects of meaning or thinking became a starting point for Peter Winch's *The Idea of a Social Science* (1958), which amounts to a new tranformation of Kantian social philosophy reflecting a sophisticated awareness of modern social anthropology (rpt. in part in Wilson et al. 1970). Winch argues very plainly that "social relations really exist only in and through the ideas which are current in society," and that such ideas and relations are capable of being learned and described in their own right, without the need for the analyst to apply his own categories to them or to confuse them with his own categories. One simply learns them. He explicitly rejects logical and analytic knowledge of, as he says, "relations between ideas" as being prior to, independent of, or having a different inherent status than, such cultural and social ideas (1958:133).

A second philosophical development has so far exercised at least as much influence on dualistic traditions in anthropology as on monism, as already suggested: phenomenology. The tradition is generally considered to descend from Hegel through Husserl to a number of modern thinkers including Maurice Merleau-Ponty and Alfred Schutz, and currently Harold Garfinkel and a number of his students and associates in sociology (see Lauer 1965 for a clear and concise review of the history of the tradition). For some, its boundaries fade off into existentialism and the "structuralism" of Lévi-Strauss. But it is not, despite this lineage, wholly dualistic. While there is a strong idealistic component, there is an equally strong, and more basic, monistic one. The tradition involves a sustained attack on what is formulated as "the problem of social order." The "problem" stems from the idea that society (or the world) is not purely objective but rather that when one says something that purports to be "about" the world that statement has an inherently "reflexive" character, equally and at the same time saying something about the sayer. The point goes right back to Kant, although this is not generally recognized by modern proponents of the tradition (Garfinkel and Merleau-Ponty [1963:159f.] being notable exceptions). The dualistic tradition enters in two main areas: general methods and concepts of consensus or communication. In Husserl's "transcendental" technique of asking the reader to put concepts in "brackets" in order to question their objectivity, one finds a precise analogue to Descartes's system of doubt that ultimately ignores the possibility that knowledge may not be a matter of individual mental or perceptive states at all—that one might be looking in the wrong place to find the basis of knowledge by this means. Alfred Schutz, in a similar vein, relied on Weber's concept of "ideal types" but generalized it into a taxonomy of types or forms of what he called "intersubjectivity": communicative exchanges predicating multiple "subjects" (*The Phenomenology of the Social World*, first German pub. 1932; English trans., 1967). But Schutz's taxonomy only raised the additional question: how do such forms become stabilized in consensus?

Lacking recourse to a Kantian idea of practical action, Schutz, in his later works, seems to have stressed that one had access to the constructed world only through language, and to have extended this idea to suggest that consensus or agreement among people's perceptions itself reflected the forms of language, in some unspecified way.

Direct reliance on idealistic assumptions must, at the point where the categories of order come to be taken as universal and not as situational aspects of specific ordering processes, cross the line from being an attack on the problem of social order to being a denial of its existence, so that the phenomenological traditions in part become entangled in the very positions they attack. But in less idealistic phenomenologists, such as Garfinkel and in some respects Erving Goffman, one finds an important series of arguments for the detailed observation of "daily behavior," the minutiae of ordinary experience, that easily and richly complements the ideas of Wittgenstein and Winch, with a level of detail they themselves do not provide.

Finally, the traditions continuing from Wundt's experimental psychology received two major restatements in the work of Merleau-Ponty (1908–61) and Jean Piaget (b. 1896). Merleau-Ponty was an early personal associate of Lévi-Strauss and Sartre, and is often described as being associated with existentialism and idealism. But his work is in fact thoroughly and self-consciously tied to the monistic tradition, descending from Kant through Wundt. His many analyses of general concepts—like that of the "horizon" and the reflexivity of descriptions—are basically attempts to connect the Kantian concept of "intuitions," as it developed through the concept of "gestalt," to specific perceptual constructions and ways of organizing discussion and description. His posthumous *The Structure of Behavior* (1963) is an extended critique of the inability of dualistic (deterministic, reductionist, and mechanistic) physiological and psychological theories, especially Pavlovian reflex theory, to deal with the generation and maintenance of such concepts. Instead, he argues for neurological theories he considers better able to accommodate the psychological facts of ambiguity and individual perceptual freedom, in the manner of Wundt, and, more especially, Wertheimer.

Piaget's interests covered the same range of topics, but his approach was through laboratory experiment rather than philosophical criticism. He focused on the development of increasingly complex versions of basic concepts in children as they age, and on analyzing such increasing complexity in a way to suggest a relationship to increasing development of the central nervous system. To do this he has argued for the same simple patterns of logic beyond many different series of communicative and conceptual behaviors—game-playing, ethical argument, concepts of the child's relation to nature, and so forth—and most scholars familiar with his work would now grant that he has shown definite and regular increases in the conceptual complexity of communicative activity throughout childhood. Merleau-Ponty's influence has as yet been slight, but Piaget has been the subject of increasing and serious discussion.

Linguistics: Back to Language and Mind

In anthropological linguistics, the return to broader and more fundamental debate came with a reintegration of American descriptive linguistics with European philology, and with a renewed interest in the *way in which* language is present in the mind—the question Bloomfield had attempted to dismiss by his reductionism, and that Chomsky answered too simply. The change has been many-sided, involving many substantive issues, many schools, and many technical issues—far too many to be reviewed in detail. But it can be illustrated.

Perhaps the widest discussion of linguistic issues revolved around the ideas of B. L. Whorf, in the middle 1950s. In the early 1940s, Kroeber and others had attributed to Whorf and Sapir the idea that language determined behavior by containing basic categories of perception. Thus construed, the so-called "Whorf-Sapir hypothesis" had been dismissed as unproved, as a vague idea only suggestively argued for but never systematically established by comparative study. Perhaps it was felt that Bloomfield's reductionism could deal with behavior more effectively; but by the middle 1950s, attempts to develop this approach had already begun to run into difficulty. The interest in Chomsky was one response. A second was to turn back for another look at Whorf and Sapir. A set of important conference papers devoted to this purpose, involving major scholars in Bloomfield's tradition, was edited by Harry Hoijer (himself a student and lifetime admirer of Sapir) and published in 1954 with the title *Language and Culture*. The overall conclusion was negative— Whorf was still considered as not having established the "hypotheses." But this time, instead of suggesting that a positivist solution to the problem was near at hand, the papers more generally suggested that either such a solution was far in the future or impossible to obtain in principle. Thus this new criticism, unlike the old, was also a rejection of the claims of positivistic reductionism as well.

In 1956, John B. Carroll answered the criticism for Whorf by editing and publishing a comprehensive collection of Whorf's often scattered works, with the title *Language, Thought and Reality*. The collection included several previously unpublished papers that greatly clarified Whorf's general orientation, as too did Carroll's own excellent introduction. This collection displayed, in a convenient and clear form, not only the inapplicability of the positivists' criticism, but the extent of the differences between positivism and the self-conscious monism that Whorf represented.

The clearest statement in the Hoijer symposium of the positivist version of Whorf's views is in the article by Joseph Greenberg titled "Concerning Inferences from Linguistic to Non-Linguistic Data." Greenberg began by saying that there was a similarity between Whorf's view of language and that of a "European tradition" exemplified by Trier and Cassirer. He characterized the tradition as considering that language "embodies the intellectual remolding of this world" (pp. 3, 4). The phrase does come very close to Sapir, but less close to Whorf.

Greenberg's own approach to this problem area becomes clear as he sets the ground rules for his criticism as "primarily analytic in scope . . . an attempt to classify the . . . assertions . . . connecting linguistic and non-linguistic behavior and, in regard to each class, to raise questions as to what types of evidence are relevant to establishing and verifying hypotheses" (p. 4). Note how "intellectual remolding" has been equated with "non-linguistic behavior," and notice too how language and non-linguistic behavior are imagined as two separate "classes" of phenomena about which a "hypothesis" is to be tested.

Greenberg proposes three kinds of questions that may be asked of any "specific attempt to connect linguistic with non-linguistic phenomena": "(1) What kinds of linguistic facts are being adduced in evidence? (2) With what other phenomena is a connection being made? (3) What is the nature of this connection?" (p. 4). Under the first heading, he explicates his own view of language and semantics (a view shared by Nida, Pike, Hockett, and others). Greenberg begins: "we can ask whether the linguistic facts pertain to phonology, to grammar, or to semantics." The first two of these terms pertain to the sounds of language and their rules of combination. In these conceptions, Greenberg agrees with Whorf in his usage, and with the tradition preceding them both. It is the treatment of the last term, semantics, that is unique, and uniquely related to modern problems.

To describe the relationship between phonology and grammar on the one hand and meaning (semantics) on the other, nine terms are introduced "distinguishing different kinds of meanings" (p. 7). Five of these are especially important and illustrate the general patterns:

1. A sememe is the meaning of a morpheme (e.g., of "hand," "ing")
2. An episememe is the meaning of a construction (e.g., possession, actor, action)

. . .

6. Elementary meaning unit (E.M.U.). This is a cover term for sememes, episememes, and macrosememes, the elementary units which in combination make up more complex linguistic forms up to sentences.
7. Complex meaning unit (C.M.U.). The meaning of a structural complex containing more than one E.M.U. (e.g., the meaning of a phrase). ["Sentential meanings" are here defined as special cases of C.M.U.s.]
8. Generic meanings. The meaning common to a specified group of E.M.U.s, e.g., "male" in English as a common meaning in the following kinship terms: father, son, . . . (1954:7).

In sum, Greenberg sees a strict parallelism between hierarchical "units" of meaning and the hierarchical units of Bloomfieldian phonology and morphology. Further, more general and fuller meanings are seen as inherent in units at more complex, higher levels of linguistic combination. By definition, this makes it impossible to discuss meaning apart from formal morphology.

With this set of definitions, Greenberg set up a plausible application of Bloomfield's earlier and vaguer idea that "the *meaning* of a linguistic form (is) the situation in which the speaker utters it and the response it calls forth in the hearer" (1933:139). Given this, the "Whorf-Sapir hypothesis" becomes a hypothesis about the prediction of such responses by single individuals facing specific situations, and/or the prediction of "non-linguistic behavior" in situations on the basis of linguistic "responses."

Greenberg concluded by detailing a number of "obstacles" in the way of providing such data for the future. Some are quite general; others pertain more narrowly to Whorf. Three of the concluding passages are especially clear in indicating the limitations of this way of trying to relate language to other things, and deserve quotation:

> It is apparent that the conditions of valid inference described in the present paper allow for no more than a *better than chance predictability* from certain semantic facts to certain particular situations. Such scattered beliefs and behavior differentials can hardly be expected to add up to anything so coherent as a "world view." Is it possible then to justify Whorf's assertion that Hopi language and culture conceal a metaphysics . . .?
>
> A basic difficulty stems from the fact that in ordinary use the term "metaphysics" refers to a set of *beliefs which take a sentential form.* But language

only gives us the meanings of elementary units together with the rules for making sentences from them. From the finite set of elements and rules it is impossible to predict which sentences will actually be used by a speech community. It is not easy to see, therefore, how we can infer any such formulations of belief.

These difficulties are, I believe, not accidental but inherent in the problem. Since natural language is not devised by philosophers but develops as a living instrument of a community in its adjustment to a variety of changing needs, one would not expect and, in my experience at least, one does not find any underlying semantic system of a language to reflect some overall world view of a metaphysical nature. (p. 18; emphases are mine—M.L.)

The conclusion that knowledge of the structure of a language can provide no more than a chance predictability of linguistic responses to situations follows not from any knowledge of situations but only from the idea that such responses consist in sentences, and that language structures do not determine the sentences that can be created from the set of basic units. Conversely, morphologically dissimilar responses may be expected to occur in any given situation except in a very few areas, like kinship, in Greenberg's opinion (pp. 17–18). The idea that Whorf's "hypothesis" is thus discredited follows further from the identification of "metaphysics" (evidently the same as the "intellectual remolding" referred to at the outset) with sentences or combination of sentences. But Carroll's collection made it clear that Whorf himself did not share these definitions, and the ones he did use do not generate these difficulties.

Benjamin Lee Whorf, a highly successful inspector in a Hartford insurance company, took his college work in engineering. His first interest in linguistics was in philology, and grew out of an initial interest in the relationship between biblical languages and biblical cosmology (Carroll 1956:7). He had begun studying Hebrew in 1924, and by 1928 had moved to Mayan hieroglyphics—in the course of much reading and communication with established scholars. His interests in American Indian linguistics began to develop from this and increased without benefit of formal training until 1931, when Sapir came to Yale (Whorf lived in nearby Hartford). Whorf then took his first formal training in linguistics from Sapir, enrolling in the Yale doctoral program in anthropology. He remained in this program and in direct contact with Sapir and his students for the next several years, and served as a Lecturer in anthropology at Yale for the year 1937–38. As Carroll has described it (1956: ch. 1), this period saw him drop many earlier interests that appear to us as pseudo-scientific in favor of a more professional framework of problems and concepts. Yet through this explicit transformation of his problems, he retained an underlying interest in the relationship between language and thought, especially between language and conceptual categories.

The major papers generally referred to in relation to the "Whorf hypothesis" or the "Whorf-Sapir hypothesis" are reproduced in *Language, Thought and Reality* and date from the period after Whorf had come in contact with Sapir. The papers focus on Whorf's work with Hopi and on his comparisons between Hopi and what he called "Standard Average European" ("S.A.E.").

Two points are basic to all of the papers. First, Whorf's view of "language" was much broader than the concept Greenberg had inherited from Bloomfield, including his view of the kind of "meaning" that could be attributed to language. Secondly, Whorf did not attempt to reduce either "thought" or "meaning" to concrete "objective" behavior, much less to responses to situations in a behavioristic frame of reference. He adheres instead strictly and consistently to the linguistic methods of seeking patterns of contrast, free variation, and complementarity. These operations, however, take a broad interpretation. Anything that contrasts in the use of language with anything else, or which complements anything else, is by that fact alone linguistic and the pattern of relations it enters defines its linguistic class or category. In this sense, if ideas can be in complementary or contrasting distribution in speech, ideas are part of language.

Whorf's broader treatment is reflected in his general distinction between "covert" and "overt" linguistic categories, described in a 1936 unpublished manuscript "A Linguistic Consideration of Thinking in Primitive Communities," and in the article "Grammatical Categories" published in *Language* in 1945. The following is from the published article:

> The categories studied in grammar are those recognizable through facts of a configurational sort, and these facts are the same for all observers. Linked with configurative data, operational descriptions become valid as possible ways of stating the *meaning* of the forms, "meaning" in such cases being a characterization which succinctly accounts for all the semantic and configurational facts, known or predictable.
>
> We may first distinguish between *overt categories and covert categories*.
>
> An overt category is a category having a formal mark which is present (with only infrequent exceptions) in every sentence containing a member of the category. The mark need not be part of the same word to which the category may be said to be attached in a paradigmatic sense; i.e., it need not be a

suffix, prefix, vowel change, or other "inflection," but may be a detached word or a certain patterning of the whole sentence. Thus in English the plural of nouns is an overt category. (1956:88)

And further:

A covert category is marked, whether morphemically or by sentence-pattern, only in certain types of sentence and not in every sentence in which a word or element belonging to the category occurs. The class-membership of the word is not apparent until there is a question of using it or referring to it in one of these special types of sentence, and then we find that this word belongs to a class requiring some sort of distinctive treatment, which may even be the negative treatment of excluding that type of sentence. (p. 89)

These are not the only categories described; others include "lexemic categories" (individual items contrasted with the entire residue of the lexicon) and categories like case and gender, which crosscut the overt/covert distinctions in that the sense of the category may be conveyed in language either by overt or covert structures.

The unpublished version of the argument included by Carroll in the collection draws the implications out more sharply: ". . . the phenotype is the 'classical' morphological category . . . a certain type of grammar proceeds as if linguistic meaning dwelt wholly in them" (p. 72). The "certain type" would evidently include Greenberg's. "Sense or meaning does not result from words or morphemes but from patterned relations between words or morphemes. Isolations of a morpheme, like 'John!' or 'Come!' are themselves patterns or formulas of a highly specialized type, not bare units" (p. 67).

The first quotation could not be more pointedly directed at Greenberg's strict parallelism of meaning with form if Whorf had had foreknowledge of what Greenberg's critique would be; the second entails an explicit rejection of the idea of such a parallelism in principle. Not that Whorf believes that the divisions Greenberg describes on his different levels are not meaningful—but that many other kinds of linguistic meanings exist as well.

Given this conception of meaning, Whorf asks: does the pattern of meanings we find in a language appear to influence the pattern of cosmological concepts in use among the speakers of that language? He proceeds to the answer by two distinct steps. The first is to try to determine if the linguistic meanings alone form any consistent pattern at all, whether cosmological or otherwise. The second is to see if the patterns they form (assuming such patterns are found) imply a consistent set of cosmological categories that can be related to the formal or explicit cosmology actually in use. The first approach is from morphology; the second is through the imposition of a limited comparative framework of conceptual categories that Whorf judges to be basic to any cosmological scheme.

Examples of Whorf's attempts to answer the first type of question include "The Punctual and Sementative Aspects of Verbs in Hopi" (1936), "Some Verbal Categories in Hopi" (1938), and "Gestalt Technique of Stem Composition in Shawnee" (1949). In each case, Whorf deals with the way generic meanings are conveyed within a portion of the language. For example, in "Some Verbal Categories . . ." the divisions are "Assertion," "Mode," "Modality," "Status," and "Other Modalizers." Each is described as relying on, and therefore conveying, a definitive mental image of the nature of that which its elements name. All of them are described as being categories "of the overt or modulus types" (the latter is a category that modifies or applies either to any word of the entire vocabulary or any word of a specific class—like the possessive case of English or German); which is to say they are the standard sorts of categories one would find in a Bloomfieldian descriptive analysis, and the kind of categories that have names in Greenberg's scheme—presumably "generic meanings." Whorf makes no claim that these are the only phenotypic categories of the language, and he specifically says at the outset that both covert (cryptotypic) and word categories (like the "parts of speech" of English) exist in the language although they are not described in the article.

The approach based on a system of cosmological concepts was used in "An American Indian Model of the Universe," where Whorf tried to describe the "metaphysics" implicit in "Hopi language and culture" (p. 57); and it was extended in "The Relation of Habitual Thought and Behavior to Language," first published in 1939. This comes closest to the kind of argument Greenberg was criticizing, and perhaps for this reason Whorf includes in it a specific denial of such an attempt. The argument begins from a simple point. Whorf believed that he had seen evidence that the names situations have can influence the behavior of people towards them. He cited the example of an "empty" gasoline drum that was treated as non-dangerous on the grounds of the association of "empty" with "null" and "inert" as synonyms in some contexts. He then wanted to consider whether class meanings of larger linguistic patterns (remember that the isolation of a single morpheme is itself a pattern) had more subtle and perhaps far-reaching relations to behavior. The first section of the analysis deals with the concepts of "Plurality and Numeration in S.A.E. and Hopi," and clearly illustrates his methods:

That portion of the whole investigation here to be reported may be summed up in two questions: (1) Are our own concepts of "time," "space," and "matter" given in substantially the same form by experience to all men, or are they in part conditioned by the structure of particular languages? (2) Are there traceable affinities between (a) cultural and behavioral norms and (b) large-scale linguistic patterns? I should be the last to pretend that there is anything so definite as "a correlation" between culture and language, and especially between ethnological rubrics such as "agricultural, hunting," etc., and linguistic ones like "inflected," "synthetic," or "isolating." . . .

PLURALITY AND NUMERATION IN SAE AND HOPI

In our language, that is SAE, plurality and cardinal numbers are applied in two ways: to real plurals and imaginary plurals. Or more exactly if less tersely: perceptible spatial aggregates and metaphorical aggregates. We say "ten men" and also "ten days." The men either are or could be objectively perceived as ten, ten in one group perception—ten men on a street corner, for instance. But "ten days" cannot be objectively experienced. We experience only one day, today; the other nine (or even all ten) are something conjured up from memory or imagination. If "ten days" be regarded as a group it must be as an "imaginary," mentally constructed group. Whence comes this mental pattern? Just as in the case of the fire-causing errors, from the fact that our language confuses the two different situations, has but one pattern for both. When we speak of "ten steps forward, ten strokes on a bell," or any similarly described cyclic sequence, "times," of any sort, we are doing the same thing as with "days." *Cyclicity* brings the response of imaginary plurals. But a likeness of cyclicity to aggregates is not unmistakably given by experience prior to language, or it would be found in all languages, and it is not.

Our awareness of time and cyclicity does contain something immediate and subjective—the basic sense of "becoming later and later." But, in the habitual thought of us SAE people, this is covered under something quite different, which though mental should not be called subjective. I call it *objectified*, or imaginary, because it is patterned on the *outer* world. It is this that reflects our linguistic usage. Our tongue makes no distinction between numbers counted on discrete entities and numbers that are simply "counting itself." Habitual thought then assumes that in the latter the numbers are just as much counted on "something" as in the former. This is objectification. Concepts of time lose contact with the subjective experience of "becoming later" and are objectified as counted quantities, especially as lengths, made up of units as a length can be visibly marked off into inches. A "length of time" is envisioned as a row of similar units, like a row of bottles.

In Hopi there is a different linguistic situation. Plurals and cardinals are used only for entities that form or can form an objective group. There are no imaginary plurals, but instead ordinals used with singulars. Such an expression as "ten days" is not used. The equivalent statement is an operational one that reaches one day by a suitable count. "They stayed ten days" becomes "they stayed until the eleventh day" or "they left after the tenth day." "Ten days is greater than nine days" becomes "the tenth day is later than the ninth." Our "length of time" is not regarded as a length but as a relation between two events in lateness. Instead of our linguistically promoted objectification of that datum of consciousness we call "time," the Hopi language has not laid down any pattern that would cloak the subjective "becoming later" that is the essence of time. (1956:138–40)

In the same manner as plurality and numeration, Whorf discusses "Nouns of Physical Quantity in S.A.E. and Hopi," "Phases of Cycles in S.A.E. and Hopi," and "Duration, Intensity, and Tendency in S.A.E. and Hopi." As with the nouns of physical quantity, there is no attempt to argue that each of these headings pertains to systematic or pervasive grammatical features, or that the sum of the features is a complete and systematic review of the grammar as a whole. Whorf simply compares the kinds of linguistic units that appear to handle each of these conceptual categories, and describes the conceptual differences that the linguistic differences seem to entail—the different ways of conceptualizing "plurality" and the rest.

The last two sections are "Habitual Thought in S.A.E. and Hopi" and "Habitual Behavior Features of Hopi Culture." In the first, Whorf brings together the separate conceptual descriptions into two contrasting "thought worlds," each a "microcosm that each man carries about within himself, by which he measures and understands what he can of the macrocosm." In the second, he illustrates his views mainly by reference to the relation of ritual to ordinary action. "Habitual" in this sense means obviously "prescribed" much more than "regularly accomplished."

Comparable to the Hopi habitual behavior, Whorf next describes "some impress of linguistic habit in Western civilization." These include an interest in records, diaries, bookkeeping, and "mathematics stimulated by accounting," an interest in chronological measures and records, and an interest in annals, history, and historical periods (p. 153). As with the Hopi rituals, these are clearly stereotypic interests—symbolic beliefs about our behavior as much as objectively observable behaviors as such. Whorf at no time attempts to speak of the kind of "objective," non-conceptualized and, especially, non-verbalized behavior apart from language that Greenberg conceives of as the physical stimulus that would trigger a linguistic "response."

The conclusion, titled "Historical Implications," shows clearly that Whorf considers that the "cause" of the order in metaphysical concepts is not language but consensus; and that consensus in fact has to explain the order in language itself:

> To sum up the matter, our first question asked in the beginning (p. 138) is answered thus: Concepts of "time" and "matter" are not given in substantially the same form by experience to all men but depend upon the nature of the language or languages through the use of which they have been developed. They do not depend so much upon *any one system* (e.g., tense, or nouns) within the grammar as upon the ways of analyzing and reporting experience which have become fixed in the language as integrated "fashions of speaking" and which cut across the typical grammatical classifications, so that such a "fashion" may include lexical, morphological, syntactic, and otherwise systemically diverse means coordinated in a certain frame of consistency. . . . There are connections but not correlations or diagnostic correspondences between cultural norms and linguistic patterns. . . . (1956:158–59)

These are the nub of the arguments for what is sometimes called "linguistic relativity." But given the sense Whorf uses for the term "language" and his sense of "behavior," the idea is not nearly so radical, or deterministic, as Greenberg and many others suggest.

Whorf's linguistic interests were themselves part of a larger concern with "mind," and it is here that his consistent—and in some ways quite original—monism comes clearly to the surface. Philosophically, in many aspects of his arguments, Whorf rejects the idea that the distinction between "subjective" and "objective" reality, and concomitant distinctions, have a universal validity over and above other distinctions that are found in varying form from one culture to another. Moreover, Carroll notes Whorf's sympathies with "the philosophy and metaphysics of India" (p. 21). In "Language, Mind and Reality," first published in the *Theosophist* (Madras, India) in 1942, the interest is specifically in an Indian philosophy of language that is related to the idea of the efficacy of certain types of prayers—an idea he calls "mantra yoga." As he described it, this idea is closely related to the fundamental conception of the world as "illusion." Put crudely, the idea is that the *mantra* as it is repeatedly uttered is effective not because it acts upon nature, like a missile striking an external object, but rather because it embodies nature and is not external to it. It exemplifies an order or pattern which is in a fundamentally Kantian sense also the order of nature.

In this Whorf is rejecting the idea of nature as an external, self-contained, object or set of objects in favor of the idea that both nature and the self take shape as an embodiment of this more general underlying fact, the fact of the existence of pattern as such. Pattern is both pattern and our pattern—a habitual pattern that appears in our recognition of nature and of ourselves "within" it. This fact of pattern is what Whorf finds in language and language behavior—like prayer. This fact is constant, although the precise content of the patterns varies from culture to culture:

> Actually, thinking is most mysterious, and by far the greatest light upon it that we have is shown by the study of language. This study shows that the forms of a person's thoughts are controlled by inexorable laws of pattern of which he is unconscious. These patterns are the unperceived intricate systematizations of his own language—shown readily enough by a candid comparison and contrast with other languages, especially those of a different linguistic family. (1942 in 1956:252)

But, he adds in "Language and Logic," first published in 1941, that:

> . . . the tremendous importance of language cannot, in my opinion, be taken to mean necessarily that nothing is back of it of the nature of what has traditionally been called "mind." My own studies suggest, to me, that language, for all its kingly role, is in some sense a superficial embroidery upon deeper processes of consciousness, which are necessary before any communication, signaling, or symbolism whatsoever can occur, and which also can, at a pinch, effect communication (though not true *agreement*) without language's and without symbolism's aid. I mean "superficial" in the sense that all processes of chemistry, for example, can be said to be superficial upon the deeper layer of physical existence, which we know variously as intra-atomic, electronic, or sub-electronic. No one would take this statement to mean that chemistry is *unimportant*—indeed the whole point is that the more superficial can mean the more important, in a definite operative sense. It may even be in the cards that there is no such thing as "Language" (with a capital L) at all! The statement that "thinking is a matter of *language*" is an incorrect generalization of the more nearly correct idea that "thinking is a matter of different tongues." The different tongues are the real phenomena and may generalize down not to any such universal as "Language," but to something better—called "sub-linguistic" or "superlinguistic"—and *not altogether* unlike, even if much unlike, what we now call "mental." This generalization would not diminish, but would rather increase, the importance of intertongue study for investigation of this realm of truth. (1956:239)

At the present time, there is once again little explicit interest in Whorf or the Whorf-Sapir hypothesis among major linguists. But the current lack of interest is quite different from that prior to 1954. It is no longer that linguistic theory cannot formulate Whorf's problems, but rather that Whorf's issues have now been broken up into a number of technical problem areas ranging from the active area broadly called "language and culture" through quite "pure" linguistic theory.

Positivistic theories still exist, and Chomsky's neo-positivistic views are still considered by many to mark the path to the future. But there are growing numbers of scholars whose attachments are closer to the traditions of Sapir, Whorf, and their philosophical and psychological counterparts. Many writers have noted that Chomsky's formulation of the idea of a "selectional class" as a restricted set of lexical items, such that the occurrence of one as a subject or object of a sentence limits the selection of the item to serve as verb or adjective (from Chomsky 1964:113, 122–23), actually opens the door to many of what Whorf would have called "cryptotypic" patterns, and such patterns often appear to show a much closer relationship to cultural meaning than larger and more overt ones. For example, Paul Friedrich's "Shape in Grammar" (1970) describes a set of "classificatory verbs" in Tarascan as representing different and contrasting ideas or concepts of shape, distinguished from one another systematically along several parameters including the idea of orifice or edge, and the trichotomy long-flat-round. Complex words and phrases are made up using these consensual distinctions in what Friedrich calls the "semantic geometry" of the language, that is creatively developed and exploited in communication. While consistent with the newer technical conceptions of grammar and syntax, the relation of this to Whorf's Hopi and Shawnee analysis is obvious.

"Language and culture" or, more recently, "ethnolinguistics," is generally considered a substantive area rather than a body of theory, and while those involved have ranged from phenomenologists to associates of Chomsky, it is the peculiar sort of area that carries something very close to theory in its basic definition. It looks to the use of language, language in communicative situations, however variously conceived. And this automatically, among other things, works against the distinction between "language" and "speech" that was so important to Chomsky, and the radical separation between meaning and form that was crucial to Bloomfield's theoretical framework—to say nothing of the necessity for viewing utterances as something other than simply acceptable sentences generated by the grammar and lexicon.

An early presentation of modern work in this area was in a special publication of the *American Anthropologist,* titled *The Ethnography of Communication,* edited by John J. Gumperz and Dell Hymes (1964). Hymes's Introduction describes the common ground of the contributions:

> For ethnographies of communication, however, the aim must be not so to divide the communicative event, divorcing message form (sign type) and context of use from one another. The aim must be to keep the multiple hier-

archy of relations among messages and contexts in view (cf. Bateson 1963). Studies of the social contexts and functions of communications, if divorced from the study of the means that serve them, are as little to the purpose as are studies of communicative means if divorced from study of the contexts and functions they serve. Methodologically, of course, it is not a question of limiting a structural perspective inspired by linguistics to a particular part of the communicative event, but of extending it to the whole. (p. 6)

But if these are one's aims, certain theoretical emphases will have to follow. Hymes spells them out:

In short, emphasis and primacy of speech over code; function over structure; context over message; the ethnographically appropriate over the ethnologically arbitrary; but the interrelations always crucial, so that one cannot only generalize the particularities, but also particularize the generalities. (p. 11)

Whether what is at stake is a matter of emphasis in technical linguistic theory or an issue of fundamental choices in the conceptualization of human mentality, human nature, and scientific procedure in general, is of course a difficult point. But it is easy to see Hymes's recommendations leading more toward the general balance of emphasis one finds in Humbolt, Sapir, Whorf, and the related orientations of Wundt and Boas, than to the conceptions of Bloomfield or Chomsky, and the related general theories of Carnap or Quine.

Since 1964, there has been accelerating interest in the research areas Hymes suggested, under the labels "ethnography of speech," "ethnography of speaking," "sociolinguistics" and in some respects "semantics" and "ethnolinguistics." There has also been greatly increased interest in the history of linguistics, which has often focused on the differences between the traditions of Sapir and of Bloomfield. Hymes has himself been a major force behind this activity, both as author (see Hymes 1971) and editor. Finally, there have been increasing numbers of publications returning to broad issues in the philosophy of languages. Relatively early in the sequence was Robert Miller's *The Linguistic Relativity Principle and Humboltian Ethnolinguistics* (1968), which returned to issues in relation to the status of analytical categories that linguists use, as well as the relationship between deterministic and nondeterministic theories. Since 1969, a monograph series titled *Approaches to Semiotics,* under the general editorship of Thomas Sebeok, has been a vehicle for a number of quite important works, often either arguing for or relying upon monistic assumptions. One recent example is Cecil Brown's *Wittgensteinian Linguistics* (1974). Directly in conflict with Chomsky and positivistic conceptions of language analysis, this attempts to develop a formalization of grammar on the basis of semantic function (word and phrase synonymy) rather than morphological function, in the context of an interpretation of Wittgenstein's idea of the language game.

Modern anthropological linguistics offers some extremely sophisticated discussions of the consequences of monistic and dualistic conceptual options in a wide range of areas, from field methods to theories of meaning. Several of these discussions are tied to ethnological arguments far more closely than in the period when Bloomfield's ideas were dominant.

Ethnology: The Focus on Process and Method

In ethnology, looking over all the nominally isolated subdisciplines that had formed or were being advocated, the situation approaching 1970 was quite different from that approaching 1955. As field work improved, more phenomena came to be sorted out and described, albeit often obliquely and without admitting that one was dealing with one special kind of thing—be it a form of money or a kinship terminology—rather than the "real" basis of culture or society as a whole. In the process, more and more ground came to be assigned to "description," and less and less to "theory." At the same time, dualistic assumptions came more and more to be restricted in their application to "theory" alone, and especially to metatheory. This set the stage for those who, finally, proposed to do without dualism altogether.

The simplest major discussion in which monistic assumptions were reasserted involved the character of the unit of ethnographic observation. With Radcliffe-Brown, Evans-Pritchard, Fortes, Lévi-Strauss, and "organic" or total system theorists in general, the unit was supposed to be society as a whole. Such a unit could only be "seen" by the field worker through a quite mysterious process of abstraction, so dualistic metatheories defending the postulation of underlying entities on an arbitrary basis were perfectly appropriate. Dissatisfaction with this type of theory, coupled with the drive to be more concrete and specific in one's observations, was one of the major features of the move into "symbolism" rather than to whole societies as the object of research. Turner, Bailey, Epstein, Geertz, and others had tried to be especially specific within even this context, and organized analyses around specific instances of behavior occurring in a natural setting. But these instances did not yet show social structure directly. They were not the units out of which social structure was built. So it was still being abstracted by the analyst, indirectly, and the dualistic conceptions applied to this process even if they no longer applied to the process of ordering the data (the instances or cases) themselves. For those who objected to the remaining solipsism that attached to abstracting patterns from even the most minute "cases," what was left? To some analysts, the obvious answer was to avoid any type of unit whatever, from which social structure was to be abstracted, and instead to elicit social structure directly. Instead of being something one observed like a tiger in the trees, structure might be treated simply and directly as something one learned, like a mathematical table or a prayer. If social structure existed through communication, and was always subject to negotiation, "cases" would always reflect only one party's opinion (the informant's) at one time anyway.

The obvious thing to do was to shift from collecting the outcomes of communicative activity to learning to engage in the communicative activities themselves. "Field method" would then be not so much seeing things from the native point of view as learning how the native came to see things from his point of view, and to convince others of it. Ethnographic description involved conveying a sense of how social structure appears and is used and created in the communicative process. This was not quite participant observation (a phrase popular in the mid-1960s). It was more like observant participation. With it, the process of "abstraction" (as opposed to simple translation) disappeared entirely, and with it went the last need for recourse to dualistic conceptions of mentality, knowledge, and scientific procedure.

In retrospect, it appears that the first to cut out dualistic assumptions deliberately and state the theoretical implications of doing so was Milton Singer.

Singer had taken his B.A. in Psychology and his M.A. in Philosophy at the University of Texas (Austin) in the early 1930s. He became interested at that time in the pragmatists, especially C. S. Peirce's anti-Cartesian theory of mind and G. H. Mead's social psychology of the self. Intending to continue these interests during his doctoral studies at the University of Chicago, he specialized in the philosophy of science and of the social sciences and wrote his dissertation on the development of formal method in mathematical logic from syntactics to semantics under the direction of Rudolf Carnap. He also served as a research and teaching assistant to Bertrand Russell in 1938–39 when Russell was a Visiting Professor at Chicago.

After joining the faculty of the College Social Sciences Staff at Chicago in 1941, Singer became closely associated with Robert Redfield, first in The Comparison of Cultures Project and, beginning in 1954–55, as a colleague in the Department of Anthropology.

In 1955, Singer tentatively described the "units of observation" for studying the "cultural tradition of India" as "cultural performances," and proceeded to treat the problem of defining the study of Indian civilization as the study of conceptions illustrated in such performances by the "cultural specialists" (such as priests or dancers) who organize and direct them and as perceived by those who sponsor and attend them. In effect, the "tradition" was described as a matter of imputed noumena, what he called "autodefinitions" (p. 36), and the techniques of portraying them. There was no recourse to universal symbols, universal meanings, universal parameters of tradition, or to a privileged position for the anthropological observer.

The 1955 essay was reproduced in a more accessible form in Singer's 1972 *When a Great Tradition Modernizes* (pp. 67–80), in the context of other essays and explanatory notes that greatly amplified its significance. One important part of this new context (itself previously published in part in 1966) was an extended critique of Max Weber's treatment of the supposed causal relation between religion and economic development, coupled with Singer's own counter-description of the way Indian industrialists managed to be perfectly "modern" while also being perfectly good "traditional" Hindus. Apart from the consistent and self-conscious rejection of Weber's deterministic presumptions, rather than just his specific contentions, the argument is notable because it adds to the analysis of cultural performances a complementary analysis of ordinary affairs. Singer argues that religious and commercial activity are related (with a great deal of free play and individual choice) to each other in the context of family purposes and goals. His own description of this treatment is:

> The distinctive approach of the industrial study, . . . to an understanding of modernization is the analysis of family "adaptive strategies." The analysis shows . . . the ways in which the industrial leaders innovate while maintaining certain aspects of their cultural traditions and social institutions. Max Weber and others . . . have not recognized . . . that the system persists and changes precisely through the specific adaptations of the old and the new that individuals and groups are willing and able to make. The particular kinds of adaptations . . . used by the industrialists may not be the only kinds involved . . . No doubt remains in my mind, however, that these are some of the important mechanisms and processes underlying the modernization of Indian cultural traditions and social institutions. Adaptive strategies have prob-

ably been operative in Indian civilization for a very long time, but the arena, material, and results of their operation at any given time may be novel. (1972:248)

Singer described himself (personal conversation, 1973) as having been first a pragmatist, then a positivist, and finally as having moved back toward pragmatism. But while this approach to the description of "tradition" is unquestionably pragmatic—recalling and in some ways extending G. H. Mead's treatment of social symbols—Singer's inserted comments indicate that he, like Whorf, was also influenced by the classic monistic philosophy of India itself.

As Singer reconstructed a kind of Chicago pragmatism from Redfield's social anthropology that had been intended to subsume it, so Victor Turner's *The Ritual Process* (1969) reconstructed a new continental monistic ethnology from the anthropological tradition associated with Max Gluckman and the Rhodes-Livingston Institute. This tradition had combined Marxism with sociological functionalism and claimed to subsume the more individualistic functionalism of Malinowski.

The Ritual Process comprises the 1966 Lewis Henry Morgan Lectures delivered by Turner at Rochester University. The first two chapters present analyses of contrastive *rites de passage,* the last three develop two complementary theoretical conceptions: "liminality" and "communitas."

The treatments of ritual continue to develop the alternative to Lévi-Strauss's "structuralism" that had begun to form in *The Drums of Affliction.* This time, however, Turner carefully avoided offering a universal scheme of symbolic meanings to replace the scheme he was rejecting. Instead, he first offered a method of interpretation, based on native exigeses of the separate symbols, and of the ritual as a whole. Once such explanations were obtained, the analyst's problem was to explain how they were adequate from the point of view of those who offered them. One important part of the approach to this part of the problem involved an explanation of the selection of the symbolic objects used in the rites. Why, after all, were such mundane objects as trees, hens, cocks, blood, water, men, women, holes, and clearings used—when presumably any object, material, artificial, or imaginary, might serve instead? Turner's exploration of this question led to the idea of the "multivocality" of symbols.

Turner agreed with Lévi-Strauss that symbols were often used in contrasting pairs, but he declined to inflate this point into the idea that symbolic contrasts were always dichotomous in their logical structure, or that all the pairs in a ritual could be aligned in a single system. Instead, he stressed that a pair that had one meaning in one ritual context might have another meaning in another. By the same token, two pairs aligned in one way in one contrast (for example, male with "hot," female with "cold") might be aligned in reverse in another context. Thus each symbol and symbolic contrast had many meanings, not just one, depending on context and purpose.

If the meaning of a symbol was thus not inherent in it, where did it come from? Turner's answer to this question was that its use in the ritual reflected its ordinary appearance in a "material integument"—the objects and artifacts of ordinary life. Objects are selected for ritual use because of their associations in non-ritual life, and conversely by their ritual uses they obtain meanings which are then imported into ordinary affairs—a point that closely recalls the nineteenth-century notion that the more abstract conceptions of religion arose by abstraction from the more "natural" significances of the ritual objects.

The end point of Turner's analysis was not any sort of schema representing the contents of detached reason, but rather an attempt to provide a characterization of certain very general features of rites of passage, designated as "liminality" and "communitas." Liminality pertains to what Kant would have called "concepts," while communitas pertains to his "intuitions"—what Turner calls "sentiments" (pp. 127, 128). Liminality refers to the contrast between the discernably different ideas that define different social positions a person may occupy—especially in rites of passage from one status to another. Still more exactly, liminality refers to the "edge" between the two statuses, the condition of being divested of one and not yet invested with the other. Its hallmark is thus consciousness of choice—and hence self-consciousness. By contrast, communitas is the feeling or sentiment of being part of humankind, a sense of common humanity that lies behind all statuses and all choices of status. It is, therefore, a force that countervails against liminality, in a sense—the basis for a kind of union (or *communion*) underlying the juxtapositions and divisions of role and position. It involves the "total individual" in relation to other total individuals, as such.

The many reverberations between Turner's concepts and the nineteenth-century monistic ethnologists pose a fascinating historical puzzle. Although he referred to Wittgenstein in *The Forest of Symbols,* and this reference understates Wittgenstein's actual importance (personal communication), the only philosopher mentioned in *The Ritual Process* was Martin Buber (whose "I-Thou" concept Turner construed much in the manner of G. H. Mead's recognition of the interchangeability of "self" as an aspect of communication). There are, however, several non-philosophical touchstones. Bachofen is cited favorably at the outset for his observation to Morgan that "to penetrate the structure of a mind different from our own, is hardy work" (p. 2). Still more space is devoted to the conceptions of ritual of Hindu and Buddhist philosophical traditions, and to gestalt psychology. But perhaps the broadest foundation of Turner's argument lies in an ancient paradox in Christian theology and social theory—the clash between communion and the sectarian creeds. As the mystical union of the individual with God, communion was supposedly universal—"catholic." But the creeds, specific articles of faith, commanded assent only to specific authorities to interpret this mystical union, and thereby pitted Christian against Christian, and Christian against non-Christian. Like many before him, Turner evidently saw this as a contradiction, and chose the sense of communion as the more basic component of ritual participation. It was apparently a parallel course of reasoning, in part, that led Kant to base his theory of perceptual truth on the perceiver's *sense* that one's perceptional categories would be universally shared, and to base his moral theory on the moral actor's *sense* of a universalized "golden rule."

Despite the many technical advances concerning the detailed collection and analysis of appropriate data, Turner's conception of liminality is remarkably like Bastian's use of Fechner's concept of just-noticeable-differences; his approach to the contextual analysis of meaning replicates Bachofen's; and he recalls both these ethnologists (and the line of thinking going back through the Scottish moralists) in his conception of the contextualization of customs in the world of everyday concerns and actions, and of individuals as using rituals to create a reasonable and humane social order.

Adhering more closely to established issues in the analysis of social structure *per se,* Roy Wagner arrived at a theoretical and methodological orientation closely akin to Turner's. In his 1967 *The Curse of Souw,* directly reflecting his background as a student of Schneider at Chicago, he concluded with a contrast between "symbol" and "model" that closely paralleled Leach's and Bailey's distinction between description and theory:

> The relationships we have been discussing have all been referred, however obliquely, to native Daribi symbolizations of the ways in which people may be grouped and the kinds of connections that can exist among them, and I submit that such considerations are relevant to the formation of models by the anthropologist for the purpose of understanding and describing a society. Specifically, there is an extent to which social structure and the relationships

within it are consciously manipulated and dealt with by members of the society, and this intersects with the symbolic system of the culture. Insofar as it suffices for the maintenance of the social structure among the people themselves, for, in fact, it determines the structure, a description of this symbolic system would suffice as an analysis of the social system. (1967:222)

And then:

. . . the constructs and distinctions of the anthropologist fall wholly within the area of "model," for they are made in terms of his comparative, analytical, interest. We may distinguish two areas within the range of concepts introduced by the anthropologist. One comprises generalized criteria, unit definition and alliance, which are purely comparative, introduced for the purpose of comparing societies, and do not vary from one culture to another. For this reason, such criteria do not express native symbolic categories, but are rather imposed from the outside as cross-cultural constants, and they are not contingent upon the area of "symbol." The other area includes principles derived by the anthropologist from native symbolic categories, relating these to the criteria of comparison between societies. (p. 224)

Since the category of "symbol" by itself can give a complete account of a social structure from the point of view of those who define themselves as placed within it, and since such accounts can be rendered in English (or other anthropological languages) and compared, an obvious next step is to ask what the "model" of comparative categories actually is needed for? Why can we not describe the process of creating and using symbols as the comparative and cross-cultural concern, and forget about "unit definition and alliance" in that connection—since they add nothing to the significance of the data or the analysis (and obviously cause a great deal of trouble). The answer is that we *can* forget them and see theory entirely in terms of the idea of a symbol and the way it is used to generate whatever types of social relations people use—which may or may not appear to designate groups and alliances. And it is precisely this position Wagner took recently in one of the clearest and most outspoken general rejections to date of deterministic theory based on the claim of a privileged analysis developing substantive models of social structure (in Leaf 1974). Instead of groups, Wagner in this essay described his concern as being with "the subtleties of how natives conceptualize their sociality" (p. 119), and he stressed the identity between the normal anthropological activity of inventing models, on the one hand, and native processes of social communication, on the other. He argued not that the anthropologists should somehow transcend this fact, but that they should rather recognize it and explicitly incorporate it among features by which they identify and describe their proper subject matter—a nice phenomenological point in both Kantian and the post-Kantian senses, which, finally, became the main theme of his *Inventing Culture* (1975).

These arguments represent a rather widespread pattern that is being formed from many diverse points of origin. James Peacock's 1968 description of the popular *ludruk* theatre of Indonesia showed how it serves as a vehicle for the promulgation of both new and traditional conceptions. It included a detailed analysis of what those ideas were, and the plot structures and dramatic devices that conveyed them. It utilized purely internal descriptive criteria and included accounts of audience reaction and performer intent as part of its sense of "symbolism." The treatment dovetails perfectly with Singer and greatly extends the possible detailed content of the idea of cultural performances.

In a more explicitly philosophical vein a remarkable essay by Neville Dyson-Hudson, "Structure and Infrastructure in Primitive Society: Lévi-Strauss and Radcliffe-Brown" (1969), accurately noted the important similarities between Lévi-Strauss and Radcliffe-Brown in their attempts to define social structure without reference to individuals, and contrasted their assumptions with those of Merleau-Ponty, especially referring to Merleau-Ponty's conception of *praxis* at the individual level as the locus of order—an idea historically and conceptually related both to pragmatism and Kant's idea of practical reason. Dyson-Hudson did not, however, argue for *praxis* as opposed to structure, but argued rather that structure had to be seen in the context of *praxis*, as something arising out of it.

Methodologically, the case for monism has been abetted by the advent of a number of anthropologists interested in symbolic process who are themselves either natives of non-western societies, of societies they are describing, or both. Such scholars have often had little patience with the claim of privileged anthropological objectivity. Especially notable was Alfonso Ortiz' *The Tewa World* (1969). In addition there is the work of a large number of South Asian anthropologists who have the special characteristic of being members of a culture whose dominant religious ideology is self-consciously not only monistic but also antidualistic.

Triloki Nath Pandey, well-trained in the classical Brahmanic literature of India before being trained as a social anthropologist, added a most interesting twist to this line of development in his work on Zuñi. Concentrating on the interaction of "subjective" and "objective" perceptions, and on the interchangeability of subject and object roles, Pandey has briefly but pointedly described the way in which Zuñi perceptions of different ethnologists who worked among them, over time, influenced the resulting ethnological accounts (1972). He also described the direct relationships between the way he was himself seen by various Zuñi (and the differences among such perceptions) and his own field experience (1975). The arguments are low-key, but leave no doubt that dualistic claims of "objectivity" cannot be taken at face value. On the other hand, it is equally clear that systematically taking into account one's own locally assigned role and position(s) while doing ethnographic field work can not only free the analyst from being tied into the implicit assumptions of his "own" culture, but can enable him to translate accurately and satisfactorily categories of one culture not his "own" into those of another, equally not his "own."

Mathematically-based analyses of kinship systems and terms, leaving aside dualistic assumptions, have shown several different patterns of logical organization in ethnographic data (cf. White 1963; Read 1974). And there is at present also widespread interest in the fine-grained analysis of conversational communication, done mainly within a phenomenological framework, but it has not yet produced works that have been widely discussed.

If I may be forgiven the appearance of immodesty, I should remark that my own *Information and Behavior in a Sikh Village* (1972) overlaps the concerns of Singer, Turner, and Wagner, complements their descriptions of symbolic communication, and is intended to extend their analytical approach beyond social organization and religion into areas normally thought of as economic and ecological. The purpose of the work was to indicate a general method for eliciting the systems of meanings underlying communicative actions in a single community, and to describe all such systems that were current in universal consensus therein. On this basis the work had four main theoretical themes: to relate the formal structure of such systems of meaning and the type of ritual symbols that were used to convey them; to extend the idea of "ritual" to include all those stereotyped behaviors and symbolic objects designed to convey such ideas; to relate the multiplicity of such systems to the problem of the balance between freedom and order; and to show how the several systems of ideas, though often combined in use, retained their separateness and integrity. The success of these arguments is best left to others to judge.

For those aware of it, the debate between dualistic and monistic positions in ethnology today is far more completely articulated than its predecessors in the 1930s, and far richer. But the monistic position seems especially advantaged now, not only by the historical unfolding of the inherent difficulties of applying the dualistic assumptions to a descriptive enterprise. The principal advantage is that the monistic position has shown itself capable of co-opting and reinterpreting the detailed findings of structural studies, and giving a better account of the way the results were obtained than the dualistic assumptions allow. And this, in turn, has permitted the studies of all types of cultural order in communicative process to be placed in the larger monistic framework, extending far beyond ethnology, in precisely the position formerly occupied by such far too vague concepts as "social symbol," "custom," "law" and, finally, the "language game." The classic issues are once again being discussed, but in a much more concrete form than before, and both the stakes in the arguments and the means of resolving them are proportionately more clear.

Archeology

In archeology, formulations conformable to monistic assumptions and interests re-emerged into prominence by a circuitous route. The formulations mainly revolved around attempts to characterize historical processes by focusing on a model of the individual in a competitive, adaptive situation instead of on cultural wholes—a model that would control the extrapolation into the past of information obtained from known or historic *processes* (rather than *cultures*)—such as the way one learns to make pots, or to select house sites. Oddly and ironically, the move toward this conception began in one of the last and most strongly stated positivistic efforts to introduce an organic concept of culture—"new archeology."

Relieved by C^{14} and the related potassium-argon dating methods from the necessity of elaborate devotion to building chronological frameworks region by region, archeology in the 1960s entered what Willey and Sabloff characterize as the "explanatory" period, whose "three pillars" are: "cultural evolutionary theory, systems theory, and logico-deductive reasoning" (1974:189). These themes are intertwined in the argument for the American reaction to earlier Americanist schemes that were classificatory but anti-evolutionary. The chief architect of the movement has been Lewis Binford, both through personal teaching and a series of important articles beginning with "Archeology as Anthropology" in 1962.

Invoking the organic conceptions of culture of Leslie White and Julian Steward, Binford argued that artifacts had to be seen not as types in their own right, but as material remains of cultural "subsystems" that were in turn part of the "total extinct cultural system" (1962:219). Referring to White's general definition of cultural as "the extra-somatic means of adaptation for the human organism" (White 1959:8) (Binford 1962:218), Binford described three "subsystems" of interest as: "technomic" ("those artifacts having their primary functional context in coping directly with the physical environment"); "socio-technic" ("having their primary functional context in the social subsystems of the total cultural system"); and "ideotechnic" ("primary functional context in the ideological component of the social system") (p. 219). Also following White and Steward, and against the anti-evolutionist conceptions of Willey and others, Binford argued strongly that all artifacts had to be accounted for by reference to general evolutionary laws, rather than "particular" historical "explication" (p. 218).

To demonstrate his framework, Binford argued that the introduction of copper tools in the "Old Copper Complex" of the Archaic period in the area of the Great Lakes could not be accounted for as a technological refinement of preceding tool types alone, but rather had to be related to an egalitarian band-organized system of social groups. There were several kinds of evidence: first the tools were not followed in the next period by more or better copper tools, but rather by a return to stone; second the tools were found only in graves; third there was little evidence of reuse or repair of copper tools, which one would expect if the material were valuable for its usefulness; and finally he argued that copper tools were in fact quite difficult to produce compared to any increasing efficiency one would expect from them. Combining critical arguments with ethnographic generalizations from Steward, Morton Fried, and others, he argued that the artifacts had to be accounted for as symbols of status in a relatively egalitarian, unstratified society. In such a society, individuals are valued because of their technical proficiency, such as might be symbolized by ordinary tools made of special materials (rather than being valued by inherited status which might be symbolized by a unique class of wealth artifacts). In the succeeding period the use of copper for ornament reflected a more stratified society. In short, the copper had to be accounted for by placing its use in the sociotechnic rather than the technomic subsystem (p. 223).

In later essays, Binford erected the third pillar of the new archeology as he argued increasingly for the use of an overall "hypothetico-deductive method," citing Carl Hempel's version of the positivistic philosophy of science as a general formulation.

A certain amount of misunderstanding has been generated by the fact that by the time Binford wrote, leading ethnological opinion had already turned to the view that one cannot specify "subsystems" in this way and expect them to have cross-cultural integrity, and that the fact that objects have ideological and social contexts does not warrant leaping to the idea of a total cultural system as an organic whole in any important sense. Further, as Binford himself recognized, Hempel's "logico-deductive" model of science does not help with the difficult problems of saying how one develops any particular ideas to test, distinguishing good ideas from bad, and in retrospect distinguishing actual explanations from verbal camouflage. Ethnologists, therefore, saw Binford's conception of "anthropology" as somewhat retrograde, and failed to share the enthusiasm of many younger archeologists.

Despite the bold contrasts Binford himself used to distinguish his metatheoretical position from others, it appears at present that his most concrete and far-reaching impact has been in providing a way to articulate a rather subtle change in the area of research design and data analysis. This change has three main elements, all quite consistent with monism: it looks at data in complete detail, rejecting in principle the possibility of ignoring features of data inconsistent with proposed interpretations; at the same time it rests on prior designation of the classes of data actually to be obtained and the methods of analysis to which the data will be subjected in relation to specific developmental or historical theses; and finally, it relies heavily on statistical inference and novel research methods designed for the project at hand, instead of standardized recovery methods and typological classifications of artifacts from which inferences later may be made.

Research designs incorporating these ideas in the early 1960s promised access to information about the social organization and ideology of extinct communities that many archeologists and ethnologists had considered irretrievable. Binford's treatment of the copper tools was one example of such a design, but he presented a more spectacular example in a departmental seminar at the University of Chicago in the spring of 1962—various versions of which have since been implemented by many researchers. Reporting on work then in progress, Binford described how he proposed to infer the rule of marriage residence from archeological materials. He would collect remains of artifacts from the surface of evident residential sites, and classify the remains first by probable sex of manufacturers (based in part on ethnographic analogy). Male goods would be separated from female goods. Then each group of objects would be looked at in detail to classify the remains by actual manufacturer, insofar as this could be inferred by similarity in motifs, execution, or possibly even fingerprints. The material would then be treated statistically to estimate the diversity of the original populations of artifacts that the collection represented, and the relative diversity would provide the basis for inferring the rule of locality. For example if the ranges of variation among the male goods tended to be bimodal, to cluster about two means, while the female goods tended to cluster about one mean, it would suggest matrilocal residence. In matrilocal residence, the women would stay in place on the site learning local traditions and passing them on, while their brothers married out and husbands came in from elsewhere. This pattern would produce, over time, at least twice as many male traditions in a site as female traditions. Conversely, if there was a bimodal clustering of design variation within the population represented by the female goods with a unimodal male group, it would suggest patrilocal residence, with one tradition of male manufacturers and at least two traditions of female, since the girls trained locally by their mothers would marry out, and other women trained elsewhere by their mothers would marry in (see Binford 1968 for a restatement of the design, credits for its origins, and a review of its use up to that time). It was easy to see how it could be extended beyond single sites to regions, and beyond this residential problem to inferring more complex organizational features.

Many elements of this scheme seem to have been "in the air" at the time, both at Chicago and elsewhere. Others working along roughly the same lines, concerned with the inference of features of social organization and ideology from archeological remains in some kind of evolutionary and adaptive frame of reference, included prominently Robert Adams, François Bordes (self-consciously in an experimental tradition, and not at all a positivist), Joseph Caldwell, Paul Martin, Fred Quimby, and Stewart Struever and, at lower time levels, F. Clark Howell and Sherwood Washburn (see Caldwell's *New Roads to Yesterday* [1966] for a good sample of relevant work that was published in *Science* at about this time; see Longacre's *Reconstructing Prehistoric Pueblo Societies* [1970] for one major group of studies focussed on a single area).

In use, this type of research design has led to an explanatory framework that is actually quite different from "organic" and "evolutionary" laws operating deterministically, and much closer to a general social-psychological model of rational actors selecting cultural tools out of a range of available options in order to exploit their environment, with a secondary sense that each adaptation creates new problems and ultimately requires still further adjustments: more an individualistic stochastic model, of the sort originally argued for by Montesquieu, than the

Spencerian cultural or global evolutionary models of White or Steward. For example, Fred Plog (in Leaf, 1974) recently explicitly rejected the organic conception of a "settlement pattern" in describing how these interests have led him to a concern with parameters from location theory in geography, which contain an implicit conception of competitive choice of sites to permit efficient exploitation of one's environment. William Longacre (in Leaf, 1974) described the related development of his concern with ethnographic observation of the way in which pottery making is actually taught by mothers to daughters in a remote present-day Philippine community.

Few of the American "new archeologists" are conscious of an inherent conflict between this orientation and Binford's "organic" and "logico-deductive" metatheory, and some, at least, confidently hope that the two "levels of analysis" will be reconciled. But in fact this type of explanatory theory fits far more consistently with the pragmatic ethnological assumptions of Singer and Wagner (and Bailey and Epstein) than Steward and White.

Physical Anthropology

Within the framework of the "new systematics," interest in physical anthropology in the current period has reflected a greatly increased concern with the biological basis of social behavior, including a shift of interests from genetics as such back to the role of gross physiology in interactive behaviors of all types. The results of these interests are still too scattered, and too many technical points are too hotly disputed, to be reviewed in detail as history at the present time. But a few major recent syntheses should be noted.

First, it now is often stressed in studies of primates, that the most striking feature of human evolution is the development of the capacity for verbal communication, connected directly to the growth in brain size. Other primates now are considered to have social organization in some form, to use and manufacture tools in some form, and even to be able to use "language" (if not speech) in some sense. But humans alone use complex generative grammatical language, and teach their social organization to one another by its means. Jane Goodall's studies of chimpanzee groups under wild conditions, Irven DeVore's work with baboon social organization, and especially K. J. and G. Hayes's experiences teaching American Sign Language to chimpanzees have been particularly important in the area, although the significance of these studies has been greatly strengthened and expanded by rigorous laboratory research of a large number of other workers (see D. Morris 1967 for a selection of recent work including several reviews).

Secondly, it is now generally agreed that the fossil record shows that the present reliance on the brain as a special product and basis of the human capacity for organization and culture goes back as far into the past as we can trace our ancestry, with expansion of cranial capacity and probably brain size being the single most striking and consistent feature of hominid development. The cranial capacities of the Australopithecines, still the first clearly recognized antecedents, were already large compared to related great apes (cf. Le Gros Clark 1967:13, Tobias 1971:92–95), and each new grade has shown progressively larger cranial capacities since, up to a peak in "late pleistocene man" (according to Tobias 1971:100–04), after which there has been a slight reduction. Within the limits of caution, Tobias considers it reasonable to expect increasing complexity of structure to have been a direct concomitant of this increasing size (1971:104, 114–16). Surely it is at least an approximate concomitant. In addition the human brain in particular appears to have a different organization (Tobias 1971:114) than that of nonhuman primates.

Reviewing the language learning experience with chimpanzees, accumulated work on the apparent physiology of the brain associated with speech in humans, the fossil record, acoustic and articulatory phonetics, and the nature of language itself (in a rudimentary way), Philip Lieberman recently suggested that the human speech capacity began to develop at a very early period in human evolution, long before the brain reached its present size, perhaps among Australopithecines and even more clearly with Homo erectus (Lieberman:1975). The human pharynx—an organ uniquely adapted to the creation of speech sounds, appears to have reached its fully modern form after the neurological capacity for speech evolved: about 200,000 b.p., the time level represented by the Steinheim skull (p. 160). Lieberman was quite explicit about the general monistic view that this developing conception both required and supported. He began his arguments quoting Montaigne on the "arrogance" of imposing our own human conceptions of intelligence on non-humans; he repeatedly returned to Darwin's theme that evolution proceeds always by small steps; he firmly rejected the idea that language had a single essential feature but saw it instead as based on several features, some of which were not at all unique to humans; he equally firmly rejected the idea of long-term deterministic "laws" of evolution; and finally he attempted to reconstruct the adaptive situation of language use at each major juncture by appropriate "experimental" demonstrations.

Especially when viewed in detail as the evidence accumulates toward the same point from many different beginnings, all this suggests that while man is less unique in many respects than formerly believed, he is more unique in his use of speech and his biological adaptation for it than previously thought. Conversely, he is more the product of evolution in a "niche" composed very largely of verbal symbols of his own (or rather his ancestor's) making than was previously appreciated in detail.

The conception of the evolutionary process that underlies these studies is, like the newer models in archeology apart from Binford's dualism, fundamentally relativistic and stochastic rather than deterministic, with emphasis on the physiological basis of flexibility of action, and of cultural and social outcomes of flexibility as parts of the evolutionary situation in turn. Selection in favor of larger cerebral cortices (controlling voluntary movement) among pre-human hominids may have been developed as a response to pressure for a more complex version of the kind of tool-using behavior and social organization that they shared with related forms, perhaps in a similar environment. The large cortex in turn may have permitted selection for modification of the larynx and pharynx that could create a wider range of physical sounds, allowing still more complex verbal signalling, and the development of generative verbal signal systems (grammatical language) could have given advantages to individuals with still further modifications of the nervous system better suited to its communicative potential. The mode of explanation and the substantive results are more than simply non-dualistic and non-deterministic. In many subtle ways, they take up where the work of Wundt and such successors as Köhler left off. In consequence, they naturally articulate closely with the modern work of Jean Piaget and his successors in the development of conceptual capacities with maturation. Piaget's genetic epistomology is in turn linked to continuing unfolding of the direct neurological processes that appear to underlie the creation of consciousness.

In his recent retrospective lectures, John Eccles, like Wundt, stressed the significance of the inhibitory aspects of cerebral motor neurone function, and stated the case for inhibition being related to concentration even more strongly than Wundt had—characterizing the function of these nervous centers as the "sculpture" of incoming impulses (1972:143). In the area of sensory neurone function, which is of still greater relevance to theories of perception, advances in experimental technology have enabled workers to demonstrate differences in neurone firing indicating that individual nerves can resolve very fine differences in spatial displacement and tonality of sound. Neff (1968), for example, has shown that neurones in the brain of a cat, receiving binaural inputs, show different patterns of response corresponding to differences of microseconds only in the time a sound reaches the two ears. This difference in time corresponds to a spatial displacement of less than two degrees. Similar work, on humans using measurements at the scalp, shows similar neurological responses to tone in the range of human speech (Moushegian, 1976), and apparently there are similar mechanisms for detecting sound-sequences (Lieberman 1975:54).

Since an inherent spatial organization of visual perception is already generally accepted, a similar spatial framework for auditory responses would go a long way toward establishing the existence of precisely the kind of inborn spatial "intuition" that Kant saw as prior to learning any specific cultural system of spatial concepts, and that were formalized by such concepts. Since, as Kant recognized, this spatial intuition was involved in much more than the perception of objects in our immediate surroundings, being a basic framework for the organization of such abstract concepts as "self," "object," and "other," this finding is of the utmost importance to the understanding of the role of communication in human thought, and of the relationships among human physiology, human communication, and the contents of the conscious mind.

The Monistic Vision

Each dualistic scheme makes a promise that dualism as a system of argument denies. Each promises to identify that one aspect of culture, social structure, or thought, or that one law of evolution or adaptation, that will explain everything, all other aspects of culture or history. Yet together, they can be described as W. B. Gallie described philosophy since Descartes: ". . . radical innovator following radical innovator, true new method hard upon true new method, so that it is small wonder if to the intelligent outsider movements . . . seem almost as variable as fashions in women's clothes" (1964:146). Monism too has its promises, but in this case, what is often modestly enough offered in each area of work is confirmed and supported, not denied and undermined, by the others.

In place of universal cosmological or symbolic categories, monism offers a conception of communicative process. In place of structural wholes that include entities unrecognizable to those supposedly "within" them, it offers methods for eliciting concepts of relation and order, and for discovering how they are employed. In place of the elusive laws of evolution that pertain to linear changes of whole cultures from one stage or configuration to another, the monistic vision offers a stochastic conception of history based on interacting creative responses to options at each point in time, that create new conditions that frame new options for the next point of decision. Finally, and most importantly, instead of isolating each of these conceptions in compartments of anthropology that are cut off from one another, they are interlinked, grounded in a common conception of human nature, human mentality, and science and scientific procedure.

The conception of human nature is, as for Wundt (and Fechner), fundamentally a conception of the human biological organism as uniquely adapted for acquiring complex and elaborate habits (where habit is understood as a pattern of behavior which is learned, but which is nevertheless largely present below the level of conscious attention when it is enacted).

The conception of mind sees it as an aspect of some of these acquired habits, related to their public and conscious coordination and control. Consciousness emerges from an "integument" of less than perfectly conscious attitudes, feelings, and intuitions just as "symbols" emerge as designated selected aspects of their own "material integument" in Turner's sense (and recalling Herder's point that the basis of language was concentration). Mind is, thus, not one homogeneous entity separated from physiological function, but an evolved aspect of physiological function, related especially to communication, that provides a series of more or less separate and often unrelated "handles" on different kinds of activities and functions.

The contents of mind are, of course, still difficult to characterize—although to avoid the idea that they must all be uniform in some respect, and ordered in a single system, relieves many problems. It is reasonably obvious that "symbols," as objects that may be made to carry meanings in a way that makes them publicly available, are different from "meanings" that they may carry. Symbols are multivocal. Meanings, or ideas, are not—although they may be vague. Symbols, because they are multivocal, are better thought of as coming in sets or groups—

like rooms full of stage properties. Ideas, which take their meanings from having regular and fixed relations to other ideas, come in systems and structures in a strict sense.

The re-emergent conception of scientific procedure is demonstrative, but now the sense of how the idea of demonstration is to be construed in ethnology is much clearer than fifty years ago. Turner, for example, lays considerable stress on the point that none of the rituals he described was staged for his own benefit. Precisely because of the overriding importance of purpose and context, social communication must be seen as it naturally arises. One participates in the events within which "mind" is created in a society—within which established conceptualizations are presented and applied—and where each participant automatically obtains assurance that this application is generally recognized by others present. The only difference is that instead of aiming to be convinced and to convince others, the anthropologist's view of the process is, in a sense, from a step back. He is concerned with *how* the participants allow themselves to be convinced, and endeavor to convince others. In effect, one is engaging in a double demonstration. The cultural event of interest is itself one kind of demonstration, for those concerned, and the analyst must learn from it just as the participants do. Then, in addition, the analyst alone uses it to convey still more about the general process of such conveyance. As in all other demonstrative sciences, the analyst's strategy is to select not only those events that are clear, but those that clearly show the most important phenomena he can find. The role of theory is, partly, to argue for the importance of the kind of event selected, be it conducting a ritual or telling a pun; and, partly, to relate the particular event shown to the other events it is taken to stand for.

The view of science as a system of knowledge which follows from this conception of scientific procedure is that of a network of linked experiments, demonstrating the nature of and relations among key phenomena. The linkages extend not only across major areas of anthropology, but also into other fields: ritual to paleoanthropology to physical anthropology to primate studies to experimental psychology to language study to speech pathology, and so on.

Throughout the last fifty years, it has been fashionable to frame the most general theoretical arguments by the notion that anthropology was the study of some specific sort of cultural or social entity or system underlying and determining individual behavior: culture, social structure, cognitive structures, or levels of energy (all variously conceived). None of these conflicting alternatives has come to be generally accepted. The re-emergence of monism is in part a rejection of all of these competing positions and, even more, a rejection of the assumptions that led to the frustrating and largely verbal pattern of competition between them. It is in part also a response to the increasing technical sophistication and increasing appreciation of the details of cultural processes that the competing deterministic schemes were equally incapable of taking into account. The response cannot, in the nature of the case, be encapsulated in a new conception of anthropology as a study of yet another determinant of thought or behavior. Rather, it calls for a new conception of anthropology as the study of free, creative activity. One way to describe this anthropology, extending Wagner's conception of social anthropology as the study of the way people create their sociability, would be to say that anthropology is the study of the ways humans create their humanity. In somewhat fuller language, it is the study of the way conscious categories of thought arise through cultural communication on the basis of the evolved capacities of the biological organism; and conversely, it is the study of the content and bases of cultural communication within this process. Since such a science is not in any way dependent on imposing categories of one culture on others, it provides an equally detached examination of any community, and by the same token is equally accessible to people of all cultural traditions. In this double sense, buttressed by the facts and methods its predecessors required but could only begin to obtain, this new monistic anthropology may truly be the beginning of a universal science of man.

Bibliography

Date in parentheses indicates year of original publication. Bibliographic data pertains to edition indicated without parentheses.

Adams, Robert McCormick
1950   "Early Civilization, Subsistence and Environment." *The City Invincible*. Chicago: University of Chicago Press.

Adkins, Douglas L.
n.d.   *The Manpower Future for Anthropologists and Sociologists.* Manu-
about   script report of project on Manpower Needs and Social Science
1974   Graduate Training, sponsored by National Institute of Mental Health.

Allison, A. C.
1954   "Protection Afforded Sickle-Cell Trait against Subtertian Malarial Infection." *British Medical Journal* 1:290–94.

Antoni, Carlo
1959   *From History to Sociology,* H. V. White, trans. Detroit: Wayne State University Press.

Aron, Raymond
1964   *German Sociology.* Mary and Thomas Bottomore, trans. New York: Free Press of Glencoe.

Asimov, Isaac
1960   *The Intelligent Man's Guide to Science.* New York: Basic Books.

Ayer, A. J.
1959   *Logical Positivism.* Glencoe, Ill.: Free Press.

Bachofen, J. J.
(1859) *An Essay on Ancient Grave Symbolism.*

(1861) *Mother-Right.*

(1870) *The Myth of Tanaquil.*

1967   *Myth, Religion, and Mother-Right: Selected Writings of J. J. Bachofen.* Ralph Manheim, trans. Preface by George Boas; Introduction by Joseph Campbell. Bollinger Series. Princeton: Princeton University Press.

Bailey, F. G.
1957   *Caste and the Economic Frontier*. Manchester: Manchester University Press.

1960   *Tribe, Caste and Nation*. Manchester: Manchester University Press.

1969   *Stratagems and Spoils*. Oxford: Basil Blackwell.

Banton, Michael, ed.
1965   *The Revelance of Models for Social Anthropology*. A.S.A. Monograph No. 1. New York: Praeger.

Barrell, Joseph, Charles Schuchert, Lorande Loss Woodruff, Richard Swan Luft, and Ellsworth Huntington
1918   *The Evolution of the Earth and Its Inhabitants*. New Haven: Yale University Press.

Barth, Frederick
1959   "Segmentary Opposition and the Theory of Games: A Study of Pathan Organization." *Journal of the Royal Anthropological Institute of Great Britain and Ireland* 89:5–21.

1966   *Models of Social Organization*. Occasional Paper No. 23. Royal Anthropological Institute of Great Britain and Ireland.

Bastian, Adolphe
1860   *Der Mensch in der Geschichte*. Leipzig: Otto Wigand.

Beidleman, T. O.
1974   "Sir Edward Evans-Pritchard (1902–1973), An Appreciation." *Anthropos* 69:553–67.

Benedict, Ruth
(1934)   *Patterns of Culture*. Boston: Houghton Mifflin.
1959

1946   *The Chrysanthemum and the Sword: Patterns of Japanese Culture*. Boston: Houghton Mifflin.

Bennett, Wendell Clark
1947   *The Ethnogeographic Board*. Smithsonian Miscellaneous Collection 107:1. Washington, D.C.: Smithsonian Institution.

Bidney, David
1953   *Theoretical Anthropology*. New York: Columbia University Press.

Binford, Lewis R.
1962   "Archeology as Anthropology." *American Antiquity* 28:217–25.

1968   "Methodological Considerations of the Archeological Use of Ethnographic Data." In R. B. Lee and Irven De Vore. eds.. *Man the Hunter*. Chicago: Aldine.

          The Revelance of Models for Social Anthropology. A.S.A. Monograph No. 1. New York: Praeger.

Bloch, Bernard
1949   "Leonard Bloomfield." *Language* 25:87–98.

Bloomfield, Leonard
(1933)   *Language*. New York: Holt, Rinehart and Winston.
1961

Boas, Franz
1889   "On Alternating Sounds." *American Anthropologist* 2:47–58.
1911   *The Mind of Primitive Man*. Revised ed., 1938. New York: Macmillan.
1912   "Changes in Bodily Form of Descendants of Immigrants." *American Anthropologist*, n.s. 14:3.
1916   "The Origins of Totemism." *American Anthropologist*, n.s. 18:319–26.
(1927)   *Primitive Art*. New York: Dover.
1955
1932   "The Aims of Anthropological Research." *Science*, n.s. 76:605–13.
(1939)   *Race, Language and Culture*. Glencoe, Ill.: Free Press.
1966

Boas, Franz et al.
1938   *General Anthropology*. Boston: D. C. Heath.

Bordes, François
1968   *The Old Stone Age*. New York and Toronto: McGraw-Hill. 3d printing, 1973.

Boring, Edwin G.
1950   *A History of Experimental Psychology*. New York: Appleton-Century-Crofts.

Brew, J. O.
1968   *One Hundred Years of Anthropology*. Cambridge: Harvard University Press.

Brown, Cecil
1974   *Wittgensteinian Linguistics*. The Hague: Mouton.

Buchler, Ira and Henry Selby
1968   *Kinship and Social Organization: An Introduction to Theory and Method*. New York: Macmillan.

Buettner-Janusch, John
1966   *Origins of Man*. New York: Wiley.

Burling, Robins
1970   "American Kinship Terms Once More." *Southwestern Journal of Anthropology* 26:1:15–24.

Burtt, Edwin A., ed.
1939   *The English Philosophers from Bacon to Mill.* New York: Modern Library.

Bynum, Terrell Ward
1972   *Gottlob Frege: Conceptual Notation and Related Articles.* Oxford: Oxford University Press.

Caldwell, Joseph R.
1966   *New Roads to Yesterday.* New York: Basic Books.

Campbell, Bernard
1966   *Human Evolution: An Introduction to Man's Adaptations.* Chicago: Aldine.

Carr, David
1967   "Maurice Merleau-Ponty, Incarnate Consciousness." In George A. Schrader, ed., *Existential Philosophers: Kierkegaard to Merleau-Ponty.* New York: McGraw-Hill.

Carroll, John B.
1956   *Language, Thought and Reality: Selected Writings of Benjamin Lee Whorf.* Cambridge: M.I.T. Press.

Catlin, George
(1844)   *Letters and Notes on the Manners, Customs, and Conditions of*
1973   *North American Indians.* 2 vols. Abridged with Introduction by Marjorie Halpin. New York: Dover.

Chafe, Wallace
1965   "Meaning in Language." *American Anthropologist* 67:5, part 2:23–26.

Childe, V. G.
1951   *Social Evolution.* New York: H. Schuman.

Chomsky, Noam
1957   *Syntactic Structures.* The Hague: Mouton.

1964   *Aspects of a Theory of Syntax.* Cambridge: M.I.T. Press.

1966   *Cartesian Linguistics.* New York: Harper and Row.

Clark, W. E. Le Gros
(1959)   *The Antecedents of Man.* Chicago: Quadrangle Books.
1960

1967   *Man-Apes or Ape-Men: The Story of Discoveries in Africa.* New York: Holt, Rinehart and Winston.

Cole, Fay-Cooper
1934   "Frederick Starr." *American Anthropologist* 36:271.

Collingwood, R. G.
(1946)   *The Idea of History*. Oxford: Clarendon Press.
1962

Commins, Saxe and Robert Linscott
1954   *Man and the State: The Political Philosophers*. New York: Wash-
          ington Square Press.

Comte, Auguste
1851,   *Système de politique positive*. 3 vols. Paris: Carilon-Gœury et Vor
1852   Dalmont.

1875   *System of Positive Polity*. Vol. 1: *General View of Positivism and
          Introductory Principles*. English trans. of 1851 ed. London: Long-
          mans, Green.

1876   *System of Positive Polity*. Vol. 3: *Social Dynamics, or the General
          Theory of Human Progress*. English trans. of 1853 ed. London:
          Longmans, Green.

Cook, Joseph
1878   *Biology, With Preludes on Current Events*. Boston: Houghton,
          Asgood.

Coues, Elliott, ed.
1965   *History of the Expedition under the Command of Lewis and Clark*.
          3 vols. New York: Dover.

Dalton, George
1967   *Tribal and Peasant Economies: Readings in Economic Anthropol-
          ogy*. Garden City, N.Y.: Natural History Press.

D'Andrade, Roy G.
1970   "Structure and Syntax in the Semantic Analysis of Kinship Termi-
          nologies." In Paul Garvin, ed. *Cognition: A Multiple View*. New
          York: Spartan.

Darnell, Regna
1974   *Readings in the History of Anthropology*. New York: Harper &
          Row.

Darwin, Charles
(1859)   *Origin of Species, a Facsimile of the First Edition*. Rpt. of Harvard
1967   University Press 1964 ed. New York: Atheneum.

1871   *Descent of Man*. London: J. Murray.

Descartes, René
(1637)   *Discourse on Method*.

(1641)   *Meditations on the First Philosophy, in which the Existence of God*
1958   *and the Distinction in Man of Soul and Body are Demonstrated.* In
          Norman Kemp Smith, ed., *Descartes: Philosophical Writings.* New
          York: Modern Library.

Dewey, John
1922   *Human Nature and Conduct.* New York: Henry Holt.

1926   *Experience and Nature.* Chicago: Open Court Publishing.

Dobzhansky, Theodosius
1956   *The Biological Basis of Human Freedom.* New York: Columbia
          University Press.

Dorsey, George A.
1926   *Why We Behave Like Human Beings.* New York: Harper.

Drake, Stillman
1953   *Dialogue Concerning the Two Chief World Systems—Ptolemaic
          and Copernican, by Galileo.* Berkeley: University of California
          Press.

Dumont, Louis
1961   "Descent, Filiation and Affinity." *Man* 61:11.

Durkheim, Emile
(1893)   *The Division of Labor in Society.* George Simpson, trans. New
1966   York: Free Press (paper).

(1897)   *Suicide: A Study in Sociology.* John A. Spaulding and George
1966   Simpson, trans. New York: Free Press.

(1912)   *The Elementary Forms of the Religious Life.* London: Allen &
1915   Unwin.

Dyson-Hudson, Neville
1969   "Structure and Infra-structure in Primitive Society: Lévi-Strauss
          and Radcliffe-Brown." In E. Donato and R. A. Macksey, eds.
          Critical Languages and the Science of Man. Baltimore: Johns Hop-
          kins University Press.

Eccles, John C.
1972   *The Understanding of the Brain.* New York: McGraw-Hill.

Eggan, Fred
(1937)   *Social Anthropology of North American Tribes.* Chicago and Lon-
1955   don: University of Chicago Press.

(1950)   *Social Organization of the Western Pueblos.* Chicago and London:
1967   University of Chicago Press.

1963   "Fay-Cooper   Cole,   1881–1961."   *American   Anthropologist*
          65:641–46.

1966   *The American Indian: Perspectives for the Study of Social Change.*
          Chicago: Aldine.

Ehrmann, Jacques, ed.
1970   *Structuralism.* New York: Doubleday Anchor.

Elkin, A. P.
1956   "A. R. Radcliffe-Brown," *Oceania* 26(4):239–51.

Epstein, T. Scarlett
(1962)   *Economic Development and Social Change in South India.* Man-
1967   chester: University Press.

Erasmus, J. C.
1950   "Patolle, Pachisi, and the Limitation of Possibilities." *Southwest-*
          ern Journal of Anthropology 6:369.

Erdmann, Benno
1882   *Reflexionen Kants.* Leipzig: Fues's Verlag (R. Reisland).

Evans-Pritchard, E. E.
1940a   "Lucien Lévy-Bruhl, 1939." *Man* 40:24–25.
(1940b)   *The Nuer.* Oxford: Clarendon.
1967
1962   *Social Anthropology and Other Essays.* Glencoe, Ill.: Free Press.
1970   *The Sociology of Comte: An Appreciation.* Manchester: Manchester
          University Press.

Faris, Robert E. L.
1967   *Chicago Sociology, 1920–1932.* Chicago and London: University of
          Chicago Press.

Farrington, Benjamin
1966   *Greek Science: Its Meaning For Us.* Baltimore: Penguin. (Rpt. of
          1961 ed. with revised bibliography.)

Ferguson, Adam
(1767)   *An Essay on the History of Civil Society.* Ed. and with Introduction
1966   by Forbes Duncan. Edinburgh: Edinburgh University Press.

Firth, Raymond
1951   *Elements of Social Organization.* Boston: Beacon.

Firth, Raymond, ed.
(1957)   *Man and Culture: An Evaluation of the Work of Bronislaw Mali-*
1960   *nowski.* London: Routledge and Kegan Paul.
1967   *Themes in Economic Anthropology.* Association of Social Anthro-
          pologists Monograph No. 6. New York: Travistock.

Fortes, Meyer
1945   *The Dynamics of Clanship among the Tallensi.* London: Oxford
          University Press.

1949   *The Web of Kinship among the Tallensi.* London: Oxford University
          Press.

1970   *Time and Social Structure and Other Essays.* New York: Athelone.

Fortes, Meyer and E. E. Evans-Pritchard, eds.
1940   *African Political Systems.* London: Oxford University Press.

Frake, Charles O.
1964   "A Structural Description of Subanun 'Religious Behavior'." *Ex-
          plorations in Cultural Anthropology: Essays in Honor of George
          Peter Murdock.* New York: McGraw-Hill.

Frankfort, Henri
1948   *Ancient Egyptian Religion.* New York: Columbia University Press.

1950   *The Birth of Civilization in the Near East.* Garden City and New
          York: Doubleday Anchor.

Frazer, J. G.
1887   *Totemism.* Edinburgh: Adam & Charles Black.

1908   *The Scope of Social Anthropology.* London: Macmillan.

(1910)   *Totemism and Exogamy.* Rpt. London: Macmillan.
1935

Freud, Sigmund
1913(?)   *Totem and Taboo.* Authorized English translation by A. A. Brill.
          New ed. New York: Dodd Mead.

1955   *Beyond the Pleasure Principle, Group Psychology, and Other
          Works.* Vol. 18 (1920–22) of *The Standard Edition of the Complete
          Psychological Works of Sigmund Freud.* Trans. under the general
          editorship of James Strachey, in collaboration with Anna Freud.
          London: Hogarth Press.

1961   *The Future of an Illusion, Civilization and its Discontents and
          Other Works.* Vol. 21 (1927–31) of the above.

Friedrich, Paul
1970   "Shape in Grammar." *Language* 46:379–408.

Gallie, W. B.
(1964)   *Philosophy and the Historical Understanding.* 2d ed. New York:
1968   Schocken Books.

Galton, Francis
1893   *English Men of Science: Their Nature and Nurture.* New York: D.
          Appleton.

Garfinkel, Harold
1967   *Studies in Ethnomethodology.* Englewood Cliffs, N.J.: Prentice-Hall.

Garn, Stanley W. and Carleton Coon
1955   "On the Number of Races of Mankind." *American Anthropologist* 57:996–1001.

Geertz, Clifford
1957   "Ritual and Social Change, A Javanese Example." *American Anthropologist* 59:32–54.

1963a   *Agricultural Involution.* Berkeley: University of California Press.

1963b   *Peddlers and Princes: Social Change and Economic Modernization in Two Indonesian Towns.* Chicago: University of Chicago Press.

1966a   *Person, Time, and Conduct in Bali: An Essay in Cultural Analysis.* New Haven: Yale University Southeast Asia Studies.

1966b   "Religion as a Cultural System." In M. Banton, ed., *Anthropological Approaches in the Study of Religion.* London: Tavistock.

1973   *The Interpretation of Cultures.* New York: Basic Books.

Geymonat, Ludovico
1957   *Galileo Galilei: A Biography and Inquiry into His Philosophy of Science.* Stillman Drake, trans. New York: McGraw-Hill.

Gibson, Gordon
1948   "The Possibility of Numerous Independent Inventions." *American Anthropologist* 50:362–64.

Glick, Thomas F., ed.
1972   *The Comparative Reception of Darwinism.* Austin and London: University of Texas Press.

Gluckman, Max
1963   *Order and Rebellion in Tribal Africa.* New York: Free Press of Glencoe.

Goldenweiser, Alexander
1910   "Totemism, An Analytical Study." *Journal of American Folklore* 23:178–298.

1913   "The Principle of Limited Possibilities of the Development of Culture." *Journal of American Folklore* 26:259–80.

Goodenough, Ward H.
1956   "Componential Analysis and the Study of Meaning." *Language* 32:195–216.

1965   "Componential Analysis of Yankee Kinship Terminology." *American Anthropologist* 67:5, part 2:259–87.

Gumperz, John J. and Dell Hymes, eds.
1964   *The Ethnography of Communication.* Special Publication of the *American Anthropologist* 66:6.

Harris, Marvin
1968   *The Rise of Anthropological Theory.* New York: Thomas Y. Crowell.

Harris, Marvin and George E. B. Morren
1966   "The Limitations of the Principle of Limited Possibilities." *American Anthropologist* 1:122–27.

Hays, Hoffman R.
1958   *From Ape to Angel: An Informal History of Social Anthropology.* New York: Knopf.

Hegel, G. W. F.
(1821)   *Hegel's Philosophy of Right.* Translation with Notes by T. M.
1952   Knox. London: Oxford University Press.

(1900)   *Reason in History; A General Introduction to the Philosophy of*
1953   *History.* Translated with Introduction by Robert S. Hartman. New York: Liberal Arts Press.

Helm, June, ed.
1966   *Pioneers of American Anthropology.* American Ethnological Society Monograph No. 43. Seattle: University of Washington Press.

Herder, Johann Gottfried von
(1772)   "Essay on the Origin of Language." In John H. Moran and Alex-
1966   ander Gode, trans., *On the Origin of Language.* New York: Frederick Ungar.

(1791)   *Reflections on the Philosophy of the History of Mankind.* Abridged
1968   ed., Frank E. Manuel, ed. Chicago: University of Chicago Press. First published 1784–91, in twenty books; T. O. Churchill, trans., 1800.

Himmelfarb, Gertrude
1959   *Darwin and the Darwinian Revolution.* New York: Doubleday.

Hobbes, Thomas
1642   *De Cive.* See Lamprecht, 1949.

(1651)   *Leviathan, Parts I and II.* Herbert W. Schneider, ed. Indianapolis
1958   and New York: Bobbs-Merrill.

Hoijer, Harry, ed.
1954   *Language and Culture.* American Anthropological Association Memoir, no. 79.

Hubert, Henry and Marcell Mauss
(1899)   *Sacrifice: Its Nature and Function.* W. D. Halls, trans.; with Fore-
1964   word by E. E. Evans-Pritchard. London: Cohen and West.

Hull, Clark L.
1943   *Principles of Behavior: An Introduction to Behavior Theory.* New
          York: Appleton-Century.

Hume, David
(1750)   *An Inquiry Concerning Human Understanding.* Charles W. Hendel,
1955   ed. New York: Bobbs-Merrill.

Hymes, Dell
1971a   Foreword: "Morris Swadesh: From the First Yale School to World
          Prehistory." In Morris Swadesh, *The Origin and Diversification of
          Language,* Joel Sherzer, ed. Chicago and New York: Aldine Ather-
          ton.

1971b   Appendix to the above cited work.

Hymes, Dell, ed.
1973   *Reinventing Anthropology.* New York: Random House Pantheon.

1974   *Studies in the History of Linguistics: Traditions and Paradigms.*
          Bloomington and London: Indiana University Press.

Jackson, Benjamin D.
1911   "Linnaeus" in *Encyclopaedia Brittanica* 16:732–33. New York:
          Encyclopaedia Brittanica.

James, William
1890   *Principles of Psychology,* 2 vols. New York: Henry Holt.

1907   *Pragmatism and Four Essays from the Meaning of Truth.* New
          York: World Publishing.

1928   *Some Problems of Philosophy.* New York: Longmans, Green.

1948   *Essays in Pragmatism.* New York: Hafner Publishing.

Jesperson, Otto
1924   *Language: Its Nature, Development and Origin.* New York: Henry
          Holt.

Kant, Immanuel
(1783)   *Prolegomena to Any Future Metaphysics.* Edited and with Introduc-
1950   tion by Lewis White Beck. New York: Bobbs-Merrill.

(1796)   *Metaphysische Anfangsgründe der Rechtslehre* (Being Part I of
1887   *Metaphysik der Sitten*). Translated into English as *Kant's Philos-
          ophy of Law* by W. Hastie. Edinburgh: T. and T. Clark.

(1798)   *Anthropologie in pragmatischer Hinsicht.* Konigsberg: Friedrich.
1974   Trans. as *Anthropology from a Pragmatic Point of View,* Mary J.
           Gregor. The Hague: Martinus Nijhoff.

Kaplan, David
1968   "The Formal Substantive Controversy in Economic Anthropology:
           Reflections on Its Wider Implications." *Southwestern Journal of
           Anthropology* 24:228–51.

Kardiner, Abram and Edward Preble
1961   *They Studied Man.* Cleveland: World Publishing.

Katz, Jerrold J. and Paul M. Postal
1964   *An Integrated Theory of Linguistic Descriptions.* Cambridge: Re-
           search Monograph No. 26 and the M.I.T. Press.

Kay, Paul
1971   "Taxonomy and Semantic Contrast." *Language* 47:4:866–87.

Kluckhohn, Clyde
1944   *Navaho Witchcraft.* Papers of the Peabody Museum 22:2. Cam-
           bridge: Peabody Museum.

Kroeber, A. L.
1909   "Classificatory System of Relationship." *JRAI* 36:77–84.

1915   "Frederic Ward Putnam." *American Anthropologist* 17:712–18.

1920   *"Totem and Taboo:* An Ethnographic Psychoanalysis." *American
           Anthropologist* 22:48–55.

1935   "History and Science in Anthropology." *American Anthropologist*
           37:4:539–69.

1939a   *Cultural and Natural Areas of Native North America.* Berkeley:
           University of California Press.

1939b   *"Totem and Taboo* in Retrospect." *American Journal of Sociology*
           45:446–51.

1943   "Franz Boas: The Man." In A. L. Kroeber et al., eds. *Franz Boas
           1858–1942.* American Anthropological Association Memoir, no.
           61.

1952   *The Nature of Culture.* Chicago: University of Chicago Press.

Kroeber, Theodora
1970   *Alfred Kroeber: A Personal Configuration.* Berkeley: University of
           California Press.

Kuhn, Thomas
1962   *The Structure of Scientific Revolutions.* Chicago: University of Chi-
           cago Press.

LaBarre, Weston
1958   "The Influence of Freud on Anthropology." *American Imago*
        15:3:275–328.

Lamarck, Jean Baptiste de
1815   *Histoire naturelle des animaux sans vertèbres*. Paris: Verdière.

Lamprecht, Sterling P., ed.
(1642) *De Cive or The Citizen*, by Thomas Hobbes. New York: Appleton-
1949   Century Philosophy Source Books.

Lang, Andrew
(1887) *Myth, Ritual, and Religion*. Vols. 1 and 2, rpt. London: Longmans,
1899   Green.

1901   *Magic and Religion*. London: Longmans, Green.

1903   *Social Origins*. (Including *Primal Law*, by J. J. Atkinson.) London:
        Longmans, Green.

Lauer, Quentin
1965   *Phenomenology: Its Genesis and Prospect*. New York: Harper and
        Row.

Leach, E. R.
1951   "Structural Implications of Matrilateral Cross-Cousin Marriage."
        *Journal of the Royal Anthropological Institute of Great Britain and
        Ireland* 81:23–55.

1954   *Political Systems of Highland Burma*. London: G. Bell.

1961   *Rethinking Anthropology*. London School of Economics Mono-
        graphs on Social Anthropology No. 22. Toronto: Oxford University
        Press.

1970   *Claude Lévi-Strauss*. New York: Viking.

Leaf, Murray J.
1971   "The Punjabi Kinship Terminology as a Semantic System." *Ameri-
        can Anthropologist* 73(3):545–54.

1972   *Information and Behavior in a Sikh Village: Social Organization
        Reconsidered*. Berkeley and Los Angeles: University of California
        Press.

1974   *Frontiers of Anthropology* (with Bernard Campbell, Constance
        Cronin, George DeVos, William Longacre, Marlys McClaren, Fred
        Plog, Jack Prost, and Roy Wagner). New York: Van Nostrand.

Leakey, L. S. B., Jack Prost, and Stephanie Prost, eds.
1971   *Adam or Ape: A Sourcebook of Discoveries About Early Man*.
        Cambridge and London: Shenkman.

LeClair, Edward E., Jr., and Harold K. Schneider, eds.
1968   *Economic Anthropology: Readings in Theory and Analysis.* New York: Holt, Rinehart and Winston.

Lehmann, Winfred P.
1967   *A Reader in Nineteenth Century Historical Indo-European Linguistics.* Bloomington: Indiana University Press.

Levi, Edward H.
1972   "The State of the University." *University of Chicago Record,* VI:2. Chicago: University of Chicago Press.

Lévi-Strauss, Claude
(1949) *The Elementary Structures of Kinship.* J. H. Bell and J. R. Von
1969   Sturmer, trans.; Rodney Needham, ed. Oxford: Alden & Mowbray.

(1952) "Social Structure." In Sol Tax, ed., *Anthropology Today.* Chicago:
1962   University of Chicago Press.

1955   "The Structural Study of Myth." *Journal of American Folklore* 68:270.

1958   *Anthropologie structurale.* Paris: Plon.

1961   *A World on the Wane.* London: Hutchinson. Trans. of *Tristes Tropique,* by John Russell.

(1963) *Structural Anthropology.* Claire Jacobson, trans. Garden City,
1967   N.Y.: Anchor Books.

1966   *Totemism.* Boston: Beacon Press.

1967   *The Scope of Anthropology.* Suffolk: Richard Clay.

Levine, Donald N.
1971   *Georg Simmel on Individuality and Social Forms.* Chicago: University of Chicago Press.

Lévy-Bruhl, Lucien
1890   *L'Allemagne depuis Leibniz.* Paris: Librarie Hachette.

(1903) *La Morale et la science des mœurs.* 6th ed. Paris: Librarie Felix
1940   Alcan.

Libby, Willard F.
1952   *Radiocarbon Dating.* Chicago: University of Chicago Press.

Lieberman, Philip
1975   *On the Origins of Language.* New York: Macmillan.

Linné, Carolia
1767   *Systema Naturae, per Regna Tria Naturae.* 13th ed. Vindo bonae. Vienna: Ioannis Thomae.

Locke, John
(1690a)   *An Essay Concerning Human Understanding.*

(1690b)   *An Essay Concerning the True Original Extent and End of Civil*
1939   *Government.* In Edwin A. Burtt, ed., *The English Philosophers
          from Bacon to Mill.* New York: Modern Library.

Longacre, William, ed.
1970   *Reconstructing Prehistoric Pueblo Societies.* Albuquerque: Univer-
          sity of New Mexico Press.

Lowie, Robert H.
1916   "Ernst Mach: A Scientist's Scientist." *New Republic* 6:335–37.

(1920)   *Primitive Society.* 2d ed. New York: Harper.
1947

1937   *The History of Ethnological Theory.* New York: Holt, Rinehart &
          Winston.

1948   "Some Facts About Boas." *Southwestern Journal of Anthropology*
          4:69–70.

1959   *Robert H. Lowie, Ethnologist: A Personal Record.* Berkeley and
          Los Angeles: University of California Press.

Lydekker, Richard
1911   "Bison." *Encyclopaedia Britannica.* 11th ed. 2:11–12, New York:
          Encyclopaedia Britannica.

Maine, Henry Sumner
(1861)   *Ancient Law.* 4th ed. London: John Murray.
1870

Malefijt, Anne Marie de Waal
1974   *Images of Man.* New York: Knopf.

Malinowski, Bronislaw
1920   "Kula: The Circulating Exchange of Valuables in the Archipel-
          agoes of Eastern New Guinea." *Man* 20:97–105.

(1926)   *Crime and Custom in Savage Society.* Patterson, N.J.: Littlefield,
1959   Adams.

1927   *Sex and Repression in Savage Society.* London: Routledge & Kegan
          Paul.

1944   *A Scientific Theory of Culture, and Other Essays.* Chapel Hill,
          N.C.: Chapel Hill Press.

Marett, R. R., ed.
(1908)   *Anthropology and the Classics.* Oxford: Clarendon. Rpt. New
1966   York: Barnes & Noble.

Mauss, Marcel
1950   *Sociologie et anthropologie*. Paris: Presses Universitaires de
          France.

McLennan, John F.
1865   *Primitive Marriage*. Edinburgh: Black.

1886   *Studies in Ancient History, Comprising a Reprint of Primitive Mar-
          riage*. New York: Macmillan.

Mead, Margaret
1959   *An Anthropologist at Work: The Writings of Ruth Benedict*. Boston:
          Houghton Mifflin.

Mead, Margaret and Ruth Bunzel
1960   *The Golden Age of American Anthropology*. New York: Braziller.

Mehan, Hugh
1972   "Language Using Abilities." *Language Sciences* 22:1–10.

Merleau-Ponty, Maurice
1963   *The Structure of Behavior*. Boston: Beacon.

Mill, John Stuart
(1865)   *Auguste Comte and Positivism*. 4th ed. London: Kegan Paul,
1891   Trench, Trübner.

Miller, Robert L.
1968   *The Linguistic Relativity Principle and Humboltian Ethnolinguis-
          tics*. The Hague and Paris: Mouton.

Molesworth, Sir William, ed.
1939   *The English Works of Thomas Hobbes*. London: John Bohn.

Montesquieu, Baron de
(1748)   *The Spirit of the Laws*. Trans. Thomas Nugent. New York and Lon-
1949   don: Hafner Press.

Morgan, Lewis Henry
1877   *Ancient Society*. Chicago: Charles H. Kerr.

Morris, Charles
1948   *The Open Self*. New York: Prentice-Hall.

Morris, Clarence
1959   *The Great Legal Philosophers*. Philadelphia: University of Pennsyl-
          vania Press.

Morris, Desmond, ed.
1967   *Primate Ethnology*. Chicago: Aldine.

Moushegian, George
1976   "Frequency-Following Responses: Preliminary Studies in Man." In

John E. Desmedt, ed., *Cerebral Evoked Potentials in Man*. Oxford: Oxford University Press.

Murdock, George P.
1949   *Social Structure*. New York: Macmillan.

Nadel, S. F.
1951   *The Foundations of Social Anthropology*. London: Cohen and West.

Needham, Rodney
1958   "A Structural Analysis of Purum Society." *American Anthropologist* 60:75–101.

1962   *Structure and Sentiment: A Test Case in Social Anthropology*. Chicago: University of Chicago Press.

Neff, W. D.
1968   "Localization and Lateralization of Sound in Space." In A. V. S. de Reuck and J. Knight, eds., *Hearing Mechanisms in Vertebrates*. Boston: Little, Brown.

Neurath, Otto, Rudolf Carnap, and Charles W. Morris, eds.
(1938)   *International Encyclopedia of a Unified Science*. Vol. 1 (combined
1955   ed.). Chicago: University of Chicago Press.

Nida, Eugene A.
(1946)   *Morphology: The Descriptive Analysis of Words*. Ann Arbor: Uni-
1949   versity of Michigan Press. Revised edition.

Ortiz, Alfonso
1969   *The Tewa World*. Chicago: University of Chicago Press.

Pandey, Triloki Nath
1972   "Anthropologists at Zuñi." *Proceedings of the American Philosophical Society* 116:321–37.

1975   "India Man among American Indians." A. Béteille and T. N. Madan, eds., *Encounter and Experience*. Honolulu: University of Hawaii Press.

Parsons, Talcott
1949   *Essays in Sociological Theory Pure and Applied*. Glencoe, Ill.: Free Press.

1951   *The Social System*. Glencoe, Ill.: Free Press.

Parsons, Talcott and Edward A. Shils, eds.
1951   *Toward a General Theory of Action*. Cambridge: Harvard University Press.

Passmore, John
1962   *A Hundred Years of Philosophy*. London: Gerald Duckworth.

Peacock, James
1968   *Rites of Modernization: Symbolic and Social Aspects of Indonesian Proletarian Drama*. Chicago and London: University of Chicago Press.

Pearson, Karl
1911   *The Grammar of Science*. 3d ed., rpt. Gloucester: Peter Smith.

Pedersen, Holger
1931   *Linguistic Science in the Nineteenth Century: Methods and Results*. Authorized translation by John Webster Spargo. Cambridge: Harvard University Press.

Pelto, Perttie and Gretel H. Pelto
1970   *Anthropological Research: The Structure of Inquiry*. New York: Harper & Row.

Penniman, T. K.
1965   *A Hundred Years of Anthropology*. London: Gerald Duckworth.

Perry, Ralph B.
1926   *General Theory of Values: Its Meaning and Basic Principles Construed in Terms of Interest*. New York: Longmans, Green.

1935   *The Thought and Character of William James*. Cambridge: Harvard University Press.

Pike, Kenneth
1954   *Language in Relation to a Unified Theory of the Structure of Human Behavior*. Glendale, Calif.: Summer Institute of Linguistics.

Polanyi, Karl, Conrad M. Arensberg, and Harry W. Pearson, eds.
1957   *Trade and Market in the Early Empires*. New York: Free Press.

Quine, W. V. O.
1953   *From a Logical Point of View*. Cambridge: Harvard University Press.

1967   *Word and Object*. Cambridge: M.I.T. Press.

Radcliffe-Brown, A. R.
1932   *The Andaman Islanders*. Glencoe, Ill.: Free Press.

1952   *Structure and Function in Primitive Society*. Glencoe, Ill.: Free Press.

Radhakrishnan, Sarvepalli and Charles A. Moore
1957   *A Sourcebook in Indian Philosophy*. Princeton: Princeton University Press.

Rappaport, Roy A.
1967   *Pigs for the Ancestors: Ritual in the Ecology of a New Guinea Peo-*
           ple. New Haven: Yale University Press.

Read, Dwight
1974   "Kinship Algebra: A Mathematical Study of Kinship Structure." In
           P. Ballanoff, ed., *Geneological Mathematics*. Paris and The Hague:
           Mouton.

Redfield, Robert
1928   "A Plan for a Study of Tepoztlan, Morelos." Dissertation, Univer-
           sity of Chicago.

(1930)   *Tepoztlan: A Mexican Village*. Chicago: University of Chicago
1974   Press. Midway rpt.

1955   "Societies and Cultures as Natural Systems." *Journal of the Royal*
           Anthropological Institute of Great Britain and Ireland 85:19–32.

Reichard, Gladys A.
1928   *Social Life of the Navaho Indians*. Columbia University Contribu-
           tions to Anthropology No. 7, pp. 1–239.

Richards, A. I.
1943   "Bronislaw Kaspar Malinowski." *Man* 43:1:1–4.

Rivers, W. H. R.
1910   "The Geneological Method of Anthropological Inquiry." *Socio-*
           logical Review 3:1–10.

(1916)   *Kinship and Social Organizations*. New York: Humanities Press.
1968

Roberts, D. F.
1955   "The Dynamics of Racial Intermixture in the American Negro:
           Some Anthropological Considerations." *American Journal of*
           Human Genetics 7:361.

Romanes, George J.
1882   *The Scientific Evidences of Organic Evolution*. London: Macmillan.

Romney, A. K. and Roy G. D'Andrade
1964   "Cognitive Aspects of English Kin Terms." *American Anthropol-*
           ogist 66:3:2:146.

Rousseau, Jean-Jacques
(1762)   *The Social Contract and Discourses*. G. D. H. Cole, trans. New
1913   York: Dutton.

Rucker, Darnell
1969   *The Chicago Pragmatists*. Minneapolis: University of Minnesota
           Press.

Russell, Bertrand
1967   *Autobiography 1872–1914.* Boston: Little, Brown.

Sahlins, Marshall D. and Elman R. Service, eds.
1960   *Evolution and Culture.* Ann Arbor: University of Michigan Press.

Sapir, Edward
1949   *Language: An Introduction to the Study of Speech.* New York: Harcourt, Brace & World.

Savigny, Friedrich Karl von
(1814) *Of the Vocation of Our Age for Legislation and Jurisprudence.*
1881   Abram Hayward, trans. London: Littlewood.

1829   *The History of the Roman Law during the Middle Ages.* Translation of vol. 1 by E. Cathcart. Edinburgh.

Scheffler, Harold W.
1972   "Kinship Semantics." *Annual Review of Anthropology,* vol. 1. Palo Alto, Calif.: Annual Reviews.

Scheffler, Harold W. and Floyd G. Lounsbury
1971   *A Study in Structural Semantics: The Siriono Kinship System.* Englewood Cliffs, N.J.: Prentice-Hall.

Schneider, David M.
1965a   "Kinship and Biology." In A. J. Coale, L. A. Fallers, Marion Levy, D. M. Schneider, and S. Tomkins, eds., *Aspects of the Analysis of Family Structure.* Princeton: Princeton University Press.

1965b   "Some Muddles in the Models." *The Revelance of Models for Social Anthropology.* Association for Social Anthropologists Monograph No. 1. New York: Taplinger.

1965c   "A Critique of Goodenough's Componential Analysis." *American Anthropologist* 67:5, part 2:288–316.

1968   *American Kinship: A Cultural Account.* Englewood Cliffs, N.J.: Prentice-Hall.

1969   "Componential Analysis: A State of the Art Review." Paper for Cognitive Studies and Artificial Intelligence Research, University of Chicago Center for Continuing Education, March 2–8, 1969.

Schoolcraft, Henry Rowe
1857   *History of the Indian Tribes of the United States: Their Present Condition and Prospects.* Philadelphia: Lippincott. (Repub. by American Indian History Press, n.d.)

Schrader, George A.
1967   *Existential Philosophers: Kierkegaard to Merleau-Ponty.* New York: McGraw-Hill.

Searle, John
1972 "Chomsky's Revolution in Linguistics." Special Supplement to New York Review of Books, June 29.

Setzler, Frank M.
1963 "Anthropology During the War and After." A memorandum prepared by the Committee on War Service of Anthropologists, Division of Anthropology and Psychology, National Research Council.

Shand, Alexander F.
1914 *The Foundations of Character.* London: Macmillan.

Shannon, C. and Warren Weaver
(1949) *The Mathematical Theory of Communication.* Urbana: University of
1964 Illinois Press.

Sibley, Elbridge
1974 *SSRC: The First Fifty Years.* New York: SSRC.

Simkin, C. G. F.
1968 *The Traditional Trade of Asia.* London: Oxford University Press.

Singer, Milton
1955 "The Cultural Pattern of Indian Civilization: A Preliminary Report of a Methodological Field Study." *Far Eastern Quarterly* 15(1):23–36.

1972 *When a Great Tradition Modernizes.* New York: Praeger.

Slotkin, J. S., ed.
1969 *Readings in Early Anthropology.* Chicago: Aldine.

Smith, Adam
(1759) *(The Theory of Moral Sentiments.)* In Herbert W. Schneider, ed.,
1948 *Adam Smith's Moral and Political Philosophy.* New York: Hafner.

(1776) *An Inquiry into the Nature and Causes of the Wealth of Nations.*
1937 Edwin Cannon, ed. New York: Modern Library.

Smith, David Eugene
1951 *History of Mathematics.* New York: Dover.

Smith, W. Robertson
1885 *Kinship and Marriage in Early Arabia.* Cambridge: Cambridge University Press.

1889 *Lectures on the Religion of the Semites.* New York: Appleton.

1912 *Lectures and Essays.* J. S. Black and G. W. Chrystal, eds. London: Adam and Charles Black.

Spencer, Baldwin and F. J. Gillen
(1899)   *The Native Tribes of Central Australia.* 1st ed., 1899, rpt. New
1968   York: Dover.

Spencer, Herbert
(1862)   *First Principles.* American ed. New York: H. M. Caldwell.
1900

1882   *Political Institutions.* New York: Appleton.

Steward, Julian H.
1955   *Theory of Culture Change.* Urbana: University of Illinois Press.

1973   *Alfred Kroeber.* New York: Columbia University Press.

Stocking, George, Jr.
1968   *Race, Culture, and Evolution.* New York: Free Press.

1971   "What's in a Name? The Origins of the Royal Anthropological In-
            stitute." *Man* 6:369–90.

1974   *The Shaping of American Anthropology, 1883–1911: A Franz Boas
            Reader.* New York: Basic Books.

Strauss, Anselm, ed.
1964   *George Herbert Mead on Social Psychology.* Chicago: University
            of Chicago Press.

Taylor, Griffith, ed.
1957   *Geography in the Twentieth Century.* New York and London:
            Methuen, Philosophical Library.

Tobias, Philip V.
1971   *The Brain in Hominid Evolution.* New York: Columbia University
            Press.

Tönnies, Ferdinand
(1909)   *Custom: An Essay on Social Codes.* A. Farrell Borenstein, trans.
1961   Glencoe, Ill.: Free Press.

Turner, V. W.
1957   *Schism and Continuity in an African Society.* Manchester: Univer-
            sity Press for the Rhodes-Livingston Institute.

1967   *The Forest of Symbols.* Ithaca: Cornell University Press.

1968   *The Drums of Affliction.* Oxford: Clarendon.

1969   *The Ritual Process.* Chicago: Aldine.

Tylor, Edward B.
(1871)   *Primitive Culture.* 2 vols., 2d ed. New York: Henry Holt.
1889

1889 "On a Method of Investigating the Development of Institutions; Applied to Laws of Marriage and Descent." *Journal of the Royal Anthropological Institute of Great Britain and Ireland* 18:245–69.

Van Gennep, A.
(1908) *The Rites of Passage.* M. B. Vizedom and G. L. Caffee, trans.
1960 Chicago: University of Chicago Press.
1911 De la methode à suivre dans l'étude des rites et des mythes. *Revue de l'Université de Bruxelles.* Brussels: M. Weissenbruch.

Voget, Fred W.
1975 *A History of Ethnology.* New York: Holt, Rinehart, and Winston.

Wagner, Roy
1967 *The Curse of Souw: Principles of Daribi Clan Definition and Alliance.* Chicago: University of Chicago Press.
1975 *Inventing Culture.* Englewood Cliffs, N.J.: Prentice-Hall.

Wallace, A. F. C. and John Atkins
1960 "The Meaning of Kinship Terms." *American Anthropologist* 62:58–80.

Webber, C. E. and Emile Garck
1911 "Railways." *Encyclopaedia Britannica,* 11th ed., 22:819–61. New York: Encyclopaedia Britannica.

Weber, Max
(1930) *The Protestant Ethic and the Spirit of Capitalism.* Talcott Parsons,
1958 trans. New York: Scribner's.

Weiner, J. S.
1955 *The Piltdown Forgery.* London: Oxford University Press.

Weiner, Norbert
(1948) *Cybernetics.* Cambridge: M.I.T. Press.
1963

Weiner, Philip E., ed.
1951 *Leibniz Selections.* New York: Scribner's.

Whatmough, Joshua
1957 *Language: A Modern Synthesis.* New York: Mentor Books.

White, Harrison
1963 *An Anatomy of Kinship.* Englewood Cliffs, N.J.: Prentice-Hall.

White, L. A.
1949 *The Science of Culture.* New York: Grove Press.
1959 *The Evolution of Culture.* New York: McGraw-Hill.

Willey, Gordon R. and Jeremy A. Sabloff
1974   *A History of American Archeology*. San Francisco: W. H. Freeman.

Wilson, Bryan, ed.
1970   *Rationality*. New York: Harper & Row.

Winch, Peter
1958   *The Idea of a Social Science*. London: Routledge and Kegan Paul.

1969   *Studies in the Philosophy of Wittgenstein*. London: Routledge & Kegan Paul.

Windelband, Wilhelm
(1901)   *A History of Philosophy*. 2 vols. New York: Harper.
1958

Winspear, Alban D.
1956   *The Genesis of Plato's Thought*. New York: S. A. Russell.

Wissler, Clark
1914   "Influence of the Horse in the Development of Plains Culture." *American Anthropologist*, n.s. 16:1–25.

1929   *An Introduction to Social Anthropology*. New York: Henry Holt.

Wittgenstein, Ludwig
1953   *Philosophical Investigations*. New York: Macmillan.

Wolf, Eric R.
1964   *Anthropology*. Englewood Cliffs, N.J.: Prentice-Hall.

Wundt, Wilhelm
(1886)   *Ethics: An Investigation of the Facts and Laws of the Moral Life*. 3
1897   vols. Translated from 2d ed., 1892, by E. B. Titchener, J. H. Gulliver, and M. F. Washburn. London: Swan Sonnenschein.

(1904)   *Principles of Physiological Psychology*. 2d ed. Translated from the
1969   5th German ed. by E. B. Titchener. Facsimile ed. New York: Kraus Reprint.

1916   *Elements of Folk Psychology*. Eduard Leroy Schaub, trans. London: George Allen and Unwin.

Index

Singer, Milton, 206, 318-20
Sitten, 55, 263; *see also* Custom
Situational ethic, Benedict on Japanese, 223
Situations: Evans-Pritchard on social, 240, 244; Parsons on, 268-70
Skepticism (skeptical tradition), 10, 13, 14, 28, 31-59; in biology, 93, 94, 96, 99; of Kant, 41-57; of Montesquieu, 32-36; of the Scottish Moralists, 37-41
Skinner, B. F., 235
Small, Albion, 204, 265
Smith, Adam, 37-39, 41, 156
Smith, Elliott, 138
Smith, George, 92
Smith, William Robertson, 124-25
Social anthropology, 2; British, dualistic tradition in, 229, 237-52; as comparative sociology, 171, 176, 177
Social contract, 22, 63
Social contract theory, 15, 18, 19, 28, 55-56, 81
Social determinism, 63, 66, 253, 256
Social evolution, 68, 73, 76-77
Social integration, 174
Socialism, Saint-Simon's concept of, 67
Social life, forms of, 176-77
Social order, 249, 250, 287; problem of, 54, 302, 303
Social organization: early anthropological theory of, 106-17; relationship between social structure and, 279-88
Social positivism, 150, 155-64
Social psychology, 36, 56, 58
Social roles, 268, 269, 285
Social Science Research Council, 275
Social situations, *see* Situations
Social structure, 2, 291, 318, 324; as abstraction of analyst, 241, 242, 244, 245, 283, 318 (*see also* Society—as abstraction of analyst); alliance-descent debate and, 291-92; culture and, relationship between, 224, 292; Evans-Pritchard on, 241, 242, 291; Lévi-Strauss on, 256, 259, 260; social organization and, relationship between, 279-88; Wagner on, 322-23
Social "symbol," 130

Social will, Tönnies' concept of, 263
Society: as abstraction of analyst, 263, 283, 317 (*see also* Social structure—as abstraction of analyst); Durkheim's view of, 156, 157, 162-63, 176, 178, 253; evolution of, 68, 73, 76-77; Freud's concept of, 135; Hobbes on, 19-22; Kant's view of, 54; G. H. Mead on, 203, 204; Montesquieu on, 35-36; organic, 67, 156, 159, 162, 176, 241, 295, 317, 326-28; Rousseau's conception of, 28-29; Simmel's concept of, 263; sociological conception of, 60; Tönnies' concept of, 262, 263
Sociological theory of knowledge, 162
Sociology (sociologists), 2-3, 60, 71, 77, 138-39, 179; comparative, social anthropology as, 171, 176, 177; Comte and, 66-69; French, 156, after Durkheim, 229, 252-61; German, 229, 261-71
Socrates, 6, 8, 13
Somatology, 100
Sophism, 13
Sound law, 88-90
Sound shift, 88-89
Spatial intuition, 46, 333
Speaker-hearer, Chomsky's ideal, 233, 235, 236
Special creation, 96-98
Speech, 315, 331, 332
Spencer, Baldwin, 160-61
Spencer, Herbert, 60, 71-77, 105, 139, 153, 162, 179, 214
Spirit, Hegel's phenomenology of, 61-65
Spuhler, James, 226-27
Stages, Comte's Law of Three, 69-70, 72, 152
Starr, Frederick, 204, 205
State, the: Hegel on, 63-66; Hobbes on, 19, 22, 24; Kant's view of, 54
Statistical inference, 100, 220, 328; *see also* Postulational method of scientific inquiry
Statistical models, Lévi-Strauss on, 260
Statistical significance, 100, 102
Status law, Maine on, 111
Stevenson, Matilda Coxe, 144, 147